ALBERT O. HIRSCHMAN

Albert O. Hirschman

AN INTELLECTUAL BIOGRAPHY

Michele Alacevich

Columbia University Press
New York

Columbia University Press gratefully acknowledges the generous support for this book provided by Publisher's Circle member Harriet Zuckerman.

Columbia University Press
Publishers Since 1893
New York   Chichester, West Sussex
cup.columbia.edu

Library of Congress Cataloging-in-Publication Data
Names: Alacevich, Michele, author.
Title: Albert O. Hirschman : an intellectual biography / Michele Alacevich.
Description: New York City : Columbia University Press, 2021. |
Includes bibliographical references and index.
Identifiers: LCCN 2020030648 (print) | LCCN 2020030649 (ebook) |
ISBN 9780231199827 (hardback) | ISBN 9780231553308 (ebook)
Subjects: LCSH: Hirschman, Albert O. | Economists—United States—Biography. |
Economics—History.
Classification: LCC HB119.H57 A53 2021 (print) | LCC HB119.H57 (ebook) |
DDC 330.092 [B]—dc23
LC record available at https://lccn.loc.gov/2020030648
LC ebook record available at https://lccn.loc.gov/2020030649

Columbia University Press books are printed on permanent
and durable acid-free paper.
Printed in the United States of America

Cover Design: Julia Kushnirsky
Cover Image: Albert O. Hirschman, 1962. Photograph by Hernán Díaz.
Courtesy of Katia Salomon.

To Elizabeth, my first reader and critic

Reformers . . . behave like the country or the chessplayer who exasperatingly fights on when "objectively" he has already lost—and occasionally goes on to win!

ALBERT HIRSCHMAN, 1963

CONTENTS

PREFACE

It ain't necessarily so.

GEORGE AND IRA GERSHWIN, *PORGY AND BESS*, 1935

Albert O. Hirschman was not, by any standard, a typical scholar. German by birth, by the age of thirty he had fought in two wars and lived in seven different countries on three continents. He spoke and wrote in five languages, used multiple pseudonyms, and could pass as a native Frenchman. He held positions at a dozen elite institutions without having earned an advanced degree. Observed superficially, his scholarly output might first appear to be a hodgepodge of topics and methodologies. Yet he is one of the most important and influential social scientists of the twentieth century.

Decade after decade throughout his long life, Hirschman made groundbreaking contributions to economics and the social sciences. Far from being a series of explorations followed without rhyme or reason, together they mark out an intellectual trajectory of startling imagination and profound coherence. His perspective was so broad that it could encompass all of the social sciences under one disciplinary umbrella, thereby changing their very parameters, so much so that he preferred to speak of *one* interpretive social science. By the end of his scholarly career, Hirschman was one of the most admired thinkers alive—and one of the most difficult to imitate.

Though Hirschman received his share of criticism during his scholarly career, evaluations of his work tend to emphasize its originality, indeed its genius, and downplay its more troubling aspects. I confess I am not entirely detached as a biographer, but I have nonetheless tried to present my analysis without shying away from the problems in Hirschman's work. Hirschman once described his way of thinking about any given analysis as "it ain't necessarily so."[1] In my way, I have tried to make Hirschman's "it ain't necessarily so" attitude my own, adopting his outlook on the world to look at him without preconceived ideas. In particular, I have tried to assess Hirschman's contribution to coeval literature: how his ideas were discussed, adopted, or rejected by colleagues and policy makers; whether they have resisted the passing of time; and how his relationships with institutions evolved. Because Hirschman was a profoundly original thinker, it is tempting to highlight his uniqueness and inadvertently put him on a pedestal. One of my major preoccupations throughout the book has been to put Hirschman in context—to look at him in a continuous dialogue with his intellectual and political counterparts, framing him not as a unique scholar (though indeed he *was* unique) but rather as a participant in the intellectual and political debates of his times.

Because this is an intellectual biography, a great part of the book deals with Hirschman's scholarly life. A very beautiful and more detailed biography appeared in 2013, *Wordly Philosopher: The Odyssey of Albert O. Hirschman*, by Jeremy Adelman, Princeton historian and personal friend of Albert and Sarah Hirschman.[2] Adelman's book is an indispensable reference for anyone interested in the life and work of Albert Hirschman. Adelman's book, however, "is not the story of the works; it is rather the story behind them . . . the biographical backstory of a life's ideas."[3] By contrast, this book is more about the works per se, the debates they sparked, and the questions they tried to address; for this reason, Adelman's book and mine are not so much alternatives as complements. Though we overlap in many respects, there are a number of cases in which we stress different elements. The same can be said about recent analyses by a group of Latin American colleagues and friends who are particularly interested in Hirschman's relationship with their region and, more generally, about a number of postmortem celebrations of his oeuvre.[4]

It is especially difficult in the case of a thinker like Hirschman to understand his work without taking a holistic approach to his life. Historical events, especially in the first part of Hirschman's life, dominated in the shaping of his worldview. Hirschman's life cannot be divided in an early phase of *vita activa* and a later one of *vita contemplativa*, though he himself proposes a sort of partition along these lines, introducing his last collection of essays with a reference to "both the adventurous and the speculative sides of my life."[5] Hirschman's work has always had a strong connection to the real world, and his scholarly output was always occasioned by specific problems to which he hoped to contribute with useful ideas. No ivory tower intellectual, Hirschman was solidly down-to-earth.

In fact, the first half of Hirschman's life was largely peripatetic, and ideas often took shape through action, such as during his participation in the antifascist resistance or when speaking with peasants and city mayors while traveling across Colombia. He was always attentive to history, which deeply influenced his thought, values, and the way he lived within his own time. Hirschman traveled frequently throughout his career, and many of his pieces were occasioned by invitations to participate in workshops around the world. These are also examples of the link between Hirschman's speculative work and his active life, but they are closer to the normal links between these two spheres that often exist in a scholar's life; smuggling pamphlets in a false-bottom suitcase, less so. The first part of this book follows in some detail the work *and* life of Hirschman; from his mid-forties onward, the focus is more exclusively on his work.

Attention to Hirschman's personal life also means that I have decided to respect his numerous changes of name. Born in Berlin as Otto Albert Hirschmann, he was Albert Hermant for several months in 1940 and Albert O. Hirschman from 1941 onward. (There is yet another nom de plume that I don't want to spoil for readers of chapter 1.) Adelman decided to do the same, and I cannot find better words than his to convey this point: "to exemplify the twists and turns of the twentieth century in the most taken-for-granted gesture of everyday life, the name we go by."[6]

The fact that this book is an intellectual biography also means that attention to Hirschman's family life is reduced to a minimum. This is particularly problematic with respect to Hirschman's wife, Sarah Chapiro Hirschman. Sarah was not only the partner of a lifetime and, as Hirschman put it in the dedication of *The Rhetoric of Reactions*, his "first reader and critic for fifty years." She was also a coresearcher on many of the trips that formed the basis of Hirschman's books, writing field notes and actively participating in discussions and interviews. His most important intellectual interlocutor, she introduced Albert to a vast new body of literature, such as the work of anthropologists, that he would use consistently in his writings.

But she was not just a dedicated researcher and empathic partner; Sarah, too, lived in the real world. She founded a program, People & Stories/*Gente y Cuentos*, to support reading activities among low-income Spanish-speaking adults. The program became very successful, spreading geographically and branching out into other languages and forms, the better to serve different groups of disadvantaged people. This was grassroots activism at its best, and it became a source of learning for Albert himself. As Adelman notes, when Hirschman wrote *Getting Ahead Collectively* in 1984, the "deep imprint" of Sarah's grassroots activity and her effort to "bridge literacy and orality" is visible both in his approach to the research in the field and in his writing style.[7]

The role of the daughters, Katia and Lisa, is also by necessity sacrificed. The only reference to their relationship with their father is in a letter he wrote to them in 1965, reproduced in chapter 4, in which Hirschman explains in detail some of his most interesting conclusions for the book he was writing. But this provides only a glimpse of a relationship that was full of affection and intellectual exchange, yet another example of the vitality with which Hirschman knitted together his scholarly and personal life.

In writing this book, I have accumulated a number of debts that are a pleasure to acknowledge here. My institutional home, the Department of Political and Social Science at the University of Bologna, and in particular its former and current directors, Fabio Giusberti and Filippo Andreatta, have been very supportive of my research and the frequent trips that it involved. I am also pleased to acknowledge financial support for overseas mobility from my department thanks to the funds provided by the program Dipartimenti di Eccellenza 2018–2022 of the Italian Ministry for University and Research.

Traveling means being blessed by the hospitality of others. I would like to thank the Global Development Policy Center at Boston University for hosting me for, alas, an all too brief period in the fall of 2018. In particular, I am grateful to the center's director, Kevin Gallagher, and his collaborators, William Kring, Rebecca Dunn, and Sarah Lattrell, for their generous and warm hospitality. I also thank the Department of History at Princeton University and, in particular, Jeremy Adelman and the chair of the department, Keith Wailoo, for very kind hospitality during the summer and fall of 2019. As a member of Columbia University Seminars, I had access on a continuing basis to the rich facilities of Columbia University, without which writing this book would have been much more difficult. Finally, I thank the World Bank Group Archives for collaborating with me in granting access to their archival documents when this was far from an easy task.

In particular, I would like to express my gratitude to the archivists and librarians I have met or corresponded with at the following institutions: the Nicola Matteucci Library and the Library of the Department of Economic Sciences at the University of Bologna; the Firestone Memorial Library and the Seeley G. Mudd Manuscript Library at Princeton University; Butler Library and the Rare Book and Manuscript Library at Columbia University; the Bancroft Library at the University of California, Berkeley; the Mugar Memorial Library at Boston University; the David M. Rubenstein Rare Book & Manuscript Library at Duke University; the World Bank Group Archives in Washington, DC; and the United States Holocaust Memorial Museum in Washington, DC.

Pier Francesco Asso, Ilene Grabel, Elizabeth Leake, George Owers, and three anonymous reviewers read the entire manuscript and offered very valuable comments. Carl Wennerlind discussed chapter 6 with me with his usual acumen and irony. I am deeply indebted to all of them. Elizabeth Leake, in addition to discussing the contents, helped me shape the form and language of the entire manuscript. Her feedback and suggestions have been enormously precious throughout. I have also benefited hugely from conversations and exchanges I have had through the years with colleagues interested, for various reasons, in the work of Albert Hirschman, some of them his personal friends. A partial list includes Jeremy Adelman, Ana Maria Bianchi, Marina Bianchi, Tito Bianchi, Mauro Boianovsky, Victoria De Grazia, Neil De Marchi, Jean-Jacques Dethier, Osvaldo Feinstein, Carlo Ginzburg, Elisa Grandi, Ira Katznelson, Axel Leijonhufvud, Joseph L. Love, Charles S. Maier, Perry Mehrling, Luca Meldolesi, José Antonio Ocampo, Marta Petrusewicz, Sherman Robinson, Roger J. Sandilands, Nicoletta Stame, Paul P. Streeten, Claudia Sunna, Judith Tendler, Carlo Trigilia, Nadia Urbinati, Miguel Urrutia, Paola Villa, and, last but not least, the PhD students in my 2019–20 departmental seminar on Social Science Classics, especially Alice Fubini and Aidar Zinnatullin. Since my interest in Hirschman dates back to my years as a university student, I hope I will be forgiven by the many others I have forgotten to mention.

I am very grateful to Katia Salomon, the daughter of Albert and Sarah Hirschman, for permission to quote from the Albert O. Hirschman papers held at the Seeley G. Mudd Manuscript Library at Princeton University and in a folder of the J. B. Condliffe papers held at the Bancroft Library at the University of California, Berkeley, as well as for providing pictures for this book and permission to use other pictures related to Albert Hirschman. I am grateful to James Fry for permission to quote from the Varian Fry papers held at the Rare Book and Manuscript Library at Columbia University and use photos from that collection. Finally, I am grateful to Richard Turnwald for permission to use a photograph from his collection. This book was initially meant to appear with Polity Press, and I am thankful to Jeremy Adelman for mentioning me in the first instance and to George Owers, commissioning editor at Polity Press, for providing the initial stimulus, as well as to Julia Davies, assistant editor at Polity Press, for her help. In the process of writing, the manuscript morphed from an introduction to Hirschman's thought to a more rounded (and longer) intellectual biography. I was fortunate enough that Columbia University Press, and *in primis* its editorial director, Eric Schwartz, showed an immediate interest in the project. I feel very lucky to have met in Eric Schwartz an editor so enthusiastic about this work—and, moreover, a scholar of Hirschman's thought himself. I am also grateful to Lowell Frye, Marielle T. Poss, and Marisa Lastres at Columbia University Press; to Peggy Tropp, who copyedited the manuscript; and to Ben Kolstad at Cenveo Publisher Services, who saw the manuscript through each stage of the production process with great professionalism and care.

ALBERT O. HIRSCHMAN

Chapter One

THE FORMATION OF AN INTERNATIONAL POLITICAL ECONOMIST

Otto Albert Hirschmann came of age in years of crisis and turmoil. Born in Berlin toward the end of the first year of World War I, on April 7, 1915, he was the second of three children and the only son in an upper-middle-class family of assimilated Jews. Although he was too young to remember the war, Hirschmann's life was deeply affected by its consequences and the transformations of the interwar period. He grew up in a well-off and open-minded family, loved by two sisters and by parents who gave him a fine education, republican values, an appreciation for culture, and plenty of opportunities to nurture his curious attitude. But the cultural and political turn of the 1930s made life increasingly difficult, and it was only a matter of months after Hitler seized power before young Otto Albert's world fell apart. In April 1932, he was a high school student in his last year at the rigorous, high-bourgeoise Französisches Gymnasium. One year later, on April 2, 1933, not yet eighteen years old, he was on a train leaving Berlin with the first wave of German exiles fleeing Nazi repression.

Throughout the remainder of the 1930s, until he left Europe for the United States in December 1940, Otto Albert was deeply involved in the political fight against Nazi fascism. He also studied, made new acquaintances, changed his country of residence five times, kept in contact with his mother and sisters, and built professional connections.

He had had to grow up quickly, but with this rapid growth came a proclivity toward intellectual and personal flexibility. From his experiences as a young man in 1930s Europe, Otto Albert assimilated a combination of trust in himself, rooted in the affection of his family and friends; a solid education and a habit of reading widely; and a mental attitude that privileged doubt and curiosity over the ideological certainties of that epoch. If Marxism was a huge, solid, and imposing intellectual edifice, Hirschmann developed instead a predilection for *petites idées*, little ideas, or what his friend and mentor Eugenio Colorni would call "castelluzzi"—little castles—with a hint of ironic self-doubt about their actual stability.

These intellectual propensities found their natural counterpart in Hirschmann's character. Tellingly, he liked the French word *débrouillard*, a term describing a resourceful and independent person, able to cope with difficult situations—qualities applicable to himself, he thought, not without pride. Moreover, in those years Hirschmann took his first steps as a scholar. Obviously, his early writings show a Hirschmann still in formation, one who was learning the craft and whose intellectual style owed much to his mentors. Yet they have more than simple documentary value as features of the portrait of the scholar as a young man. Indeed, they reveal a trajectory in Hirschman's thought, prefigure some of Hirschmann's later interests, and also reveal his ability—a gift, really—to create professional opportunities for himself in order to move ahead. These years of study and antifascist activism in Europe between 1933 and 1940 were crucial to Hirschmann's formation and fundamental for understanding his entire intellectual biography.

One final note is in order before plunging further into Hirschmann's early adult years. With the benefit of hindsight, we already know how the story ends. Hirschmann not only survived the war and migrated to America but is now recognized as one of the most stimulating and creative social scientists of the twentieth century. In reading this brief account of his life, however, it should be remembered that the Otto Albert Hirschmann of the 1930s was not simply the promise waiting to become reality. Otto Albert was a talented, ironic, sensitive, and intelligent adolescent and young man who, like many intelligent and sensible people he met, could nonetheless have lost his way or worse. If he managed to survive, thrive, and contribute to the world, it was not simply because of the qualities that we recognize in the accomplished Hirschman-the-scholar but because of an imponderable mix of chance, resilience, luck, the twists and turns of history, intuition, and intelligence that blessed that young man. Hirschman understood as much, which is one important reason why he gave history such a central role in his system of thought.

BERLIN YEARS

Otto Albert's father, Carl Hirschmann, was a respected neurosurgeon with a deep aspiration to assimilation, both in the German nation and in the upper echelons of the bourgeoisie, the profession, and the civil service, of which his wife's family had been a part for generations. His origins, on the contrary, were humble, and he did not like to talk about them. The son of farmers or small merchants, he came from the Eastern provinces, the region from which the poor and unlearned members of the Jewish community originated. But he had studied, and he belonged to an important and highly assimilated profession. Indeed, his political hero was the late first chancellor of the German Empire, Otto von Bismarck, after whom he named his son. His daughter Ursula remembered him as "humble and dominated by Prussian morality as if it were the Gospel."[1] He applauded the decision of Kaiser Wilhelm II to declare war on Russia and France; in domestic politics, however, he was moderately progressive. But most of all, he was a quiet and studious person. Though at times prone to depression and melancholy, he was always a dedicated and affectionate parent, especially with his son, with whom he engaged in gymnastic exercises and discussed readings.

The mother, Hedwig, called Hedda, had studied medicine and then art history at university. Passionate about opera and theater, disinterested in books, and suspicious of political radicalism, she was the central figure of the family, energetic, happy, and a party organizer, though also considered difficult and "overbearing" by her children.[2] Unlike the Hirschmanns, Hedda's branch of the family, the Marcuses, financiers and businessmen, had been integrated and prosperous for generations.

Otto Albert was closely attached to his sisters. Toward Eva, five years younger, he always maintained a very protective attitude. Ursula, one and half years older, became an intimate friend. The children had been baptized as Lutherans, and in fact the Hirschmann family had considered itself "nondenominational" since the nineteenth century, though Jeremy Adelman warns us that conversion was often more a way to join a national culture than it was indicative of a specific religious transformation.[3] "Christian and Jewish families lived side by side and often they had been friends for several generations. Whether one belonged to a Christian or a Jewish family was easily understood from the surname, but many Jews were by then baptized," Ursula wrote in her memoir. "The Lutheranism of the families I knew then was very liberal, and the Jews, almost all of them belonging to the professions, were also not really observant, or only superficially. In both Christian and Jewish houses the same candles were lit, and the same old German hymns were sung around the Christmas tree."[4]

Carl and Hedda established the family on one floor of an urban villa in the elegant Tiergartenviertel, an area close to the Tiergarten Park where wealthy Berliners once had their summer homes. By the 1910s, the neighborhood had become the district of doctors, lawyers, university professors, and government officials. Besides the tony neighborhood, love for the arts was another attribute of status, and the Hirschmanns cultivated their passion for classical music, the opera, and theater. Music lessons—piano for the daughters, cello for the son—were a basic staple of the children's education, and professional artists were commissioned to paint portraits of the family members. Family friends were doctors, lawyers, art dealers, and artists. One was the famous photographer Gerty Simon, whose portrait subjects included Albert Einstein and the actress and singer Lotte Lenya, Kurt Weill's wife and principal interpreter of his operas. Carl also had a photo taken by Gerty.[5] The winter brought skiing holidays in Switzerland and the Dolomites, while the summer saw the family head to the beaches of the Baltic, the North Sea, and Holland.

As Adelman notes, however, there was a sort of fragility, or precariousness, to this elegant lifestyle. The Hirschmanns "lived at the cusp of the establishment, not in it."[6] They did not own an automobile or the house where they lived, and a mixture of pride for what they had achieved and aspiration for further consolidation seems to have been a dominant note in the lives of Carl and Hedda. Ursula, Otto Albert, and Eva belonged instead to the generation that "grew up in the apex of the Republican dream," absorbing all the features of a "vibrantly cosmopolitan, civil, bourgeois-republican-upbringing," which in some way informed their entire lives.[7]

Otto Albert, in particular, was "well-knit and healthy and loved our parents' proposals for long walks or museum visits."[8] He enjoyed physical activity but was also committed to doing well in his studies. A self-reflexive

FIGURE 1.1 Otto Albert Hirschmann, 1924. Courtesy of Katia Salomon

and at times sly adolescent, as his sister recalled him, he was very jealous of his independence and freedom, endowed with strong and methodical intelligence, and determined to build for himself a well-rounded culture.

Between 1923 and 1932, Otto Albert studied at the Französisches Gymnasium, a school imbued with the spirit of cosmopolitanism and tolerance, intellectual rigor, and a commitment to classical studies. In those years, Otto Albert read Thomas Mann, Fyodor Dostoevsky, Hegel's *Phenomenology of Spirit*, Nietzsche, and most of all, history books. His best friend was Peter Franck, nephew of the famous impressionist painter Philipp Franck and son of a chemistry professor at the Technische Hochschule. Peter's sister, Ingeborg, Albert's first infatuation, would later become an accomplished sculptor in East Germany. Another dear friend was Alfred Blumenfeld, in the postwar years a high diplomat in West Germany. Together with the Hirschmanns, most of their friends would later join the ranks of German émigrés fleeing the Nazis.

EYEWITNESS TO CATASTROPHE

Otto Albert's interest in politics began at the end of the 1920s, when he was fourteen or fifteen years old. By then, the economic, social, and political landscape of the Weimar Republic was changing quickly. His growing interest in political issues was nurtured by some initial readings of Marx, Lenin, Kautsky, Max Adler, and Otto Bauer. Bauer, in particular, made a lasting impression on Hirschmann at a political rally at Berlin's Sportpalast in the winter of 1930–31. There, Bauer explained the crisis that had hit Western economies in terms of long-term economic cycles, offering a compelling interpretation of the economic roots of the social unrest and political extremism that pervaded the republic. That was Hirschmann's first discovery of political economy as a powerful analytical tool. "If there was a single event that convinced him to study economics," Adelman wrote, "it was that night at the Sportpalast; five decades later, Hirschman could still close his eyes and reconstruct Bauer's performance."[9]

This wide array of readings was important as a formative experience, for it allowed Hirschmann freely to explore many different cultural territories. In Adelman's words, "the German language may have been his mother tongue (*Muttersprache*), but it was not his home (*Heimat*)."[10] At the same time, the German tradition of shaping one's own education, the tradition of *Bildung*, remained a core attitude of Hirschmann's.

The Weimar Republic was characterized by economic and political turbulence, unstable institutions, and weak governments. The immediate postwar years were characterized by political turmoil and an economic crisis that culminated in the hyperinflation of 1921–1923. A contemporary witness recollected that people were "dazed and inflation-shocked and did not understand how it happened to them . . . they had lost their self-assurance, their feeling that they themselves could be the masters of their own lives . . . and lost, too, were the old values of morals, of ethics, of decency."[11]

Politically the republic remained an unfulfilled promise, and even if the second half of the 1920s were years of economic prosperity and cultural frenzy, the recovery rested on very fragile foundations.[12] German industrialists were often more interested in mergers than in new investments to increase productivity. Moreover, capital came mainly from foreign sources, primarily from heavy inflows from the United States.[13] When, at the end of October 1929, the New York Stock Exchange crashed, the repercussions in

Germany were enormous. American banks began withdrawing their funds, prompting German banks to take out short-term loans from the industrial sector. Industrial production began to fall, and by 1932 it was only 61 percent of what it had been in 1929. In Europe, only Poland had done worse.[14]

Unemployment skyrocketed. By 1932, approximately one worker in three was registered as unemployed. In absolute numbers, five million workers were unemployed at the end of 1930, six million one year later. In 1932, the unemployed and their dependents were about one fifth of the entire German population. Not only industrial workers but also white-collar workers, government employees, all kinds of middle-class occupations, and small family businesses were hit. Social safety nets were hugely inadequate, especially because the crisis went on for a good three years before starting to relax its grip. The slump was so long and deep, the lack of jobs so hopeless, Mark Mazower has noted, that the very pace of social life started to change. "For the men, the division of the days into hours has long since lost its meaning," wrote a report on the unemployed of the small city of Marienthal. "Getting up, the mid-day meal, going to bed, are the only remaining points of reference. In between, time elapses without anyone really knowing what has taken place."[15] Misery and desperation were widespread, "a hint of potential violence and criminality always in the air."[16]

The crisis took a serious toll on the Hirschmann family. Carl retained his job, but the family's savings had evaporated. The Marcuses—Hedwig's family of origin—were also hit, and Hedwig's mother had to move in with the Hirschmanns. Moreover, for Carl, things were turning sour at work. In a phase abruptly characterized by quickly growing identity politics, Jewish and Christian hospitals began to prefer, respectively, Jewish and Christian doctors. Though highly respected, Carl saw his career come to a halt as he was passed over for senior positions by younger candidates with "impeccable" religious credentials.[17] The choice of assimilation was becoming a liability.

The political landscape was quickly crumbling. The Social Democrats, though the largest party, were in retreat. The grand coalition they led between 1928 and early 1930 had not fared well, and their hesitant and myopic political positions were leaving a growing number of electors deeply disillusioned. On their left, the Communist Party was growing and turning increasingly extremist. The Nazi Party, tailoring its political message to many different and competing constituencies and interest groups, was winning support among conservatives, nationalists, anti-Semites, and the ranks of the small and middle bourgeoisie, as well as the inhabitants of rural areas—"a catch-all party of social protest," in the words of historian Richard J. Evans.[18] The traditional conservative and centrist parties, on the contrary, were hemorrhaging consensus, and the elections of September 1930 delivered them a decisive blow. The Nazi Party, which in 1928 had obtained 2.6 percent of the votes, by 1930 had become the second most powerful party with 18.2 percent of the votes. The democratic institutions of the Weimar Republic were more and more fragile. Street violence and clashes between opposing paramilitary groups rose dramatically, with hundreds of political riots and tens of dead every year. At the elections of July 1932, the Nazi Party became the largest party in the legislature with 37.3 percent of votes, distancing the second party by more than 15 points (the Social Democrats, at 21.6 percent).

The 1930 elections were the first that Otto Albert followed closely. His immersion in the writings of Marx began at this time, under the mentorship of an older friend at the Französische Gymnasium, Heinrich Ehrmann. As Adelman notes, "Marxism offered to Hirschmann and his classmates a new key . . . to make sense of the confrontations unfolding around them."[19] But more than Marx the revolutionary or Marx the economist, it was Marx the historian (for example, *The Eighteenth Brumaire of Louis Bonaparte*) who captivated Hirschmann: "his historical books were much less orthodox than his economic ones."[20]

Hirschmann also began to read Lenin, whose political analyses, which highlighted the unpredictable turns of history and put on full display a profound skepticism about inviolable historical laws, fascinated Otto Albert deeply. Marx's and Lenin's writings would have a lasting influence on Hirschman's views of how history unfolds, as well as on processes of policy making. Lenin's influence, Hirschman recalled sixty years later, "can be noted in some parts of my work—for example, in *Journeys Toward Progress*, when I speak about how to carry out reforms in Latin America. The idea of 'reform mongering' goes back in some way to my early reading of Lenin."[21]

Otto Albert and Ursula began political activism in 1931 in the youth organization of the Social Democratic Party, the target not only of Nazi aggression but also of Communist contempt; Communists used to label the Social Democrats as "Socialfascists." This was "absolutely the worst thing imaginable to say about your enemies," Hirschman said. Despite the strong divergences in vision and attitudes between the SPD and the Communist Party, he was convinced that the only hope for the republic was a collaboration between these two forces in a common front against the Nazis.[22]

In 1932, Otto Albert graduated from the gymnasium and decided to enroll in the law faculty, where economics was taught at the time. He managed to do some reading in classical political economy (he wrote short essays on Smith and Ricardo), but the general situation was far from conducive to studies. Political confrontation, nationalism, and anti-Semitism were rampant, and in May 1933 right-wing extremist students stormed the library, building a bonfire with tens of thousands of books. Hirschmann dedicated himself almost full-time to political militancy.[23]

When Hitler became chancellor of Germany on January 30, 1933, the republic collapsed in a matter of weeks. Political violence by Nazi stormtroopers exploded everywhere against trade union, Social Democrat, and Communist offices and at the homes of prominent left-wingers. Episodes of anti-Semitism were rampant. On February 27, the Reichstag, Germany's parliament, was set on fire by a lone outcast. Hitler seized the opportunity to issue a decree abolishing freedom of expression, freedom of the press, and freedom of assembly. The decree also allowed the police to detain individuals indefinitely without a court order. Preceded and followed by massive acts of intimidation and violence, the elections called by Hitler on March 5, 1933, gave the Nazi Party 43.9 percent of the votes. Shortly after the elections, Himmler announced that a concentration camp for political prisoners would be opened at Orianenburg. On March 23, the Reichstag passed the so-called Enabling Act, which enabled the chancellor to rule by decree, deviating from the constitution without the approval of the parliament and the president. What was presented as a temporary piece of emergency legislation became "the legal, or pseudo-legal basis for the permanent removal of civil rights and democratic liberties."[24] Hitler had become Germany's dictator.

As political and personal freedoms quickly shrank, political activism became increasingly dangerous. In the absence of a free press and with public assemblies forbidden, Otto Albert, Ursula, and their group decided they would prepare mimeo leaflets for door-to-door political proselytism. Their duplicating machine was installed in the room of Eugenio Colorni, an Italian philosopher and friend of Ursula's then in Germany to study with Erich Auerbach for a thesis on Leibnitz. His hotel room, Hirschman later recollected, "became a nerve center for antifascist activities and publications."[25] Meanwhile, Otto Albert's friend Peter Franck was arrested, and his papers, with the names of his fellow activists, were confiscated. Hirschmann was in direct danger.

EXILE

Albert's father died of cancer on March 31, 1933. On April 1, Jewish students were expelled from German universities. Otto Albert, baptized as Lutheran, became overnight "a Jew by decree."[26] On April 2, a few days before his eighteenth birthday, the young Hirschmann left Berlin—not to return until 1979. His knowledge of French and "a good dose of Francophilia," as he later put it, made him choose France as his destination—not an uncommon choice for an antifascist émigré.[27] His mother remained in Berlin with Ursula and Eva, although Ursula joined him that summer. Supported partly by small amounts of money sent by his mother, partly by his own income from a student scholarship, and partly by giving German lessons to the sons of bourgeois Parisian families (many of whom became friends), Hirschmann thus began his new life as a political expatriate. Perhaps because of his young age but certainly because of his attitude, Hirschmann neither rejected nor embraced his new condition in a total and exclusive way. As Adelman put it, "Hirschmann was neither a cast-away Odysseus struggling to get home nor an immigrant determined to make himself anew in another place." There was more of "a wandering quality" in his expatriate condition.[28]

In October 1933, Hirschmann entered the École des Hautes Études Commerciales (HEC). Though not as famous as Sciences Po, which was more oriented toward the formation of high governmental officers and diplomats, careers admittedly impossible for a young German émigré, the HEC was nonetheless another grand école. Adelman claims that the education Hirschmann received there was "miserable" and that HEC, in the 1930s, was virtually a failed institution, characterized by very low enrollments, a small budget, and a basic disconnectedness from the real world.[29] In the late 1980s, Hirschman expressed a less negative view, but this might have been the simple effect of circumstance (Hirschman received an honorary degree from Sciences Po, and it would have been improper to criticize HEC on that occasion). What is certain, however, is that HEC offered at least one important opportunity to the young Hirschmann: he was able to study economic geography with Albert Demangeon.

Demangeon explained trade not as an abstract model but as a complex activity taking place between different regions. Geography and distances mattered, as well as the economic landscape in which trade unfolded. Hirschman had already followed some courses in political economy at the University of Berlin, but it was at the Parisian HEC that he received crucial imprinting for his subsequent approach to economic studies. "This early schooling in physical geographic concreteness," he later commented, "is probably at the bottom of my later refusal to explain growth and development exclusively through macroeconomic aggregates, such as savings, investment, income, and capital-output ratios."[30] Those aggregates, wholly abstracted from any geographic dimension, seemed to Hirschman insufficient to analyze the actual mechanisms that can explain the economic dynamics of a country. Hirschman's first book on development issues, *The Strategy of Economic Development*, though not without recourse to models and abstractions, was based on in-depth knowledge of the geographic characteristics of a specific country, Colombia. As Hirschman pointed out later, in Colombia he developed a deep understanding of how investment decisions were affected by the specific topography of the country. "Perhaps," he noted, "it was the interaction of the Colombian experience of the fifties with the still lively Parisian memories of the thirties that made me hit on the notion of backward and forward linkages," one of his most fertile and fortunate propositions as a development scholar.[31]

The world of émigrés in Paris was not particularly exciting for Hirschmann. "In many respects," Adelman writes, "he did not even consider himself an exile, but rather a 'foreign student.' "[32] He was, of course, in contact with expatriates, and some of them, like Rafael Rein (known also as Rafael Abramovitch), were important points of reference for the young Ursula and Otto Albert. But in general, Hirschmann preferred to remain apart from that world. The political scene was also disappointing. Though a few people were undoubtedly interesting and inspiring, such as the many Italians militating in the nondogmatic group *Giustizia e Libertà* (Justice and Liberty) or a few Marxists such as the Austrian Kurt Landau and the German Walter Löwenheim, many leftists (especially the Communists) were totally absorbed by theoretical feuds and internecine fights—a most depressing view.

In 1935–36, after graduating from HEC, Hirschmann crossed the Channel to attend courses at the London School of Economics. There, after the few classes in Berlin in the fall of 1932 and the unorthodox teaching of economic geography by Demangeon, Hirschmann was exposed not only to a full diet in economics but also to cutting-edge debates in the discipline. The "effervescent LSE atmosphere," as Hirschman remembered it, was a welcome change from the Paris years. He attended the courses of Abba Lerner on economic theory and P. Barrett Whale on international trade and foreign exchanges. For the latter, he prepared an essay on the interwar monetary history of France, focusing particularly on the franc Poincaré—from the name of the prime minister under whose government the franc was devalued and pegged to gold in 1928—that dominated French monetary and political discourse during the Depression. The franc Poincaré represented the commitment of French monetary authority to the gold standard, but in fact it was based on delusional premises, such as those illustrated by remarks made in July 1930 by the founder of the luxury department store Galeries Lafayette: "There is no crisis; the crisis does not exist. It is a phantom invoked by the incompetent and the eternally discontented."[33] But even those who acknowledged the crisis, like the distinguished economist Charles Rist, interpreted it as a problem of overproduction whose only remedy was a deflationary policy to eliminate marginal producers, exhaust inventories, and reduce production costs, including wages.[34] The result was that by the mid-1930s, while other countries that had depreciated their currencies were experiencing recovery, France was locked in depression, and only after the victory of the Popular Front in 1936 was the franc Poincaré finally devalued. This was a very important topic for French recent economic history, and Hirschmann's work on it would later serve as the starting point for his PhD thesis.[35]

In London, Hirschmann frequented fellow refugees such as Hans Landsberg and George Jaszi—both would become important pioneers in statistical studies—and had the opportunity to visit Piero Sraffa in Cambridge as well as to attend one of Keynes's lecture.[36] Keynes's *General Theory* was published during Hirschmann's year in London—he later recollected the long queue that formed outside the LSE bookstore—but, interestingly, the diatribe that followed did not thrill him.[37] Hirschmann, it should be remembered, did not arrive in London with a strong preparation in economics. As a consequence, he did not view the work of LSE economists such as Lionel Robbins and Friedrich Hayek as an old and well-known orthodoxy torn down by Keynes's "revolution." Moreover, Hayek's individualism and appreciation for the inscrutability of individual behavior, as well as his reflections on the limits of knowledge in economic processes, struck a chord with Hirschmann.[38] Instead of taking sides in the debate over the *General Theory*, Hirschmann absorbed new perspectives, amalgamating them in his own eclectic way.

In June 1936, Hirschmann moved back to Paris, but only one month later, Francisco Franco revolted against the Spanish Republican government. Hirschmann joined the international brigades that supported the Spanish Republic, fighting in the Asturias and Catalonia. When Mussolini came to power in 1922 and Hitler in 1933, democratic forces had not taken up arms to defend democratic institutions. Many felt that Spain offered an opportunity to react at last. As Hirschman later recollected, "when I felt that there was the possibility of doing something I seized the opportunity."[39] He spent around three months at the front, his unit suffering "enormous losses" in a "heavy fight."[40] But Hirschman recounted little more than this; Adelman reports that throughout his life, Hirschman was very reluctant to discuss his experience in the Spanish Civil War. "His wife Sarah," he reports, "found him silent on the topic, and sensing his unease, she didn't press him for detail."[41]

After Hirschmann returned to Barcelona from his first experience at the front, he was supposed to join the International Brigades in Madrid. These, however, were falling under the control of the Communists, and Hirschmann felt increasingly uneasy. Instead of going to Madrid, he took a train through France to Trieste, on the northeastern coast of Italy.

NOVICE ECONOMIST

In Trieste, Otto Albert joined his sister Ursula, who by then had married Eugenio Colorni. Whereas in Berlin, Colorni was mainly Ursula's friend, in Paris a strong bond also developed between him and Otto Albert. Colorni became a close friend and mentor to the young Otto Albert, and thus the trip to Trieste was as much an occasion to strengthen his relationship with Colorni as to reconnect with his sister.

For this and other reasons, the two years in Trieste were particularly important for Hirschmann's formation. He was able to continue his studies with some of Italy's most talented economists, demographers, and statisticians, graduating from the University of Trieste in 1938. He also managed to produce his first publications and scholarly works. But perhaps more important, he forged a strong friendship with his brother-in-law. The brevity of their connection (Hirschmann was able to spend time with Colorni only occasionally in 1935 and then more continuously in 1937–1938) did not make it any less important. Colorni had a strong influence on Hirschmann's maturation and the shaping of his values and human, political, and intellectual attitudes.

In June 1938, Hirschmann graduated with a thesis on the vicissitudes of the franc Poincaré, building on research he had begun at the London School of Economics under Barrett Whale.[42] This was not, in fact, a formal doctoral thesis, as PhD programs did not exist in Italy at the time, but Hirschmann received credits from his studies at HEC in Paris, took a few additional courses, and thus was able later to present this work as a doctoral dissertation. As he wrote in 1983 to one of his old professors in Trieste, "In retrospect, I must say, you (and my brother-in-law, Eugenio Colorni whom you will recall) gave me exactly the right advice which was to take by all means the laurea: in this way, when I came to the United States . . . I already was a 'doctor' and could take the decision *not* to go for a Ph.D., but rather to *write* . . . my first book, *National Power and the Structure of Foreign Trade* which was much more fun than writing another dissertation."[43] In Trieste, Hirschmann's supervisor was Renzo Fubini, a professor of political economy with strong interests in financial economics, financial history, and the history of economic thought.[44]

In his thesis (161 typescript pages plus an annexed table), Hirschmann finely intertwined the monetary history of the franc Poincaré with the political and economic history of France, as well as relevant theoretical debates (for example, on the elasticity of demand in relation to the exchange rate).[45] Hirschmann's analysis is kept to the essential in both style and structure: no information is offered that is not directly relevant to the discussion, and the sections are tight and strongly interconnected. Nonetheless, Hirschmann was able to unveil in incremental steps the complexity of the French economic and political situation that its monetary history between the 1920s and the 1930s revealed.

Hirschman discusses the sterilization of foreign exchange in 1926–28, the banking crisis of 1930–31, the deflation of 1934–35, and the reflation of 1936–37, as well as the budgetary issues, the growth of public debt, and the vagaries of discount rates policies, always in relation to the needs, constraints, and ideologies of the French governments that followed in rapid succession throughout the decade (twenty-two, from the government of Raymonde Poincairé in 1926–28 to the last *Front Populaire* coalition headed by Léon Blum in 1938). In the parsimonious style that characterized the entire work, Hirschmann presented his own opinion on specific debates or policies—as, for example, when he debunked English criticisms of the French monetary policies of the late 1920s or pointed out the limits of automatic adjustments of wages to inflation:

The inconvenience of the index-linked pay scale is that . . . the authorities predict and accept the increase in prices, workers consider it with indifference for they know they will not suffer from it, and sellers feel authorized to implement it, knowing, furthermore, that demand will not decrease. In this way, this mechanism becomes an important psychological factor in favor of a rise of prices, whereas the latter should be maintained within its natural limits, set by the prices of imported products.[46]

In general, the thesis showed with extreme clarity Hirschmann's "political economy" approach to the analysis of monetary and economic episodes and the role of unexpected events and unpredictable developments in the unfolding of political and economic processes. He often highlighted the political factors at the base of monetary crises. At the same time, he was alert enough to avoid explaining this complex story exclusively in terms of political agency. In a telling passage, Hirschmann endorsed the French position on the limited importance that should be attributed "to the monetary factor in the economic system, as well as the influence that the government can exercise upon the former."[47] As he put it in a subsequent chapter, "One must not forget that the situation of public finance, the fall of revenues, are in turn nothing more than effects, whose roots are in the economic crisis."[48] Hirschmann thus devoted many interesting pages to the predicament of the real economy and, in particular, to the specific dynamics of the agricultural and industrial sectors. As Marcello De Cecco has noted, the thesis is written in the style of a governmental report on monetary issues. Indeed, in style and content, it is the natural precursor to an actual report that Hirschman wrote one year later, for the International

Institute of Intellectual Co-operation of the League of Nations, on exchange control in Italy.[49]

In addition to defending his thesis, Hirschmann published his first scholarly article.[50] Starting from the discrepancies between two recently published nuptiality tables, Hirschmann discussed the theoretical implications of these discrepancies and how different formulas should be used to different ends. Though a strictly statistical exercise on a narrow topic, the article is one of the first instances of Hirschmann's gift for statistical analysis, an early passion of the young economist.

Also in the pipeline was a broader work on nuptiality and fertility issues, in which Hirschmann demonstrated the decreasing returns of survival rates in relation to number of births per woman in Italy. He noted, for example, that whereas an average of four out of a woman's six children survived, a woman who gave birth to seven children would see only three survive. In other words, as the number of births per woman increased, the number of surviving children decreased. Giorgio Mortara, a renowned demographer and statistician, editor of the well-established *Giornale degli Economisti*, accepted the former, more pedantic work on nuptiality tables but advised Hirschmann against publishing the latter, more imaginative and interesting study. Clearly, a statistical demonstration that debased Fascist demographic policies aimed at increasing fertility and privileging large families was not an easy argument for publication, as Mortara well knew. Only the year before, Pierpaolo Luzzatto-Fegiz—one of the most important Italian statisticians and Hirschmann's mentor for his 1938 article—felt obliged to hide the claim that pro-nuptiality and pro-fertility incentives adopted by the Fascist government had only a negligible impact on demographic trends behind a smokescreen of distinctions between the limitations of scientific analyses and the visionary power of "the Duce's political genius."[51]

It was sufficient simply to circulate the idea on which he was working for Hirschmann to be immediately attacked by the most important Italian newspaper, *Corriere della Sera*, whose article was promptly reported by the principal Italian racist magazine, *La difesa della razza*. Commenting on the arrest of Colorni and other antifascists in early September 1938, the article focused also on Colorni's brother-in-law, who had "infiltrated the university and very recently had defended a thesis on *How a mother who has more than four children will give birth to children prone to die or live in illness*," though the actual subject of Hirschmann's thesis, as we have seen, was French monetary policy. The confusion between the topics of Hirschmann's thesis and his article, however, was instrumental to an attack against Jewish university professors. Indeed, the article continued: "That the Jew Otto Albert Hirschmann has, more or less proficiently, written the abovementioned thesis does not come as a surprise. But we would be curious to know the name of the professor who accepted this thesis topic."[52] The reference to Fubini and Luzzatto-Fegiz was immediately legible to those who needed to know. Luzzatto-Fegiz, who belonged to a formerly Jewish family that had converted to Catholicism, managed to remain in the university, though he was accused by a colleague of belonging, together with Fubini and Hirschmann, to a "Sionist international."[53] Fubini, who had not hidden his Jewish identity in the questionnaire for racial profiling distributed to faculty in August 1938, was expelled from the university in October.[54] Arrested in February 1944 and deported to Auschwitz, he died there in the fall of that year.[55]

In addition to his studies in population statistics, Hirschman also acquainted himself with the broader Italian economic and financial situation, producing a report that was published, unsigned, by the *Bulletin Quotidien* of the Paris-based Société d'Études et d'Informations Économiques as "Les finances et l'économie italiennes—Situation actuelle et perspectives." For the same journal, Hirschman later prepared a report on "L'Industrie textile italienne et l'autarcie."[56] As Hirschman later recalled, the first report attracted some attention in Paris, for it described Italian economic and financial developments that were surrounded by official secrecy. Besides enjoying "outwitting the Fascist authorities" by circulating information that the regime would rather keep unknown, Hirschman earned recognition as an expert on the Italian economy and landed his first job when he had to move back to Paris in mid-1938.[57]

During this time, Hirschmann became increasingly close to his brother-in-law, Eugenio Colorni.[58] It was under Eugenio's guidance that Otto Albert continued to expand his reading, from Flaubert to Laclos, from Croce to Leopardi, and, above all, Montaigne. "A foundation was laid," Adelman wrote, "for Hirschman's interest in the psychological processes lurking behind individual and group behavior." Montaigne's "highly personal vignettes, meditations, and moral reflections shook Hirschmann to his core. . . . Montaigne's affection for the aphorism, for accumulating quotes, rubbed off on Hirschmann instantly, and he began to stockpile his own."[59] The influence of these readings was evident from Hirschman's first book, *National Power and the Structure of Foreign Trade*; but it is especially Hirschman the essayist, in later works such as *The Passions and the Interests*, *Shifting Involvements*, and *The Rhetoric of Reaction*, who evinces the crucial imprinting of those works' style.

During his two years in Trieste, Hirschmann continued his antifascist militancy, this time working actively for the underground resistance, often smuggling documents across the French border. He used a false-bottomed suitcase—or rather "a false-topped one. He knew the customs officers . . . would soon grow wise to a false bottom. So he simply switched. They never thought to look."[60] Emilio Sereni, an economic historian of agriculture and a cousin of Colorni's, who was also one of the leaders of the Italian Communist Party (PCI), then illegal, asked Hirschmann to work as a courier. In the factious and suspicious atmosphere of those years of dangerous underground activity, however, even this unquestionably highly orthodox acquaintance was not sufficient to save young Otto Albert from diffidence from other members of the party. A PCI memo denounced that "a certain Hirschmann or Kirschmann" brought a suitcase filled with party documents to Colorni, an out-of-the-closet Trotskyite Socialist and thus highly suspect. According to the memo, "this Hirschman, also a Trotskyist scoundrel . . . openly expressed Trotskyist ideas, speaking against the political line of the Communist International, claiming that this line will doom the labor movement, and in particular he attacked Stalin." The memo continued: "The fact of having used this rascal, who apparently was not even hiding his opinions, is of the utmost gravity. This scoundrel was, until 1932, a member of the German socialist youth, from which he was expelled, he claims, for pro-Communist tendencies. Then he spent two or three months in Spain—why it is unclear—moved to Paris . . . always with his regular German passport, and finally came to Italy where he has remained for a long time."[61]

On September 8, 1938, Colorni was arrested and sent to internal exile on the island of Ventotene, where Ursula, by then pregnant with their second daughter, followed him. Just a few days before, Otto Albert had been urged by Giorgio Mortara, who had published his first article in *Giornale degli Economisti*, to leave the country (Mortara was also expelled from the university and in 1939 moved to Brazil). Otto Albert moved back to Paris—his "second emigration," as he defined it.[62] Meanwhile, his little sister Eva had managed to expatriate to Britain, where she began to work as a nurse in Dover. After Kristallnacht (November 9–10, 1938), when civilians and paramilitary troops stormed Germany with a pogrom that caused the death of hundreds of Jews, the destruction of thousands of Jewish houses, hospitals, and synagogues, and the incarceration of tens of thousands of Jewish males, Hirschmann's mother Hedda also decided to leave and, in July 1939, reached Eva in Britain.

MONEY AND TRADE IN THE INTERWAR YEARS

Hirschmann arrived in Paris with a reputation as an expert on the Italian economy. Robert Marjolin, the managing editor of the quarterly bulletin *L'Activité Économique*, invited him to publish regular reports on Italy. The job was interesting, came with a paycheck, and helped Hirschmann expand his network: *L'Activité Économique* was a joint publication of the Institut de statistique de l'Université de Paris and the Institut scientifique de recherches économiques et sociales, whose president was Charles Rist.[63] Marjolin, who in 1948 would become the first secretary-general of the Organization for European Economic Cooperation, would be an important contact for Hirschman when, during the years of the Marshall Plan, he was employed in the research division of the Board of Governors of the Federal Reserve.

In the late 1930s, Marjolin and Rist also contributed to *L'Europe Nouvelle*, a weekly magazine of political commentary. In the November 12, 1938, issue, an article by a certain Jean Albert appeared on the crisis of Italian colonization of eastern Africa. It was none other than Otto Albert Hirschmann, showing with visible pleasure the collapse of Italian imperial plans in Africa. Not only had the region not been pacified three years after the Italian invasion, he gloated, but the exploitation of resources and Italy's enrichment had remained totally chimerical. Though the regime claimed its "place au soleil," Italian workers did not believe it: in March 1937, there were 115,000 Italian workers in eastern Africa; that number plummeted to 36,000 in March 1938, and to 21,000 four months later. "So this is hardly an optimistic picture of the current situation of the new Italian colony," Jean Albert/Albert Hirschmann wrote. "From an already serious crisis of slow growth, its economy has passed almost without respite to a crisis of negative growth, the end of which we cannot yet see." He thus concluded the article: "And it is not the least instructive side of this development that a State boasting of a regulated economy and subject to the rigorous control of corporate bodies . . . had to record fluctuations in economic activity of a violence unknown so far in the annals of colonial history."[64] *In cauda venenum.*

Hirschmann's reports for *L'Activité Économique* were approximately five-page statistical summaries of the main macroeconomic trends of the country, discussing the trimestral data of agricultural and industrial production (and, when possible, of subsectors such as textiles, metallurgy, chemicals, and so on), employment rate, imports and exports, banking and monetary policies, and the progresses and results of autarkic policies. Brief references to the international situation (the *Anschluss*, the invasion of Ethiopia, the evolution of international trade) or to the influence of weather on crops helped put the information in context. What is evident from reading these reports is the intimate knowledge that the drafter must have had of the Italian economy and, in particular, his ability to look behind the government's opaque statements and find useful sources to extrapolate actual economic trends. In late 1938, Hirschmann captured the deep weakness of the Italian economy:

The Italian economy . . . is at a level substantially below the maximum level attained in 1937. Due to the control of the economy by the state and the many programs currently under way, a more marked fall seems unlikely; but after three years of considerable effort in all fields, the present stagnation is destined to continue for a long time unless external events make it possible to resume growth both in Italy and in her African possessions.[65]

These were solid works of economic commentary. Despite his fragmentary and incomplete course of studies, the young economist was cutting his teeth on serious economic analysis, showing a particular ability to accumulate data and, more important, to discuss the trends behind the data.

If the encounter with Marjolin provided Hirschmann with a job, another meeting would prove even more important. In Paris, Hirschmann met John B. Condliffe, an economist from New Zealand who had studied at Cambridge and was deeply involved in applied economic and statistical research, especially for the Economic Intelligence Service of the League of Nations, for which he had written the first six editions of the *World Economic Survey*, from 1931–32 to 1936–37.[66] In 1938 Condliffe was professor of commerce at the London School of Economics, but in 1939 he accepted a position at the University of California, Berkeley—a professional change that arguably had even more momentous consequences for Hirschmann than for Condliffe himself.[67]

Condliffe involved Hirschmann, among many others, in the preparation of some preliminary documents for an international conference to be held in August 1939 in Bergen, Norway, under the auspices of the International Institute of Intellectual Co-operation (IIIC), for which Condliffe was the general rapporteur and most important scholar on the program committee. The IIIC was a Parisian subbranch of the more famous (but mostly ineffective) International Committee on Intellectual Co-operation—the forerunner of UNESCO. In the 1930s, the IIIC hosted a number of biennial conferences on international issues (The State and Economic Life, Milan, 1931, and London, 1933; Collective Security, Copenhagen, 1935; and Peaceful Change, Paris, 1937). The 1939 Bergen conference would discuss the theme of national economic policies in relation to world peace.

The reports prepared for the conference discussed the trade policies of more than twenty countries selected for their commercial and political relevance, including Canada, the United States, Mexico, Brazil, and Argentina in the Western Hemisphere; many Western, Northern, and Eastern European countries; Australia; and Japan as the sole representative of Asia. Not unexpectedly, there were some notable absences; for example, no African region was represented.[68] It was hoped that the comparative effort would offer a novel analysis of the increasing conflict of economic and political forces in the modern world.[69]

A more specific but very ambitious goal of the conference was to prepare a series of studies of exchange controls in Europe and a number of countries in the Western Hemisphere. After ten years of growing controls, it was difficult to continue to consider them as mere "emergency measures," and it was time to accept that a new monetary system had in fact taken the place of the gold standard.[70] This study was launched in late 1937 as the "major project" of the forthcoming conference, in the hope that it would provide the basis for more effective international trade agreements and thus for some relaxation of exchange restrictions—in sum, as a first step in enhanced international economic cooperation. Though this policy goal became increasingly unrealistic amid growing international tensions, the topic nonetheless remained crucial, as a programmatic document put it, "to understand how the exchange restrictions in various countries have grown up, how they operate and how they have recently been modified, together with the possibilities of further modification and of the introduction of more flexibility."[71]

At the preparatory meetings held in Prague in May 1938, Condliffe insisted that the reports for the Bergen conference be "concise, factual and descriptive" and that each national subcommittee should prepare a synthetic analysis of its country's foreign economic policy, as well as of its major motivations and the administrative machinery with which it was carried out.[72] Except perhaps for its lack of conciseness (his report was ninety-three pages long, one of the most voluminous), Hirschmann's memorandum on exchange controls in Italy was a perfect application of those instructions.

As he had done with his reports for L'Activité Économique and his article in L'Europe Nouvelle, Hirschmann decided to hide his identity: his memorandum was the only one unsigned. His studies on topics critical of Italy's economic and demographic policies had already been noted by the regime's thugs, and his analyses of the faltering economy of Italy and its colonies, as well as of its questionable economic policies, were circulating sensitive information. As the 1937 assassination of the Justice and Liberty leaders Carlo and Nello Rosselli in Normandy had shown, the Fascist regime was ready to hunt and kill its political opponents abroad. Hirschmann was a much less distinguished opponent of fascism, but the regime kept him under strict surveillance. On September 8, 1938, the very day of Colorni's arrest, the chief of police in Trieste sent a "very confidential" note to the Division of Political Police of the Italian Ministry of Interior to communicate the new Parisian address of "the German Jew Hirschmann Otto": rue de Turenne no. 4.[73] In subsequent reports, Hirschmann was described as an "extremely dangerous element" because of his "conspiratorial activities," and Italian border authorities and police offices in northern Italy were informed that Hirschmann was forbidden to reenter the country. An urgent note from the Ministry of Interior added that "in the eventuality that he nonetheless manages to enter the [Italian] Kingdom and were to be discovered in any of [your] jurisdictions, especially while His Eminence the Chief of Government is still on his tour, you are requested to arrest him immediately and alert this Minister."[74] In those weeks, Mussolini was touring northeast Italy for a series of public appearances, and apparently

Hirschmann was considered a serious threat to the Duce's safety. Obviously Hirschmann could not have been aware of the police documents just mentioned. Nonetheless, he must have felt that unnecessary publicity was unwise when he wrote about Italy.[75]

Hirschmann's report for the Bergen conference offered a detailed reconstruction of the process through which exchange control had been established in Italy, as well as of its administrative organization, the role of the banking system and of the central bank, and the payments system. Hirschmann noted that, compared to other countries, Italy was a latecomer in adopting exchange-control legislation—mid-1934 instead of 1931. This was not strange, considering that Italy belonged to the so-called gold bloc and that the lira did not show the particular weaknesses that had forced Britain to devalue and Central European countries to establish exchange controls.[76]

Indeed, Hirschmann's first major contention, which he highlighted at the very beginning of his memorandum, was that one should not commit the mistake of believing that exchange-control policies in Italy were the natural outcome of the authoritarian and aggressive character of the Italian government and, in particular, the first step on the path to the invasion of Abyssinia. As he put it, "Such a retrospective interpretation would be too easy and even false."[77] More simply, exchange control in Italy emerged as a reaction to the deterioration of the balance of payments, and the Italian government adopted it only "à contre-coeur."[78] Though adopted reluctantly, this policy was inevitable, given the joint effects of the deflationary attitude of the Fascist government and the world crisis that followed the 1929 crash. A further deflation in 1934 would have fatally damaged industrial growth. The alternatives were thus devaluation and exchange control.

These were not new political dilemmas in Hirschmann's eyes. Indeed, he had studied many of the same problems for his thesis, as France had experienced both deflation in 1934–35 and devaluation in 1936.[79] Italy opted for a policy of exchange controls, but this was another way to reach the same result of devaluation. Both strategies, as Hirschman put it, would safeguard economic recovery by removing the monetary obstacle—via devaluation in a direct way, and via exchange controls in an indirect way. In a sense, then, exchange control was like "an indirect, veiled, and fragmented devaluation."[80] In the end, however, the lira was devalued in October 1936, following the devaluation of the franc Poincaré the previous month[81]—a further sign, as though another were needed, of the fragility of the Italian economy.

Hirschmann also analyzed how the growing machinery of exchange controls interacted with trade policies. In particular, he showed the unavoidable influence of the real economy on monetary dynamics. Though in 1937 the lira underwent a huge devaluation, imports still grew more than exports because of the need for raw materials for the industrial sector and for agricultural produce (the latter caused, in turn, by a particularly poor harvest the year before.) "Knowledge of these various 'real' factors is essential to explain the dynamics of foreign trade."[82] The strength of Hirschmann's analysis rested not only on his deep knowledge of the machinery of controls in Italy but also on his ability to master convincingly the many different statistical, juridical, institutional, political, and economic aspects of a demanding topic such as exchange controls. As a term of comparison, the work of American economist Howard S. Ellis on German monetary issues, which was considered a fine piece of scholarship, was much less sophisticated in its discussion of German foreign exchange policies.[83]

In addition to the memorandum on exchange control in Italy, Hirschmann prepared another study for the Bergen 1939 conference: a statistical note on equilibrium and bilateralism in international trade.[84] In this short study, Hirschmann first highlighted that the tendencies of world trade toward equilibrium and bilateralism, considered two sides of the same coin, were in fact often unrelated outcomes. As he wrote, "the trend toward equilibrium does not necessarily mean the abandoning of triangular exchanges," while at the same time "bilateralism does not necessarily entail the equilibrium of trade balances."[85]

Hirschmann's statistical study was novel in many respects. As Pier Francesco Asso has shown in a masterful analysis of the literature on bilateralism in the 1930s, Hirschmann's note was one of the first attempts to construct a synthetic representation of the hundreds of bilateral agreements that had been concluded after the 1929 crash.[86] Moreover, the study showed two striking facts about the readjustment process of the depression years. First, the rush toward bilateralism had been less than successful in creating a new, reasonably stable system of international trade relations. Second, the processes of adjustment to bilateral trade relations were very similar among countries, irrespective of their very different political systems. In other words, bilateralism was not yet another negative attribute of politically rogue nations, as opposed to liberal democracies. Asso summarizes:

Totalitarian Germany . . . often identified with bilateralism, not only did not emblematically stand out to lead Hirschman's intercountry bilateral ranking, but throughout the decade systematically lagged behind her European rivals. Quite significantly Great Britain—the utmost upholder of multilateralism—had taken Europe's lead toward bilateralism: the very country that no less than three years previously had pompously replied to a League of Nations' inquiry that she could provide no useful information on bilateralism since "no clearing agreements had been concluded by H. M. Government."[87]

In this respect, Asso concluded, Hirschmann's statistical note confirmed the increasingly accepted view that British external trade had a strong bilateral flavor.[88] In particular, the United Kingdom experienced a continuous path toward bilateralism in trade relations from 1929 to 1937. Other countries, such as Germany, the Netherlands, and Sweden, saw instead an increase in multilateralism for another couple of years, followed by a decrease.[89] Specifically, as Hirschmann summarized, "although Germany has adopted bilateralism as the dogma of her commercial policy, she has not managed to lower her index [away from multilateralism] any more effectively than the other countries."[90]

The rapid deterioration of the international political situation made it impossible for many national delegations to be in Bergen on August 27, 1939. The reports, however, had been produced in advance. They constituted the basis for an informal exchange of ideas among the few conference attendees and had the more lasting effect of providing the material for a study on the predicament of world trade published by Condliffe one year later.[91] Condliffe's volume would later prove fundamental to understanding the intellectual coordinates of Hirschman's first book, *National Power and the Structure of Foreign Trade.*

RESCUE OPERATION

Only five days after the IIIC conference opened in Bergen, Germany invaded Poland and World War II began. Hirschmann, who had been among the many unable to travel to Norway, joined the French army. As he told an acquaintance during his military training, that was the third time his scientific work had been interrupted—first in Germany, then in Italy, and finally in France, "and fundamentally always by the same reason."[92]

Yet Hirschmann did not see any "real break of continuity" between scholarly research and military service against Nazi fascism. As he wrote to Condliffe, "I feel intensely that our present 'métier' is absolutely necessary for our future work."[93]

Germany's *Blitzkrieg* forced Hirschmann's company, mostly German and Italian volunteers, to disband. Paris was occupied on June 14, 1940, and France fell on the 22nd. An understanding officer summoned the foreign volunteers to distribute demobilization papers in names of their own choosing, lest they be shot as traitors if the German or Italian armies ever caught them. Hirschmann decided his pseudonym would be Albert Hermant. He then headed toward unoccupied France—the puppet Vichy government—stopping over in Nîmes and finally reaching Marseille. There, Hirschmann/Hermant spent six months as one of the principal organizers of an illegal operation led by the American journalist Varian Fry to help Jewish and leftist refugees flee Nazi-Fascist Europe.[94]

Under Article Nineteen of the Franco-German Armistice, the Vichy government committed to "surrender on demand" to the Nazis all Germans (and Poles, Hungarians, Czechs, Austrians, and Italians) living in France and its territories. At the same time, the Pétain government closed the borders. The émigrés who had sought refuge in France found themselves trapped and at risk of being incarcerated and sent to Germany at the Nazis' whim.

In New York, a small group of journalists, religious leaders, intellectuals, artists, and activists established the Emergency Rescue Committee (ERC) to assist refugees trapped in France. Varian Fry, a journalist and editor of magazines and paperbacks, with no diplomatic experience—not to mention experience in underground activities—was the only one who volunteered to move to France and start operations as the ERC representative. Virtually the only port on the continent from which ships still sailed for the United States was Lisbon. Fry's work was to help refugees financially and, most of all, to assist them in acquiring the necessary visas for the trip. While transit visas for Spain and Portugal were relatively easy to obtain, it was impossible to obtain an exit visa, so getting out of France had to be done illegally.

The major problem, paradoxically, lay at the end of the trip. Refugees needed an entry visa to the United States, but American immigration policy was very restrictive and rigidly applied. Obtaining an entry visa was

FIGURE 1.2 Otto Albert Hirschmann's false identity card under the name of Albert Hermant. United States Holocaust Memorial Museum, Washington, D.C.

very difficult. During the first months of the occupation, approximately seven out of a hundred applications received a positive response; later this figure actually decreased.[95] One of the major sources of frustration for Fry's operation was the attitude of the American consulate in Marseille. Anti-Semitism and a general lack of concern, even intolerance, for refugees were widespread in American public opinion and in governmental offices, and the consul general in Marseille was an active opponent of the Fry operation. Indeed, at the State Department, Assistant Secretary of State Breckinridge Long instructed his staff regarding the release of immigration visas: "postpone and postpone and postpone."[96]

Fry arrived in Marseille in mid-August and established a cover office, the Centre Américain de Secours, pretending he was merely assisting refugees with local necessities, such as food and clothing.[97] The important part of the job was hidden: finding illegal routes out of France, creating new identities for those who were smuggled to Spain (many had fought in the civil war on the Republican side and feared for their safety), buying passports and other documents on the black market or forging them outright, changing dollars into francs (again on the black market), corrupting consulate officers, and in general keeping contacts with all the peripheral figures involved, including smugglers, informants, the occasional agent provocateur, even Corsican gangsters—in sum, the typical demimonde of a large Mediterranean port city. As Fry recollected, "Marseille was such a confusing mass of interlocking combinations of all sorts—the gangsters with the police—the police with the Gestapo—the Gestapo with the gangsters, etc. etc. that I never knew whether I was talking to a friend or an enemy."[98]

Hirschmann/Hermant, recruited by Fry shortly after his arrival in Marseille, quickly became Fry's second-in-command, screening the left-wing refugees, whose milieu and networks he knew well, and most of all running the covert operation—"my specialist on illegal questions," as Fry put it.[99] Hirschmann/Hermant, by then twenty-five years old, knew the languages, had some direct experience with covert antifascist operations, was well-acquainted with German and Italian émigrés and with French antifascist circles, and was politically alert. His "impish eyes and perennial pout, which would turn into a broad grin in an instant," Fry remembered, earned him the nickname Beamish.[100] Blessed with a "sweet, boyish smile," it seems that Beamish could be "irresistible to women . . . and a charmer with men," but he was also "elusive and always one step ahead."[101] A female colleague at the Centre described him as "a handsome fellow with rather soulful eyes . . . that demon of ingenuity with the puckish smile."[102] In a word, Beamish was captivating and *débrouillard,* "someone who knew how to slip through the net, evade controls and generally take care of himself"— a perfect profile for the operation.[103]

Hirschmann found several points along the border where crossing appeared feasible and not excessively risky, and established contacts with local people who were willing to help.[104] One of these routes went from Bourg-Madame down to Barcelona, another from Perpignan or Banyuls-sur-Mer to Portbou. He even tried to arrange transfers by ship, though in those early months that proved impossible. Frustratingly, new routes soon became obsolete, not only because the border police discovered them but because the refugees themselves often divulged the particulars of their past or prospective escape. "Plenty of talk [was] making the rounds of the cafés and the Vieux Port, where informers swarmed," lamented a collaborator of

FIGURE 1.3 Otto Albert Hirschmann / Albert Hermant in Marseille with an unknown person. Varian Fry Collection, Columbia University

Fry's.[105] Hirschmann also convinced the Polish and Lithuanian consuls to sell to him some passports (one of which he would eventually use himself), and is even credited with having invented the "tubogram," a secret tool to send illicit reports across the Atlantic—a toothpaste tube containing a message wrapped in a condom.[106] In short, as one report summarized, "all kinds of illegal activity were practiced."[107]

This adventurous dimension should not obfuscate the sense of fear and despair that oppressed the world of émigrés. This human distress is rendered vividly in a letter written by Varian Fry in September 1940 about the vicissitudes of David Schneider, his wife, and their two children:

They have valid Polish passports issued in Paris four or five years ago. After weeks of waiting, they finally obtained their American visitors' visas; they then got their Portuguese and Spanish transit visas and because they were born in the part of Poland occupied by Russia, they obtained the French "sortie" visas, they went down to Cerbere and through the tunnel to Port-Bou. There they were "refoulés" [pushed back] by the Spanish four times. They tried again at Bourg-Madame and were also "refoulés." This, after weeks of effort getting all the necessary visas. They are still here in a state bordering on despair. Another one of our clients, Benjamin Walter [sic; here Fry is obviously referring to Walter Benjamin], committed suicide a few days ago, after going through the same procedure as Schneider. This makes the third suicide on our list—the other two being [Walter] Hasenclever and [Ernst] Weiss.[108]

The list of suicides did not end there, and there were also other failures. Fry, for example, was unable to help Rudolf Breitscheid and Rudolf Hilferding, among the best-known statesmen of the Weimar Republic, safely escape. Breitscheid, who had been president of the German Social Democratic Party and a member of parliament, was considered "one of the best-known personalities in German foreign affairs before Hitler."[109] Hilferding, the German minister of finance in Hermann Müller's cabinet and a member of parliament, was also the author of the classic work *Finanzkapital*. Breitscheid and Hilferding tried all possible legal ways to obtain exit visas but, fatally, refused to exit illegally. After almost a year spent between Paris, Marseille, and Arles, they were arrested, brought to Vichy, and then handed over to the German authorities on February 10, 1941.[110] Hilferding committed suicide in Paris shortly after; Breitscheid was sent to Buchenwald and never returned.

In December 1940, the police visited the Centre looking for Hermant. He was out of town and managed to avoid arrest, but it was clear that his time in Marseille had come to an end. Following one of the routes he knew so well, Hirschmann crossed the Pyrenees to Portbou and, via Barcelona and Madrid, reached Lisbon. From there, with an entry visa to the United States attached to a Rockefeller Foundation fellowship sponsored by John B. Condliffe, he embarked on the SS *Excalibur* of American Export Lines and sailed to New York.[111] Exit to the United States, when he was twenty-five years old, marked for Hirschmann the beginning of a new phase in his life. "I had suffered so many defeats," he later said, "that I was only too glad to be on the side of the victors for once!"[112] At the immigration window, Otto Albert Hirschmann became Albert O. Hirschman.

Fry was deeply affected by Hirschman's departure. "My closest friend was Hirschmann," Fry wrote to his wife. "He was the best of them all [i.e., Fry's collaborators], and I got to be very fond of him and very dependent on him."[113] In his 1945 memoir, Fry noted "how completely I had come to rely on him, not only for solutions to the most difficult problems, but also for companionship. For he was the only person in France who knew exactly what I was doing and why, and was therefore the only one with whom

FIGURE 1.4 The SS *Excalibur* of American Export Lines, 1940. The U.S. flags on the side indicated that the ship belonged to a neutral country. Collection of Richard Turnwald

I could always be at ease. . . . With Beamish and Beamish alone I could be perfectly candid and natural."[114]

The spring months proved very effective for the Centre, but Fry's operations in Marseille were increasingly difficult. The State Department put heavy pressure on the ERC to terminate Fry's appointment, and the American general consul openly sabotaged his work. Fry was arrested on August 29, 1941, and accompanied to the border in early September.[115] The Centre remained active for another year, until it was closed by the French police in early June 1942.[116]

It is roughly estimated that, in its two years of activity, the Centre handled approximately two thousand cases, or a total of more than four thousand individuals. The Centre managed to find a way out of France for more than one thousand people, either to the United States, to Latin American countries, or to French Africa. Another three thousand people were assisted financially, helped get out of jail and hide, and provided with false documents. Among those assisted by Fry and his group were Marc Chagall, Arthur Koestler, Marcel Duchamp, Sophie Taeuber, Alberto Magnelli, Max Ernst, Wanda Landowska, Hannah Arendt, Roberto Matta, André Breton, Golo and Heinrich Mann, Hertha Pauli, Jacques Chiffrin, Franz Werfel, Otto Meyerhof, Max Ophüls, Jean Arp, Otto Klepper, and Heinrich Ehrmann, Otto Albert's old mentor in Berlin.[117] Varian Fry, long forgotten, was posthumously celebrated by the United States Holocaust Memorial Council in 1991, and in 1996 he was inducted as a Righteous Among the Nations in the Yad Vashem Memorial in Jerusalem.

Chapter Two

THE POLITICS OF POWER

On January 14, 1941, the SS *Excalibur* moored in the port of New York. "To-morrow," Hirschman wrote, "I shall—most probably—set foot on the American soil."[1] Less than two weeks later, delayed in New York to report to the Emergency Rescue Committee about operations in Marseille, he was eager to resume his work. Daydreaming that he could "take at once . . . the Transcontinental Airplane to San Francisco," he sent to Condliffe a list of the many projects he had in mind, among them a statistical investigation on trends in world trade, an article on capital movements between closed economies, and the population problems in which he had specialized in Italy. In fact, the specific topic was not that important; as he put it, "the main thing is to get back to work."[2]

When Hirschman arrived in Berkeley in 1941 (by train), he found a very lively and fertile intellectual environment in Jack Condliffe's circle. Condliffe, who only a couple of years earlier had involved Hirschman in the Bergen conference, was the newly appointed chair of the Bureau of Business and Economic Research at the University of California, Berkeley, where he had launched the Trade Regulation Project, financed by the Rockefeller Foundation. This project was the continuation of the research initiated for the Bergen conference to study the effects of the breakdown of international trade. Hirschman and his fellow researchers were expected to produce reports and possibly bring them to publication. Indeed, Hirschman joined a very interesting cohort of scholars.

Among these was Ukrainian-born Alexander Gerschenkron, ten years older than Hirschman, who had studied economics in Vienna, then worked as commercial representative of a Belgian motorcycle firm and entered politics with the Austrian Social Democrats. After the Anschluss, he moved to the United States, where he would become one of the most important economic historians of the second half of the twentieth century. At Berkeley, Gerschenkron was working on a huge report on "State Trading Monopolies, or the State as a Trading Agent." One chapter of that report later evolved into Gerschenkron's first book, *Bread and Democracy in Germany*.[3]

Nonny Wright, then thirty-one years old, was preparing a second report on the role of the state in international trade, exhaustively titled "State Philosophy in International Trade, Including the Conflicts Arising out of Power Politics and the Effects of State Trading Monopolies on Business Organization." After studies in political science and economics in Paris, Copenhagen, and Oxford, she had worked for the National Bank of Denmark, for the Danish Ministry of Foreign Affairs with special competence on currency and commercial issues, and for the Brookings Institution as its financial correspondent in Geneva. Later, she would become the second female ambassador in Danish history, and arguably one of the first female diplomats in world history.[4]

Another member of the group was Antonín Basch, a Czech economist who, after economic studies in Prague, Vienna, and Berlin, had built a long and successful career as industrial manager and civil servant for the Czechoslovak Chamber of Commerce, Ministry of Commerce, and National Bank. For eight years (1926–1934), Basch was the director of the research department of the Czechoslovak National Bank, after which he became the general manager of one of the largest heavy industries of the country, the United Chemical and Metallurgical Works.[5] In 1939, Basch left Europe for the United States, joining first Brown University and then Columbia University. For the Condliffe project, Basch wrote a report on the "Economic Relations of Germany and Central Europe," which would later evolve into his 1943 book, *The Danube Basin and the German Economic Sphere*. Peter Franck, Hirschman's old friend from the 1920s in Berlin, was also at Berkeley. Finally, rounding out the group was Alexander Stevenson, who after the war would join the World Bank and,

FIGURE 2.1 Meeting at the Faculty House, University of California at Berkeley, 1941. Albert Hirschman is the young man looking at the camera from the opposite side of the table. The man at the table holding a pipe is John B. Condliffe. Courtesy of Katia Salomon

in the early 1970s, become the director of its development economics department.

But more important than all of these contacts was Sarah Shapiro, a student of literature and philosophy six years his junior, whom Hirschman met while queueing for lunch at the dorm cafeteria. The daughter of an affluent bourgeois family of assimilated Lithuanian Jews, Sarah had lived in Paris and escaped Europe for the United States only a few months before Albert. "In Sarah, Albert found a kindred spirit," Adelman writes.[6] They shared the same culture, passions (novels, poetry, and music), and fears for their devastated Europe. Together they spoke French, a language they both commanded as a second mother tongue. In a few weeks' time, they were engaged, and on June 22, 1941, they married. Their first house, at the border between the Berkeley campus and the hills, was just a small bungalow, but they did not need anything else. "With nature, Sarah, and books," Albert wrote to Ursula, "I feel very autarkic."[7]

Hirschman, one of the two youngest members of the group (along with Stevenson), contributed several statistical analyses on world trade, which

FIGURE 2.2 Albert and Sarah Hirschman, June 1941. Courtesy of Katia Salomon

formed the backbone of a report titled "Quantitative Analysis of Trends in World Trade, Especially Bilateral," an intermediate step between the "Étude statistique sur la tendance du commerce extérieur vers l'équilibre et le bilateralism" that he had prepared for the Bergen conference and the statistical analysis of part II of his 1945 book, *National Power and the Structure of Foreign Trade*.[8] He also took the courses of William Fellner, a Hungarian economist who had recently moved to Berkeley after ten years of running the family manufacturing company in Budapest, and Howard S.

Ellis, a Harvard PhD with expertise in monetary issues and international economics. Hirschman continued his studies in applied statistics as well, which would lead to his first two publications in English: one on the relationship between dispersion measures for an entire distribution and for its subseries, and one on the commodity structure of world trade.[9] The second article was particularly important, for it tried to offer a better description of actual world trade flows—a necessary step, Hirschman noted, to reconstruct a postwar international economic order on a more solid basis. This article would later become the third statistical study of his book.

NATIONAL POWER AND FOREIGN TRADE

Hirschman's major project in Berkeley was the preparation of his first monograph, *National Power and the Structure of Foreign Trade*, written mainly in 1941–1942 and published in 1945. With that work, he entered a lively debate on the crisis of the interwar period and plans for a postwar international order.[10] Of particular concern in the debate was the question of how to avoid the mistakes made after World War I that had ultimately led to a second world conflict. Gerschenkron, for example, maintained a strictly national focus, arguing that the German Junkers, the aristocracy owning large agricultural estates in the territories east of the Elbe River, were responsible for the collapse of democracy in their country and Germany's aggression against its neighbors. He posited that the only possible path for democracy to thrive in postwar Germany passed through "the destruction of the Junker class."[11] Hirschman instead focused on the international dimension of economic aggression. As he put it in a letter to Condliffe during the drafting of the book, "My digging into economic post-war planning during World War I has much enhanced my confidence in the utility of the kind of work we have been doing. Nearly all the disasters of the later period can be deduced from faulty planning or lack of planning during the war."[12]

National Power shows all the limits of a first book, as well as the specific conditions in which it was written. Its structure is somewhat loose: a long, eighty-page essay (part I of the book) and three statistical notes on specific aspects of world trade (part II). The essay in part I, which justifies the book's title, *National Power and the Structure of Foreign Trade*, is in turn organized into four chapters, two of which are rather cursory historical introductions to the more substantive analysis in the following two chapters. Chapter 1 discusses how political philosophers in the eighteenth and nineteenth centuries addressed the relationship between foreign trade and national power, and chapter 2 develops a more general theoretical examination of this relationship, based on contemporary economic literature. Chapter 3 asks how the question of economic aggression was discussed before and during World War I, and chapter 4 aims at providing a solution to limit economic aggression after World War II.

The results of Hirschman's first book-length effort were uneven. In the end, only a few chapters have resisted the passing of time, most notably the statistical inquiries that form part II of the volume—in particular a statistical index that became quite popular in the early 1960s—and the core chapter of part I, rediscovered in the early 1970s as a foundational analysis for the then nascent discipline of international political economy (IPE). Despite its limitations, the book's longevity is no small accomplishment, and the analysis offered in the strongest chapters is remarkably influential even today. Even the less compelling chapters of the book present a number of very productive intuitions, some of which would blossom decades later, as well as a literary style and a method of scholarly inquiry already recognizable as the hallmarks of Hirschman's scholarship.

The work of Condliffe is essential to understanding Hirschman's first book. In his 1940 volume based on the Bergen conference, Condliffe noted the fundamental conflict in the modern world between political and economic forces, as well as between states, on one side, and economic activities that increasingly transcended national boundaries, on the other. "There was a long period," he wrote, "when Nationalism and Industrialism seemed to march together."[13] In the nineteenth century, these twin forces proceeded hand in hand, and government did not exercise much interference in private economic activity. "In the modern world, however, Industrialism and Nationalism are in sharp conflict," as national states started to react against the growing transnational dimension of the world economy and indeed used economic international relations to pursue goals of national power.[14] Combining the analysis of resurgent nationalism and power politics of British historian Arnold J. Toynbee with American economist Eugene Staley's theory of a shrinking world and globalizing economy, Condliffe discussed the "politization" of the economy and its subordination to nationalistic political goals.[15] Condliffe, an acute observer of the connection between political and economic dynamics, correctly interpreted the Nazi invasion of eastern European countries in terms not only of military expansionism but also of economic imperialism. As he put it in 1943, "The second world war began on this economic front."[16]

Hirschman opened *National Power* on very much the same note: "The extensive use of international economic relations as an instrument of national power policies has been . . . one of the main characteristics of the period preceding the outbreak of the present war."[17] To the vast literature investigating this interconnection, Hirschman sought to add the analysis of one specific and fundamental issue: the inherent weaknesses in the international trading system that made it prone to political manipulation. In other words, instead of focusing on the political motives of economic aggression and imperialism, Hirschman was interested in investigating the specific mechanisms through which this aggression was made possible, offering a systematic analysis of "why and how foreign trade might . . . be used as an instrument of national power policy."[18] Part of the originality of this book resides precisely in this effort to use tools typical of international economic analysis to discuss not the usual economic questions (e.g., gains from trade and welfare issues), but the highly *political* question of power. As we will see, the inextricability of the economical and the political would remain central to Hirschman's thought. Hirschman's inquiry was consciously limited to one causal vector: how trade relations can create the economic conditions for the political domination of one country over another. Though Hirschman was aware that the opposite causal relationship is also important—that an imbalance in the distribution of power affects trade relations and produces cumulative effects—his interest lay in exploring the elements of foreign trade that make it a potential instrument of domination. In a sense, this was a "structuralist" approach *ante litteram*, which is how it was read and appropriated by later generations of scholars, especially in Latin America.

It had been long known that foreign trade can be instrumental to national power by increasing the supply of goods that enhance a country's military power. Hirschman called this relationship the *supply effect* of foreign trade. More important to Hirschman's analysis, however, is its *influence effect*—that is, the "politicalization" of trade, a term he coined by translating the German *Politisierung* (and one that recalled his mentor's 1940 study as well).[19] Through the analysis of a number of stylized cases characterized by different bargaining imbalances between countries, the central chapter of Hirschman's book offers a detailed casuistry of this influence effect.

For example, Hirschman discussed how manipulation of the terms of trade by a country that seeks to increase its own importance as trading partner for another country can have a negative impact on its own supply effect, by reducing its purchasing power in the international markets. This trade-off makes other strategies relevant, such as developing trade relations with partners that may have an urgent need for the specific exports of the power-seeking country. This often translates not only into reinforcing trade relations with poorer and smaller countries, making their economies highly complementary to that of the more powerful country, and pursuing strictly bilateral trade relations; it also offers a compelling argument for the more powerful country to prevent poorer and smaller countries from industrializing or from diversifying their internal production and foreign trade relations.[20]

In particular, Hirschman examined the sequences through which a power-seeking country first maneuvers to enter into stricter trading relations with other countries and then progressively changes the overall political and economic gains in its own favor, when it is too late for the trading partners either to dispense with foreign trade or shift toward other markets. The geography of trade, then, becomes important for the way it can make neighboring countries probable victims of power-seeking nations.[21] As an example, Hirschman proposed German-Bulgarian trade: in 1938, trade with Germany represented 52 percent of Bulgarian imports and 59 percent of its exports; at the same time, trade with Bulgaria accounted for only 1.5 and 1.1 percent, respectively, of German imports and exports.[22] Clearly Germany had the upper hand—and used it. Indeed, Hirschman referred to the trade policies of Nazi Germany as the textbook example for all of the theoretical cases he discussed.

This was of course an obvious case study, and the most prominent one. Jacob Viner, one of the great students of international economic relations of the twentieth century, thus described Germany's interwar strategy:

Germany's first overtures to the Balkan States for special trading arrangements on the exchange control or barter basis appeared very attractive to the Balkan countries. In the first year or two or three most of the Balkan countries were thoroughly satisfied, on the whole, with the outcome of their trade arrangements with Germany. . . . But gradually, as Germany made these countries more and more dependent on the German export market by taking more and more of their exports, it became a stronger and stronger bargainer.[23]

Germany, Viner summarized, used its power "with discretion and finesse but without scruples."[24] Viner, who was at the Bergen conference, recollected the tone of the discussion then:

At the International Studies Conference which took place at Bergen, Norway, last August, it was interesting to hear one representative after another of the smaller European countries tell very much the same story on the whole. While they first entered into bargaining negotiations with Germany with misgivings and fears, there was general satisfaction with their outcome after the first two or three years of the experience. But gradually increasing pressure was applied, and soon the pressure became not merely economic, not merely a pressure for better terms of trade for Germany . . . but for acceptance of a measure of German control over national policy in the various countries, including authority over direction of production . . . away from manufactures and toward the provision of the foodstuffs and raw materials in most urgent demand within Germany.[25]

Hirschman concurred. In a synoptic table, he showed how Germany had made use of virtually all available strategies to strengthen its hold on central, eastern and south-eastern Europe.[26] Recapitulating all the possible variations of the supply effect and the influence effect, Hirschman concluded his principal analysis on a note of scholarly pride: "It is . . . only natural that by examining in a general way the processes through which these two sources of power through foreign trade could be best developed, we should at the same time have described the actual policies of a state which had made power the primary object of its actions in every field."[27] As Hirschman's Bergen statistical exercise on bilateralism had shown, however, the growing trade imbalances based on bilateral trade agreements were not "inherently 'teutonic,'" but part of a general systemic change that involved both democratic and totalitarian states.[28]

Having described the ways foreign trade can be turned into an instrument of national power, Hirschman addressed the question of how to defuse the problems of mutual diffidence, increasing restrictions, and enhanced economic nationalism after the war. He asked: "How can we escape from a process of causation leading directly from one war to another?" The virtues and beneficial effects of free trade were, for Hirschman, not simply unrealistic but "entirely fantastic."[29] The world would be safe from the evil consequences of foreign trade only if it were populated by a multitude of states of the same economic importance, with similar volumes of foreign trade and domestic productive diversification, and if each of them was unable to exercise any monopolistic power. But the real world was full of imbalances; if anything, Hirschman noted, situations of dependence are generally cumulative: dependency creates further and deeper dependency.

Hirschman's solution lay in a gigantic systemic transformation, from a world of sovereign states to a world in which economic sovereignty would be surrendered to supranational institutions. The logic was as unexceptionable as an Aristotelian syllogism: if the "politicalization" of trade was primarily rooted in the power of a state to dominate weaker partners through trade policies, and if this power is an attribute of national sovereignty, then the only way to avoid the manipulation of trade for the aggrandizement of international political power is to curb national economic sovereignty. As Hirschman wrote while drafting this chapter, his aim was to insist on "the necessity of *denationalizing* the administration of international economic relations."[30] (We might recognize the influence of Colorni and Spinelli's project for a European federation here.) Hirschman's plea for this political program conveys both the urgency and the visionary dimension that informed this kind of analyses in those years:

The Nazis have merely shown us the tremendous power potentialities inherent in international economic relations, just as they have given us the first practical demonstration of the powers of propaganda. It is not possible to ignore or to neutralize these relatively new powers of men over men; the only alternative open to us is to prevent their use for the purposes of war and enslavement and to make them work for our own purposes of peace and welfare.

This can be done only by a frontal attack upon the institution which is at the root of the possible use of international economic relations for national power aims—the institution of national economic sovereignty.[31]

As we will see, the older Hirschman would be quite critical of "frontal attacks" and comprehensive, all-encompassing revolutionary solutions—even though in this case the revolution was meant to take place only at the institutional level. At the same time, Hirschman would never abandon, even in later years, the idea that visionary proposals may be in fact opportune and even feasible. In 1968, for example, Hirschman and his coauthor Richard Bird would advance a proposal fully to reorganize the institutions of foreign aid. They did not refrain from highlighting the feasibility of their new aid mechanisms, "however Utopian they may appear at first sight."[32]

In any case, according to Hirschman, the power to organize and regulate trade should be taken out of the hands of nation-states and transferred to an international organization that could provide the essential mechanisms on which international trade would be based. Only in this way, Hirschman thought, could the supranational authority exercise actual control and non-nationalistic power on international trade relations.

Hirschman's belief in the possibility of overcoming national sovereignty was not as farfetched as it might appear at first sight. Condliffe had already argued in his 1940 volume, for instance, that the nationalistic drift that had resulted in two world wars could not be undone by simply restoring laissez-faire policies, which would only reinstate the conditions for nationalistic economic aggression. As he argued, "the advocacy of international economic cooperation by laissez-faire arguments beats vainly against the inescapable fact that government regulation is firmly rooted in national markets. This being so, national economic policies independently pursued are in practice bound to issue in strained international economic relations that cause recourse to measures of economic nationalism."[33] The system of modern national states was clearly the wrong basis for the construction of a truly cooperative mechanism of international trade. "The world at present," Condliffe wrote, "consists of a curious conglomeration of large States and small, which differ in economic development in almost every respect but which are alike in claiming to exercise unfettered sovereignty"—a point repeated almost verbatim by Hirschman in *National Power*.[34]

"Hard political thinking" and "political imagination and invention" should instead be put to use to plan the postwar period, Condliffe wrote. The concluding chapter of his book was entirely devoted to discussing the fundamental need to reconsider the concept of national sovereignty. Irrespective of whether Germany or Britain won the war—Condliffe was writing in 1939–1940, when the final outcome of the war was still uncertain—one thing was clear in his eyes: "If international co-operation is to be effectively organized, long steps must be taken in the direction of a world-state. This means the transfer to some international authority of many aspects of economic sovereignty."[35] At about the same time, the chair of the department of political science at the University of Chicago, Walter Laves, called for "voluntary limitations upon the traditional sovereignty of states," and E. H. Carr—that extravagant and blind supporter of realism in the study of international relations—considered the establishment of a European Planning Authority as "the only alternative to a recrudescence of the economic nationalism of the past twenty years."[36]

Thus, Hirschman's proposal for a supranational authority was not an isolated idea. And although the most radical proposals for surrendering national sovereignty, such as Hirschman's, were soon forgotten, the problems they tried to address were indeed real; in due course, they prompted solutions that had at least a distant family resemblance to these early elaborations, though usually on a much smaller scale. Hirschman's work on the European Payments Union in 1949–1950 would have been considerably more difficult without these early exercises in envisioning radically new postwar institutional organizations.

Indeed, every major social scientist dealt with these kinds of problems. In 1940, British economist and future Nobel laureate James Meade put forth a very detailed proposal for an International Bank that would have the power to act as a worldwide central bank—issuing an international currency, controlling the money supply in every member state, and engaging in open market operations. This bank would work in tandem with an international organization with the power not only to control the foreign trade policies of national states, including ensuring that the principle of the "open door" was applied to colonial territories to remove possible grievances by countries without colonies (part of what Meade called "a just and efficient system of international economic relations"), but also to supervise production, sales, and prices within the different national markets.[37] Meade's premises and their axiomatic flavor anticipated Hirschman's position: "Without some form of International Organization no international regulation of economic affairs is possible," Meade wrote, adding that it was "doubtful whether the economic bases of an International Organization can be firmly laid unless the Member States which constitute it restrict their freedom of national action in the economic sphere and grant corresponding powers of economic decision to the appropriate organs of the International Organization."[38]

These were undoubtedly radical positions, but the necessity of international cooperation was underscored even by those who preferred to see international relations regulated by a hegemonic power rather than surrender sovereignty to a supranational authority. "The automatic functioning of the world economy which prevailed before 1914," Basch wrote, "must be replaced by an organized cooperation, in regard to credit and international finance, in the development of backward areas, in control of raw materials, and so on. All of this presupposes indeed a real solidarity of all the important factors in the world economy, with the United States assuming such responsibility, as is appropriate to its economic and political power."[39] The debate evolved quickly and, as the negotiations between Harry D. White and John M. Keynes on postwar multilateralism showed, a general surrender of sovereignty on trade and economic issues was soon put aside as impractical. But more limited goals, such as the coordination and control of exchange rates by a multilateral organization, were widely agreed upon.[40] Indeed it was this vision that prevailed in the postwar world.

Part II of *National Power* consists of three statistical studies on specific trade dynamics. The first study describes an index of preference by power-seeking countries for trading with countries characterized by a small amount of foreign trade. In other words, this index serves to test Hirschman's claim that power-seeking countries tend to direct their foreign trade toward smaller and poorer countries. The reaction of these small or weak countries is the subject of the second index. This is a concentration index; it measures the concentration of a country's trade with other countries. Concentration is total (and the index at its maximum value of 100) when a country's trade is entirely monopolized by another country. The index would be at its theoretical opposite value of zero if an infinite number of countries possessed an infinitesimally small share of trade with the country under consideration (in practice the index will always be at a value higher than zero). As mentioned, this index acquired a new popularity in the early 1960s.[41]

Finally, the third statistical study focuses not on the geographical distribution of trade but on its sectoral distribution—that is, whether world trade is mainly between producers of raw materials on one side and producers of manufactured goods on the other, or between industrial countries on both sides of the exchange.[42] This question has been widely discussed by economists and economic historians in recent decades, but in the

1940s Hirschman's study was one of the first statistical analyses available. Hirschman's results also added a new perspective to the issue. By his calculations, manufactures against raw materials accounted for less than one-third of total world trade; however, the opposite thesis, that manufactures were mainly exchanged against manufactures, was not validated either, as this exchange actually accounted for approximately one-fifth of world trade. Instead, Hirschman discovered that the largest part of world trade consisted of another exchange that had been much less studied: foodstuffs and raw materials against foodstuffs and raw materials. "The traditional view that world trade is based primarily upon the exchange of manufactures against foodstuff and raw materials is not even approximately correct," he argued.[43]

This conclusion refuted the idea that the international division of labor between industrial and agricultural countries was the only possible basis for the expansion of world trade. Just as Hirschman's conclusions demonstrated that, in principle, trade was not necessarily an instrument of domination, they also preempted the analysis, soon to become fashionable, of the deteriorating terms of trade between "core" and "peripheral" countries.[44]

Hirschman's conclusions added a degree of complexity to the study of trade relations between powerful and weak countries that helps explain the ambivalent relationship between Hirschman and dependency theorists. According to the latter, whose theories gained momentum in the 1950s and 1960s, international trade is structured between "core" and "peripheral" countries in a way that enriches core industrial countries at the expense of peripheral economies, keeping them in a state of dependency on advanced economies. Dependency theorists would concur with Hirschman's analysis of asymmetrical power relations in international trade. At the same time, however, their conclusions would seem to Hirschman excessively gloomy and deterministic, for the most interesting part of his research demonstrated that many different equilibria were possible—that power politics through economic policies was not a deterministic game because there were ways for the weaker actor to defend its own interests.[45]

Hirschman's analysis of the time dimension is also valuable. Threats to stop or reduce trade with a country, he argued, will bring very different outcomes depending on the nature of the adjustment to the new situation for the country targeted by the one seeking power. Hirschman noted that classical theorists of international trade, though aware of the difference between the short-term and long-term reorganization of the domestic productive system, in fact studied only the latter. But if one considers that the disruption of foreign trade can have significant social and political repercussions, and that politicians predominantly have a short-term horizon, the short-term dimension becomes much more important than usually thought. "The influence which one country exercises upon another through foreign trade," Hirschman concludes, "is therefore likely to be larger the greater the *immediate* loss which it can inflict by stoppage of trade," especially in modern democracies and "within the framework of a national policy aiming at full employment" (it is worth highlighting this reference to the relevance of full employment for domestic policy, for it is particularly prescient of a sensitivity that would grow only in the postwar period).[46]

With the exception of one reviewer, who found the discussion "frequently disappointing" and lacking originality, reactions to the book were in general quite favorable.[47] It was described as "thought-provoking," "very interesting," and a "valuable" and "very precious" contribution to the study of international trade relations.[48] Bert Hoselitz considered the book "excellent"; Manuel Gottlieb, "remarkable."[49]

What left the reviewers unconvinced, besides the "somewhat miscellaneous" structure of the book, was the author's tendency to be highly selective in his analysis and in his choice of references to support it. This left the impression that Hirschman's argument might appear more convincing than it actually was, at the expense of completeness of analysis.[50] On the other side, it was recognized that these choices in content and style helped open new vistas with remarkable clarity. This kind of ambivalent reaction would also apply to Hirschman's subsequent books. The lack of comprehensiveness of the analysis and an excessive linearity in following a specific train of thought, together with a very selective use of sources, would become standard criticisms by readers skeptical of Hirschman's style of inquiry. Indeed, Hirschman himself admitted as much. But the point, in subsequent books as in *National Power*, is that Hirschman was less interested in discussing a topic from all possible perspectives than in picking a particular viewpoint that would shed new light on important questions. Hirschman's many stimulating contributions to the analysis of social change stemmed from this very attitude. His personal genius resided in his ability to conduct these difficult exercises with lucidity and acumen.

Unanimously considered the weakest part of the book were the conclusions to part I. Readers found them unrealistic and naïve. As one reviewer noted, Hirschman's proposal for a supranational economic authority "has not the slightest chance of being acted upon within any predictable future, if ever."[51] Another reviewer argued that "surely the abolition of national economic sovereignty implies the prior or simultaneous achievement of world peace through the creation of a world state," but how would that come into existence?[52] Some twenty-five years later, Hirschman conceded that his proposal was, in retrospect, "infinitely naïve." As he recognized, "I invoked a *deus ex machina*; I wished away the unpleasant reality I had uncovered instead of scrutinizing it further for some possibly built-in modifier or remedy."[53] Moreover, his proposal could not guarantee that the *deus ex machina*, the supranational sovereign, would not use its privileged position to act politically to its own advantage. A lucid commentator highlighted this problem when the book came out: "When trade is highly manipulated and closely controlled . . . 'political' considerations are almost certain to enter into many of the decisions of the controllers. In large measure this would still be true if an international authority wielded the power of control."[54] In any event, in a couple of years it became clear that the "drift toward state control of foreign trade," as one commentator put it, was irreversible.[55] By 1949, the International Trade Organization, already a much weaker authority than those initially envisaged by Hirschman, had failed to materialize.

THE BELATED FORTUNE OF A CLASSIC

As Adelman notes, the book was quickly forgotten, to Hirschman's disappointment. It is worth highlighting a number of intuitions and characteristics, however, that explain why, despite its limits, *National Power* remains a valuable study and a notable first monograph in Hirschman's career.

The first thing a reader notices is Hirschman's acquaintance with the moral philosophers and classical economists from the sixteenth to the nineteenth century and his reliance on the history of economic thought. This is at once an unusual starting point for a study of international trade relations and a perfectly natural move, for classical political economists were used to discussing power and economic issues together. This same perspective remains a central proposition in Hirschman's analysis, and the basis of his lack of interest in narrow economic approaches. "Purely economic relations" or the "purely economic man," Hirschman wrote in *National Power*, are abstractions perhaps useful for economic inquiries, but they are "seldom encountered in real life, especially in dealings between sovereign nations."[56] He insisted on this point time and again throughout his long scholarly career.

Hirschman also highlighted that classical economists considered trade beneficial not so much because humans are inherently peaceful as because it is in the nature of trade to build a web of interrelationships so wide and complex that states become increasingly unable to pursue their power ambitions without deeply damaging their own interests. As Hirschman noted, a long line of thought, from Montesquieu to John Stuart Mill, had insisted on this beneficial effect of trade. This idea later became the core of one of Hirschman's highest scholarly achievements, his 1977 book, *The Passions and the Interests*.

One particularly important feature of unbalanced trade relations that Hirschman discussed is their cumulative effect. The division of the world into large and small, rich and poor, industrial and agricultural countries not only explains trade imbalances but also produces increasing power disequilibrium. As Hirschman demonstrated, "the dependence on one or a few markets and the dependence on one or a few products are generally cumulative. In this way, foreign trade brings about a maximum degree of dependence for certain countries which is by no means always the result of conscious policy on the part of other countries."[57] With this analysis, Hirschman pioneered ideas that would gain wide currency in the new field of development economics and, later, of economic geography.

Finally, working on the book reinforced Hirschman's conviction that there was value in exploring perhaps improbable, yet possible processes of social change instead of focusing only on the analysis of what is probable. The latter path aimed at the big target—what would probably happen, the big regularities of history. The former, more difficult and less frequented, attempted instead to reveal less visible and often counterintuitive mechanisms that nonetheless promised to open new perspectives and solutions. After all, as Paul Valéry wrote in one of his aphorisms, which Hirschman reported at the end of part I of his book, "Peace is a virtual, mute, continuous victory of the possible forces over the probable appetites."[58]

National Power went through two different waves of notoriety. One, more limited and technical, gained momentum in the early 1960s, when a number of scholars rediscovered Hirschman's statistical studies as important and useful insights into the concentration mechanisms in economic geography and international trade.[59] A precursor of this interest in Hirschman's indexes was Wolfgang Stolper, coauthor of the famous Stolper-Samuelson theorem, who in 1946 argued that "the heart of the book consists of the three important statistical studies."[60] He was so adamant about this that his review, published in the *Journal of Political Economy*, was entirely devoted to part II of the book. No reference whatsoever was given to the essay of part I, not even to acknowledge its existence.

The second wave came in the 1970s, when the collapse of the Bretton Woods system, the oil shocks, discussions about a New International Economic Order, and negotiations at the United Nations Conference on Trade and Development made the book's core subject relevant again. If, in the international "embedded liberalism" of the 1950s and the 1960s (John G. Ruggie's famous expression), foreign aid policies and capital flows had shaped the political discourse of international economic relations, in the 1970s, "trade and the institutional framework within which it is carried on have come back into the picture."[61] In the area of international relations, until the 1960s, economists and political scientists had followed rigorously separate paths. In the words of British scholar Susan Strange, they had displayed a stubborn "academic astigmatism."[62] The quick disappearance of *National Power* from scholarly debates had been the result of this lack of interdisciplinary contamination. David A. Baldwin, one of the first to rediscover the book in the mid-1960s, considered its presence in the bibliography of textbooks in international relations a convenient indicator of their analytical and theoretical depth on economic statecraft. But, he noted, of the sixteen textbooks in print at the end of the 1960s, only one passed the test. Between 1950 and 1970, the flagship journal *International Organization* did not contain a single citation of the book.[63]

Toward the end of the 1960s and more powerfully in the 1970s, however, the divide between economists and political scientists was reduced, thanks especially to political scientists who became aware of issues of concern that had previously been the exclusive reserve of economists. As a result, international economics and world politics were reunited in the new and thriving field of international political economy (IPE). In the words of one of its founders, IPE focused on "the reciprocal and dynamic interaction in international relations of the pursuit of wealth and the pursuit of power."[64]

Hirschman's book was rediscovered as an early precursor of this strand of studies. In particular, *National Power* opened the door to modern work in IPE that focuses on structural imbalances in international financial relations, on the practical impact of ideas, and on the ability of national and international actors to shape preferences (for example, through the "influence effect"). Not unexpectedly, the book has had a much lesser impact on IPE scholars who take what is known as the Open Economy Politics approach, which adopts a more standard neoclassical economics framework. As a recent history of IPE put it, in any case, *National Power* today is "rightly regarded as a classic."[65] Hirschman's focus on asymmetrical interdependence would be the subject of one of the foundational texts of the new IPE, Robert Keohane and Joseph Nye's *Transnational Relations and World Politics.*[66] The rediscovery of *National Power and the Structure of Foreign Trade* as a classic was so obvious that another IPE pioneer, Stephen Krasner, titled his important survey of the relationship between hegemony and trade "State Power and the Structure of International Trade."[67]

Interestingly, another foundational book of the new field, Charles Kindleberger's *The World in Depression*, also discussed the crisis of the 1930s—not as a recent matter, as was the case for Hirschman in 1941–1942, but from a historical perspective.[68] Kindleberger's seminal study on the interwar depression underscored the importance of a hegemonic power for international stability. With the benefit of hindsight, after three decades of American hegemony, Kindleberger's volume provided a solution to Hirschman's dilemma of thirty years before: how the international trade system can operate without being open to the malfeasances of any country's politics of power. Instead of Hirschman's impractical solution of a supranational sovereign, Kindleberger highlighted the role of a national sovereign in stabilizing the international order through its hegemonic role.

The rediscovery of *National Power* by IPE scholars also occasioned a reflection on the points of contact and the differences between Hirschman's structuralist study of international economic relations and the analyses of another group of structuralists, the Latin American theorists of *dependencia*. The similarities rested mainly on three interrelated elements. The first one, predictably, is the notion that power issues are inherent to international economic relations. The second is the significance that both Hirschman and the dependency theorists gave to these power issues. The political consequences of foreign trade were not just a side effect but a core feature of the analysis of both Hirschman and the Latin American structuralists. The third element is that both considered the relationship between different countries to be asymmetrical.

Hirschman, however, also highlighted some important differences—if not between the dependency theorists and his younger self, then certainly between them and his mature self. Whereas dependency theorists considered the asymmetrical relation immutable and to the full advantage of the more powerful country, Hirschman pointed out that gains, though asymmetrical, accrued also to the weaker country. As we will see in chapter 8, he would later highlight this difference between his own analysis and that of the dependency theorists to claim, rather exaggeratedly, that the latter did not belong to the field of development economics.[69] Most important, however, Hirschman argued that dependency theorists, by considering the structural dimension as immutable and incapable of reform, persevered in the error he himself had made as a young scholar: evoking a *deus ex machina* to solve the asymmetry. For Hirschman, the *deus ex machina* had been the surrender of national sovereignty to a supranational organization. For the theorists of *dependencia*, it often meant revolution.[70] But what if one looked for mechanisms of change intrinsic to asymmetrical relations? Hirschman listed a number of instances in which initial dependence can activate built-in mechanisms in the direction of more independence. For example, a poor country rich in natural resources often has little bargaining power with a foreign firm planning to exploit them. But once foreign firms have built their plants, they become, in a sense, "captives" of the poor country, increasing that country's bargaining power.[71]

More generally, Hirschman noted that often the asymmetrical relation implies that the more powerful country is less vested in the relationship—that it has a much lower economic importance for the stronger than for the weaker country (remember, for example, the asymmetrical relationship between Germany and Bulgaria). As a consequence, "economic disparity generates a disparity of *attention,*" this time in favor of the dependent country, which will "pursue its escape from domination more actively and energetically than the dominant country will work on preventing this escape."[72] Hirschman recognized that these outcomes are just "possibilities rather than certainties," but that was precisely his point: dependency theory had, in his words, an "antipossibilist" intellectual orientation that condemned it to "decreasing intellectual returns."[73]

FIGURE 2.3 Albert O. Hirschman, Berkeley, 1943. Courtesy of Katia Salomon

David Baldwin underscored another important difference between Hirschman's discussion of trade dependence and that of *dependencia* theorists. A powerful implication of Hirschman's analysis was that dependence is directly—not inversely—correlated with gains from trade. Thus, the claim of dependency theorists that dependent countries derive no or negative gains from trade was difficult to maintain. As Baldwin concluded, "Hirschman's discussion of the relationship between dependency and the gains from trade is certainly not the last word on the subject, but it is difficult to see how intelligent discussion can proceed far without at least taking account of his position."[74]

These debates were, in any case, very much in the future. On Sunday morning, December 7, 1941, the Japanese attacked the U.S. naval base at Pearl Harbor and other U.S. and allied territories. Less than two months later, Hirschman enlisted in the U.S. Army. While waiting to be called up, he presented his manuscript at seminars at Harvard, Princeton, and the University of Chicago, where he met Viner. Meanwhile, Condliffe was lobbying for Hirschman to land a professorship. He introduced Hirschman to Robert Gordon Sproul, the president of Berkeley and the architect of the multicampus system of the University of California (as well as its first president). Though it was impossible for Sproul to hire Hirschman directly because Hirschman, despite his Lithuanian passport, risked being considered an enemy alien, Sproul joined Condliffe in supporting Hirschman for a position at the Department of Economics at UCLA. After a long series of ordeals, Hirschman was indeed very close to a job he had always dreamt of, thanks in no small part to Condliffe's sponsorship. "May I tell you again how much I have to thank you for all you are doing for me?," Hirschman wrote to Condliffe, and continued: "To become a professor one day is a very old dream of mine which I had abandoned but which I had never succeeded in burying completely. I do not remember who said that it is more important to save our dreams than to save our lives. But I dare say that you have nearly saved both for me."[75]

Nothing came of those efforts, however, and Hirschman started to study literature and periodicals on Chinese monetary policies for a project that Condliffe was organizing, eventually producing a forty-page report.[76] But in April 1943, his quest for a new occupation was "suddenly solved," as he put it, when he was finally inducted into the U.S. Army.[77] Because of his language abilities, he was assigned to the Office of Strategic Services (OSS). In February 1944, he was sent to Algiers and from there, after languishing for several months, to Italy, where he worked as an army translator.

While still in Algiers, Hirschman learned that Colorni, by then separated from Ursula, had been killed on May 30, 1944 by a Nazi gang in Rome, less than a week before American troops liberated the city. This was a terrible blow for Hirschman. It left him "completely broken," and he mourned his loss to Sarah: "What a fount of hope Eugenio still represented for me—what an example, what an idol I had."[78] Despite their relatively brief acquaintance, Colorni had been a true and dedicated mentor for Otto Albert, confirming in him, through example, affection, and shared political and intellectual passions, some of Hirschman's deepest and most cherished values. Twenty-five years later, on the cusp of scholarly celebrity, Hirschman would dedicate his most famous book to Eugenio, "who taught me about small ideas and how they may grow."[79]

Yet not all was loss. In October 1944, Albert and Sarah's daughter, Catherine Jane, called Katia, was born in Santa Monica. After months in which Hirschman felt deeply depressed by the loss of Colorni and forced inactivity in North Africa, the news of Katia's birth finally lifted his spirits. At the end of the war, Hirschman managed to visit Paris and then went to London to see his mother after a separation of almost thirteen years (she, along with her daughter Eva, would later move to Rome), back to Rome to reconnect with Ursula, and finally back to the United States. He met Katia for the first time in February 1946. Nine months later, in October 1946, Katia would be joined by her new sister, Elisabeth Nicole, called Lisa.

THE FED YEARS

Upon his return to the United States, Hirschman found it very difficult to find a job. Despite the swelling of governmental offices and the birth of several new organizations, Hirschman's applications were invariably rejected.[80] As Adelman has shown, unbeknownst to Hirschman, his activism in the youth movement of the German Social Democratic Party, then as a fighter in the Republican Army in Spain, and finally in Italy as a courier for the antifascist resistance made American authorities suspicious of possible communist sympathies. U.S. government officials felt "unable . . . to establish that [Hirschman's] primary loyalty was to the Government of the United States," reported an FBI file declassified by Adelman in 2006.[81]

Despite these suspicions, personal connections eventually worked. After a short stint at the Clearing Office for Foreign Transactions at the Department of Commerce, Hirschman landed a much more interesting position at the Federal Reserve Board in Washington, DC. Alexander Gerschenkron, Hirschman's colleague at Berkeley, had joined the Fed and had quickly become the head of the International Section of the Division of Research and Statistics, headed by J. Burke Knapp, who would later move to the World Bank and become an important sponsor of Hirschman there. Gerschenkron could hire his own staff and did not have patience for unsubstantiated loyalty issues. He put Hirschman in charge of the Western European desk.

Hirschman's expertise on Italy and France was particularly useful for his work at the Fed. Initially, his reports focused principally on monetary policies in these two countries, but he soon broadened his focus to other countries, to questions related to the Marshall Plan, and even more important, to matters of European integration.[82] We have already noted Hirschman's deep knowledge of the Italian economy as it emerged from his prewar analyses. The same proficiency is evident in Hirschman's reports for the Fed, further improved by a much more solid and conscious analytical ability. Hirschman was in the late 1940s the same shrewd "detective" of economic data he had been in the late 1930s, but he was also a more fully formed and well-rounded scholar.

In particular, his direct, long-term knowledge of some of the most important European economies made him particularly sensitive to the specific problems they were encountering in the immediate postwar years. The studies on exchange controls, foreign trade, and bilateralism that he had pursued between 1938 and 1942, moreover, provided him with a powerful conceptual framework for discussing how to foster the recovery of international trade. Inventiveness, flexibility, and lack of dogmatism were important qualities in addressing these problems.

Hirschman's study of the evolution of exchange controls in Italy between 1946 and 1947 is a perfect example of his approach.[83] Exchange controls in Italy were a particularly difficult subject of analysis.[84] Data were either unavailable or unreliable, and their collection was difficult. In a geographically divided country like Italy, which had experienced very diverse inflationary dynamics in its southern, central, and northern areas, the problem was compounded by a patchwork map of regional specificities. Moreover, legislation on exchange controls and rates of exchange changed quickly. Italy had regained sovereignty on foreign trade only at the end of January 1946. Less than two months later, in March 1946, a decree authorized Italian exporters to keep 50 percent of the foreign exchange proceedings they were formerly obliged to surrender to the Italian exchange control agency. The goal, clearly, was to facilitate foreign trade and redress some of the major distortions caused by very rigid regulations. How this partial liberalization would work in practice, however, was a completely different matter. The decree had to be modified several times in more or less restrictive directions in order to be effective, and it became the basis for a renegotiation of the official exchange rate with the U.S. dollar.

Hirschman's analysis is remarkable for its ability to summarize lucidly the major systemic characteristics of this so-called 50 percent system, offering a fresh perspective on its goals and results. Hirschman highlighted the somewhat casual emergence of the system. It was not so much the result of a process of policy making as the outcome of the sum of many deficiencies, from totally inefficient state controls on foreign exchange to the lack of Italian authority over its most essential imports, which were controlled not by the Italian government but by the United Nations Relief and Rehabilitation Agency. Once the system was in place, however, Hirschman judged it to have fared remarkably well. Most of all, it had transferred excessive profits from importers to exporters, thus helping reallocate resources in favor of exports, to the disadvantage of domestic consumption, with only limited inflationary pressure. Though apparently a small redirection of resources, this result was of paramount importance in a situation characterized by a chronic and generalized dollar shortage.

The system, Hirschman noted, had many opponents, among them, for different reasons, "Italian bureaucrats and 'total planners' to whom any kind of economic freedom is anathema"; countries with which Italy had clearing agreements; Britain and countries of the pound area; and, at least in principle, the International Monetary Fund, which Italy would soon join.[85] Hirschman, however, dismissed their criticisms in the face of a successful strategy at once unorthodox and flexible: "While it is true that even a nation's currency system cannot indefinitely remain 'half slave and half free,' it would appear better to leave it provisionally in this condition pending the creation of the bases for a system of total freedom—when the only practical alternative is a return to total regulation."[86] In subsequent months, Hirschman likewise praised Italy's devaluation of the lira by more than 20 percent as particularly expedient for the country's balance of payments. He wrote, "The least that can be said about postwar Italian exchange rate and exchange control policies is that they have displayed remarkable inventiveness."[87]

Likewise, Hirschman proposed a highly innovative interpretation of monetary and industrial policies in Italy. Many observers had criticized the credit restrictions issued by the Minister of the Budget Luigi Einaudi in August 1947 on the grounds that these restrictions, which resulted in severe shortages of cash, would have a negative impact on industrial recovery. Indeed, the danger of a sudden collapse of Italian industrial production forced the government to start a program of industrial subsidies. Hirschman recognized the resulting contradiction, for the Italian government, "of having its Minister of Industry undo what had been done by its Minister of the Budget."[88] But, he added, "the combination of deflation with expansionary measures in specifically selected fields was a logical economic policy for Italy to follow after the violent inflation it had undergone."[89] Instead of siding with one or another policy approach—those supporting deficit spending on one side, and those supporting orthodox monetary stabilization on the other—Hirschman found both appropriate in different phases of the process of Italian reconstruction. First, an open postwar inflation permitted a rapid pace of recovery, though at the price of monetary instability. Then, as inflation quickened and investments became increasingly wasteful, a credit restriction became "easier *and possibly tempting*."[90]

Moreover, Hirschman noted, the temporary recession would also be beneficial in the long run, for it had the positive effect of exposing the deep structural problems of Italian industry, which the previous inflationary pressures had hidden. As he discussed in several reports, this situation presented European countries with the unexpected opportunity to carry out necessary readjustments to their industrial structure.[91] In fact, Hirschman argued, certain standard targets praised by conventional economic theory, such as curbing inflation and a substantial equilibrium in the balance of payments, might be reached "*too soon*, i.e., before the more fundamental economic and social conditions have been improved to an extent consonant with the broad objectives of the European Recovery Program."[92]

Hirschman's convictions about the inherent uncertainties of development strategies, as well as his ability to recognize inverted or somehow unorthodox sequences for monetary and industrial policies, were thus greatly honed during his years working on postwar European reconstruction at the Fed. Skeptical of excessive faith in the virtues of planning, he noted that "even when the national accounts of a country are known with good approximation, it is not easy to indicate the 'correct' amount of investment. . . . *A priori* deductions, while instructive, can only yield extremely rough guesses and are not able to replace as yet the method of trial and error."[93] If looking for the "correct" aggregate volume of investments was a "futile search," then "one should concentrate upon locating those investments which permit the breaking of important bottlenecks and will thereby lead to increases of output and improvements of performance out of proportion to the investment itself."[94] In sum, in these reports Hirschman was anticipating many themes that would be at the core of the theory of unbalanced growth for which he would become famous ten years later in his work as a development economist.[95]

Two interrelated problems contributed to slow economic recovery in the early postwar years: a generalized dollar shortage—that is, the lack of hard currency to import goods and raw materials—and currency inconvertibility, which limited trade to a quasi-barter basis. The European governments, jealous of their very limited exchange reserves, imported from a country only what they could pay with exports to that specific country.[96] Hence, no country was able to improve its own reserves of foreign exchange, and in any case, because of currency inconvertibility, the currency obtained from trade with one country would be useless for trading with another country.[97] This also held true between major currency areas. As one European executive director of the International Monetary Fund put it, "We had British pounds. We needed dollars. We could not exchange the former into the latter."[98] As a result, intra-European trade was a huge "spaghetti bowl" of more than two hundred bilateral agreements, de facto a huge, slow, and highly inefficient barter market.[99]

This economic and social predicament conflated with the worsening relations between the two superpowers and the onset of the Cold War. The U.S. response was the launch of the Marshall Plan—a massive program that, between 1948 and 1952, would bring to Europe more than twelve billion dollars of aid. This was supposed to overcome a quintessentially Catch-22 situation, in which European countries had to export to build reserves but had nothing to export if they could not import raw materials and machinery. As Hirschman noted, budgetary deficits were "the most recalcitrant of all postwar problems."[100] Everywhere, the budgets were low, the fiscal systems in disarray, and reconstruction expenditures very high. Thus, it was not surprising that European governments resorted to inflationary finance—that is, to printing money. But the dollar shortage was another, no less pressing problem.[101] With reduced exporting capacity and opportunities, the huge import surplus resulting from humanitarian and productive needs could be financed only with massive foreign aid from the United States.

The provision of materials and machinery was the first channel through which the Marshall Plan helped jump-start the European economies. But the second and, according to many commentators, the most important channel was the promotion of intra-European cooperation, which took the form of the Organisation for European Economic Cooperation (OEEC) and, from 1950, of the European Payments Union (EPU). From his desk at the Fed, and armed with a deep knowledge of the economic and political limits of bilateralism gleaned from his studies for the 1939 Bergen conference and his recently published *National Power*, Hirschman was a strong and sophisticated supporter of intra-European cooperation, and specifically of the EPU.

As Richard Bissell, the second in command at the Economic Cooperation Administration (ECA), the agency that administered the Marshall
Plan, later wrote, the key achievement of the Marshall Plan was "the resto-
ration of functioning market economies within *and among* the participating countries."[102] In the late 1940s, ECA officers warned with increasing
alarm that the failure of economic European integration would jeopardize international security. The tight compartmentalization of national
economies was to be overcome by the reorganization of multilateralism.
To achieve this aim, it was necessary to create the institutional machinery
that "by its very functioning" would create a tighter bond among European
governments, until then unreassuringly lukewarm toward intra-European
cooperation.[103]

The European Payments Union, established in 1950, was a major step
forward in the reconstruction of multilateral trade in Europe. Indeed, the
head of the OEEC, Robert Marjolin, regarded it as the most important
achievement of the Marshall Plan, for it "created powerful ties and a habit
of working together."[104] Marjolin found a strong ally in Paul Hoffman, head
of the ECA, and his collaborators Richard Bissell, Harold Van Buren Cleve-
land, Robert Triffin, and Theodore Geiger. Hirschman was in tune with his
old acquaintance Robert Marjolin and with his new ECA colleagues—at
times more than with his direct employer, the Fed.[105]

In December 1949, Hirschman circulated a "Proposal for a European
Monetary Authority." This monetary authority was intended to develop in
the "interstices" of national sovereign prerogatives and exercise both moral
suasion and veto power over the monetary and credit policies of European countries, as well as centralize foreign exchange reserves and manage
exchange rates in their relations with extra-European regions. Hirschman
was aware that such an authority would have limited powers and that a
common European currency would be totally impractical in the absence
of a fiscal union. Nonetheless, he was not shy in arguing that this was an
important step toward the explicit goal of European political unification.
He claimed that even the possible failure of the monetary authority would
bring positive spillovers, to the extent that failure would open the eyes of
European governments to the fact that unequivocal political acts were necessary prerequisites for economic integration.[106]

Two elements of his document are worth underscoring. The first is the
visible echo of the federalist vision of Europe, which Hirschman knew well,
having absorbed it directly at its source, first from Colorni and Ursula and

eventually from Ursula's new companion, Altiero Spinelli. The second is the way Hirschman's interest in inverted sequences and in building arguments for what is possible and desirable—not only for what is probable—was taking shape. In the end, Hirschman argued, a European Monetary Authority would prove useful in case of success *or* failure. In the first case, it would be a direct step toward political federation; in the second, it would show how important political federation was.

The European Monetary Authority did not see the light, but European countries took a fundamental step in the direction of multilateral trade relations with the establishment of the European Payments Union. This was, and not only in Hirschman's judgment, a "radical innovation," for it wiped away from Europe, in one big stroke, the major limits of bilateralism.[107] Crucial to the EPU project was the support of the ECA and, in particular, of its deputy director, Richard Bissell. The draft proposed by the ECA to the OEEC countries, known as the Bissell Plan, would permit countries to offset a trade deficit with one partner with a trade surplus with another partner and provide a settlement mechanism for the net balances from multilateral trade.[108]

After the birth of the EPU, Hirschman's principal task, in collaboration with the ECA group, was to evaluate how the coordination of monetary and economic policies among European countries was proceeding. Characteristically, he took a very eclectic position. On monetary issues, though in general not afraid of inflationary pressures, he valued orthodox caution. In a number of reports, he repeatedly urged avoiding "even moderate inflationary ventures." At the institutional level, he warned against excessive "harmonization" of intra-European policies that might transform the payments union in an excessively rigid instrument.[109] But he also recognized that only the adoption of the same anti-inflationary policies by all EPU countries would make the payments mechanism work; thus, he favored a certain amount of rigidity in forcing all countries to adopt anti-inflationary fiscal and credit measures and abandon direct controls. A difficult equilibrium between different and partially conflicting impulses required an eclectic combination of policies and continuous readjustments.[110]

Despite its success, the birth and functions of the EPU were highly contested in some U.S. quarters, especially because it restored the convertibility of European currencies into each other but not into the dollar. This caused a de facto discrimination against U.S. products on the European market. Not unexpectedly, U.S. agencies such as the Departments of Agriculture and

Commerce, the Treasury, and to a lesser extent, the Federal Reserve, opposed the scheme.[111] The International Monetary Fund was also opposed, not so much to the EPU itself as to its discriminatory practices. As Diebold wrote, "Formation of the EPU was a potential challenge to the Fund, an agency dedicated to the achievement of convertibility and to the elimination . . . of controls over current payments among members."[112] The EPU, in contrast, would provide limited convertibility based on discrimination against the dollar. It was not surprising, therefore, that Treasury officers were "infuriated."[113]

The establishment of the payments union and increasing European integration were fundamental elements of the recovery, which after 1950 appeared increasingly solid. As Hirschman noted in a March 1951 internal memo for the board of governors, the EPU had been very successful in developing its clearing function. In spite of many technical complications, the clearing operations managed by the Bank for International Settlements proceeded so smoothly it seemed an easy and routine task. The liberalization of trade and payments, in contrast, had lagged behind. According to Hirschman, however, this was not difficult to understand, given the changing economic climate, the drive toward rearmament, and the price increases and fears of an incipient shortage of raw materials because of the Korean War.[114]

The establishment of the EPU was the culmination of the work of the ECA group. Paul Hoffman left in 1950, and Bissell and others in early 1952. Interagency collaboration between the Fed and the ECA became increasingly difficult. Meanwhile, the Cold War intensified, as did the anti-Communist climate in the United States. The Loyalty Review Board of the Civil Service Commission shone a spotlight on Hirschman, and he understood he might lose both the job and the U.S. citizenship he had obtained at the end of the war. He started to look for alternatives.

Among the many acquaintances he contacted was Manlio Rossi-Doria, an agrarian economist who had been a close friend of the Colornis, with whom Rossi-Doria had a shared history of antifascist activism and prison.[115] Hirschman's letter to Rossi-Doria reveals the sense of uncertainty and anxiety about his job prospects that haunted him in this period of his life. Hirschman did not spare the use of emphatic adverbs and of deferential etiquette—using a capital Y in You—to present himself in a positive light:

As You can see from the attached curriculum, I am highly specialized in monetary policy and international economy. During these last four and a half years at the

Federal Reserve Board I have been much absorbed by the many aspects of American economic aid to Europe. I have worked in very strict contact with ECA, I have been one of the pioneers of the European Payments Union, and so on. At the same time, I have published a number of articles, and I believe I can say I have built a pretty solid reputation in the "profession."[116]

He concluded, "At the Federal Reserve Board I have a fine and solid position, which I could keep until the end of my life."[117]

Yet Hirschman was planning to trade it all for a one-year position, possibly supported by the Fulbright program, at the Institute of Agrarian Economics and Policies of the University of Naples, chaired by Rossi-Doria. Hopefully, he added, during that year, "I could try to make myself useful by giving some talks on issues of international political economy; it is even possible that I might become a consultant to the World Bank (I know well Rosenstein-Rodan and Stevenson)."[118] Clearly, despite his optimistic tone, Hirschman felt that his position at the Fed was increasingly difficult and, in any case, a source of unbearable stress.

Hirschman offered an articulated list of reasons behind his decision:

First of all, I would like to live for a while in Italy. Second, I would like to work on issues less anemic than the balance of payments. Third, I would like to learn something about the great question of the economic development of "backward areas," and I am convinced that in this field one does not learn anything from mulling over it in Washington or participating in those famous missions of experts that last only three weeks. Finally, I would like to be more independent than I currently am from the great bureaucracies of this world.[119]

The attraction of a new and thriving field of inquiry was of course an important motive, but other reasons, as we have seen, were also relevant. Whatever the combination of dissatisfaction with an increasingly uninteresting job, his growing concerns about the worsening political climate, and the attraction of a new enterprise, Hirschman was determined to leave. As he recollected forty-five years later: "When . . . the opportunity arose to leave Washington, I seized it with much relief."[120]

Chapter Three

PIONEER OF DEVELOPMENT

As with many things in Albert Hirschman's life, his career as a development economist was not the outcome of any planning. Though in his work for the Federal Reserve Board he formulated many ideas that would become central in his subsequent work on development, development issues per se were nonexistent in his work, nor could one predict that they would ever emerge. Before leaving the Fed, Hirschman made only one reference to underdeveloped countries, in a 1950 report he presented at a conference in Chicago the year after. Hirschman would later describe that paper as his first contact with the development field, but in fact its exclusive focus was on the structure of foreign trade and its effects on the markets and export capacities of *industrial* countries in the event of a general industrialization of underdeveloped countries.[1] Another report, coauthored with Robert Solomon, dealt indirectly with underdeveloped countries, but it too focused on the influence of an economic power (the United States) on the foreign trade of less developed countries. Written very much from the perspective of *National Power*, this report attempted to analyze the consequences of "the dominance of the United States as the foremost producing and consuming nation of the world," while "the rest of the world is highly dependent on the United States both as a market and as a source of supply."[2]

Hirschman's recollection of this passage in his life is very nonchalant. In Colombia "there was a new planning council that had been established on the recommendation of the World Bank. . . . But the Colombians said, 'If you want us to set up a new planning council, send us an economist who is capable of advising us.' The Bank looked around, my name was mentioned, and I was ready to come—and in fact did come."[3] His contact at the World Bank was his old colleague from Berkeley, Alexander Stevenson, who had moved to the Bank's Economic Department in 1947. Stevenson mentioned to Hirschman the collaboration between the Bank and Colombia and suggested that Hirschman get in contact with the Colombian ambassador in Washington, DC. As it happened, the ambassador offered Hirschman the job on the spot.

COLOMBIA ASSIGNMENT

To a twenty-first-century observer, Colombia in the early 1950s may seem a rather peripheral destination, not as important as other developing countries, such as India or Indonesia. But in the early postwar years, Colombia appeared as a country rich in natural resources and full of potential. Its government was deeply committed to modernizing the country, and in 1949 it hosted the first "general survey mission" ever sent by the World Bank to a developing country, with two very ambitious goals: to formulate "a development program designed to raise the standard of living of the Colombian people," and to establish the model for future World Bank missions to less developed countries.[4] Colombia, in sum, was seen as a laboratory for the definition of development policies.

The 1949 mission to Colombia was headed by Lauchlin Currie, a prominent former New Dealer, top Fed officer in the 1930s, and later the economic adviser to Franklin D. Roosevelt and Roosevelt's envoy to China. Under Currie's leadership, the mission prepared a thorough study of the social and economic conditions of the country and published a voluminous report envisioning a major comprehensive investment plan.[5] As Currie remarked at a conference in Washington, "Economic, political and social phenomena are so inter-related and interwoven that it is difficult to effect any significant and lasting improvement in one sector of the economy while leaving the other sector unaffected. . . . Poverty, ill health, ignorance, lack of ambition, low productivity are not only concomitants—they actually reinforce and perpetuate one another."[6] To these problems, one should add the widespread political and social violence that vexed Colombia for ten years after the assassination of the opposition leader Manuel Gaitán in April 1949—a low-intensity civil war known as *la violencia*.

In 1950, an Economic Development Council (the Comité de Desarrollo Económico) was established to turn the mission's recommendations into policies. Currie was appointed as economic consultant to the council, acting as its technical secretary and marking the continuity between the study phase of the mission and its implementation. At the suggestion of the World Bank, Hirschman was hired as economic adviser to the Colombian government. He and his family would remain in Colombia for four years, from 1952 to 1956.

In his advisory role, Hirschman was initially meant to replace Currie— at least that was the World Bank's idea. But with Currie as the new government adviser to the Comité, they overlapped, and it was not long before the two economists reached the point of mutual intolerance. Contrasts between Currie and Hirschman revolved initially around the inflationary potential of the Colombian 1953 budget, but the conflict soon became more general, as the two economists felt that their visions of the economic development process and of policy-making dynamics were mutually at variance. The conflict was based not so much on theory as on practical divergences. Nor did they click at the personal level, as each fought for influence and visibility.

Letters from Hirschman to the World Bank headquarters in Washington, DC, render a vivid picture of his frustration. As he wrote a few months after his arrival, things moved "not only slowly, but on occasion also erratically. . . . Since we are not always in agreement, we have already had several open discussions between ourselves during Council meetings on such matters as fiscal and monetary policy. I need hardly say that this is not only unpleasant . . . but also serves to confuse the Council members."[7] Hirschman was initially tasked with the analysis of monetary trends, but he grew increasingly impatient. "I did not give up my Federal Reserve position to advise on the raising or lowering of reserve requirements in Colombia," he wrote to J. Burke Knapp, his former boss at the Federal Reserve, who was by then the World Bank manager in charge of the Western Hemisphere and thus, once again, Hirschman's direct superior.[8]

The clashes were not simply unpleasant. As Hirschman remarked, they made his work (and that of Currie) much less effective than it could be. "I am convinced," he wrote to Knapp, "that our Colombian friends do not mind very much if the possibility of conflict is built into the staff organization of the Council. They just love to play one foreign expert out against the other . . . it permits them to make their bow to foreign expert opinion and at the same time provides them with an alibi for doing exactly what they want."[9] That this was an interesting insight into a mechanism of the sociology of organizations was cold comfort; Hirschman had the unpleasant feeling of being manipulated.

The relationship between Hirschman and the World Bank, on the contrary, remained solid, possibly on the strength of Hirschman's previous very positive working relations with Alexander Stevenson in Berkeley and even more with Burke Knapp at the Fed. The latter was very sympathetic: "Albert, the main purpose of this letter is to let you know that we in the Bank feel that . . . you have had a rotten deal and that we understand and sympathize with the extraordinary difficulties which you have had to confront. I find myself wondering to what extent your experiences have soured you on the general situation in Colombia and your prospects for satisfactory future work there."[10] In fact, the bank's powerful director would have been happy to bring Hirschman to Washington: "I want you to know, if you decide to leave, that I would be eager to have you join the regular staff of the newly created Western Hemisphere Department in the Bank."[11] From Berkeley, Condliffe wrote to offer Hirschman a faculty position (ten years after his first attempt), but Hirschman let the proposal drop. As long as he had reasonable prospects to do interesting research on real problems, Hirschman was happy to stay away from university teaching; as Adelman reports, teaching for Hirschman was "traumatic," an "aversive task," a "source of anxiety he would never dispel," and "utterly foreign." As one of Hirschman's admiring students at Harvard later told Adelman, Hirschman remained "a catastrophically bad teacher." He would refuse reiterated offers from Condliffe and Howard Ellis again in 1956 and 1957, preferring a temporary position at Yale without teaching duties.[12]

After two years as an adviser to the Economic Development Council, Hirschman had had enough and decided to resign. As a last statement as government consultant, he published a short article on the nature of his job. He used an admittedly trite simile—the "money doctor"—that had been in circulation at least since the Latin America missions of Princeton University economist Edwin Kemmerer in the 1920s. But unlike Kemmerer, famous for applying the same prescription of strict adherence to

FIGURE 3.1 Albert and Sarah Hirschman with Yves Salaün of the United Nations in the Llanos, Colombia, 1953. Courtesy of Katia Salomon

the gold standard, automatic budgeting stability, and independent central banks, Hirschman emphasized " 'clinical sensitivity', made of intuition and experience" as the indispensable skill for economic policy making. As he remarked, statistical and economic information alone cannot produce any meaningful strategy. "Ultimately," he wrote, "there is always an area of ignorance, of different possible interpretation of the facts and of possible hesitation and discussion, which the economist must be capable to address thanks to his good judgment."[13]

In that obscure publication, Hirschman was exposing one of the methodological beliefs most valuable to him—namely, the idea that both the diagnosis and the prescription for a problem, though based as much as possible on "objective" data gathering and analysis, rely crucially on a perhaps ineffable but nonetheless indispensable "feeling" and "sensitivity" for what is happening and what must be done. We have seen this attitude in Hirschman's analysis of postwar policy making in Europe, and we will find it similarly applied to development issues, democratic processes, monetary and fiscal policies, and other areas. The Colombian experience deeply reinforced Hirschman's view on the nature of the policy-making process.

Instead of joining the World Bank in Washington, DC, as Burke Knapp had proposed, Hirschman decided to stay in Bogotá as a private economic and financial adviser, working for banks, firms, and publicly owned utilities interested in obtaining public funding.[14] Joining forces with George Kalmanoff, another American economist who had consulted for the council, Hirschman offered his services as an economic analyst on topics such as the financial prospects for the expansion of the municipal facility companies of the city of Cali, the market for gas in Cali and Valle del Cauca, the market for paper and pulp in Colombia, and levels of remuneration for managerial positions in the private sector. (Kalmanoff and Hirschman would cross paths again in the late 1950s and early 1960s, when they both joined Columbia University; Hirschman considered Kalmanoff a "remarkably pleasant and intelligent person with a lot of critical common sense [and] initiative," and supported his application for a job at the World Bank, where he would become the deputy director of the Industrial Projects Department.)[15]

One wonders whether the decision to let Knapp's proposal fall and to remain instead in Bogotá, reinventing himself again as a private consultant, was due to the unattractive prospect of moving back to a United States ravaged by McCarthyist hysteria. In mid-1954 McCarthy was already under attack for his methods, but he was still a force to be reckoned with. Hirschman surely remembered well how, only two years earlier, the situation at the Fed had become difficult in a matter of months. At the same time, Colombia had been a beautiful discovery for the Hirschmans; they had made new friends and led an interesting life. Moreover, having had his experience with large organizations at the Fed, it is very probable that Hirschman truly relished the prospect of more independent work. If one conviction had taken root in him from his experience in the army, it was a

FIGURE 3.2 Albert O. Hirschman with daughters Lisa and Katia (wearing the ponchos, left to right) and young friends in Colombia, 1953. Courtesy of Katia Salomon

FIGURE 3.3 Albert O. Hirschman with daughters Lisa and Katia in Tunjuelito, Colombia, 1953. Courtesy of Katia Salomon

"dislike of mastodontic organizations and the appreciation of private initiative and responsibility."[16]

Certainly, his increasing frustration was one important reason for leaving the council (by then renamed the Planning Office). As Hirschman
wrote to Knapp, the Planning Office was not functioning. Having failed
to establish any effective working relationship with relevant ministries, the
office was constantly ignored and left out of the loop. Hirschman reported
a scene of irrelevant and wasteful administration at its worst:

The Office has taken the line of least resistance by spending practically its entire
time on regional programs. It's so much pleasanter: one travels, one is feted by
the local authorities still thrilled by foreign experts whose glamour has worn a bit
thin in the capital, and one escapes the thorny problems of collaborations with the
Ministers. Then one throws together in a few weeks a report about how many road
kilometers, kilowatts, schools, hospitals, houses, etc. are to be built in that province
during the next five years, tells the benighted population that they should long ago
have moved from the slopes to the tropical plains and the whole thing is sent to the
President and published.

The entire process was totally inconsequential, based on the unrealistic
conception that the voice of the Planning Office carried weight with the
president, who instead "*at best* gives the report, unread, to the competent
Minister," who in turn trashes it without further ado. Hirschman concluded, "The whole procedure raises tremendous hopes which soon evapo-
rate leaving a very bitter taste behind."[17]

The sense of disappointment that Hirschman felt for the ineffectual work
of the development planning authorities was mutual, at least for some. Perhaps because of continuing conflicts with an economist who had already
won the trust of the Colombian government, Hirschman apparently never
managed to convince his Colombian counterparts of the value of his work.
Emilio Toro, executive director of the World Bank for a constituency of several Latin American countries and president of the Colombian Economic
Development Council, was particularly disappointed by Hirschman. In late
1952, he synthesized the view of Colombian high officials to the Bank's vice
president, Robert Garner:

Hirschman is a good man in his restricted field of monetary matters, but as Director of Programs, to plan the development of a country in all its aspects, he falls

short and very short. He lacks broadness of concept, leadership, initiative, personality and has difficulties in expressing and getting consideration for his ideas. When
I compare the work done by the [World Bank's] Economic Mission to Colombia in
four months, the task accomplished by the Administrative Mission in five months
and the service rendered by the Committee of Economic Development in nine
months, all under the direction of Currie, with the work that the planning office
has accomplished in seven months, under Hirschman, I feel appalled.[18]

It would be difficult to imagine a more abrasive brush-off of one's work. A
discrepancy of judgments this wide between Bogotá and Washington suggests that Hirschman and the council started on the wrong foot, and then
things simply went from bad to worse.

The contrasts, however, took the shape of a clash between opposing visions of policy making. On one side, Currie and other World Bank
economists advocated broad and balanced policies of intervention, which
encompassed a variety of sectors and required the development of strong
planning skills by government bodies. On the other side, Hirschman
favored investments on specific projects that would in turn trigger further
investments via the stimulation of what he would later call "backward and
forward linkages."

Linkages provided an interpretive lens to observe the many and unpredictable concatenations of investment decisions that characterize a development process. Hirschman's starting point was a vigorous opposition to
the rhetoric of the comprehensive plan that characterized development
economics in the 1940s and 1950s. His first published criticism appeared
in a 1954 article in which he described integrated development planning
as a "myth" and a futile exercise, based on heterogeneous, tentative, and
imprecise budget figures. According to Hirschman, the rhetoric of the plan
had little to do with the policies that were actually implemented, and at
times that rhetoric was used to hide a lack of vision and utter confusion:
"the pretense of total, integrated economic planning could and often does
coexist quite amicably with, and may serve to cover up, unregenerated total
improvisation in the actual undertaking and carrying out of investment
projects."[19] Hirschman also knew how to be abrasive.

In his view, the comprehensive approach envisioned by Currie bore the
same flaws as the theories that were driving development economics in
those years. Hirschman's critique of these theories took full shape in his

book *The Strategy of Economic Development*, written after he and his family had returned from Colombia to the United States, when he was Visiting Research Professor in Economics at Yale in 1956–1957 and (with support from the Rockefeller Foundation) 1957–1958, and published by Yale University Press in 1958.[20]

As shown in the final section of this chapter, however, an exclusive focus on the theoretical debate between conflicting theories does not do full justice to the experience of development policy making that was pioneered by Hirschman, Currie, and many others. What in theory appeared as a conflict between diametrically opposing doctrines, in practice was a much more nuanced discussion about specific and limited policy options.

HIGH DEVELOPMENT THEORY: *THE STRATEGY OF ECONOMIC DEVELOPMENT*

On various occasions, Hirschman offered a number of hints on the circumstances that generated his approach to development issues. In the preface to *The Strategy of Economic Development*, Hirschman stated that the main goal of his book was "to elucidate my own immediate experience in one of the so-called underdeveloped countries"—that is, "to reflect on my Colombian experience."[21] His observations during his stay in Colombia, he wrote in the 1980s, "remained key elements of the conceptual structure that I erected three years or so later in *Strategy*."[22] What is certain is that the gestation of the book was long. As early as the spring of 1953, reflecting on what to do at the end of his job for the Economic Development Council, Hirschman prepared a research project to study specific cases of successful industrial, agricultural, and financial ventures in order to "derive some general lessons for developmental policy" in less developed countries.[23] The history of specific projects as the basis for broader generalizations, which would become the explicit premise of Hirschman's subsequent books on development, was thus already present as an assumption for his earlier analyses and for *Strategy*. Perhaps even more significant was that, very early on, Hirschman conceived his approach as distinctly different from standard development theories: "through such studies one might find out more about the process of economic development than through theories dealing with aggregates only or through statistical manipulation involving the division of every conceivable economic variable by the National Income."[24]

Prevailing doctrines in development economics stressed, in one way or another, the need for the different sectors of a developing economy to remain in step in order to avoid difficulties originating from structural imbalances on the supply or the demand side. With a broad generalization, these analyses were subsumed under the banner of the "balanced growth" doctrine. As Hirschman highlighted, referring again to his Colombian experience, "it was the experience of finding myself instinctively so much at variance with this theory that made me aware of having acquired a distinct outlook on development problems."[25] To leave no doubts about his opposition to what he considered a flawed development orthodoxy, Hirschman called his approach the theory of "unbalanced growth."

The first major statement of the vision that would become known as the balanced-growth approach to development was a seminal 1943 article by Polish economist Paul Rosenstein-Rodan on the problems of industrialization in eastern and southeastern Europe. Writing during World War II, with the aim of defining a blueprint for the development of a region whose political, social, and economic weaknesses had destabilized the entire continent twice and aroused the imperialistic appetite of Nazi Germany, Rosenstein-Rodan discussed a number of concepts that would become standard elements of the development discourse in the postwar years.

The political economy of a pacified postwar Europe was *the* question that captured the attention of many scholars in the Allied countries. Hirschman, in *National Power*, studied the trade relations between Germany and its weaker neighbors. Gerschenkron focused on which socioeconomic changes should be realized within Germany to defuse its structural aggressiveness, thus proposing the eradication of the eastern Junkers. Rosenstein-Rodan's attention was devoted to strengthening the regions that had been the target of Germany's eastward imperial appetites. As his work was the synthesis of a research effort he had coordinated for the London-based Royal Institute for International Affairs, also known as Chatham House, the focus on eastern and southeastern Europe was not surprising. Many European governments in exile had relocated to London, so a huge network of scholars and diplomats existed sources of information about those areas. Even more important, Britain had a direct interest in building a hegemonic role for itself in the postwar reconstruction of eastern Europe. The Soviet takeover of that area would frustrate British plans, but in 1941–1943, when Rosenstein-Rodan conducted his research, that scenario was still open.

Rosenstein-Rodan highlighted the problem of "agrarian excess population" that characterized central and southeastern Europe, as well as the condition of "disguised unemployment" in the agricultural sector that made productivity of the agrarian excess population equal or close to zero.[26] The solution, as he saw it, lay in the transfer of this excess population to a newly established industrial sector. In order to avoid imbalances in supply and demand that would endanger the profitability of the new factories, this industrial sector would have to be treated "like one huge firm or trust."[27]

Even though Rosenstein-Rodan did not explicitly mention a policy of "balanced growth," this is what he was de facto proposing when he suggested considering the industrial sector as an indivisible enterprise. As an example, he used a shoe factory. If taken individually, such a factory would quickly fail because of insufficient demand, as peasants would not have the income to buy shoes on the market and the shoe factory workers did not provide a large enough market to absorb its entire production. What was doomed to fail at the micro level, however, could succeed at the macro level. As Rosenstein-Rodan put it, "If, instead, one million unemployed workers were taken from the land and put, not into one industry, but into a whole series of industries which produce the bulk of the goods on which the workers would spend their wages, what was not true in the case of one shoe factory would become true in the case of a whole system of industries: it would create its own additional market."[28]

Rosenstein-Rodan also insisted that this new industrial sector ought to be established through huge investments in a limited amount of time, lest it die in the cradle. This concept was later christened the "big push"—that is, a concentrated effort to reach a stage of self-sustained growth before inertia and diminishing returns fatally doom the plan.

Rosenstein-Rodan's article was the first of a long series of studies in the same vein. In one of the most influential articles of early development economics, W. Arthur Lewis built his model of a dual-sector economy on the same premises as Rosenstein-Rodan's—namely, the existence of excess population in a stagnating sector (mainly agriculture but, in Lewis's model, also urban casual jobs, petty retail trading, and domestic services) and the migration of this unproductive labor force to a newly established industrial sector. In Lewis's words, economic development occurs through the transfer of excess population from the "subsistence sector," characterized by low productivity, to the "capitalist sector," which uses reproducible capital and is characterized by high productivity.[29] Equally fundamental, in Lewis's view, was the acceleration of capitalist growth. In a widely quoted sentence, he stated, "The central problem in the theory of economic development is to understand the process by which a community which was previously saving and investing 4 or 5 per cent of its national income or less, converts itself into an economy where voluntary saving is running at about 12 to 15 per cent of national income or more."[30] This shift from a low to a high rate of savings and investments was the main feature of the economic "takeoff" of a less developed country.[31]

Columbia University economist Ragnar Nurkse elaborated on the concept of complementarities first put forth by Rosenstein-Rodan, again emphasizing the crucial importance of synchronized investments in a wide range of industries: "Here is an escape of the deadlock; here the result is an over-all enlargement of the market."[32] As Nurkse concluded, "a frontal attack . . . a wave of capital investments in a number of different industries" was profitable where individual investments would not have survived the limitation of the market.[33] This was an approach very distant from standard laissez-faire economic policy. But, as Hirschman noted, these reflections, "while being themselves novel and heterodox, were rapidly shaping up in the 1950s as a new orthodoxy."[34]

In the early 1950s, Hirschman was witnessing the construction of that orthodoxy in real time. Nurkse's volume on problems of capital formation in underdeveloped countries caused a sensation in the field when it appeared in 1953, and the sensation was even stronger when Lewis's article appeared one year later. At a time when Hirschman was trying to make sense of how to trigger industrial and economic growth in Colombia, these scholars were shaping the field by offering broad analyses of the fundamental mechanisms of development processes and ways to break out of vicious circles. If the development literature offered important food for thought, it was often served in terms of broad generalizations.

Hirschman found himself confronting this literature while learning from a very localized and specific context. This was, no doubt, also the experience of the Lewises, the Nurkses, and the Rosenstein-Rodans, who had taken their experience in the field seriously and had elaborated their analyses on that basis. Hirschman's characterization of development experts as people comfortably seated at Washington desks, as he had depicted them in his letter to Rossi-Doria, did no justice to the practitioners and scholars who were frantically exploring "the field"—at least, it did not do justice to that early generation of development economists. But during his Colombia years, Hirschman must have felt that those early attempts at tackling the problems of economic backwardness were overemphasizing certain processes while missing an entire spectrum of different possibilities. In fact, Hirschman would later summarize his attitude as a "passion for the possible," in contrast to analyses that he regarded as limited and often excessively focused on what is simply "probable."[35]

Perhaps Hirschman was also connecting some missing dots in his 1945 work, *National Power and the Structure of Foreign Trade*. The historical background of that study was the Nazi policy of economic imperialism toward eastern and southeastern European countries. When he wrote his manuscript in 1942, he analyzed the dynamics between Nazi Germany and its weaker neighbors to discuss how to reorganize postwar trade policies in ways less conducive to political manipulation. In the same months, Paul Rosenstein-Rodan was studying the same subject and for the same reasons—that is, envisioning a stronger international equilibrium that would make the economic aggression of one country against its neighbors impractical. The novelty of Hirschman's study lay in using the traditional theory of international trade to make sense of cumulative asymmetric power relations between countries. Rosenstein-Rodan and the Chatham House working party, instead, referred to a very different tradition, deeply rooted in the work of central European economists who were the first to discuss the economic conditions of their countries in term of backwardness and underdevelopment, such as the German Friedrich List (whose major volume was published in 1841) and the Rumanian Mihail Manoilescu (whose main contributions appeared between 1929 and 1942).[36] Most of all, they completely turned the standard laissez-faire argument on its head. Since the central European countries lacked any comparative advantage in industrial production, laissez-faire supporters argued that their path to prosperity could only pass through the export of agrarian products. Rosenstein-Rodan claimed instead that, precisely because of their poor agrarian economies, what these countries needed was a huge state-sponsored industrializing effort. In other words, Rosenstein-Rodan put aside the question of foreign trade to focus on the internal development of eastern European countries. His important article was based on this innovative shift—and Hirschman, of all people, could appreciate the power of Rosenstein-Rodan's 1943 unorthodox study to set the tone for a new field of inquiry.

The common trait among the analyses of the first generation of development scholars was thus the insistence on the need to break the interdependent mechanisms that kept a country in a state of poverty and backwardness. A multipronged attack against these many obstacles to development was often proposed. A sustained and balanced effort was the standard strategy to break the vicious circle. A conference in Rio de Janeiro in 1957 was the occasion for Rosenstein-Rodan to summarize this strategy with the metaphor of the "Big push," which Nurkse, intervening at the conference, described as an "interesting new term."[37] By then, Hirschman was writing his manuscript at Yale, but he also attended the Rio conference, and as Adelman notes, this was for him "an eye-opener," as Latin American social scientists highlighted structural imbalances and disequilibria as growth-inducing opportunities.[38] In an explicit reaction to the orthodoxy of the Rosenstein-Rodans and the Nurkses, some researchers viewed the process of economic development as substantially *un*balanced. The two main supporters of "unbalanced growth" would become, one year later, Albert O. Hirschman and the Austrian-born British economist Paul P. Streeten.

In *Strategy*, Hirschman questioned the very fundamentals of the theory of balanced growth, writing:

My principal point is that the theory fails as a theory of *development*. Development presumably means the process of *change* of one type of economy *into* some other more advanced type. But such a process is given up as hopeless by the balanced growth theory which finds it difficult to visualize how the "underdevelopment equilibrium" can be broken into at any point. . . . The balanced growth theory reaches the conclusion that an entirely new, self-contained modern industrial economy must be superimposed on the stagnant and equally self-contained traditional sector.[39]

Unbalanced growth, on the contrary, was based on the assumption that because of the interdependence of inputs and output between different sectors and subsectors of the economy, the growth of one sector ahead of others would trigger rebalancing mechanisms, such as changes in relative prices or more direct public policies. Figure 3.4 offers a simple description of the two policies.

Hirschman, however, later recognized that the unbalanced growth of a sector, in the admittedly common situation of lack of excess capacity of, say,

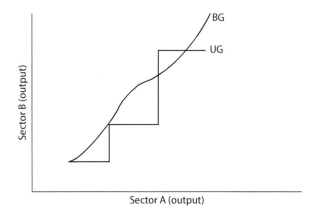

FIGURE 3.4 Balanced and unbalanced growth. *Source*: Hirschman 1984a, 107

power and transportation facilities, would leave other sectors deprived and thus actually retrogressing. Hirschman defined this possibility as antagonistic growth. This is not the same as a zero-sum game: the economy progresses, though making two steps ahead in one sector and one step behind in another, as depicted in figure 3.5.

With the concept of antagonistic growth, Hirschman was pointing to a case of limited resources, in which, as Deirdre McCloskey later noted, the production possibility curve does not move out fast enough, therefore causing huge shifts of demand along it (figure 3.6).

But Hirschman's case for unbalanced growth, though obviously related to the availability of resources (as the discussion of antagonistic growth has shown), relied on yet a different perspective. Indeed, Hirschman's main

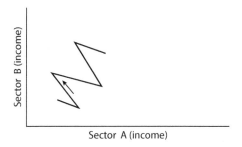

FIGURE 3.5 Antagonistic growth. *Source*: Hirschman 1984a, 107

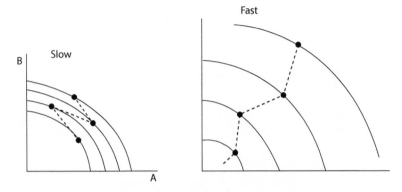

FIGURE 3.6 D. McCloskey to Albert [Hirschman], November 9 [1982 or 1983], AOHP.

point was that posing the problem in terms of insufficient resources—
primarily capital—was misleading. He considered the resources and the
elements necessary for development as latent, hidden, but nonetheless
existent. In a famous passage, he asserted that "development depends not
so much on finding optimal combinations for given resources and factors
of production as on calling forth and listing for development purposes
resources and abilities that are hidden, scattered, or badly utilized."[40]
Thus, the problem was not that factors allegedly necessary for development were missing, but rather that ways of summoning and combining
existing elements must be put in motion. As Streeten wrote, "One aspect
of the case for unbalance is that it highlights the spots where action is
needed most urgently, and thus economises in a resource often in short
supply, viz. the power to take decisions."[41] Hirschman put it only slightly
differently. The special characteristic of the diagnosis by theorists of
unbalanced growth was that, instead of being concerned with the lack of
one or more factors, they were concerned "with the deficiency in the combining process itself."[42] In a remarkable consonance with Streeten's view,
Hirschman added that underdeveloped countries "find it difficult to take
the decisions needed for development in the required number and at the
required speed."[43] The scarcity of different factors of production or elements conducive to economic growth, often highlighted by development
economists as crucial obstacles to development, was thus reduced to only
"one basic scarcity"—that is, the ability to make development decisions.[44]

This *reductio ad unum* and the privileged status conferred on decision-making mechanisms implied that the usual litany of the many obstacles to development said to plague backward regions was being overemphasized. In *The Strategy of Economic Development*, Hirschman denied the importance of "obstacles" highlighted by most of the existing literature on development, which to him conveyed the flawed idea that it was sufficient to remove one or several obstacles to release hitherto repressed energies, "much like race horses after the lifting of the starting gate."[45] Indeed, in a later article Hirschman argued that the very idea of obstacles in the development field was conceptually weak. Alleged obstacles may in fact reveal themselves as positive assets. The extended family is one such case. Western economists

FIGURE 3.7 Albert O. Hirschman experiencing alternative horizons in Pacho, Colombia, 1952. Courtesy of Katia Salomon

have usually considered the extended family as an obstacle to development because it disincentivizes individual entrepreneurship, assuming, as Hirschman put it, that "no one in his right mind can really care for the welfare of his third cousin."[46] "But suppose 'they' do?," Hirschman retorted. In that case, the extended family may liberate resources for cooperative entrepreneurship, or facilitate transactions, that would not be available to nuclear economic units. Of course, this is not necessarily so. The extended family may still reveal itself as an obstacle to development. But Hirschman's objection demoted it from its ahistorical and acontextual pedestal, opening horizons for a variety of different possible cases.

Not all obstacles turn out to be positive assets, of course. Many obstacles remain obstacles, no matter from which point of view one observes them. Yet their removal is not imperative as one might think: in many cases, they can simply be overcome by following an alternate route. Capital accumulation is a case in point. The great majority of economists, economic historians, and development economists considered capital accumulation a prerequisite of industrialization and economic growth. But Alexander Gerschenkron, in a series of studies published in the 1950s—of which the most important was presented at the 1952 conference organized by Hoselitz and attended by Hirschman—demonstrated that countries lacking primitive capital accumulation had in many cases found alternative ways to bypass the problem through what he called "substitute factors."[47] The long capital accumulation that fueled the industrial revolution in England was accomplished in a much shorter period by banks in Germany and by the state in Russia. The obstacle might be there, but it was bypassed, not removed. Finally, in the case of obstacles that remain detrimental to development and that cannot be turned into an asset or bypassed, Hirschman noted that often their resolution can be at least postponed. Moving the economy forward in the presence of an obstacle, Hirschman argued, would either prompt stronger efforts at removing it—if it proved to be truly a hindrance—or confirm that it was correct, after all, to postpone a head-on attack on it, if the obstacle appeared not to be that important.[48]

Returning to the core problem of underdevelopment—which does not consist primarily of a lack of resources or the presence of insurmountable obstacles, but is a more fundamental scarcity in the ability to make development decisions—one must also recognize that the specific resource, the ability to make decisions, cannot be economized. Each development move (private investment, trade agreement, managerial strategy, and so on) needs a decision informing it. Hirschman's book was thus primarily concerned with discussing the "inducement mechanisms" that would trigger as much decision-making ability as possible.[49]

The search for inducement or pressure mechanisms made Hirschman particularly sensitive to all possible sequences conducive to investment decisions irrespective of their apparent improbability. This is why, in Hirschman's vocabulary, terms such as "hidden rationalities," "inverted" or "disorderly sequences," or "cart-before-the-horse sequences" became so prominent.[50] They all referred to his goal of building a development strategy that expanded the possibilities for triggering development decisions. Because of the nature of these concepts and their structuration as variations on a theme, it is impossible to give a sense here of the richness of the volume. But it is worth devoting a few words to how Hirschman reasoned about effective ways to induce sequences of investment—a concept he fully explored through the idea of "backward" and "forward linkages." The concept of linkages implied dismissing synchronic solutions to the problem of industrialization and replacing them with sequential solutions, much more realistic in light of the limited ability to take decisions in developing countries—and also less risky, precisely because they distributed financial and administrative resources through a sequential process instead of committing them all at once in a comprehensive plan, and because they left space for adjustments along the way.[51] It should be noted that this alleged limited ability to take decisions was not meant to have any patronizing connotation or imply any judgment on the ability of individuals, political elites, entrepreneurs, or grassroots cooperatives to take decisions; rather, it emphasized that institutional and economic constraints might make the decision-making process more difficult. As we will see in the next chapter, Hirschman was the first to acknowledge that this was an oversimplification, so much so that he would devote his next book to the study of processes of decision making in Latin America.

The linkage effects, per se, were not outright innovative ideas. They amounted to a rationalization of the idea that most economic activities stimulate the production of inputs needed either in those activities or as inputs for other activities. The former relationship is called backward linkage because it emphasizes how a certain economic activity induces the establishment of a new activity for the production of inputs useful to the former.

Thus, it triggers new activities upstream in the production chain. The latter relationship is called forward linkage because it shows how a certain economic activity induces the establishment of new activities downstream.

The power of Hirschman's analysis lay in the way he used these simple concepts to develop an analytical framework to interpret the process of development and possibly inform investment decisions. As Hirschman later summarized the role of the linkage approach for development strategies, "development is essentially the record of how one thing leads to another, and the linkages are that record."[52]

Measuring linkages from a quantitative perspective proved very difficult. Input-output analysis tried to do that, but even cutting-edge research such as the studies of Hollis Chenery and Tsunehiko Watanabe offered only a coarse-grain analysis of some intersectoral connections.[53] The linkage concept is thus more useful as a general framework for thinking about development strategies than as a precise tool for planning development investments. This approach, in particular, shifted the focus about the value of investment decisions from their immediate contribution to output to a broader assessment of both their direct contribution to output and their *inducing potential* for further investment decisions.[54]

The linkage framework made it possible to recognize certain patterns typical of industrialization in underdeveloped countries, such as early specialization in the transformation of imported semimanufactured goods into final goods. Only at a later stage would these countries venture into the domestic production of intermediate goods and finally of capital goods. In this respect, the linkage framework offered valuable insights into the role of imports for industrialization.

The very presence of imports in a specific sector signaled, as Hirschman emphasized, a demand for certain products. If imports grew enough, then it would become convenient to produce the imported products domestically. Contrary to usual analyses, then, imports were not so much an alternative to domestic production as a preliminary phase carrying important information for the domestic process of economic policy making. Seen from this perspective, imports were not simply the result of a static distribution of comparative advantages among trading nations, as the standard theory of international trade would put it. Nor could they be interpreted as the instrument through which industrially powerful countries colonized foreign markets, as theorists opposed to free trade would maintain.

The linkages approach proposed a more varied story: imports had a fundamental signaling role that provided crucial information to importing countries about possible industrialization strategies. Once the break-even threshold for domestic production was reached, this would start in earnest, and at that point, but only at that point, protectionist policies would help prevent destruction of the infant industry by international competition. As Hirschman, with an only apparent paradox, argued, "countries tend to develop a comparative advantage in the articles they *import*."[55] Protectionist policies should be phased according to the inducement mechanisms they trigger or inhibit: if the "infant industry" stage called for protectionist policies, the "prenatal" stage called for open market treatment.[56]

The pursuit of backward linkage dynamics—their phased, sequential path from final products to capital goods and the role of protectionist policies in the development of the various phases—became widely known as import-substituting industrialization, or ISI, policies. These had an important role in many less developed countries in the 1950s and 1960s, especially in Latin America. Also, as the name immediately makes clear, they revealed a bias in favor of the industrial sector.

In this regard, it is worth considering the role of agriculture in Hirschman's analysis. As he admitted, agriculture in general, especially subsistence agriculture, is characterized by a structural scarcity of linkage effects. Backward linkages cannot exist, except for inputs such as chemical products and machinery in modern large estates. Forward linkages are often limited to some processing, but a large part of the production is destined for either domestic consumption or export.[57] The only linkage mechanism easily observable in the agricultural sector is what Hirschman, based on the fine analysis of Canadian economist Melville H. Watkins, would later call a "consumption linkage." In this case, and especially in poor countries, an income increase originating from a boom in primary exports would be mainly directed toward further domestic consumption of food and other primary products, thus leading to additional food production.[58]

Whereas in *Strategy* Hirschman discussed the linkage concept primarily with reference to the industrial sector, the concept was later broadened to include a number of further variations, such as consumption linkages, fiscal linkages, inside linkages, outside linkages, and so on.[59] Hirschman also mentioned the negative linkages that might emerge and sabotage the development process but, characteristically, decided not to elaborate on them.

This is an appropriate entry point to one important aspect of Hirschman's approach to his book *Strategy* and, more generally, his personal attitude throughout his scholarly career—namely, his deep commitment to reform-ist-oriented democratic policy making.

Potentially disruptive linkages and tensions were, according to Hirschman, unavoidable. The development process, he noted, could be represented as a basic "grand tension" affecting entire societies. Less widely understood, however, was that new strengths could emerge from the tensions created by the development process. He saw his task as explaining the importance of these strengths and positive sequences, analyzing them under the cat-egory of linkages and inducement mechanisms. One consequence of this endeavor, he hoped, was to broaden the analytical horizons of foreign aid practices. He wrote wishfully:

Economic advisers would be far less given to determining priorities from the out-side . . . they would instead be intent on discovering under what pressures people are operating and toward what forward steps they are already being impelled. Instead of laying down "first things first" rules, they would try to understand how progress can at times meander strangely through many peripheral areas before it is able to dislodge backwardness from the central positions where it may be strongly entrenched.[60]

This insight alone was a result of the greatest magnitude for the devel-opment field. But Hirschman had an even deeper concern. The failure to refine the analysis of underdevelopment and to make development policies more effective, he feared, might open the door to potentially disastrous alternative solutions. "Economic policy may be worse than ineffectual," he wrote, "futility can be abruptly replaced by brutality, by utter disregard for human suffering, for acquired rights, for lawful procedures, for tradi-tional values, in short for the 'thin and precarious crust of civilization.' "[61] Hirschman had witnessed no less than that during the years of *la violencia* in Colombia. Futility and brutality were in a sense two faces of the same malaise, in which the failure to accept the incremental nature of change led either to comprehensive development plans that were as grandiose as they were futile or to violent revolution and antidemocratic regimes.

Hirschman's goal was to broaden the space and sharpen the analytical instruments for a third way, an intermediate and deeply reformist agenda between these two extremes, by discussing the possible mechanisms through which the process of change could advance—sometimes through inverted, nonlinear, and otherwise unorthodox sequences.

We have already mentioned this reformist dimension of Hirschman: the way he embedded the moral and political dimension into his scholarship is a crucial element of his contribution to development economics and social science. Indeed, this point was so important to Hirschman that he emphasized it in later reassessments of *Strategy*. In an article that further discussed the linkage approach twenty years later, Hirschman noted an apparent paradox: the similarity of this concept to the "staple thesis," according to which the development of underdeveloped countries is deeply shaped by the specific characteristics of the primary products they export, but also to the thesis of the "development of underdevelopment," according to which it was precisely the successful exportation of primary products that made the underdevelopment of many peripheral countries so formidable a problem.

It would be difficult to find two theses more mutually opposed. If the staple thesis described how primary exports had made development possible, the development-of-underdevelopment thesis emphasized the underdeveloping function of primary exports. Hirschman argued that the linkage approach overcame this antithesis and, more important, emphasized its reformist imprinting. Though the linkage approach recognizes that development processes can go awry, it nonetheless shows their positive potential. Hirschman argued, therefore, that the linkage approach "has a claim to be more truly dialectical than the development-of-underdevelopment thesis, which misses altogether the intimate connection between the various phases of what ought to be understood as a dynamic process."[62] Hirschman, of course, was not really interested in discussing which approach had more dialectical potential. Rather, for Hirschman, the dialectical potential was a test of the reformist, as opposed to the revolutionary, nature of this specific analytical framework.

The publication of *Strategy* positioned Hirschman firmly at the center of the development debate, and his terminology, first and foremost the concept of linkages, entered immediately into the standard vocabulary of development economics.[63] No less important, from a strictly professional perspective, the book secured him tenure at Columbia University. *Strategy* was reviewed not only by economists but also by political scientists and sociologists, confirming the wide horizon that characterized Hirschman's analysis, as well as the broad spectrum of sources he had used. Reviewers highlighted that the book was "full of fresh ideas and new angles of looking at economic phenomena," that it was "highly readable . . . [and] well worth the careful attention of the profession," and that it had an "original and thought-provoking approach . . . [and showed a] healthy skepticism."[64] Most of all, reviewers praised Hirschman's analysis as "a powerful contribution to the theory of development as a process" and a truly "dynamic" theory.[65]

Jacques Polak, one of the most experienced economists at the International Monetary Fund, declared himself "profoundly fascinated by the book throughout," and complimentary letters, many of them with long comments prompted by the book, came from François Perroux, Gustav Ranis, John E. Sawyer (an economics professor at Yale and future president of Williams College and the Andrew W. Mellon Foundation), Jack Condliffe, Hans Singer, and Wolfgang Stolper, among others.[66] Roy Harrod was a late but enthusiastic reader. In 1963, he wrote to Hirschman that he had finally read *Strategy*, finding it "the most interesting book that I have read on economics for years, perhaps the most stimulating book that I have read on any subject for some time," and concluded, "I have now put it back on my pile of *legenda* for a second reading, so that I can work more deeply into your system of thought."[67]

The reactions, though, were not unanimously enthusiastic. If everyone recognized Hirschman's novel perspective, more than one reader raised doubts about what they considered an exaggerated one-sidedness. "Has he perhaps not gone a bit too far at times?" asked one reviewer.[68] The same idea was reiterated by Canadian political economist Melville Watkins: "Iconoclasm is itself a useful corrective, but it can be pushed too far."[69] If Hirschman's criticism of the excessively static balanced-growth perspective was considered useful and refreshing, his insistence on investment-inducing mechanisms as *opposed* to other shortages left many unconvinced. Stanford development economist Hollis Chenery was particularly hard on this:

Hirschman's emphasis on the ability to make investment (or development) decisions leads to a theory of development which is more applied psychology than economics. Since in this view capital and other input limitations are illusory, the economist is left with nothing to economize except the elusive quality of decision-making. . . . Whatever the merits of including motivational factors in a theory of economic development, Hirschman surely overstates his case. Even if all his speculations about the responses of investors, managers and bureaucrats are correct, the scarcity of decision-making ability cannot be made to serve as the sole guide to development policy any more than can capital scarcity or the other criteria that he rejects.[70]

As Chenery concluded, "a policy-maker maximizing induced investment would run into shortages of foreign exchange, saving, or skilled labor unless he had taken them into account in setting his priorities."[71]

Hirschman, in fact, had not excluded the possibility of the usual shortages of capital resources and the like. Rather, his point had been to deemphasize that exclusive focus. Chenery was ungenerous in his reading of *Strategy*, though there is no doubt that Hirschman's tone had often been provocative. As one reviewer wrote, "in style it appears deliberately polemical. . . . In good Ricardian fashion Hirschman argues the extreme position, adding the caveats almost as afterthoughts."[72]

It did not help that Hirschman's book lacked almost entirely any quantitative analysis, thus leaving many of the questions that he raised ultimately unresolved. One reviewer quipped, "More scarce than capital in underdeveloped areas is the data necessary for testing [Hirschman's] hypothesis."[73] Benjamin Higgins, who otherwise highly appreciated the book, wrote that it was "impressionistic, imaginative, and intuitive rather than rigorous and systematic."[74] But this was hardly Hirschman's fault. As we have seen, he had a trained eye for statistical analysis. This had been an important element of his scholarship since the years in Trieste, in his studies of the Italian economy, in his reports for the Bergen conference, and in his previous book, *National Power*. But statistical data about less developed countries were often missing or very difficult to recover. With regard to Colombia in particular, statistical series of national income and capital formation and basic data about many different sectors of the economy were first assembled by the Currie mission in 1949. Hirschman simply did not have the numbers to give a quantitative basis to his study, and the few available were too aggregate to be used for Hirschman's elaboration of the linkage effect and inducement mechanisms.

THE POLITICAL ECONOMY OF DEVELOPMENT PLANNING

The mainly theoretical conflict between supporters of balanced versus unbalanced strategies overlapped with a more practical discussion about the loan policies of foreign aid organizations—specifically, about the need to fund comprehensive plans of investments or, on the contrary, to make loans targeting only specific and directly productive projects.

Balanced development was conducive to more comprehensive planning policies. We have already seen that Rosenstein-Rodan recommended treating the entire industrial sector "like one huge firm or trust." The theoretical emphasis on capital accumulation by Lewis and others led likewise to the application of a planning perspective. Even if Lewis refused "detailed central planning," considering it "undemocratic, bureaucratic, inflexible, and subject to great error and confusion," he was a strong supporter of what he labeled "piece-meal planning." This, however, implied the need to control and manipulate significant macroeconomic variables such as capital formation, the level of exports, and the level of industrial production.[75] Moreover, Lewis envisioned a major role for state intervention in the economy. "The little man can improve his own house, or his small farm," he wrote, but "the biggest lump of investment has to be in public works and public utilities," especially infrastructures such as roads, railways, harbors, and electric power.[76]

Planning, of course, was not a novel argument. Starting at least in the 1930s, planning was often advocated as a necessary policy for all mature societies, be they Communist dictatorships or liberal democracies. Planning promised tremendous progress in social organization. In the interwar years, for example, Karl Mannheim illustrated how "a co-ordination of social techniques" would multiply social resources and opportunities.[77] If the Soviet experiment was for most a clearly negative example of very restrictive planning, scholars of liberal perspectives such as Eugene Staley advocated planning as a synonym for "conscious control of economic activity."[78]

In the postwar years, and with specific reference to underdeveloped countries, development economists who supported planning mainly underscored the need to increase investment and labor productivity, whereas a growth in consumption that reduced investment was considered highly dangerous.[79] John K. Galbraith argued that planning was the only policy available to countries where private entrepreneurship was anemic and market mechanisms weak: "Perhaps—just perhaps—if development were left to markets incentives, it would proceed as rapidly as under public auspices, or more rapidly. But suppose it did not. Suppose the private vision and entrepreneurship were lacking. Or the capital. Who can be sure? . . . Then to count on free enterprise now would be a dreadful risk."[80]

From a planning perspective, therefore, injecting capital into a backward economy was necessary but by no means sufficient. Given the distortions and weaknesses of markets, a planning authority should take care of the allocation of resources and of strategic decisions about the future path of growth of a country's economy. In the words of Rosenstein-Rodan, planning was necessary to provide "guidelines or principles for determining the amount, the composition and the timing of public investments," as well as to define "the system of incentives and disincentives needed to orient the private sector's amount and composition of investment." He concluded: "A specific vision [of] which sectors should grow at what rate is needed. General principles of 'sound' economic policy alone are ungrammatical prose."[81]

It will not come as a surprise that Hirschman was among the most vocal opponents of this approach. His writings on development show a constant skepticism about the promises of planning. He summarized the main points in an article published ten years after *Strategy*, in which he systematized ideas he had been elaborating since the mid-1950s.[82] Hirschman's first concern was that aid to finance a comprehensive plan would be excessively intrusive. Having to address such macroeconomic categories as, say, the relationship between investment and consumption, or exchange rates and price levels, the plan would directly benefit certain groups and harm others. As a consequence, an overall program would probably stimulate internal opposition at levels that a single project, even an important one, would not.

Second, Hirschman argued that aid programs would often risk being either redundant or useless. A government receiving an aid package in return for a promise to pursue certain macroeconomic policies might in fact already be committed to them, irrespective of the promise of aid. Foreign aid, in this case, would only seem useful for "rewarding virtue . . . where virtue appears of its own accord."[83] Sensible though this consideration was, it should be noted that it did not make specific projects immune from the same kind of criticism.[84]

Alternatively, Hirschman argued, financial aid could be used to push a government to pursue macroeconomic policies that would otherwise not be included in the government's agenda. In this case, the task would become "infinitely more difficult," for it would entail not just rewarding existing virtue but "bringing virtue into the world," definitely a noble endeavor, but one usually destined to fail.[85] As Arnold Harberger observed about the U.S. foreign aid agency (the Agency for International Development, or AID), "friction is a natural concomitant of program and sector loans. . . . The more deeply AID becomes involved in what the recipient countries consider to be their internal affairs, the greater this friction is likely to be."[86] Usually, to avoid an open deterioration of the relations between donor and recipient, "continued reluctant accommodation" became the game of the day, resulting in an exhausting series of negotiations and postponement of deadlines, prolonging the duration of the aid program virtually endlessly.[87]

Hirschman noticed all these dangers during his years in Colombia, and this is why he focused instead on "how not to plan."[88] Specific project loans, in his view, had the advantage of being locally focused, subject to less politically biased technical evaluation, and most important, respectful of the strategic policy decisions of the recipient country. As Hirschman and many advocates of project loans maintained, an aid policy centered on specific investment projects would be less ambitious in goals and means but, for those very reasons, also more feasible and more efficient. This was all the more important for a recently established aid organization such as the World Bank. The bank needed to gain the confidence of North American investors—practically the only source of financial resources for international operations—and only specific and well-monitored projects, so it was thought, would guarantee American investors that loans were being administered according to sound criteria of responsible economic management.

Other scholars, however, argued that linking a loan to a single, well-defined project was wishful thinking. Rosenstein-Rodan, who after leaving Chatham House became a World Bank economist and then left the organization just before Hirschman moved to Colombia, argued that a project loan would finance not the project for which it was formally disbursed but the *marginal* project that the beneficiary country would have abandoned had it not obtained a line of credit from the Bank. Because the Bank did not want to finance risky endeavors, it directed its aid toward projects that were sound enough to be fairly high on the agenda of the beneficiary country. In other words, Bank funds would finance a project that the country would probably have financed out of its own budget anyway. This corresponded to Hirschman's concept of remunerating existing virtue. But it also meant that the Bank, by financing a project that would have been financed by the recipient country irrespective of the Bank's intervention, was freeing domestic resources for other projects that had previously been excluded from funding (usually riskier projects than the Bank would have been willing to support). Project loans, in other words, were vulnerable to the problem of "fungibility" of funds—that is, the transferability of funds from one project to another. As Rosenstein-Rodan put it in an interview, the Bank might think it was financing a dam, when in fact it was financing a brothel.[89] Indeed, this outcome would amount not simply to a failed attempt to bring virtue into the world (Hirschman's worst case criticism of program aid), but to a successful attempt to introduce evil!

Even critics of program loans, such as Hirschman and Harberger, admitted that the issue of fungibility was a serious one.[90] The solution, from their perspective, lay not in any comprehensive plan but in a dramatic improvement in the ability to monitor the execution of projects. It was more than a decade, however, before project evaluation became a relevant topic in foreign aid; Hirschman, as we will see in the next chapter, also had a pioneering role in that endeavor.

The controversy over balanced growth versus unbalanced growth, with its practical equivalent of program loans versus project loans, was, in the words of one participant and observer, "the most prominent of all in the development literature of the 1950s."[91] In development-economics histories, readers, and encyclopedias, this controversy is referred to as a milestone in the foundational years of the discipline.[92] Probably the only issue of comparable importance was W. Arthur Lewis's elaboration of a dual-sector model in 1954. Indeed, Paul Krugman referred to those pioneering debates as "the glory days of high development theory," significantly dating them from the 1943 article by Paul Rosenstein-Rodan, which inaugurated the literature on balanced growth, to the 1958 publication of Hirschman's *Strategy*, which attacked it.[93]

DEVELOPMENT ECONOMICS IN THEORY AND PRACTICE

The conceptual structure of *Strategy* was based on Hirschman's experience in Colombia, where he found himself deeply at odds with other economic advisers to the government, in particular Lauchlin Currie. As Hirschman put it in the introduction to his book, in Colombia he felt a strong dissatisfaction with the existing theories of growth in developing countries; at the same time, he began to see his own reflections "more and more like variations upon a common theme"—in other words, as elements of an internally consistent new approach.[94]

The clashes between balanced and unbalanced growth, and between planning and project approaches, have been recounted here mainly as they emerged from published work, where the two positions seem mutually irreconcilable. If, however, one observes the actual policy-making experiences of the supporters of those irreconcilable approaches, the picture becomes substantially less neatly defined. There are, in fact, many overlaps and points of agreement between analyses that, in principle, pointed in opposite directions. In other words, the nature and the real extent of those conflicts have usually been overemphasized.

This is less puzzling than it may appear. To be sure, differences did exist. But a more complete account of how things actually happened must also recognize that the logical and rhetorical leap from practice in the field to theoretical elaboration allowed for both remarkable convergence in the practice and divergence in the theory. Partly, this had to do with the premium originating from differentiating oneself from the positions of others. More important, however, it is an inherent feature of abstract thinking. To understand these dynamics better, it is worth observing in detail how Hirschman and Currie, stationed in Colombia, examined one of the standard icons of a country's economic industrialization: the iron and steel industry.

Domestic steel production is often regarded as an overriding strategic national interest, and postwar Colombia was no exception. The World Bank mission headed by Currie studied the issue with particular attention: in 1949, when the mission arrived in Colombia, a project for an integrated steel plant close to the city of Paz del Río, in the internal region of Belencito, was in an advanced stage of implementation. As it happened, the mission judged negatively both the choice to build an integrated steel plant, a capital-intensive solution whose break-even point would be reached only at very high volumes of output, and its location in the interior of the country, notwithstanding the presence of coal seams. Technological and geographical considerations—in particular, the low quality of the raw materials, the lack of waterways with the capacity to feed the cooling system, and the high altitude, which would have made combustion particularly difficult—contributed to making implementation of the project unadvisable. Moreover, the Belencito region was far removed from the country's main lines of communication, making it arduous and expensive to bring the output to its final destinations. The World Bank mission claimed that, because of its location, Paz del Río would never become an attractive location for other heavy enterprises, thus inhibiting the formation of a "growing point" and the harnessing of by-products of steel production.[95]

Whereas an integrated plant in the interior was uneconomical, the Bank's mission suggested, a smaller steel plant for the processing of imported scrap metal in Barranquilla, on the northern coast of the country, would make good economic sense. Without a coking plant and blast furnaces, it would be simpler and less expensive. Moreover, its location on the Caribbean coast at the terminus of one of the country's main railway lines put it in a strategic position to supply both domestic and international markets.[96] Various considerations made this solution politically unpalatable to the Colombian government, so the mission proposed a compromise. The Paz del Río integrated plant would be built, but it would be smaller and the technology simpler than originally conceived, so that it could be supplied by Colombian firms.[97] This way, the national need to produce a strategic good without depending on the foreign supply of scrap metal was guaranteed, without embarking on an investment of gigantic proportions and dubious economic sense. Moreover, because of the possibility of producing most of the machinery internally, the loss of foreign exchange would also be reduced. Finally, a smaller and simpler plant would help management and local workers acquire expertise without incurring major mistakes. The principle of learning by doing would be the basis of an incremental strategy, from small to large dimensions, and from relatively basic to more sophisticated technology.[98]

Hirschman presented his own reflections on the Paz del Río controversy in an article published in 1954.[99] Criticizing both the general trend toward "overall plans" and the specific decision of the Currie mission not to support the integrated steel plant, Hirschman wrote:

In spite of all the insistence on "overall" planning, I have yet to see a project that is thus [sic] well conceived rejected . . . on the ground that the investment required is too high considering the need for monetary stability and for "balanced" development. In Colombia, the only case to my knowledge into which this kind of consideration has thus far entered at all was that of Paz del Rio steel mill.[100]

Hirschman argued that, because of the effects of "backward" and "forward linkages," the development of the new industry had to be examined dynamically, taking into account the satellite and nonsatellite industries created as a consequence of establishing the main factory.

The considerations of a technical and geographic nature in the Currie report, however, underlined the weak impact that the investment in Paz del Río would have as a stimulus for other industrial sectors. As noted, it would have been very difficult to form a "growing point," which was considered the most desirable result by both Currie and Hirschman, who dedicated an entire chapter of *Strategy* to this concept.[101] When it became clear that construction of the plant in Paz del Río could not be avoided, an attempt was made to envision an incremental development of the plant. This would limit the disadvantages of the unfortunate location and at the same time allow the business to gain strength despite this initial handicap. There would have been gradual growth as staff and workers acquired competencies and the plant itself gained a bigger market share.

This reasoning was not too different from Hirschman's attempt to unfold the "hidden rationalities" of a development process. The Currie mission took a mediator's role between political-ideological or lobbying needs, on the one hand, and technological and economic issues, on the other. In other words, it positioned itself at the center of a process of structuring decision making—exactly what Streeten and Hirschman highlighted as the most necessary (as well as the rarest) element to trigger development sequences in backward countries.

In sum, the fundamental approaches of the World Bank mission and of Hirschman were more similar than the *ex post* reconstruction of the debates among development economists may suggest. Clearly, the agreement was not total. But different positions were not so clearly mutually opposed, and the fundamental visions about development were much more similar than their individual advocates were ready to admit. For example, the report of the Currie mission supported a number of other useful projects with arguments substantially equivalent to concepts such as linkages and agglomeration processes, widely used by advocates of an unbalanced growth approach, and showed a strong focus on specific projects. In general, the relevance of projects in the perspective of a planning approach was that projects were cornerstones of planning when it came to its implementation. In India, for example, advanced planning reports presented detailed lists of industrial projects.[102] An analysis of how theoretical reflections merged and intertwined with the practice of economic advising thus reveals a much less clear opposition between apparently irreconcilable approaches. In confronting the issue of the iron and steel industry in Colombia, both Currie and Hirschman reflected on mechanisms of industrial polarization, inducive mechanisms, and forward and backward linkages. One of them framed them as elements of a "balanced" development program, while the other underlined their economically "unbalancing" role. Yet, in the practice, both were seeing pretty much the same things, and their differences were stronger in accent than in language.

Sociologist of science Robert K. Merton has argued that many conflicts among social scientists have less to do with substantive, mutually exclusive assumptions and more to do with specific, rather limited issues about whether intellectual resources should be devoted to one or another problem. Often, when a conflict becomes public, it transforms into a battle for status. "The consequent polarization," Merton notes, "leads each group . . . to respond largely to stereotyped versions of what is being done by the other."[103] Of course, these stereotypes have some bases in reality, but they can be amplified into unrecognizable caricatures. Social scientists in each camp

develop selective perceptions of what is actually going on in the other. They see in the other's work primarily what the hostile stereotype has alerted them to see, and then promptly mistake the part for the whole. In this process, each group . . . becomes less and less motivated to study the work of the other, since there is manifestly little point in doing so. They scan the out-group's writings just enough to find ammunition for new fusillades.[104]

The debate between supporters of a balanced approach and supporters of an unbalanced approach is a good example of this Mertonian pattern. Differences existed. The positions, however, quickly radicalized, fossilizing their understanding of their opponent's claims into stereotypes. As one development economist once remarked, "it is the inevitable fate of authors to be remembered by their central ideas and not by the qualifying clauses they so carefully insert."[105] Indeed, the first to forget the qualifying clauses were colleagues in the discipline. Thus, debates on the possible policies to be followed in one case or another—often very context-specific and limited in range—became the basis for broad analytical positions that appeared to be polar opposites. This may have been particularly important to the generation of pioneers of the discipline of development economics. The new field was still in formation, and their claims to intellectually legitimacy were considered, as Merton said, "mutually exclusive and at odds."[106] Indeed, Hirschman's challenged the very legitimacy of the theory of balanced growth. It will be remembered that he argued that the balanced theory "fails as a theory of *development*"—thus depriving it of the basic right to contribute to the discipline.[107]

Contemporary readers noticed as much. In a perceptive analysis of *Strategy*, Amartya K. Sen confessed to be "a little puzzled" by the balanced versus unbalanced growth controversy. "Put in their native forms," he wrote, "both the doctrines look right; examined from the other's point of view, each looks totally inadequate." Yet his impression is that both doctrines had "a considerable amount of common ground."[108] Indeed, Sen highlighted one of the strategies that Merton analysed: "One cannot . . . help feeling that Professor Hirschman is overstating his case. . . . I have no doubt that this is how economic thought progresses: we discover a hitherto concealed aspect of the problem, and make it the *essence*, if not the *whole*, of the problem."[109]

In the preface to the second edition of *Strategy*, Hirschman substantially accepted this point, presenting the two approaches less as mutually opposed theories than as complementary perspectives on the analysis of development processes. "I do not deny by any means the interrelatedness of various economic activities of which the balanced growth theory has made so much," he wrote. "On the contrary, I propose that we take advantage of it, that we probe into the structure that is holding together these interrelated activities." If the balanced growth approach thus offered a macro perspective of development dynamics, "to look at unbalanced growth means . . . to look at the dynamics of the development process *in the small*."[110]

Apparently, time and distance have proven Sen's reading correct. William Diebold, who had known Hirschman for decades, commented on a 1980s paper in which Hirschman revisited his unbalanced growth theory: "Given your past differences with Lauch Currie I was much struck with the fact that some of the points you make . . . are quite similar to points that Lauch makes in his book."[111] Diebold, who was referring to a recent book by Currie on the experience of economic advisers in developing countries, concluded that "somehow some further exchange of views between you two and some comparison with what is now a long time ago would be instructive for all of us."[112] Diebold's suggestion remained unheeded.

Even one of Hirschman's most important allies in the unbalanced growth camp, Paul Streeten, scaled down the theoretical relevance of the diatribe that defined development economics in the 1950s. He decided to do this in an essay for a Festschrift in honor of none other than his old ally, Albert Hirschman. Streeten focused specifically on the important differences between policy making and theorizing. "Our notions and policies," he wrote, "grow out of praxis and experience," and "grand theories only distill these practical experiences, or spin a theology above the real day-to-day tasks, mistakes and achievements."[113] Streeten further highlighted some differences in strategy between practitioners and academic development economists. In policy making, agreement on a certain course of action is often reached by "blurring distinctions and avoiding subtlety," especially on value premises. Economic theory, on the contrary, is not aimed at reaching a practical agreement on a course of action. "Clarifying concepts" and "drawing finer and sharper distinctions" among different theories thus becomes particularly important in the theoretical realm—but is barely possible in the practical one.[114]

Many development economists belong to both worlds—that of practitioners and that of academicians—and their work is shaped by these different and at times conflicting impulses. These conflicts are part of the nature of their job, as alert economists well know. A problem arises only when observers, failing to recognize the double dimension, theoretical and practical, of the work of development economists, presume to describe development economics as a fierce struggle between incompatible theories. But when we take into consideration both the theories and their practical counterparts, we discover that they co-define the field of development economics in complex ways. As Paul Streeten put it, "In retrospect, much of the balanced versus unbalanced growth controversy seems to me a sham dispute. . . . Often in practice there was much more agreement than in theory."[115] This insight can also elucidate current debates in contemporary development economics.

Chapter Four

REMAKING DEVELOPMENT ECONOMICS

Early postwar development theories were highly abstract. They discussed general sets of typical "conditions" of underdevelopment and attempted to offer general frameworks through which to attack economic backwardness. By the mid-1960s, however, the development field was starting to change in profound ways. Broad, overarching development theories were giving way to more detailed, country- and time-specific analyses.[1]

Development economics had by then moved beyond its foundational phase, and a new wave of studies brought increased complexity to the analytical landscape. Broad generalizations were considered inadequate to address country-specific bottlenecks; much more specific and targeted analyses were needed to tackle underdevelopment successfully. Furthermore, the centrality of per capita income as an indicator of development began to wane as additional factors were taken into consideration, such as nutrition, public health, education, and housing.[2]

NOVEL APPROACHES IN DEVELOPMENT STUDIES

Hirschman was among the leading figures of this new season of development economics. In keeping with his role as a dissenter in the "old generation," he was among the first to form new hypotheses to frame and test the process of development and the causes of economic and social backwardness. Alexander Gerschenkron's historical studies on capital accumulation in Europe, mentioned in the previous chapter, had persuasively shown that the process of economic growth had not followed the same pattern in different countries but had unfolded in a different way for each country. Hirschman aimed at a similar research project with regard to development issues. Increasingly convinced that thorough historical reconstruction was the only way to unravel the mechanisms of development, he explicitly addressed this issue in his foreword to Judith Tendler's book on the economic and political consequences of technological choices in Brazil's electricity sector:

Underdevelopment having been diagnosed as something so multifaceted, tangled, and deep-rooted, it was often concluded that the situation called for revolution, massive redistribution of wealth and power from the rich to the poor countries, or at least coordinated attack on pervasive backwardness through highly competent central planning.

But what if none of these *dei ex machina* are available to take matters properly in hand? What if the fortress of underdevelopment, just because it is so formidable, can not be conquered by frontal assault? In that unfortunately quite common case, we need to know much more about ways in which the fortress can be surrounded, weakened by infiltration or subversion, and eventually taken by similar indirect tactics and processes. And I suggest that the major contribution to our knowledge of economic development must now come from detailed studies of such processes.[3]

Judith Tendler's 1968 book, the final output of PhD research conducted under Hirschman's supervision at Columbia University, was another study that pioneered this new approach. The book discussed how hydro versus thermal power generation and distribution affected Brazilian economic development between the 1950s and the 1960s. Following in Hirschman's footsteps, Tendler developed a historical analysis of a sector's development, taking into consideration technological choices and opportunities, professional incentives, and political behaviors.[4]

The first major installment of Hirschman's new focus on the detail of development processes was his 1963 volume, *Journeys Toward Progress*. Two-thirds of the book consists of a detailed historical analysis of how three specific economic policy problems in three different countries evolved over a long period of time. Hirschman examined the questions of drought in Northeast Brazil, land reform in Colombia, and inflation in Chile. As he put it, "the essence of this volume is in the flow of the three stories."[5]

Hirschman felt that, in attempting to understand the problems faced by economic policy makers in Latin America, "the best method of looking for answers was to scrutinize the record of a few specific, documented, protracted, significant policy problems."[6] This propensity for historically grounded analyses and even for much despised *histoire évéénemetielle*, would remain an important feature of Hirschman's approach. As he suggested at a 1980 conference:

Following in detail the process of a revolution gives us a strong feeling, as the structuralist approach does not, for the many might-have-beens of history, for narrowly and disastrously missed opportunities as well as for felicitous and surprising escapes from disaster; as a result, the event-minded historian is less likely than the sociologist to declare that, given such and such a structural condition, the outcome was preordained. [This] emphasis on the revolutionary process . . . in effect promises to restore a few degrees of freedom we were in danger of losing to the structuralists.[7]

The research that resulted in Hirschman's subsequent book, *Development Projects Observed*, published in 1967, followed the same approach. Although the book does not contain the stories of the individual projects analyzed, the research had an "intensive concern with 'cases,' " and the projects the book examined were selected because they had "an extended history." "Immersion in the particular," Hirschman concluded, "proved . . . essential for the catching of anything general."[8]

This tension between the particular and the general emerged from the widespread disorientation, among practitioners and scholars, regarding the state of knowledge about development. After almost twenty years of development assistance, the results were inconsistent, and early postwar development economics was considered wanting as an effective analytical tool and a basis for aid policies. Perhaps even more fundamentally, the record of what had been done, and with what results, remained unclear.

THE HISTORICAL TURN: *JOURNEYS TOWARD PROGRESS*

In *Journeys Toward Progress*, Hirschman's interest lay in the development and functioning of the problem-solving capabilities of public authorities in Latin America. This was, in a sense, a natural evolution of his reflections about the development process. In *Strategy*, Hirschman had focused on the inducement mechanisms and backward and forward linkages that could work as substitutes for the ability to make investment decisions. In *Journeys*, his attention turned from the economic sector to the political sphere. How did *political* decision making work when addressing *socioeconomic* problems?

Hirschman thus embarked on a detailed analysis of three major policy problems in Chile, Colombia, and Brazil. However idiosyncratic the historical record of specific problems might be, Hirschman was interested in finding elements that would improve the effectiveness of policy reform in the future. While he did not believe that any "iron law" governed social, economic, and political dynamics, his research aimed at understanding the characteristic features underlying the policy-making processes he had analyzed in detail in his country studies.

Hirschman's terminological choices indicate his awareness of the difficulties of drawing generalizations from specific cases. He predicted that his analysis would produce only "tentative" and "dispersed" findings, and stated that his goal was not to produce a theory of policy making but to delineate "a Latin American 'style' in handling, learning about, and moving toward the solution of large-scale policy problems."[9] The search for a "Latin American style" was different from speculations about the nature of a continental character. In Hirschman's perspective, it was based on the deep structure of the continent's problems and societies. "Style," Hirschman suggested, "should be made to arise, to the greatest possible extent, out of the characteristics of the problems and of the problem-solving process itself."[10] Hence, Hirschman's analysis focused on what kind of problems usually made their way to the top of the policy agenda, and the characteristics of the process of policy-making in response to those problems.

Underdeveloped societies, Hirschman noted, are characterized by rudimentary and often ineffectual communication between the public and the government. In such a situation, violence and mass protest are in many cases the only way for long neglected problems to get the attention of governing elites. If a particular problem does not prompt public protest, it is likely to remain unconsidered. The only exception to this bottom-up binary situation is, of course, a top-down initiative, when previously unaddressed and forgotten issues are brought to general attention by the direct initiative of policy makers, either because fixing these issues appears to be the solution to other problems that have caused public protest or because new

political scenarios make it convenient for policy makers to address problems that were previously considered secondary and whose solution could
be easily postponed with no political backfiring.

This pattern of how problems rise to national attention also influences
how these problems are dealt with. Problems that are felt as "pressing,"
either because they are the cause of social and political turbulence or
because they are considered major obstacles to the modernization of the
country, will often produce some reaction and an attempt at solving them,
not necessarily based on a real understanding of the roots of the problem. In other words, as Hirschman summarized, "motivation" often pulls
ahead of "understanding." The effects of this dynamic are easily apparent in
underdeveloped countries: a certain grandiose tendency to attack big problems frontally, disregarding more limited but perhaps more manageable
targets; the launch of comprehensive plans to solve all problems at once; the
frequent establishment of new organizations dedicated to solving once and
for all a deep-rooted problem; an excessive reliance on imported solutions
that appear to be salvific only because they are "foreign"; and finally, huge,
abrupt policy shifts and major ideological clashes.

Ideology in particular was, according to Hirschman, a fundamental lens
through which to understand the development debate in Latin America and
the Latin American style of problem solving and policy making. Hirschman
had specifically touched upon the role of ideology in Latin America in the
introductory chapter to his 1961 edited book, *Latin American Issues*.[11] The
book collected a series of essays on the problems of inflation, regional trade,
and land reform in Latin America. Interestingly, despite the very practical
nature of these problems, Hirschman's introduction focused on the role
that ideology had played in shaping the debate itself. As Jeremy Adelman
put it, "if economists were accustomed to thinking of themselves as outside
societies looking in, like a doctor examining a patient, Hirschman turned
them into the subject."[12]

When Hirschman analyzed ideology and the other elements of policy
making in *Journeys*, he discovered that they presented several interesting
and promising characteristics. Apparently dysfunctional features of Latin
American policy making, far from being hopelessly negative, actually functioned as byways through which countries lacking a political system capable of assuring a dialogue between the public and policy makers became
aware of certain problems and committed, though perhaps bumpily, to their

resolution. At a conference in Rio de Janeiro a few months before the publication of *Journeys*, for example, Hirschman offered an interpretation of the different views of monetarist and structuralist scholars about inflation, based on the specific ways of problem solving that the two groups had developed in their specific sociopolitical contexts. Whereas the monetarist perspective came largely from countries where virtually all interest groups have channels of communication with policy makers, the structuralists came from countries in which neglected problems could hope to be considered only if they were somehow connected to those under the attention of policy makers. Hence, the former proposed strictly monetarist and fiscal policies to tackle inflation, whereas the latter insisted on the links between inflation and supply anelasticities, institutional rigidities, and structural bottlenecks.[13] Their differences, Hirschman seemed to imply, were based less on theoretical differences than on the ideological framework they had formed in different institutional settings.

In this perspective, comprehensive plans proved particularly useful in linking neglected problems to a pressing problem already under the spotlight. Thus the "comprehensive plan"—the idea that no solution can come to any specific problem unless a whole group of questions is addressed in a coordinated way—became, in Hirschman's perspective, "a generalized device for indirectly achieving recognition for the stepchild problems."[14] At the Rio conference, Hirschman highlighted another advantage of a comprehensive plan, somewhat opposed to the one just mentioned: a plan, because of the large financial commitment involved, would prove a useful "tactical weapon" for policy makers attempting to stop pressures for additional uncoordinated and haphazard expenditures.[15] A comprehensive plan, in other words, would help policy makers define a perimeter dividing two huge groups of policies and problems—namely, those to be addressed now (within the perimeter of the plan) and those that must be postponed (outside that perimeter).

Hirschman's praise, in *Journeys*, of comprehensive plans is quite startling when compared to his position of only five years earlier. It will be remembered that Hirschman's aversion to comprehensive development plans prompted his harsh critique of the balanced-growth approach and his proposal of an alternative, unbalanced approach in *The Strategy of Economic Development*. But whereas in that case Hirschman was engaged in an analytical debate on the mechanisms of industrial development in less developed countries, in *Journeys* he was discussing a very different set of questions. The comprehensive plan, economically inefficient if not useless, was, from the perspective of policy making, an important strategic device. As pointless and rigid as a comprehensive plan might seem when the question was how to induce economic entrepreneurship, it turned out to be a rich and flexible instrument when the question was how to advance political decisions.

In the same vein, other characteristics of this "Latin American style" had their uses. Exaggerated reformist promises, Hirschman opined, are usually followed by disappointing results. Yet, a "utopian phase of policy-making" often has the merit of producing legislation which, although initially unenforced, nonetheless exists "on the books." In a subsequent round of reformist efforts, this dormant legislation will probably come to fruition, securing

FIGURE 4.1 Albert and Sarah Hirschman visiting the Instituto Colombiano de la Reforma Agraria (INCORA) during their field trip for *Journeys Toward Progress*, 1962. Courtesy of Katia Salomon

the legislative basis for policy initiatives that would otherwise have been considered unrealistic. As an example, Hirschman noted that postwar land reform initiatives in Colombia found unexpected providential support in a forgotten article of the Constitution of 1936, which permitted, in certain circumstances, land expropriation without compensation. Utopian though that article may have been when it was approved, it turned out to provide a solid basis for land expropriation (with compensation) decades later.[16]

Likewise, the strange combination of outright criticism of previous policies with blind faith in new initiatives that characterized huge policy swings in many Latin American countries presented a number of unexpected positive sides. First of all, the habit of considering all government attempts at reform eventually doomed made opposition to reforms less strong than it might have been. But in this way, the rhetoric of failure opened up spaces for actual reform. At the same time, the bombastic announcements that accompanied new policies, even when they were unrealistic, had an energizing effect on policy makers; a selective amnesia on previous failures made it possible to embark on new attempts.

Hirschman's optimism seems here to have taken the lead, for the positive combination of the rhetoric of failure and the rhetoric of success was only one possible outcome. In principle, it might just as well produce an outright reactionary result. For these two effects to work together in favor of reform, the rhetoric of failure must predominantly apply to the opponents of reform, while the rhetoric of success must apply to those in charge of reformist policy making. But what if opponents of reform were convinced that the new policy proposals might actually be realized as promised by their proponents, while the proponents of reforms, who paid lip service to the rhetoric of success, were actually convinced that nothing would really change? In this case, one could expect a strong preemptive reaction in defense of the status quo.

Yet there was a method in Hirschman's optimism. *Journeys* must be read as an attempt at explaining the mechanisms of economic and social reform *short of revolutionary events*. We should not forget that revolution, in early-1960s Latin America, was a rather fashionable concept, whose most successful example was the recent Cuban revolution. Hirschman, however, was no revolutionary; he considered revolution not only unnecessary but also analytically flawed. Instead of understanding and addressing the question of social change, revolution was a "cataclysmic interlude between two

static societies": the prerevolutionary one, rotten and unjust and unrespon-
sive to reform, and the postrevolutionary one, just and harmonious and no
longer in need of further improvement.

As in his criticism of the balanced-growth approach, which, according to Hirschman, superimposed the dream of a developed society upon
a backward reality but had nothing to say about how to move from one
to the other, Hirschman found the revolutionary perspective unable to
explain the truly interesting question—that is, how social and political
change happens. Hirschman's study was a way to unravel material for a
sort of "reformmonger's manual," or a manual for the staunch, unremitting
reformist. As he put it, "perhaps it is time that such a text be written and
offer some competition to the many handbooks on the techniques of revolutions, coups d'état, and guerrilla warfare."[17] In this sense, *Journeys* was
the natural follow-up to the research that Hirschman had begun five years
earlier in *Strategy*. In both cases, Hirschman delineated a middle position
between maintaining the status quo and launching a revolution (in the terminology of *Strategy*, between "futility" and "brutality"). In *Strategy*, the
focus was on processes of economic development; in *Journeys*, it was on
processes of political reformmongering.

Hirschman did not shy away from analyzing certain forms of violence
and found that, in some sequences of policy making, "elements of both
reform and revolution" were present.[18] Apparently, there were cases in
which violence itself could become an ingredient of reform. Colombian
peasants, for instance, had often occupied uncultivated lands. But those
eruptions of violence, far from being conducive to revolution, made it
possible for reformist governments to legislate about land redistribution in ways that would have been unthinkable had not the peasants
triggered a reform process through violent land seizures. Hirschman
was amused by the "highly disorderly sequence" the Colombians had
invented. Instead of the predictable sequence from revolution to land
redistribution within the framework of a new postrevolutionary order,
Colombian peasants had first enacted decentralized and illegal redistribution, which was later legalized thanks to the intervention of a reformist government.[19] More generally, Hirschman highlighted the enormous
complexity of reformist action in Latin American countries and the
mixed character of reform policies, which appeared to be made of both
nonantagonistic and antagonistic dynamics.

The whole book and the research on which it was based—which Hirschman had conducted in a series of trips to Latin America with his wife, Sarah, and his colleague and friend, the political scientist Charles E. Lindblom—was an uncompromising attempt at introducing public-policy analysis into the realm of development economics. Dissatisfied with the relegation of functioning public decision-making mechanisms to the mere role of "preconditions" for economic growth, in *Journeys* Hirschman was determined to show how processes of decision making and problem solving, disorderly and counterintuitive as they might be, nonetheless played a decisive role at all stages of development. He explicitly connected this goal to his previous book, *Strategy*, in which he had investigated a variety of inducement mechanisms able to summon up entrepreneurial resources to advance economic development. Although in *Strategy* he had criticized the tendency of governments to frame decision-making processes in the perspective of comprehensive plans, Hirschman had not ruled out the contribution that public decision making could make to the development process. As he wrote in *Strategy*, "The assertion was made that non-market forces, e.g., the response of public authorities to an electric power shortage, are not necessarily or intrinsically less automatic than the response of private entrepreneurs to a rise in the price of their product."[20] The desire to document this assertion led Hirschman to the core question of *Journeys*—namely, "the investigation of the behavior of public decision-makers in problem-solving situations."[21]

Hirschman's attempt at connecting economic and political analysis, perhaps not unexpectedly, was appreciated mostly by political scientists, whereas fellow economists advanced more than one criticism. Mancur Olson considered *Journeys* probably the best book published in several years on the topic of the two-way relationship between economic development and political processes. As Olson noted, this nexus was very important yet very rarely studied.[22] A number of economists, however, criticized the economic analysis of the three case studies as wanting, at times unconvincing, and in any case excessively limited. As Dudley Seers put it in an otherwise positive review, "it is one thing to say that economic theory needs to take account of political factors, another to leave economics very largely out of the picture."[23]

In his acute review, Seers praised the novelty of Hirschman's approach, his determination to analyze political and economic issues together, and his sensitivity to the complex evolution of political and social processes and their frequently counterintuitive patterns. In a nutshell, Hirschman's book was "a useful manual for the reformer—a 'progressive' counterpart to Machiavelli's *The Prince*."[24] At the same time, Hirschman's confidence in the usefulness of deciphering the unexpected and the counterintuitive in Latin American political economy seemed to Seers problematic at best. In a sense, Seers wondered whether Hirschman's attempt at predicting the unpredictable would not ultimately risk irrelevance at the practical level.

As we will see in the discussion of *Development Projects Observed*, Hirschman's fascination with the unpredictable, the uncertain, and the unexpected would often make him vulnerable to the critique of irrelevance. Seers observed:

Perhaps Hirschman's picture of the way society changes is also simplistic; one of the motive forces of progress is precisely a belief that change will result predictably from a certain political program, and that this will be an easier and quicker process than is in fact at all likely. Both the public and political leaders need a somewhat naïve view of the world if significant advance is to be achieved (just as Columbus had to believe that Asia lay out in the Atlantic if he was to 'discover' America). To take away people's illusions may make it quite impossible not merely for these illusions to become reality, but for conditions to be even slightly improved.[25]

Ironically, Seers's criticism of Hirschman's vision of social change relied on what would later become the main idea behind Hirschman's Principle of the Hiding Hand.

The publication of *Journeys Toward Progress* consecrated Hirschman as one of the most perceptive and interesting scholars in development, and even before reviews started to appear, the Department of Economics at Harvard informally inquired whether Hirschman might be interested in joining its faculty. Gerschenkron, Hirschman's old colleague at Berkeley and the Fed and in the mid-1960s one of the most influential and esteemed professors at Harvard's economics department, insisted on stealing Hirschman from Columbia.[26] Though Columbia was ready to meet Harvard's offer, in March 1964 Hirschman accepted a position as Professor of Political Economy in Cambridge, Massachusetts. Since arrangements had already been made with the World Bank and the Brookings Institution for

FIGURE 4.2 Albert O. Hirschman, 1962. Photograph by Hernan Diaz. Courtesy of Katia Salomon

a long research trip on development projects around the world, Harvard granted Hirschman a very soft landing: during 1964–65 he would be on sabbatical, the subsequent year he would be in Cambridge but teach only a graduate seminar on his research and write his book, and he would take up a regular teaching load only in 1966–67.[27]

Cambridge was also where Sarah began a small pilot project to introduce Puerto Rican adult women to reading literary texts. Sarah read a short story aloud to the women, who followed on their own copy, and then she facilitated a conversation. The initiative, called *Gente y Cuentos*, was first conducted in Spanish in a Massachusetts housing project in 1972. In time, it expanded to New Jersey, the city of Quilmes on the outskirts of Buenos Aires, Florida, Texas, New York, and Puerto Rico, and from the mid-1980s it was conducted in both Spanish and English, as People & Stories/*Gente y Cuentos*.[28] The program has since established a youth initiative and programs for prison inmates, victims of sex trafficking, residents of homeless centers, and low-income adults in an increasing number of places.

THE PROJECT FOCUS

As soon as *Journeys* was hot off the press, Hirschman began to make plans for his next project. In the spring of 1963, he contacted Burke Knapp, by then vice president of the World Bank, to propose an in-depth, world-wide field investigation of specific Bank-financed projects in developing countries in order to test the hypotheses elaborated in *Strategy* and *Journeys*. Hirschman's plan was to conduct extensive on-the-ground investigations, paying attention "to the upkeep and performance of the project itself, to the economic activities that it has stimulated (or destroyed?), and very much also to the wider economic, social and political ramifications of the project such as its educational effects and its contribution to the formation of new local or national elites." An additional purpose for Hirschman, after two books heavily based on Latin American cases, was to expand his expertise in development issues by becoming acquainted with Asia and Africa.[29] From the early months of 1964, Hirschman's study was reframed as a Brookings Institution initiative endorsed by the World Bank and financed by the Carnegie Corporation and the Ford Foundation.

The principal purpose of Hirschman's study was, in his words, "to explore in detail the direct effects as well as the broad repercussions of a project on economy and society," in order to reach "some improvements in the process of project evaluation and selection."[30] The aim was to gain a deep understanding of the salient features of a project, both at the planning stage and after its completion. That Hirschman chose to analyze projects financed by the World Bank was not unexpected; the Bank's twenty-year-long experience constituted "the most ample, varied, and detailed source of information and documentation in this area."[31] Also, none of the selected projects had developed without encountering serious problems. Therefore, this sample, albeit limited in size, could prove useful to the goal of building generalizations about the problems arising in project lending. More fundamentally, a comparison of the different projects would highlight similarities and differences in project experience, so as to discover whether they could "be traced to what . . . may be called their 'structural characteristics.' "[32] These structural characteristics included economic, technological, administrative, and organizational features and were closely connected to the broader sociopolitical environment.

Hirschman identified three areas for questions and analysis of project effectiveness. The first was the decision process in the recipient country. Who took the initiative for the project? What political and interest groups were for or against it? Did any of these groups shift their initial position about the advisability of the project? A second focus area was the decision process within the World Bank. Here, too, Hirschman underscored the importance of comparing the Bank's initial positions with *ex post* considerations. More specifically, his goal was to shape a method by which project planners could navigate the intrinsic uncertainties of a project's performance and predict probable lines of behavior.

A third focus area was the project in retrospect. Relevant questions included a review of the effects of the construction phase (from a description of unexpected events to the direct and indirect capacity-building effect on local engineering, managerial, and planning capabilities) and the project's ultimate impact on the society and economy of the recipient country. Of course, Hirschman's curiosity dwelt on the linkage effects that could originate from the construction or the operation of the projects. For example, had the construction or the operation of a project triggered the establishment of other economic activities? Finally, Hirschman recommended analyzing even the most far-reaching consequences, such as the effects of projects on the distribution of wealth, income, and power in the recipient country; the development of new entrepreneurial and administrative capabilities, in both the public and private sectors; and the introduction of "fundamental structural changes."[33]

Candidate projects for inclusion in Hirschman's study had to meet three basic criteria: they had to be diverse in sector and geographical area; they had to have been operational for several years, in order to enable a reconstruction of their historical evolution (detailed historical analysis, as we have seen, was crucial); and, finally, they had to be identifiable activities that required continued maintenance and brought about identifiable linkage effects. Hydroelectric projects, specific highways, or industries were the natural candidates, as opposed to loans for general highway reconstruction and maintenance activities, for the purchase of agricultural machinery, or for balance-of-payments purposes.[34] With the help of World Bank officers, Hirschman selected a list of projects.

Feedback from inside the Bank was in general extremely positive. Dragoslav Avramovic, a senior and highly respected economist, remarked that "probably for the first time, the contemporary theory and practice of project appraisal in infra-structure will be subjected to a systematic *ex-post* methodological scrutiny on a wide basis."[35] Because of these high expectations, the Bank became unusually involved in the research, especially considering that it was being conducted by an external researcher. Robert Asher, a major officer at the Brookings Institution who worked with the Bank on the Hirschman study, noted that "it is an extraordinary thing for the Bank to open its project files to an outside researcher, to provide an assistant for the outside researcher, to request the collaboration of its member governments, and to do the other things the Bank has agreed in this case to do."[36]

Some officers, however, were doubtful about the representativeness of the small and heterogeneous sample that Hirschman intended to examine: "one wonders," wrote an officer, "whether in relation to the wide variety of projects and the widely differing economic and political backgrounds of the Bank's . . . member countries, such a small sample as a dozen projects out of about 300 will be sufficient to bring out valid general conclusions."[37] Along similar lines, the economist Robert F. Skillings proposed focusing on a specific sector (such as power or roads) and implementing a thorough analysis of all the projects financed by the World Bank in that particular sector.[38] This suggestion was not followed at the time, but it was not forgotten: among the first studies sponsored in the early 1970s by the Bank's new Operation Evaluation Division was a thorough analysis of the Bank's results in the power sector.[39]

The coming together of the World Bank and Hirschman under the umbrella of the Brookings Institution's research was a timely joint venture. Like several other institutions, the World Bank was increasingly recognizing the need to establish and refine methods for evaluating the impact of its policies on less developed countries. Early exercises in project evaluation were based on a thick description of the cases under examination, often written in a narrative style. "In the old days," recalled a future head of the evaluation department, officers "would write a book about the history of the Bank's relationships with a country. It was a beautiful history, actually, a very solid piece of work."[40] The problem, however, was that it did not permit any kind of generalization or combination of information and offered only a limited basis for comparative analysis.

Albert and Sarah Hirschman spent one year, between July 1964 and August 1965, traveling to four continents. Sarah was not simply an accompanying spouse but, as often in Albert's work, a partner in field research and an important intellectual interlocutor. Her contribution had already been fundamental in *Strategy*, helping Albert to incorporate anthropological literature that was particularly relevant to development studies. Likewise, she participated in field research during the summer of 1960 in Mexico, Colombia, Chile, Argentina, and Brazil that would serve as the basis for *Journeys*.[41] In 1964–1965, Sarah was again "a member of the 'team.'"[42] The archive digger will find her handwriting in many field notes.

Upon their return from the field trip, Hirschman circulated a memo with some preliminary observations, focusing on what he called the "behavioral characteristics" of development projects in a number of different sectors. "Having learnt in fairly rapid succession about a wide variety of projects," he wrote, "I became alerted to the characteristic advantages or handicaps under which power projects, say, proceed as compared to irrigation projects."[43]

The principal aim of Hirschman's interim observations was clearly methodological. Far from addressing questions such as the economic return on the Bank's loans or the traditional distinctions of, say, infrastructure

TABLE 4.1
Hirschman's journey and project loan purpose

El Salvador	July 20–August 1, 1964	Electric power
Ecuador	August 3–20, 1964	Roads in Guayas Province
Peru	August 21–Sept 11, 1964	San Lorenzo irrigation
Uruguay	Sept 20–Oct 7, 1964	Pasture improvement
West Pakistan	Oct 28–Nov 8, 1964	Karnaphuli paper mill
India	Nov 9–Dec 16, 1964	Damodar Valley development
East Pakistan	Dec 17–Jan 3, 1965	Karnaphuli paper mill
Thailand	Jan 4–28, 1965	Chao Phya irrigation
India	Jan 29–Feb 25, 1965	Selected ICICI-financed industries in Mysore
Italy	Apr 26–May 28, 1965	Irrigation in Southern Italy
Uganda	May 29–June 18, 1965	Electric power transmission and distribution
Ethiopia	June 21–July 9, 1965	Telecommunications
Nigeria	July 10–Aug 12, 1965	Railways modernization and Bornu extension

Source: Albert O. Hirschman, "A Study of Selected World Bank Projects—Some Interim Observations," August 1965, World Bank Hirschman Folders Vol. 1.
Note: Italy was added to the list only as an afterthought, on the advice of several World Bank officials who maintained that the bank's loans to the Italian Cassa per il Mezzogiorno—the Italian agency for the development of Southern Italy—would be very relevant to Hirschman's study; see Douglas J. Fontein to Prof. Gabriele Pescatore, April 9, 1965, World Bank Hirschman Folders Vol. 1.

versus agricultural and industrial projects or human versus physical capital, Hirschman emphasized the need for a change in perspective. What really affects projects, he claimed, is their degree of uncertainty: "the element of the unknown, the uncertain and the unexpected which deflects projects from the originally chartered course is considerable in all projects. But it is far more important in some projects than in others and it may be of interest to the Bank to gain an approximate idea about the principal determinants of this uncertainty."[44]

Among these determinants, Hirschman listed the ability to map out the project completely upon its launch (for example, electricity projects can be mapped out more easily than agricultural improvement projects); the direct link between the new supply produced by the project and the actual demand to absorb it (a power station will present different degrees of uncertainty depending on the level of economic development of the region where it is established); and the degree to which economic, social, and political change can interfere with a project's implementation (for example, to what degree a rise in labor costs affects irrigation projects, or to what extent it is possible to insulate projects from political interference).[45] Notes taken during the field trip also elaborate on the difficulty of computing and quantifying benefits in several types of projects. Hirschman, referring to Ethiopia, underscored the case of telecommunications: "how do you compute benefits of easier communications, ability of scarce managerial talent to spread itself over wider areas, better information of market information, etc."[46] Hence, these kinds of projects are often ignored, even if they may be the most productive.

This change in perspective called for a corresponding change in the Bank's behavior. The World Bank, Hirschman wrote, should avoid that "air of pat certainty" that emanated from project prospects and instead expose the uncertainties underlying them, exploring the whole range of possible outcomes. Moreover, the Bank should take into account the distributional and, more generally, the social and political effects of its lending. As a matter of fact, an excessively uneven distribution of the benefits of a project, besides jeopardizing political and social stability, would likely create threats to the project itself. A new road project, for example, would open up new land for agricultural exploitation. According to Hirschman, the Bank should have explicitly addressed the issue of ownership of that land, with the aim of spreading the benefits of the project to the largest possible population. Of course, Hirschman was aware that spreading the benefits might require time: frequently, a project initially contributes to the development of the most advanced segments of a country, and only in a second phase does it reach larger segments of the population and disadvantaged areas. This diffusion mechanism was even clearer, for example, in the establishment of a power station, usually conceived to serve the largest city and only subsequently capable of broadening the supply to smaller cities or the countryside. Still, Hirschman thought it important that "such a second benefit-spreading phase of projects . . . either be explicitly foreseen or at least its possible emergence be carefully watched and seized upon when it occurs."[47] Hirschman also criticized the inadequate consideration of social and political factors in project analysis. In his opinion, many projects had encountered huge difficulties during their implementation because of too cursory an analysis of their political and social context. Regional, tribal, or center-periphery antagonisms, and the political power of specific interest groups, are important elements that affect the success or failure of a specific project.

In addition to the influence that social and political factors might have on a project, Hirschman was interested in studying the reverse: was it possible to identify projects that would help the development of political skills and facilitate intergroup agreements? In their travels, the Hirschmans noted that irrigation projects often brought in new resources that initially were believed to be available in strictly limited quantities: irrigation almost immediately creates disputes over the distribution of water, along with related problems of administration and coordination between engineers and farmers, as well as between different farmers' organizations, extension services, and so on. At the same time, these problems may have an unexpected, positive spillover, as they become "a veritable school for bargaining, adjustment, etc."[48]

The case of an electrification project in Uganda provided another example of possible community building to come out of project management. In the town of Masaka, Indians and Africans lived completely separate lives, carrying on distinct economic activities and following different patterns of urban migration and settlement. The Indians all lived in town and could connect to the electric power network for a nominal fee; the Africans, on the other hand, lived scattered throughout the countryside, and in order to connect to the power network, they were required to make a capital contribution that could be more than five times the fee paid by Indians. The Ugandan project of power distribution had thus highly exacerbated the conflicts between ethnic groups in the country. At the same time, Hirschman noted, there was room to restructure the project, bringing Indians and Africans together to cooperate in managing the project or coordinating management by the two communities in different areas: "the technical nature of the common task," the Hirschmans ventured to hope, "helps in making both [ethnic groups] 'forget' about the other's skin."[49] If properly reorganized, the Ugandan electric project would yield strong social benefits.

At the opposite end of the spectrum of projects with institution-building potential, one might consider highways. Highway construction always left ample margins for improvisation, sloppiness, the cutting of corners, and the sacrifice of quality for quantity, without any specific inducement to develop more structured and effective institutions.[50] Moreover, no natural or technical constraint limited road construction, thereby making it particularly prone to political pressures and the disrupting effects of political struggle on national cohesiveness. This characteristic was shared by thermoelectric, as opposed to hydroelectric, power. While hydroelectric power generation is limited by the availability of natural resources, a thermoelectric plant can be built virtually anywhere. Investments in thermoelectric plants therefore appeared to be much less protected from political pressures. In Hirschman's terminology, this was an opposition between "foot loose" (roads and thermoelectric power generation) and "resource tied" public utilities.[51] If one considered projects from the point of view of institution building, irrigation would produce the maximum effect and highways the minimum, with railroads and electric power falling somewhere in between.[52]

Highways were nonetheless an interesting case study for the links between social phenomena and economic development. Often, Hirschman argued, road maintenance is prompted by a combination of physical deterioration and public protest: truck drivers' refusing to pay road tolls because of the roads' poor condition will negatively affect the financial resources needed to repair the roads; at the same time, their actions signal that the roads have reached an unacceptable level of deterioration, and this will probably induce a reaction (road maintenance).[53] In *Strategy*, Hirschman had discussed at length the fact that in less developed countries, often the resource that was lacking was not capital or any other physical asset, but rather the ability to make decisions, and he thus urged the individuation of "inducement mechanisms" that function as substitutes for this missing ability. The circular mechanism of (1) road use, (2) lack of maintenance, (3) road disruption, (4) public protest, and finally (5) road maintenance was one of these inducement mechanisms. This observation was the seed for a particularly productive yield in Hirschman's intellectual journey. As we will see in the next chapter, it would become the starting point for the discussion of "voice" in Hirschman's analysis of social interactions in his 1970 book, *Exit, Voice and Loyalty*.

In his "Interim Observations," Hirschman argued that the World Bank had ignored important questions and that "the projects appear to be judged wholly on their technical merits."[54] Moreover, as Sarah wrote in their notes, "Profitability alone is no yardstick for social desirability of investment."[55]

Hirschman also focused on some specific World Bank policies usually set forth as preconditions of lending: the Bank's preference for dealing with development agencies independent of the national government and with contractors selected through international bidding; its insistence that governments should profit from public utilities established through its loans; and its insistence on exerting strict control over the internal administrative processes of the borrowing country. Hirschman underscored instead the need to adapt the loan procedures to local circumstances.[56]

During his travels, Hirschman had noticed that certain agencies, which in principle were supposed to be autonomous from the national government, were actually limited in the effectiveness of their decision making by chaotic and disunited boards, whereas more streamlined chains of command in governmental ministries could prove to be more effective. In other cases, autonomous authorities were turning into semifeudal centers of power.[57] Administrative independence of development agencies was not positive by default but had to be assessed on a case-by-case basis. As for the Bank's attempts to control the internal administrative processes of borrowing countries, Hirschman noted that very often this was plainly impossible: internal difficulties within recipient governments and intragovernmental conflicts were common characteristics of borrowing countries, and the first casualty of these difficulties was reliable and open communication with external subjects.[58]

Most of Hirschman's observations were dismissed by Bank officers as either obvious or wrong. Some critics underscored that on several occasions,

Hirschman had based his conclusions only on partial analyses of specific matters. "As for the tendency 'to clothe the prospects of all projects with an air of pat certainty,' " said one comment, "the Doctor may have a point, but it must be remembered that our project reports are not economic dissertations. They must be brief and many points considered are not always included in the reports."[59]

In a less acrimonious tone, Duncan S. Ballantine, a Bank officer and former professor of history at MIT and Harvard University, elaborated convincingly on the apparent bias of many reports: "in presenting a positive recommendation for action to the [Executive] Directors, a report must be positive . . . at some expense to the uncertainties. Nevertheless, during the process of appraisal leading up to the inevitable simplification of the issue, the staff . . . does 'make a sustained effort at visualizing' the uncertainties."[60] Considering that Hirschman, in his studies, had traditionally been interested in processes of decision making and "reform mongering," it is noteworthy that reactions from Bank officers underscored his apparent inability to understand the need to calibrate messages to the audience and the situation.

Had Hirschman taken more elements into account, the critics pointed out, he would probably have discovered that his proposals were actually very much in line with the Bank's thinking and practices or, as another officer put it, that "there is relatively little in [Hirschman's] observations which has not normally been taken into account by Bank staff during project work."[61] For example, when addressing the conflict that might arise between the World Bank and a borrowing country over the borrower's obligation to consult the Bank prior to key personnel changes, Hirschman had emphasized that "efforts should be made to limit requirements of prior consultations to a few matters deemed essential."[62] It was easy for a critic to note that the Bank was already doing what Hirschman proposed: "Dr. Hirschman is not well aware of the Bank's practice concerning consultation. In the 253 loans and credits made in the last five years . . . only 40 loan and credit agreements required consultation . . . These were 'deemed essential.' "[63] Campbell Percy McMeekan, a senior agriculture specialist in the Division of Technical Operations who was responsible for the appraisal of agricultural development loans, remarked that "the Bank does do just what is suggested."[64] Hans Adler, an authority on transportation projects (and, like Hirschman, a refugee from Nazi Germany) concluded: "some of his suggestions are now a regular part of our appraisal. It might therefore be useful for Hirschman to read some of our recent reports."[65]

In other cases, Hirschman's assumptions were considered plainly wrong. In his "Interim Observations" he had stated that the Bank's task was "to undertake projects that are unattractive to private capital because uncertainty surrounding their success is too high."[66] One officer sharply noted that "it has been the policy of the Bank *not* to make loans for projects where uncertainties surrounding their success were high on the ground that the borrower's welfare and development would be best served if his investments were made, and Bank money used, only for sound projects."[67] As for how the Bank negotiated with development agencies, several officers noted that their approach was far from doctrinaire, and those most familiar with Hirschman's chosen examples considered them "singularly inappropriate."[68] Some officials also doubted that it would be useful for the Bank to explicitly address political and social factors in project appraisal. The World Bank was perceived by its staff as relatively free from political pressures and driven by a technocratic approach. An explicit inclusion of political and social considerations in project appraisal meant that the Bank would be "vulnerable to every variety of reaction from member countries and would lose its fortunate position."[69]

An important cause of criticism was that Hirschman showed a complete disinterest in quantitative evaluations, focusing instead on a qualitative analysis or, as he wrote, on "comparing 'personal profiles' of projects in different sectors."[70] To a bureaucracy that expected Hirschman's study to shed some light on issues such as the measurement of the indirect economic benefits of projects and the feasibility and effects of applying shadow prices for products and factors of production, this was most disappointing.[71] Furthermore, criticism may have intensified in reaction to Hirschman's claim that his reflections were "strictly policy-oriented," and thus had immediate consequences for the Bank's loan policies, whereas many staff members considered that they did not have any application.[72] A World Bank engineer commented that Hirschman was "not well aware of the choices facing the Bank."[73]

THE CONUNDRUM OF DEVELOPMENT KNOWLEDGE: *DEVELOPMENT PROJECTS OBSERVED*

Despite the barrage with which Bank staff met Hirschman's interim observations, their reaction to the final output of his research, published in 1967 by the Brookings Institution as *Development Projects Observed*, was not particularly critical; rather, as one officer put it, Hirschman's conclusions "have only very limited applicability."[74] One senior manager considered the book's first chapter, "The Principle of the Hiding Hand," "a bit thin, particularly with respect to relevant guidance for those who must decide whether to undertake, continue, or complete a proposed project."[75] A senior researcher at the Brookings Institution concurred, noting that Hirschman's theses were "disconcerting . . . to those in quest of clearer criteria to govern eligibility for foreign aid."[76] In "The Principle of the Hiding Hand," Hirschman stated that the underestimation of problems is a powerful mechanism that induces the implementation of projects that, had all the difficulties been foreseen, would never have been initiated in the first place. According to Hirschman, the problems that arise when a project is under implementation usually trigger a creative effort that leads to their solution. Differing from Toynbee's theory of challenge and response, Hirschman's principle posited that "people undertake some new task not because of a challenge, but because of the assumed *absence* of a challenge."[77] Toynbee's thesis, according to Hirschman, was an *ex post* rationalization, "*per fare bella figura.*"[78]

Though rhetorically forceful and "Hirschmanesque" (Walter Salant's term), this principle left many unconvinced. Even the members of the Brookings Advisory Committee who were more favorable to Hirschman's approach, such as Walter Salant or Edward Mason, considered the principle one-sided.[79] Salant, for example, noted that this principle, far from offering a general analytical framework as Hirschman seemed to imply, was only one of many possible associations between the estimation of problems and the estimation of one's own ability to solve them: of course problems might be underestimated, but they might also be either correctly estimated or overestimated, and the same would be true for the ability to solve them. Nine outcomes were actually possible, from the successful Hiding Hand to sheer disaster (when an underestimated problem is coupled with an overestimated ability to solve it).[80]

Years later, Hirschman admitted that his opening chapter "was close to a provocation. Nothing could be less 'operationally useful' than to be told that underestimating the costs or difficulties of a project has on occasion been helpful in eliciting creative energies that otherwise might never have been forthcoming."[81] But this was the point: the Principle of the Hiding Hand, based as it was on the actor's ignorance, was not intended to be a policy tool. It was a way for Hirschman to elaborate on the need to include uncertainty and limited rationality in the Bank's epistemology. While this principle received its final name in juxtaposition to Adam Smith's "invisible hand," its original name was perhaps more revelatory: in January 1965, from East Pakistan, Hirschman wrote to his two daughters in New York, Katia and Lisa, a detailed explanation of what he then used to call the "theory of providential ignorance":

The Pakistan project, the Karnaphuli paper mill, is perhaps most interesting because it shows that it isn't so easy to "transfer" an industry from one country to another. It *looks* easy—why shouldn't the same machines perform just as well in East Pakistan as in Sweden? The fact is, however, that there are many differences, from the raw materials (bamboo instead of pine) to the demand in the market which require far more "creative" adaptation than the country had probably expected it would to be. One almost feels that had they known all the troubles they were headed for, they would never have founded this industry, but having founded it they managed to solve their problems one by one. The secret of creativity is then to place yourself in situations where you've got to be creative, but this is done only when one doesn't know in advance that one will have to be creative. This, in turn, is so because we underestimate our creative resources; quite properly, we cannot believe in our creativity until we experience it; and since we thus necessarily underestimate our creative resources we do not consciously engage upon tasks which we know require such resources; hence the only way in which we can bring our creative resources into play is by similarly underestimating the difficulty of a task.[82]

Here Hirschman was confronting the inescapable conundrum of development knowledge at its most micro level. By its nature, development knowledge is not a capital resource already available to the development community or to entrepreneurs, and even less it is easily transferable. From his fifteen-year-long experience in the development field, Hirschman had learned how difficult it was to carry on successful endeavors. In *Strategy*, he had focused on how to trigger and facilitate economic decision making precisely because the problem was not so much the lack of any specific factor of production but the lack of a more fundamental ability—the ability to make development decisions. Put another way, Hirschman focused on inducement mechanisms as a way to bypass the unavailability to economic actors of implementable development knowledge. The research at the basis of *Journeys* was a variant of this question, only applied to processes of policy making. In *Development Projects Observed*, Hirschman confronted the problem of the creation of development knowledge at the basic level of the project, with a focus not so much on the development sequences per se as on the fundamental building blocks of those sequences—that is, the acts of creativity that make it possible to find solutions to the specific problems that are scattered throughout the development path. Thus, it is not strange that Hirschman found particularly interesting the question of which conditions are more conducive to trigger creative responses, and the question of the very nature of creativity.

Hirschman also underscored what he called "the centrality of side-effects," and in *Development Projects Observed* he described project appraisal as the art of visualizing them. In his definition, side effects are not just "secondary effects," mere spillovers or repercussions of a project. More often than not, they turn out to be "inputs essential to the realization of the project's principal effect and purpose."[83] They are called "effects" instead of, for example, "conditions" or "prerequisites" because they are "eventual requirements"— not needed from the inception, but essential for the project to survive after the start-up and mature into a long-lived endeavor. A project for the development of highways (as opposed to railways) would serve as an example.

It is commonly held that investment in highways develops the trucking industry and therefore enhances entrepreneurship. But this secondary effect may have much wider consequences: "entrepreneurship means political power, which in turn means the ability to change the rules of the transportation game decisively in favor of the highways." What might seem a mere secondary effect (enhanced entrepreneurship) becomes a decisive element, making the decision to develop motorways instead of railways irreversible.[84] Side effects are at the same time necessary and unpredictable, and central in Hirschman's approach: "a search for the indirect effects is to be recommended if only as a heuristic device, as a means of identifying some of the basic conditions for the project's success."[85]

Cost-benefit analysis and its attempt to make precise calculations of the secondary effects of investments, according to Hirschman, turned this search for indirect effects into an excessively rigid process, hampered by too many arbitrary assumptions, and made the quest for a unique ranking a futile exercise. "How could it be expected," Hirschman protested, "that it is possible to rank development projects along a single scale by amalgamating all their varied dimensions into a single index when far simpler, everyday choices require the use of individual or collective judgment in the weighing of alternative objectives and in the trade-off between them," especially when the aim of cost-benefit exercises seems to be not to facilitate the decision maker's informed judgment, but to make him dispense with such judgment altogether.[86] The following passage captures Hirschman's unsystematic approach, his idea that it is impossible to detect a set of criteria uniformly applicable to all projects:

Upon inspection, each project turns out to represent a *unique constellation* of experiences and consequences, of direct and indirect effects. This uniqueness in turn results from the varied interplay between the structural characteristics of projects, on the one hand, and the social and political environment, on the other. To facilitate the understanding of this interplay I focused . . . on various properties of projects—primarily uncertainties and latitudes—that condition their *total* behavior and career. . . . There was no intention to erect these manifold aspects of project behavior into full-fledged criteria that should be applied to all projects; rather I was seeking to provide project planners and operators with a large set of glasses with which to discern probable lines of project behavior, in the expectation that the analysis of each individual project would require different and rather limited subsets of the full set of glasses which has been exhibited.[87]

By the time Hirschman was drafting the manuscript of his book, it had become clear that his research agenda was at total variance with the World Bank's. A senior officer noted that the book did not contain "any operationally useful analysis" and concluded on a note of disappointment: "I for one gained no significant new insights into the process of project preparation and evaluation."[88]

Hirschman's approach to project appraisal was a natural evolution of his previous work, which had marked an increasing distance from the early debates in development theories. The "failure of several of the earlier ideas as *practical* policy solutions," as Tony Killick put it, prompted Hirschman's detailed inquiries into the mechanisms of economic policy making, as well as the early evaluation studies that the World Bank undertook in the 1960s and the convergence of the Bank and Hirschman on the need to develop a more systematic method for appraisal.[89] But the shared perspective on what was needed did not become a shared perspective on how to meet that need.

Hirschman tried to transform the *Weltanschauung* of the World Bank and its approach to project design, management, and appraisal. In this effort, rather than focusing exclusively on building evaluation procedures, he added questions that were more ample and strategic in nature. Moreover, while some of his insights were pathbreaking and innovative, such as the need to consider carefully the social and political factors that could affect a project, other reflections appeared excessively academic—for example, his discussion of the degree of independence of regional development agencies from the political sphere.

Ultimately, Hirschman neglected the eminently practical needs that were at the basis of the Bank's effort to discuss evaluation procedures. The World Bank expected Hirschman to analyze its projects without any revolution in perspective, to work on making project design and management somehow more measurable, predictable, and possibly replicable. Herman van der Tak suggested that Hirschman "summarized the positive and negative aspects of various types of projects" into "a more operational 'summary and conclusions,' . . . which would provide practitioners with guidelines."[90] The Bank's Economics Department eventually made an attempt to write this operational guide, resulting in a hybrid between a "summary and conclusions" for practitioners, as proposed by van der Tak, and a series of "annotated questions" about projects, as proposed by Hirschman. However, a proper operational version of Hirschman's study never saw the light.

While the World Bank was struggling with the seeming inapplicability of Hirschman's reflections, cost-benefit analysis received a tremendous boost from research pursued by other multilateral organizations. Cost-benefit analysis had taken shape in the 1920s and 1930s as a technique in water resources development, cultivated mostly by engineers, subjecting public investment decisions to economic analysis and evaluating alternative projects in terms of the maximization of public "utility." However, the intrinsic difficulties of quantifying the projects' effects, compounded with competing views among the different bureaucracies that had authority over water management in the United States, made it impossible to agree on a standardized method of cost-benefit analysis until the 1960s.[91]

Moreover, as Stephen Marglin observed, "benefit-cost analysis was introduced as a means of project 'justification' alone . . . not as a tool for project planning; in American practice (as distinct from theory) it often has served as window dressing for projects whose plans have already been formulated with little if any reference to economic criteria."[92] A push toward standardization and uniformity came only in the late 1940s, and especially the 1950s, as a way to overcome conflict among agencies and because of the increasing interest in cost-benefit analysis among economists. The development of the new welfare economics after World War II gave intellectual legitimacy to the attempt to turn, as one critic put it, "a useful way of roughly assessing the promise of a particular project, or comparing various ways of carrying out a project," into "a precision tool for attaining general economic efficiency."[93]

Between the late 1960s and early 1970s, a new wave of studies in cost-benefit analysis appeared. In 1968, the Development Centre of the Organisation for Economic Co-operation and Development (OECD) published the second volume of its *Manual of Industrial Project Analysis in Developing Countries*. Whereas the first volume had focused on the profitability of industrial investments from the firm's point of view, the second volume, authored by Ian M. D. Little and James A. Mirrlees, centered on social cost-benefit analysis. The Little-Mirrlees volume, republished in a deeply revised version in 1974, was immediately regarded as a groundbreaking contribution to project appraisal in developing countries, especially in their use of shadow prices—prices that were meant to reflect the social effects of projects, as opposed to their private profitability.[94] In the span of a few years, this approach had become a "school" that directly influenced "the thinking of economists engaged in planning in developing countries."[95] In 1972, the United Nations Industrial Development Organization (UNIDO) published another milestone volume in project appraisal, authored by Partha Dasgupta, Stephen Marglin, and Amartya Sen.[96] Although the differences from the Little-Mirrlees's approach were important, the two approaches still had enough in common to be viewed "in some immediate sense [as] similar" or having "a similar spirit."[97] To be sure, both these approaches discussed the role of uncertainty in project design and appraisal. But in practical matters, they tended to conflate this term with what is usually meant by "risk"—that is, something subject to measurement. Hirschman, following the Knightian (and Keynesian and Hayekian) dichotomy between "risk" and "uncertainty," considered uncertainty a quality that was impossible to measure. In an article from the early 1960s, coauthored with political scientist Charles Lindblom, Hirschman elaborated more generally on the unavoidable unknowns in policy making: "it is clearly impossible to specify in advance the optimal doses of . . . various policies under different circumstances. The art of promoting economic development . . . consists, then, in acquiring a feeling for these doses."[98]

Reflections about the limits of cost-benefit analysis beyond Hirschman's of course existed. The final report of a UNESCO meeting of experts, for example, underscored not only the limits of reducing all the factors of social choice to a single measure, but the actual impossibility of reducing to a financial measure social objectives that are in fact not marketable, such as the acquisition of new values and the strengthening of social relationships. In particular, the UNESCO report reinforced Hirschman's major criticism of cost-benefit analysis as a deeply antipolitical approach: "Reducing all factors to a common denominator winds up by substituting for the complex processes of political and social debate the arbitrary balancing and measurement of the technocrat. The instrument of rationality appears used as a means of evading political choice."[99] Bernard Schaffer and Geoff Lamb, of the Institute of Development Studies at Sussex University, elaborated further on the limits of cost-benefit analysis, such as its inability to gauge the redistribution effects of development projects.[100] Peter Hall, an expert on urban and regional planning, dedicated the first chapter of his sensationally titled *Great Planning Disasters* to the role of uncertainties, suggesting that planners develop scenarios that incorporate Hirschman's work on uncertainty in project appraisal.[101] These, however, were minority positions with only limited impact on the development debate.

By the early 1970s, Hirschman's book had been completely forgotten. The 1974 Little-Mirrlees book dismissed it as "a stimulating essay on the theme that any assessment leaves things out," and the rest of the literature almost completely ignored it.[102] When, in 1975, the World Bank published its own reference text in project appraisal—very much in the tradition of Little-Mirrlees—it did not include a single reference to Hirschman's work for the Bank.[103] The head of the Evaluation Department of the Overseas Development Administration of the British government described *Development Projects Observed* as "entertaining and provocative reading" but, conflating the whole book with the first chapter on the Hiding Hand, dismissed it as unfounded speculation: "all too often a basic mistake in the original concept or design of a project has crippled its subsequent chances of success."[104]

Clearly, giving pride of place to the Principle of the Hiding Hand was a strategy that backfired. The chapter's focus on the beneficial role of unexpected problems was impossible to introduce into organizational routines, and thus did not convince readers. Another issue may have accounted, if not for the oblivion into which Hirschman's book fell, at least for the reaction it prompted at the World Bank—a reason that has more to do with the sociology of organizations than the history of development economics. The dismissal of Hirschman's work by several Bank officers may have been due to his being an outsider to the institution who commented on (and criticized) its core activity, as well as the ability of its staff to read and interpret development patterns. This distrust first appeared in the "Interim Observations" that Hirschman had circulated. On that occasion, a staff member dismissed Hirschman's observations on bank policies as "the echo of some of the most frequently recurring beefs we heard from the other side of the fence, but only from some people on the other side of the fence, not necessarily representative people," and accused Hirschman of having been heavily one-sided and uninterested in the Bank's viewpoint.[105] Another staff member commented:

What [Hirschman] is trying to do is to call our attention to some of the pitfalls inherent in our operations. . . . It is useful to have an outsider's reminders and the advantage of his perspective. But we should be sure that Mr. Hirschman has access to all the facts, and all the points of view, before completing his book. In the academic and literary professions, criticism seems to draw higher marks than does praise, and while Mr. Hirschman is very knowledgeable and capable, he may not be above succumbing to this temptation.[106]

Even when there was no suspicion that Hirschman might be fishing for praise through indiscriminate criticism, there remained concern that his academic perspective would render his effort irrelevant to the operations of a development institution like the World Bank. Duncan Ballantine, a former academic himself, noted that Hirschman was attempting a "marriage between two inherently incompatible points of view—that of the decision maker and that of the academician or seeker of truth."[107] While he recognized the value of such an exercise, the prevalence of the academic perspective carried a high risk of irrelevance. The common note was that an outsider was not equipped to understand the Bank's operations.

Except for the reaction against the comments of an outsider, much of the criticism by World Bank officials seems plausible and sensible: there is no question that, no matter how insightful Hirschman was, he nonetheless failed to provide any concrete tools for operations evaluation. At the same time, and beyond the Hirschman case, the legitimacy of comments, criticisms, and advice from external subjects is a sensitive issue at the heart of the evaluation function; the reactions of Bank officials highlight that feedback mechanisms are a soft spot in most organizations. Even for the World Bank's internal (but independent) Operations Evaluation Department—its current name is Independent Evaluation Group—balancing independence and objectivity with collaboration and communication between operational and evaluation staff has always been a major challenge. This equilibrium is highly unstable, and subject to recurrent swings. At times, the evaluation function has seemed insufficiently independent and credible. As a Bank officer underscored in 2003, lack of independence undermined the credibility of the evaluation function in principle *and* in practice: "the latest review by the Bank's Quality Assurance Group shows that among the Bank projects entering the portfolio last year, 93 percent were satisfactory. If you put out a report showing that 93 percent of your projects are satisfactory, do you have a credibility problem?"[108] At other times, independence has come at the price of antagonistic reactions. As a director of the Bank's Operations Evaluation Department (OED) wrote, the typical reaction of operational staff was "to dispute the factual details and to question the usefulness of the findings, and to attack OED's methodology."[109] No wonder that Albert Hirschman experienced similar criticism.

The publication of a new edition of *Development Projects Observed* by the Brookings Institution Press in 2015 has triggered renewed, if somewhat polemically overheated, attention to the book. In an enthusiastic foreword to the new edition, Harvard professor Cass Sunstein has highlighted the similarities between the Principle of the Hiding Hand and more recent insights of behavioral economics, such as the "optimism bias" and the "planning fallacy." According to Sunstein, Hirschman "can easily be seen as an early behavioral economist," and *Development Projects Observed* "can plausibly be counted as a work in behavioral economics."[110] While the choice of Sunstein as the author of the foreword makes immediate sense—Sunstein had very positively reviewed Jeremy Adelman's biography of Hirschman in the *New York Review of Books*—it was also somewhat paradoxical, given Sunstein's longtime work on cost-benefit analysis in the study of the modern regulatory state.[111] With *Development Projects Observed*, Hirschman had specifically tried to counter the emergence of cost-benefit analysis as the standard approach to project appraisal. As we know, his attempt resulted in utter failure. Now a longtime advocate and major proponent of cost-benefit analysis was celebrating that very book as a classic.

Actually, in his writings, Sunstein offers a sophisticated version of cost-benefit analysis, aware of the controversial nature of judgments of value that intervene in it, as well as our limited knowledge of many crucial variables. Sunstein also highlights that the effects of regulations cannot always be expressed in monetary terms and that qualitative description of relevant effects should remain of primary importance.[112] Yet, as Sunstein put it in a recent book, unequivocally entitled *The Cost-Benefit Revolution* and based on his experience as administrator of the Office of Information and Regulatory Affairs in the Obama administration, "Cost-benefit analysis reflects a firm (and proud) commitment to a *technocratic conception of democracy*."[113] As much as Hirschman valued competence, one cannot help noticing that it was precisely this technocratic pride that Hirschman considered ill placed and misleading.

The recent polemics about the book revolved once again around the Principle of the Hiding Hand. The major critic was Bent Flyvbjerg, a professor of management and an expert on megaprojects at Oxford University, who set out to test Hirschman's principle on a large data set of more than two thousand projects located all over the world (against Hirschman's eleven projects). In a number of publications, Flyvbjerg claimed that Hirschman's Hiding Hand had historically provoked many more negative effects than positive responses.

This kind of criticism was not new, as several other scholars have highlighted the possibility that the Principle of the Hiding Hand can end in disaster and not in creative beneficial reactions. In 1984, Paul Streeten forged the "Principle of the Hiding Fist, which is related to Murphy's law, according to which 'if anything can go wrong, it will,'" while Robert Picciotto noted that in several instances the Hiding Hand becomes "a sleight of hand activated by rent seekers and development con artists."[114] Picciotto sensibly remarked that "the paths to development are strewn with the carcasses of failed schemes sponsored by leaders who overestimated their capacity to overcome problems and underestimated project risks and costs"—which is actually the optimism bias mentioned earlier by Sunstein and already highlighted by Salant in 1967—and warned that, in evaluating the possible effects of the Hiding Hand, "it is vital to distinguish . . . *what* is being hidden and *who* is doing the hiding and *why*."[115] Sunstein evoked a "Malevolent Hiding Hand," the evil twin of Hirschman's principle, "which also hides obstacles and difficulties, but in situations in which creativity does not emerge, or emerges too late, or cannot possibly save the day," while Roger Sandilands of the University of Strathclyde and the biographer of Hirschman's adversary adviser in Colombia, Lauchlin Currie, described *Development Projects Observed* as "not only bad economics but even worse morality."[116] Apparently equating, as Sandilands did, Hirschman's mainly descriptive principle with a strictly normative one, Picciotto questioned the opportunity of using the Hiding Hand in development projects: "In the short run, it may be expedient to secure support through overoptimistic goal setting. But to achieve staying power, social frustrations must be kept to a minimum and trust preserved through realistic objectives and transparent exposition of their risks and costs."[117]

Flyvbjerg's attack caused a little brouhaha, with replies from other scholars countercriticizing Flyvbjerg's premises and conclusions. The virtuoso effect in the quarrel came from Sunstein, who managed to praise the Principle of the Hiding Hand in his preface to Hirschman's volume and criticize it in an article coauthored with Flyvbjerg. The latter concluded the exchange by reiterating that the principle is at best a special case, not a typical one.[118]

This may indeed be the case. But one cannot help considering the entire discussion a tempest in a teapot. A much more equanimous approach is that of Des Gasper, who, as a PhD student at the University of East Anglia, in 1986 wrote that the Hiding Hand was to be taken "only as an entry point for discussing project realities." According to Gasper, Hirschman's main intention was "to draw on project experience to better understand project processes and hence improve project design, selection, and management."[119]

More generally, the 2015 debate missed a broader point. Apparently, all discussants took it for granted that the Principle of the Hiding Hand is Hirschman's most important contribution to project appraisal. This is a questionable proposition. Actually, the Principle of the Hiding Hand provided a captivating introduction to a broader, and much more important, question—that is, the ineliminable presence of deep-rooted uncertainties in project design and implementation. Hirschman's discussion of uncertainties takes many pages, discussing their pervasive presence on both the supply and demand sides, and in different areas such as finance, administration, technology, and research and development. Likewise, Hirschman discusses at length which specific characteristics of a project could help reduce uncertainty and enhance control in design and implementation—hence his discussion of spatial, temporal, and institutional "latitudes" and "disciplines," of "trait-taking" and "trait-making" in project design, and of the "centrality of side-effects" in project appraisal.

Nobody, not even World Bank critics of Hirschman, thought that Hirschman was proposing to rejoice in false starts, the underestimation of costs, and unexpected crises. More to the point, they questioned how it was possible to routinize Hirschman's interpretation of projects that he saw as a "*unique constellation* of experiences and consequences, of direct and indirect effects," and of unexpected creative responses in organizational processes. This was Hirschman's unresolved problem, and it is still an important question for World Bank officers and development agencies today.

Having left behind the polemical accents that characterized the first circulation of the book fifty years ago, World Bank staff members have returned to use Hirschman's reflections as a sounding board to reflect on the relationship between their field experience and the Bank's production and routinization of useful knowledge from appraisal and evaluation processes. Having abandoned the hubris of overconfident modernizers, development practitioners are on the lookout for a better understanding of processes of institutional learning. Two World Bank officers recently described their research as the quest for "a process of structured, cumulative experimentation that admits the existence of uncertainty but at the same time acknowledges and builds on existing knowledge." They concluded, "In this context, Hirschmanian themes of social learning continue to be of relevance."[120]

Chapter Five

AN INTERDISCIPLINARY SOCIAL SCIENCE

The second half of the 1960s were years of tremendous productivity for Hirschman. After the publication of *Development Projects Observed*, his third book-length installment on development, he published several other important contributions to the field in essay form. The seven articles he published between 1965 and 1970 were so close in time and contents to one another that, as Hirschman put it, "increasingly they became chapters of a book in formation."[1] At a length of about 180 pages, they might well have constituted a book on their own, but eventually Hirschman decided to assemble them, together with other writings on development from previous years, in a larger collection, *A Bias for Hope: Essays on Development in Latin America*, published in 1971.[2]

But the late 1960s were also the crucial years in which Hirschman moved beyond the regional and disciplinary borders of the development field to discuss some basic processes of social action that applied to a wide array of cases, in both developed and underdeveloped countries, private and public spheres, and states and markets. The general issues Hirschman wanted to address were how individuals respond to different kinds of "deterioration" in public services, market products, and organizational behaviors; under which conditions individuals come together to voice their discontent or, at the opposite end of the spectrum, prefer quietly to "vote with their feet" (what he calls exit); and what mechanisms of "recuperation" different cases of deterioration allow. As this admittedly abstract synthesis of Hirschman's new research project shows, the task was very general in scope and truly interdisciplinary. The result was Hirschman's 1970 slender essay *Exit, Voice, and Loyalty*, arguably his most famous and important book.[3]

That volume marked Hirschman's transformation from political economist to all-around, deeply interdisciplinary social scientist. From then on, his contributions to the scholarly and public debate, though always in contact with the discipline of economics and the field of development, touched on an impressively wide spectrum of themes, offering compelling and novel analyses and continuing to demonstrate the potentialities and power of truly interdisciplinary scholarship.

Because of the chronological overlap between Hirschman's old and new interests and, at the same time, the clear differences between these two phases in his scholarly career, it is difficult to synthesize all these analyses in a cohesive chapter. In a sense, Hirschman's writings from the late 1960s on development gravitate toward the preceding period, whereas his work on exit and voice is the first manifestation of the next phase. The deep continuities between the two phases have to do with Hirschman's persona, writing and scholarly style, *forma mentis*, curiosity, attitudes, and so many other intangible elements that it would be vain to try to enumerate them all.

An explicit *trait d'union* is, however, the introduction to *A Bias for Hope*, whose first part was dedicated to the relationship between economics and politics. Written in 1970, just when *Exit, Voice, and Loyalty* was going to press, this introduction, titled "Political Economy and Possibilism," programmatically addressed what had in fact been a fundamental element of all Hirschman's previous research—the dismantling of disciplinary divisions between economics and political science. In it, Hirschman asked, "How is it possible to overcome the parochial pride of economists and political scientists in the autonomy of their respective disciplines and to go beyond the primitivism of . . . efforts at linking them?"[4] *Exit, Voice, and Loyalty* was, for Hirschman, first and foremost a new analysis aimed at breaking the "fundamental schism" between economics and political science, though it was by no means the first.[5]

In "Political Economy and Possibilism," Hirschman noted that the obvious connection between the two perspectives is evident in large-scale phenomena such as the link between inflation and mass unemployment, on one side, and political consensus on the other. But these large-brushstroke analyses are either too easy and uninteresting or so complex in their analytical details that they become unfathomable and inconclusive. A more promising approach, according to Hirschman, lies in the analysis not of the rough outline, but of the "fine features of the economic landscape," with great attention to historical detail and the specific functioning of well-circumscribed social mechanisms.[6] Not surprisingly, Hirschman dated his interest in the political implications of economic phenomena at least from his 1945 book *National Power and the Structure of Foreign Trade*, but also noted that his discussions of program and project aid (which we examined in chapter 3), of policies of import-substitution industrialization, and of the discrepancies between the changing economic scenario and the perceptions of policy makers (to be discussed in the first part of this chapter) are all examples of "interactions between market and non-market forces," and all provide "considerable food for political thought."[7]

The unifying principle of this transitional period can therefore be detected in Hirschman's increasing urge to address head-on and explicitly the problem of the separateness of economic and political analysis. Hirschman was very parsimonious with programmatic pieces, at least until the turn of the 1970s. Thus, the decision to write a methodological essay can be read as further confirmation of his growing desire to broaden the disciplinary boundaries of his inquiry, and that the time was ripe for an explicit statement of his intentions.

This chapter is dedicated to this complex transitional period, starting with Hirschman's late-1960s articles on development issues and ending with his 1970 masterpiece, *Exit, Voice and Loyalty*.

THE REFORMIST PATH: AGAINST *FRACASOMANIA*

As we saw in chapter 4, by the mid-1960s practitioners in the field of development economics were increasingly frustrated with the results of development efforts. To start with, the record of achievements was unclear. Not only individual scholars but entire organizations lacked a legible map of which policies worked and which did not, which institutional settings were conducive to development and which were not. Even at the level of individual projects—the basic unit of development aid—the picture was far from clear. The World Bank, for instance, measured the success of its operations from returns on investment, but recipient governments virtually always repaid their debts to the bank, and that did not say much about the actual working of the projects. Returns on investment measured not so much the economic usefulness of funded projects as the political power of the World Bank in relation to member countries, for no country would dare to default on its debt to the Bank.

The debates about project appraisal and evaluation, discussed in the previous chapter, were an attempt to react to this lack of clarity. Interestingly, the evaluation question arose more or less at the same time in many different development organizations between the late 1960s and the early 1970s. This was not by chance. In his history of the United Nations Development Program, Craig Murphy reports a revelatory statement by the UNDP's first chair (and former head of the Marshall Plan) Paul Hoffman: "if we do our jobs well, we will be out of business in twenty-five years."[8]

Of course, things did not work out that way. But the vitality of the "glory days of high development theory" was possible precisely because the solution to the development question always seemed close at hand. Perhaps, had the formidable difficulties of fostering development been evident from the beginning, many scholars would have felt totally discouraged even before attempting to address the task, and the initial wealth of intellectual energy devoted to development would have been much smaller. In this sense, Hirschman could perhaps have consoled himself that if his Principle of the Hiding Hand failed to become an analytical instrument in the toolbox of foreign aid and project appraisal, it nonetheless helps explain the somewhat belated birth of project appraisal, when early optimism waned and development economics underwent its first serious crisis.

The crisis unfolded as both a crisis of understanding and one of confidence. From the late 1940s well into the 1960s, a number of underdeveloped countries were considered "laboratories" of development policies or "test cases," under the assumption that they would serve as blueprints for more systematic action worldwide. Unfortunately, development laboratories often produced overconfident diagnosticians proposing unjustifiably generalized solutions. The only evident and widely agreed upon conclusion was that the category of "underdeveloped countries" comprised so many different cases that it was in fact useless.

Less developed countries, Hirschman lamented, had become "fair game for the model-builders and paradigm-moulders, to an intolerable degree."[9]

To these overconfident development "experts," less developed countries appeared clearly intelligible, their "laws of movement" regular and predictable, and the solutions to their predicament easily definable—in fact, Hirschman argued, too easily definable. "Why should all Latin America find itself constantly impaled on the horns of some fateful and inescapable dilemma?" he protested. "Any theory or model or paradigm propounding that there are only two possibilities—disaster or one particular road to salvation—should be prima facie suspect. After all, there *is*, at least temporarily, such a place as purgatory!"[10]

Moreover, and related to the difficulty of evaluating outcomes, development policies were also a bone of contention. Major debates in the 1950s and 1960s involved the policies of industrialization and the role of foreign direct investment in less developed countries. Hirschman felt there was not enough public awareness about either the limits of these policies or the positive results obtained, and made a series of important interventions to try to redress this information deficit. Throughout the 1960s, in essay after essay, he was building a reformist path between the two extremes of total defeatism and denial of the evident limits of the development edifice.

The tendency that Hirschman observed among his Latin American colleagues to exaggerate criticism was, in his view, the specular attitude of what he had called, borrowing an expression from Flaubert, "la rage de vouloir conclure," or the rage for wanting to conclude.[11] Once tested against the complexity of reality and the fact that actual problems are less malleable than models predict, this urge produces natural by-products in the form of disappointment, frustration, and a sense of total failure. Hirschman considered this highly volitile cyclical pattern of the rage-to-conclude followed by a sense of failure to be typical of Latin America and other less developed regions, often accounting for the very polarized political cycles seen in those countries. The recurrent experience of excited enthusiasm followed by utter disappointment had ingrained in Latin American development thought a failure complex, which Hirschman eventually dubbed *fracasomania*, or "the insistence on having experienced yet another failure."[12]

Contrary to this *fracasomania*, Hirschman's reading of industrial policies in Latin America was much more optimistic. He recognized the limits, but also saw the positive sides, of past growth policies. Among these, import-substituting industrialization (ISI) had been a very fashionable strategy in the 1950s. According to the thinking at the time, Latin American economies from the middle of the nineteenth century to the Great Depression were marked by a long phase of growth, based on the export of foodstuff and primary products. The collapse of international trade caused by the two world wars and the 1929 crash showed all the limits of economies heavily dependent on the international markets for raw materials and on the import of manufactures. After World War II, Raúl Prebisch (at the Economic Commission for Latin America, ECLA) and Hans Singer (at the United Nations) produced important studies on the secular deterioration of the terms of trade of primary products vis-à-vis manufactured goods in international markets. Though their thesis was later challenged by economic historians, in the 1950s it provided a fundamental basis for the argument that *crecimiento hacia afuera* (export-led growth) should be abandoned in favor of *crecimiento hacia adentro*—growth led by an expansion of the domestic market.[13] The latter strategy would help overcome both deterioration in the terms of trade on the international markets (a demand side problem) and excessive domestic specialization on primary products (a supply side problem).

In a long 1968 article on "The Political Economy of Import-Substituting Industrialization in Latin America," Hirschman rejected this simplistic phasing of different policies. In the first place, he argued, the preponderance of ISI policies was not so absolute as critics depicted it, for export-led growth had been a fundamental and successful strategy for a number of countries in postwar decades as well. Second, and more important, ISI policies had very distinct origins in different countries. In some cases, they had been triggered by balance-of-payments problems; in other cases, they were the outcome of a gradual growth of income; in yet other cases, they had been put in place by deliberate and direct government action. Different origins meant different trajectories: ISI policies originating from government planning were usually more prone to the production of capital goods; those originating from balance-of-payments difficulties had instead a tendency to favor the domestic production of nonessential luxury goods. It made little sense to criticize ISI policies in general. In certain countries, they helped expand the industrial sector and the incomes of large strata of the population; in others, they caused only a limited development of manufacturing and an increase in income inequality.

Hirschman also noted that ISI policies, far from having turned ineffective because of an alleged exhaustion of import-substitution possibilities (the thesis of prominent Brazilian economist Celso Furtado, among others), had in fact fostered a series of new investment opportunities, either because growing income created demand for new consumption products or because new production triggered backward linkages (that is, created additional demand for inputs whose domestic production eventually became viable).[14] From this perspective, even niche or luxury products could have a beneficial effect, if they were able to provide the additional demand that opened the door to the establishment of a new import-substituting industry. Hirschman's analysis of "bottleneck industries," or of the (seemingly paradoxical) necessity of nonessential production for industrial expansion, was thus an elaboration on the concept of linkages.[15]

If one common characteristic of ISI policies could be detected behind the various experiences of different countries, it was a certain tendency to unfold in phases. ISI usually started with the production of manufactured consumer goods and only at a later stage moved to the production of intermediate and eventually capital goods (the duration and importance of the different phases varied according to country). This made the process highly sequential and smoother than in early industrial countries such as Great Britain and France, where the production of intermediate and capital goods had to be pursued at the same time as consumer goods manufacture. Early industrial countries could not import capital goods from other countries.

This sequential character, Hirschman noted, accounted not only for the relative ease with which ISI policies were introduced in many Latin American countries but also for certain typical limits to the process of industrialization in those countries. One was the lack of training in technological innovation, because most technologies were imported. Perhaps even more important was the disconnect between the transformation of a country's industrial sector and that of its social and political structure.

The idea of an all-around transformation of the economic, social, and political structure of industrializing countries had long been a basic tenet of modernization theory. The idea was that economic development would bring with it a deep transformation of the social fabric (from extended to nuclear family, from interpersonal relations based on kinship to relations based on contract, from religious to secular values, and so on) as well as the development of a modern party system and democratic institutions. But the reality of industrial growth in many developing countries had shown modernization theory for what it was: interesting analysis paired with normative prejudice. As Hirschman put it, "the fact that import-substituting industrialization can be accommodated relatively easily in the existing social and political environment is probably responsible for the widespread disappointment with the process. Industrialization was expected to change the social order and all it did was to supply manufactures!"[16]

This unremarkable character of import-substituting industrialization, according to Hirschman, obscured from view the positive changes it brought.[17] As he wrote in another article from 1968, "Obstacles to change are intertwined in Latin America and in other less developed areas with considerable obstacles to the *perception* of change."[18] This line of reasoning was related to the reflections that Hirschman had developed in *Journeys Toward Progress*, strengthened by a renewed interest in social psychology during his sabbatical at Stanford in 1968–69. Just as in *Journeys* he had tried to identify the characteristic features of a Latin American "style" of policy making, in these later reflections he paused to consider whether there existed a typical style of perceiving change (or a structural inability to perceive it) in less developed countries.

According to Hirschman, one additional issue made the perception of change more difficult in underdeveloped countries than in advanced ones. Being in some way "dependent" on one or another superpower, less developed countries needed to introduce change in small doses or in surreptitious ways in order to avoid excessive interest (if not direct intrusion) in their domestic affairs from the powerful ally. This is why dependent countries often "dissimulate change," Hirschman suggested. They show a *"stealthy* style of change" precisely to avoid the interference of leading countries.[19] (Twenty years later, Hirschman noted that commentators who considered the end of the Cold War bad for the Third World because of the diversion of Western capital, entrepreneurship, and attention to newly opened Eastern European countries failed to see the beneficial side of this "neglect effect."[20]) But when dissimulation is too successful, it also obliterates the perception of opportunities for change.[21] In a sense, successful dissimulation risks turning into a self-fulfilling prophecy.

In the late 1960s, Hirschman's defense of ISI policies was addressed largely to leftist Latin American economists, such as Celso Furtado, Maria da Conceição Tavares, and Santiago Macario, and organizations such as ECLA, a powerhouse of structuralist thought in Latin America.[22] In a few years, however, the major critiques of ISI policies would start to come from scholars focusing on patterns not so much of national industrialization as of international trade. The opening salvo in this debate was a landmark 1970 OECD volume by Ian Little, Tibor Scitovsky, and Maurice Scott, *Industry and Trade in Some Developing Countries*, followed by a veritable deluge of similar studies, which criticized not so much the decreasing efficacy of ISI policies as their very theoretical foundations, emphasizing the distorting effects that they had on trade and domestic patterns of industrialization.[23] In the 1970s, however, the international economic landscape was changing quickly, and ISI policies became less sustainable not only because they were under attack from an ideological perspective but also because of the increasing liberalization of international capital movements.

THE REFORMIST PATH: FOR A NEW FOREIGN AID POLICY

The rejection of what Hirschman considered excessively gloomy interpretations of industrial policies in less developed countries did not mean that he saw no space to improve those policies. At various points throughout his career, Hirschman advanced imaginative policy proposals with a clearly provocative bent, in order to kindle discussion and possibly enhance the space for reformist policies. This was one of those moments. He identified as the main problems the role of direct foreign investments and the functioning of foreign aid organizations.

Foreign investments had a contested history. On one side, their positive contribution to the economies of host countries was unquestionable, because they supplied factors such as capital, entrepreneurial and managerial capacity, technology, and market connections. In the best-case scenarios, they even functioned as vectors for the transmission of useful knowledge and thus helped improve the quality of domestic factors of production. Among the negative aspects, Hirschman and others highlighted the effects that these investments had on the domestic entrepreneurial climate, especially the displacement of local abilities, as in the case of local businesses crowded out by foreign investments.[24]

Hirschman's most novel contribution to this issue involved policy conclusions. First, in what we now recognize as his signature style of reasoning, Hirschman differentiated between separate phases of the development process and showed how the negative effects of foreign investment characterized only certain phases, but not others, of a country's economic growth. Hirschman's criticism targeted not foreign investment in general, but its effects in specific phases of the development process. His second contribution was the deeply institutional proposal that he advanced to redress the problem.

According to Hirschman, foreign investments had different effects depending on when they intervened in the process of a country's economic growth. At an early stage of the development process, he argued, direct foreign investments usually have a preponderantly beneficial effect, because of their capacity to supply factors of production and abilities that are either missing or complementary to those present in the country. In subsequent phases, negative effects overcome the positive ones. As is often the case in Hirschman's analyses, his point was to move away from either-or questions (are foreign direct investments positive or negative?) to focus instead on developing a sensitivity about which policies to implement at various phases of the process. As we have seen in chapter 3, Hirschman (and Lindblom) argued against reliance on any precise recipe for policy making: "it is clearly impossible to specify in advance the optimal doses of . . . various policies under different circumstances," they wrote. "The art of promoting economic development . . . and constructive policy making in general consists, then, in acquiring a feeling for these doses."[25]

In the same vein, Hirschman noted that foreign investment "can be at its creative best by bringing in 'missing' factors of production, complementary to those available locally, in the early stages of development of a poor country. The possibility that it will play a stunting role arises later on, when the poor country has begun to generate, to a large extent no doubt because of the prior injection of foreign investment, its own entrepreneurs, technicians, and savers."[26] Every phase, in other words, carried within itself the seeds of its own destruction (a Marxian concept of which Hirschman was fond), and each new phase originated from the previous one. The difficulty was to develop the feeling for how the sequence would unfold. Hirschman concluded, "It is, of course, exceedingly difficult to judge at what point in time foreign investment changes in this fashion from a stimulant of development into a retarding influence, particularly since during the latter stage its contribution is still ostensibly positive."[27] Foreign investment was thus for Hirschman a mixed blessing, whose contribution to the development of a country had to be delicately calibrated.

In any case, if the fine-tuning of foreign investment was difficult in principle, there was little doubt that by the end of the 1960s the time had come for liquidating a substantial part of it—or divesting, as Hirschman put it. This should be done by using "institutional imagination" to design an agency that would function as financial intermediary, arbitrator, and guarantor to help foreign investors divest while awaiting domestic investors to take their place.[28] As Hirschman's focus was principally on the relationship between the United States and Central and South American countries, he proposed the establishment of an Inter-American Divestment Corporation that would act as a buffer to overcome problems of coordination between divestors and new investors. The corporation would also help governments diagnose which sectors were in most urgent need of divestment: "Just as the doctor asks the patient where it hurts, so the corporation could periodically inquire among governments which are the firms where foreign ownership is felt to be irksome."[29]

The establishment of a divestment corporation, according to Hirschman, would make it possible to reach goals more ambitious than simply transferring ownership from foreign to domestic investors. For example, it would create the conditions to broaden the basis of industrial ownership, involving small investors in the purchase of shares. The structure of industrial ownership and wealth would become more democratic and egalitarian, and entirely new sources of capital, until then unavailable because they had previously been considered too small and disaggregated, could be successfully tapped.

Finally, through careful reorganization of the ownership of firms, an Inter-American Divestment Corporation could create a network of financial and managerial ties among industrial sectors in different countries, thus laying the basis for the development of truly Latin American multinational corporations. As Hirschman put it, "Divestment, combined with a measure of 'Latinamericanization,' rather than mere nationalization, could impart a much needed momentum to the integration movement."[30] A divestment corporation, Hirschman implied, would make it possible to transform a phase of relative stasis for Latin America into an opportunity to reconfigure wealth distribution at the national level, as well as the economic landscape of the entire continent.

This was indeed institutional imagination on a large scale. It was also a more detached version of a number of highly political critiques that Hirschman had been making for a decade about U.S. foreign policy toward Latin America. One early occasion for public criticism was the disastrous "goodwill" visit that Richard Nixon paid to several Latin American countries in 1958. Nixon was angrily challenged by demonstrators at many stops throughout his itinerary. According to a detailed analysis of the trip, in Caracas "hundreds screamed for the Nixons to go home and spat and threw garbage on them from an overhanging airport terminal observation deck."[31] Trying to downplay the effects of what journalist Walter Lippman called a "diplomatic Pearl Harbor," Nixon nonchalantly declared that the United States should have "an *abrazo* for democratic leaders" in Latin America, and Milton S. Eisenhower, the president's brother and an important adviser on Latin American affairs, went so far as to recommend that this "embrace" become "official policy in relation with Latin American leaders and nations."[32]

Hirschman was appalled by the "naïveté" of this proposal. "It did not occur to anyone," he wrote, almost incredulous, "that the 'democratic leaders' might not particularly care for our *abrazo*."[33] Hirschman reiterated this point in reaction to John F. Kennedy's speech of March 13, 1961, in which Kennedy proposed to the Latin American ambassadors a new "Alliance for Progress . . . a vast cooperative effort, unparalleled in magnitude and nobility of purpose, to satisfy the basic needs of the American people for homes, work and land, health and schools—techo, trabajo y tierra, salud y escuela."[34] Hirschman denounced the presumptuousness of these proposals, but even worse he thought they would be counterproductive. The insistence on the rhetoric of inter-American solidarity or, worse, the display of top-down benevolence, would probable irritate many reformist groups within Latin American countries and push them away from policies endorsed or directly imposed by the United States toward its poorer southern neighbors. With his interest in the political economy of reformmongering, Hirschman was highly alert to the political realignments of forces as a consequence of U.S. foreign policy toward Latin American countries. "The fight for social reforms," he reflected, "called forth a certain type of supporters, some of whom may well lose interest once the fight has the blessing of all the authorities. Nationalist elements will certainly find fault with any reform the United States espouses and will shift either to defending the status quo or to advocating more radical measures."[35]

Far from strengthening its relations with Latin American countries and changing its image for the better, the United States would end up playing the role of the bull in the china shop, missing the opportunity to take more meaningful steps—whether highly visible actions, such as turning the Panama Canal over to a multilateral inter-American organization, or less ambitious problem-solving activities. Far from an *abrazo*, what was needed was a respectful and collaborative distance.

Another late-1960s proposal to reform a basic mechanism of international economic relations was elaborated by Hirschman in conjunction with Richard M. Bird, a former student of his at Columbia University and then a lecturer in economics at Harvard, following the input of Hirschman's old friend at the World Bank, Alexander Stevenson.[36] The starting assumption was Hirschman's old interest in the relationship between national power and economic international relations, only in this case the focus was on foreign aid, not foreign trade. "In a world of sovereign nations," Hirschman and Bird wrote, foreign aid "is an instrument of national policy which can be used by the rich to acquire influence and to increase their power."[37] The paper, titled "Foreign Aid—A Critique and a Proposal," consisted of two rather disconnected parts. We have already discussed the critique in chapter 3; it is an attack on program lending in defense of lending for specific projects.

The proposal was another very imaginative exercise aimed at revolutionizing the international organization of foreign aid. The essence of the plan was to transfer decisions about foreign aid spending by rich countries from government to individuals. Standard practice was for the national governments of rich countries to tap a portion of tax revenues to fund foreign aid programs; in the Hirschman-Bird scheme, the decision would stay with individual taxpayers, who would decide how much of their income should be funneled to which foreign aid projects (with an upper ceiling of, say, 5 percent, to prevent wealthy individuals from becoming unduly influential). In return, taxpayers would receive from the national revenue service a tax credit and, as an incentive, a "share in development" yielding a small annual return. Foreign aid would be disconnected from the rich countries' pursuit of international influence because funds would be directly channeled by individual taxpayers to specific regional development corporations (World Development Funds, in Hirschman and Bird's final version) in competition among themselves to incentivize efficiency.[38]

As Hirschman and Bird admitted, leaving the ultimate choice of the destination of funds to individual taxpayers left the door open to very erratic and unpredictable results. Yet, they argued, it would be impossible to do worse than the current state of affairs, in which aid policies were a mere instrument of Cold War strategies. In the past twenty-five years, they noted, the highest share of per capita U.S. bilateral aid had been disbursed to Korea, Taiwan, Jordan, and Greece.[39] Clearly, national power preoccupations had strongly influenced the structure of foreign aid. Hirschman and Bird tried to imagine a system that would shift the focus from national power to the development of less developed areas.

Hirschman and Bird circulated a draft among members of the Study Group on Foreign Aid, which used to convene at Harvard, bringing together a small Olympus of development studies. Among the participants who discussed the Hirschman-Bird paper in early December 1967 were Edward S. Mason (former dean of the Graduate School of Public Administration at Harvard, now known as the John F. Kennedy School of Government, and the founder, in 1963, of the Development Advisory Service, now the Harvard Institute for International Development); Gustav Papanek (a former manager of the State Department's technical cooperation in Asia and then the director of Harvard's Development Advisory Service); Francis Bator (the former deputy national security adviser to Lyndon Johnson and a senior economic adviser at USAID, new to Harvard); Walter P. Falcon (an expert of international agriculture, then at Harvard and later at Stanford); Paul Rosenstein-Rodan (then at the MIT Center for International Studies); and a cohort of younger economists, including the rapporteur, Sherman Robinson (then a PhD student in economics at Harvard and later a professor at LSE, Princeton, and UC Berkeley).[40]

The discussion must have been heated. As Robinson summarized the discussion of the "critique" part of the paper in the transcripts, "When all the feathers had settled, there seemed little left in H&B's distinction between project and program aid." The proposal did not meet better reactions: "politically unrealistic," "science fiction," and "harebrained" were among the terms used.[41] World Bank officers emphasized the "sterile" nature of the discussion and the "misconception" of aid policies, and cast serious doubts on the new scheme. "Is this really a 'starter' politically?" wondered the more generous of the commentators.[42] Stevenson warned his friend that World Bank reactions to the paper were "somewhat explosive."[43] More positive reactions came from Princeton. The director of the International Finance Section of the Department of Economics at Princeton University, distinguished economist Fritz Machlup, found the reader's report on the paper so favorable that, as he wrote to Hirschman, he accepted it for publication "even before reading it myself."[44]

But this was only partial consolation. To be sure, Hirschman and Bird did not expect their proposal to be easily adopted in any one donor country. Yet they had hoped to be able to trigger more constructive and imaginative discussion than just comments ranging from scorn to disdain. After all, as Hirschman wrote, the crisis of foreign aid and development economics was in front of everybody's eyes, so "utopian thinking may once again have a role to play."[45] As Hirschman elaborated in a letter to Robert Heilbroner, he approached the two articles as essays in persuasion. He was prepared to see most of his proposals rejected but also saw a place for "this kind of 'naïve' utopianism," since all the constraints of existing interests and power positions might eventually become less binding than they were or appeared to be. Hirschman's proud utopianism was not just tongue-in-cheek polemical positioning against vested interests; it was also based on his deep belief that "change comes about as a result of extraordinary historical constellations when the normal constraints suddenly cease to operate, so it is good to be ready then with proposals that look utopian the day before."[46]

But utopian thinking it remained, and once again Hirschman's reformist position did not satisfy either the supporters of the status quo or, at the opposite extreme, the revolutionaries. Hirschman had been proposing institutional mechanisms for divestment in less developed countries for years, but the response of large multilateral organizations, such as the World Bank–affiliate International Finance Corporation (IFC), had been lukewarm at best.[47] In contrast, left-wing colleagues, such as the young Sam Bowles, saw Hirschman's reformism as a way to reinforce national bourgeoisies and thus to reinforce capitalistic development. But, Bowles suggested, "an alternative view might hold that the weakening of the national bourgeoisie by the predominance of foreign investment is a good thing, as it virtually insures that the nationalist movement in the country will be anti-capitalist as well as anti-imperialist."[48] It was not an easy task for the reformist to avoid being squeezed between these two extremes and to preserve an autonomous political space. As Hirschman explained to Bowles, whom he held in great esteem, his goal was not so much to rule out revolution as to remove it as "an absolute prerequisite"—very much as he had always fought against the idea of necessary prerequisites for capitalistic modernization. Hirschman simply wanted to "try to increase the number of options," for if revolutions may be a solution, "they don't happen often. So, in the meantime, it is worth thinking about other ways of achieving forward movement."[49] In any case, Hirschman was not a revolutionary and knew quite well that grand transformational plans could and did induce severe human costs.

Despite all these efforts, neither an Inter-American Divestment Corporation, nor a new scheme to fund and manage foreign aid, nor smaller reforms saw the light in the development field in those years. In fact, in development economics, the late 1960s were the eve not of reform but of a veritable counterreform.

Hirschman would never abandon his interest in development issues, and he wrote passionately about them until the end of his active scholarly career. But from the end of the 1960s, development was no longer at the forefront of his reflections. The political and social unrest of the late 1960s, both in the United States and internationally, called into question Hirschman's reformist agenda of the past fifteen years. For Hirschman, revolutionary shortcuts remained unappealing, but he also perceived his reformist position to be increasingly weak. Adelman's book offers a detailed and dismaying description of Hirschman's sense of disconcertion in 1966–1968 and his difficulty in framing this feeling into a manageable question.[50]

It was about that time, in preliminary conversations with his colleague Gerschenkron on issues of competition versus monopoly, theories of consumption, and consumer behavior, that Hirschman began to elaborate on the broader question of how individuals shape and manifest their discontent before the deterioration of organizations—not necessarily firms on the market but also public services, neighborhood or ethnic communities, political parties, churches, states, and universities.[51] As he wrote to his sister Ursula, his reflections were going "in some unforeseen directions," though he realized in an increasingly clear manner that he needed to break down disciplinary boundaries, and even went so far as to assert that cross-fertilization between different disciplines was fundamental to address the social and political upheaval of the late 1960s.[52] The invitation to join the Center for Behavioral Sciences at Stanford during the 1968–69 academic year offered a welcome opportunity to shape these ruminations into a small volume that would be immediately recognized as a classic in the social sciences—*Exit, Voice, and Loyalty*. In this work, Hirschman explored much vaster intellectual territories, but the point of entry was still development, specifically an observation he had made in *Development Projects Observed* about rail transportation in Nigeria and the response of local users to a deterioration in its performance.

THE PROBLEM OF POOR PERFORMANCE

In a world inhabited by project planners deceived by the Hiding Hand, Hirschman believed that an important question for improving project design was how to navigate between the Scylla of projects that fully accept the underdeveloped conditions of the region in which they operate, and thus are inherently incapable of effecting any change in the status quo, and the Charybdis of projects entirely oriented toward changing the status quo but with no consideration for existing constraints. To be successful, Hirschman wrote, paraphrasing terminology from price theory, the behavior of a project should offer a combination of "trait-taking" and "trait-making" characteristics. The project, in other words, should be able to incorporate or accept (take) those traits of the social, economic, and human reality in which it will be embedded that are considered unchangeable, and at the same time to modify (make) some other, more malleable traits. Not unexpectedly, for Hirschman the problem resided in developing a sensitivity for what activities fall on the "take" or the "make" side of the equation, and under which conditions.

One particularly insidious problem, Hirschman noted, arises with projects that are only *implicitly* trait-making—that is, projects that appear to be safely trait-taking but will require substantially more changes to the socioeconomic environment than initially envisaged. The quintessential case that Hirschman offered was that of subsidies for the Bornu Railway Extension as opposed to highway construction (and development of the lorry business) in Nigeria. A number of characteristics of Nigerian society, including high tribal antagonism, widespread corruption, and the rough transition to independence in the early 1960s, made new investments in railway expansion problematic because small lorry businesses adapted much better to intergroup antagonism and corruption than did a much more centralized and fragile system like a railway network. As Hirschman concluded, "the chances for the railways to become a school for noncorruption, for coexistence among the various tribes, and for similar fundamental shifts in behavior must be considered rather poor."[53]

Indeed, in January 1966, a mere five months after the Hirschmans had visited the country, a military coup initiated a period of escalating instability and mass killings that resulted in the secessionist attempt of Biafra, in the southeastern region of the country, and the civil war of 1967–1970. The Hirschmans had not seen the crisis coming. As Adelman suggests, one could argue that "Hirschman's optimism blinded him to the simmering tensions . . . his wish for surprising, positive effects overwhelmed what he saw and heard."[54] Indeed, not only was the railway extension unlikely to help interethnic coexistence, it had "disastrous consequences," directly contributing to increasing strife among different regions and factions of the country.[55]

In addition to the shock and humanitarian concerns provoked by Nigeria's descent into civil war, Hirschman continued to reflect on another element that made railways a poor competitor to highways. In particular, he noticed that certain services do not tolerate poor performances, whereas others allow much more latitude for deterioration. Air transportation is a very good example of the former; roads are an example of the latter. If airplanes are not well maintained, disaster is almost certain. Road deterioration, in contrast, leads to greater wear and tear on vehicles, lower average driving speed, and an increase in the number of small accidents, but rarely a major catastrophe.

Services that offer no latitude for deterioration are strong trait-makers, because they impose their own characteristics on the socioeconomic environment. People often accept road deterioration for a long time before public protest erupts, but in the case of a deadly incident to an airliner, one can expect an immediate response from the authorities, as well as strong public pressure for the problem to be addressed and solved without delay. In *Strategy*, Hirschman had briefly discussed this sort of "compulsion to maintenance," built into specific technologies, as one example of an inducement mechanism. In that case, he also mentioned railways as a case of stronger compulsion to maintain than highways, "as the accidents resulting from nonmaintenance are more serious."[56]

Nigeria, however, seemed to defy this conclusion. As far as Nigerian railways were concerned, the presence of a well-developed network of roads and road transportation businesses made the trait-making feature of railway transportation much *less* compelling, because the presence of a ready alternative made it easier to indulge the weaknesses of the railway system. As Hirschman wrote, "with truck and bus transportation available, a deterioration in rail service is not nearly so serious a matter as if the railways held a monopoly for long-distance transport—it can be lived with for a long time."[57] Moreover, state subsidies protected the railways from a decrease in revenues. This, in turn, meant that improvements in the efficiency of railways could be postponed without any serious consequences.

This apparently minor observation, this *petite idée*, was the seed for a major breakthrough in Hirschman's thought. Without realizing it yet, he had stumbled upon an analytical insight with the potential to illuminate a wide range of economic, political, and social phenomena. Public protest against the deterioration of the railway service was an example of what Hirschman would call "voice." The choice of an alternative to the disappointing service—in the Nigerian case, highways instead of railways—he would call "exit."

Hirschman wrote his new manuscript in 1968–69 during a sabbatical at the Center for Advanced Study in the Behavioral Sciences at Stanford University. In 1970, *Exit, Voice and Loyalty* was published. The subtitle—*Responses to Decline in Firms, Organizations, and States*—clearly refers to the roots of Hirschman's reflection, but, as we will see in the next section, the narrow question of how railways and highways interact in a fragmented and conflictual social environment exploded to embrace a much larger scale and scope of applications.

THE MOST FAMOUS TRIAD: *EXIT, VOICE, AND LOYALTY*

As Hirschman wrote in his introduction to *Exit, Voice, and Loyalty*, his goal was to propose a "unifying way of looking at issues as diverse as competition and the two-party system, divorce and the American character, black power and the failure of 'unhappy' top officials to resign over Vietnam."[58] The project did not lack for ambition.

Such grandiose claims usually came from "economic imperialists," economists committed to broadening the territories of neoclassical economic analysis to include areas that usually fell outside their bailiwick, such as the family or racial group dynamics. This was a particularly original example of the position of the Economics Department at the University of Chicago, on the frontlines of a disciplinary turn toward increasing focus on the micro-foundations of economics. Gary Becker started what an enthusiastic

commentator called his "imperialistic crusade" with a doctoral dissertation in economics on racial discrimination, published in 1957.[59] Considering the "taste for discrimination" as part of an individual's utility function,
Becker analyzed discrimination like any other good: rational and maximizing individuals would be willing to pay in order to obtain, or exercise,
discrimination.[60]

At first sight, Hirschman's boldly "unifying" approach might be said to
resemble that of economic imperialists. Nevertheless, when asked in an
interview if it was true that he was "somewhat critical" of economic imperialism, Hirschman used "much stronger terms" to describe his opposition:
"I am definitely hostile to that approach."[61] After all, in his previous books,
Hirschman had consistently shown a propensity for mutual contamination of different perspectives rather than analyses under a single methodological umbrella. Hirschman's "unifying" approach was predicated not on
any imperialism of one discipline over the other but on its opposite: truly
interdisciplinary cross-fertilization. Using the concepts of *exit* and *voice*,
his goal was to overcome the "fundamental schism" between economics
and politics.

The book begins with the observation that in the face of disappointing
performance by an organization, some individuals leave it (or stop buying its products); in Hirschman's vocabulary, they exercise the exit option.
Typical of a market environment, *exit* has the features of choices made in
the market: it is discrete (one either buys or does not buy, one either leaves
or remains), impersonal (no explanations are necessary), and indirect (by
exiting, one simply signals to the organization that something is wrong). A
different option is *voice*, which presents opposite characteristics to *exit*. It is
continuous, as it can vary from low-volume grumbling to loud protest; it is
personal—that is, articulated face to face; and it is direct—that is, it carries
contents, not simply signals. *Voice*, Hirschman summarized, "is political
action par excellence."[62]

But Hirschman noted that economists and political scientists seemed
not only incapable of, but totally disinterested in, analyzing both market
and nonmarket mechanisms, or, in Hirschman's new vocabulary, both
exit and *voice* options. Economists focused exclusively on expanding the
market mechanism, as in Milton Friedman's famous proposal to give parents vouchers to be "spent" on educational services by shifting their preferences from one provider to the other instead of expressing their views

through "cumbrous political channels."[63] Political scientists tended instead to emphasize political conflict, disparaging exit as a purely antisocial option. Hirschman hoped to show how both perspectives were in fact useful. Addressing the economists in particular, Hirschman argued that "in a whole gamut of human institutions, from the state to the family, voice, however 'cumbrous,' is all their members normally have to work with."[64] In other words, market and nonmarket mechanisms, instead of belonging to different disciplinary realms, exist side by side. The interplay between these different mechanisms would show "the usefulness of certain tools of economic analysis for the understanding of political phenomena, *and vice versa*," leading to a more complete and balanced understanding of processes of social change than could be provided by economic, sociological, or political analyses in isolation.[65]

Hirschman's aim was first and foremost to elucidate response pathways used by consumers and citizens. But he was also clearly keen to promote a true commingling of different disciplines—to demonstrate "to political scientists the usefulness of economic concepts, *and to economists the usefulness of political concepts*."[66] As the selective use of italics demonstrates, *Exit, Voice, and Loyalty* was also an attempt to redress the imbalanced relationship among social sciences caused by the rising tide of economic imperialism. By applying the analytical framework of economics to political phenomena such as power relations and democratic processes, Hirschman wrote, economists "succeeded in occupying large portions of the neighboring discipline while political scientists—whose inferiority complex vis-à-vis the tool-rich economist is equaled only by that of the economist vis-à-vis the physicist—have shown themselves quite eager to be colonized."[67]

This has proven to be true. More contentious, however, is whether Hirschman managed to accomplish his goal of redressing the balance between the two disciplines. He was undoubtedly successful in mixing elements often analyzed separately in the different disciplinary realms of economics and political science. In particular, his analysis of *voice* elevated this concept to a central position in both political science and economics discourses. This was particularly important for Hirschman, because, as he put it at a 1973 seminar, his goal was "both positive and normative": he wanted to show the conditions under which *voice* emerges, but he also argued that there are situations in which "the proper balance of institutional incentives ought to be adjusted so as to strengthen *voice* in relation to *exit*."[68]

But alerting economists to the importance of the political concept of *voice* did not necessarily mean bringing the two disciplinary perspectives onto even ground. On this point, political scientists were divided. Brian Barry, one of the leading political philosophers of his generation, argued in an insightful review that to show the relevance of political *concepts* is not the same as building a truly interdisciplinary *method of analysis*. Barry claimed that Hirschman's goal of having economists look at political concepts and political scientists at economic concepts and how they are intertwined rested nonetheless on a clearly recognizable "economic viewpoint" of both market and nonmarket mechanisms, and in particular on an economic viewpoint of the peculiarly political mechanism of voice.[69] The president of the International Political Science Association Stein Rokkan, in contrast, insisted that Hirschman's essay was "more than just another attempt to make use of the conceptual apparatus of economics in the analysis of political processes" but represented instead "perhaps the first systematic effort to make effective use of models of political response in the analysis of economic behaviour."[70]

The entire analysis of *Exit, Voice, and Loyalty* rests on the fundamental observation that processes of deterioration are pervasive and unavoidable in human societies, and that no concept of maximization, rationality, and efficiency can cancel out this unpleasant truth. Hirschman articulates this concept on the first page of his introduction to the book:

Under any economic, social, or political system, individuals, business firms, and organizations in general are subject to lapses from efficient, rational, law-abiding, virtuous, or otherwise functional behavior. No matter how well a society's basic institutions are devised, failures of some actors to live up to the behavior which is expected of them are bound to occur, if only for all kinds of accidental reasons. Each society learns to live with a certain amount of such dysfunctional or mis-behavior; but lest the misbehavior feed on itself and lead to general decay, society must be able to marshal from within itself forces which will make as many of the faltering actors as possible revert to the behavior required for its proper functioning. . . .

While moralists and political scientists have been much concerned with rescuing individuals from immoral behavior, societies from corruption, and governments from decay, economists have paid little attention to *repairable lapses* of economic actors.[71]

Two interrelated reasons explain this neglect. One is that economic models assume perfect rationality. Decay or deterioration of the performance of an economic actor is thus the consequence of some exogenous event that is, by definition, intractable. The second reason is that, in a competitive economy, a decaying actor leaves room for new actors to emerge. Repairing lapses, in other words, is unnecessary as the economy, in the aggregate, is not subject to lapses—or, from a Schumpeterian perspective, economic progress proceeds precisely because of waves of "creative destruction." Yet Hirschman's reformist and social democratic vision permitted him to observe market mechanisms from a different perspective. "Even when vigorous competition prevails, unconcern with the possibility of restoring temporarily laggard firms to vigor is hardly justified," he wrote, for "mechanisms of recuperation would play a most useful role in avoiding social losses as well as human hardship."[72]

Simply by assuming the new perspective of repairable lapses, Hirschman was able to reexamine several aspects of the market behavior of firms and consumers. Take, for example, a competitive market in which consumers shift their preference from one product, produced by a certain firm, to another product produced by another firm because of a deterioration in the quality of the former. Under what conditions will recuperation be possible? If consumer demand is highly inelastic with respect to changes in quality (that is, if aggregate demand remains basically the same, irrespective of the quality of the product), management will have no reason to react to deteriorating quality. Insofar as management relies on demand trends to gauge the public's appreciation of their product (a proxy for its quality), management might not even notice that a decrease in quality has occurred. If, on the contrary, demand is highly responsive to quality deterioration (demand is elastic, in economic jargon), consumers will shift to other products before management has time to react. The firm will be out of the market before it can recover. Hirschman thus concluded that, if we are interested in understanding the mechanisms of recuperation from temporary lapses, the elasticity of demand to quality deterioration must be at an intermediate level—not so low as to produce insignificant changes in demand, not so high as to bankrupt the firm before a reaction can be organized. This middle way can be described as a situation in which a firm has a mix of different kinds of customers, some of them highly alert to quality (they will immediately exit, providing the signal that quality recuperation is needed) and some inert to changes in quality (they will provide the loyal demand necessary for the product to remain on the market while measures for recuperation are taken).

As this example makes clear, the common wisdom according to which competition is the master mechanism of functioning markets must be recast in significant ways. There is no direct linear correlation between perfect competition and market efficiency. On the contrary, Hirschman argued, "consideration of competition as a recuperation mechanism reveals that, although exit of some customers is essential for bringing the mechanism into play, it is important that other customers remain unaware of, or unperturbed by, quality decline."[73]

What about competition when the decline in quality expands to an entire industrial sector? Then the usual market mechanism based on the exit of consumers will merely result in the mutual exchange of each other's dissatisfied customers by the competing firms. In this case, the quest for a better product by disappointed consumers will be both frantic and vain. Instead of relying on ineffectual exit, it would be better for customers to rely on a different mechanism—that is, direct pressure for quality improvements. As Hirschman noted, this situation is often witnessed not only in markets but also in political systems, in which the major competing parties seem to many dissatisfied citizens to offer no real choice. These considerations bring us to the second term of Hirschman's analysis, voice.

Voice should be defined in broad terms as any attempt to change an objectionable situation "from within"—that is, without recourse to exit (leaving an organization or deciding to buy an alternative product). Thus, at first glance, voice is a residual of exit, since those who do not exit will remain and articulate their discontent. Voice, however, can be better viewed as an alternative to exit. For voice to offer a reasonable chance of success, members of an organization must choose to remain and fight for change from within instead of leaving. Choosing to remain is, of course, another way to say that one decides to be loyal. This is a common experience in the life of political parties.

Hirschman was principally interested in the complex interactions between exit and voice. It is on these grounds that he managed to show how economics and political studies could best interact and offer useful analyses applicable to many different situations. The great complexity and nuance of Hirschman's analysis can be gleaned from his case studies, such as his discussion of how exit and voice help visualize the dynamics of the difficult process of emancipation of the black population in the United States, or how exit illuminates certain ingrained elements of American ideology, what Hirschman refers to as "the curious conformism of Americans."[74]

A simple interaction has to do with whether voice is actually strengthened or weakened by the presence of the exit option. The possibility of leaving will obviously make some individuals opt for exit instead of facing all the troubles of using voice. At the same time, voice becomes more credible when an exit option is available. But a more complex analysis immediately unfolds if we try to draw a profile of those who tend to exit and those who tend to exert voice, and on what occasions.

Standard economic analysis claims that when a price increase occurs, marginal customers drop out first. "Marginal" here refers to the position of customers with respect to price. In other words, marginal customers are those who are willing to buy a certain product at a certain price but would not pay one additional penny for it. If the price increases, they exit. In this case, the customers who are less interested in the product, or who cannot afford a price increase, leave. When, however, it is not the price that increases but product quality that deteriorates, customers who care most about the product and its quality leave first (provided an alternative product exists and they can afford a higher price). In economic terms, it could be argued that for them a deterioration in quality corresponds to a huge increase in price, but the point here is the different sensitivity that different groups have with regard to price increases, on one side, and quality deterioration, on the other. As the subsequent examples will make clear, Hirschman was also influenced by the literature on social psychology and the exchanges he had with Stanford psychologists such as Leon Festinger and Philip Zimbardo.[75]

Consider the case of schools. If the quality of a public school deteriorates, parents who either are uninterested in the quality of their children's school or cannot pay for a private school will leave their children at the public school. Affluent parents interested in providing their children with high-quality education, in contrast, will immediately react to the deterioration of the public school by moving their own children to a private school that can offer at least the same quality as did the public school before it deteriorated. Several consequences follow. First, the strength of voice of parents at the public school is reduced, because many of them have left with their children. Moreover, those who have left are all, by definition, quality-driven; therefore, their voice would have been particularly important as a reaction against quality deterioration.

Hirschman was building his analysis in an attempt to complicate the standard economics perspective, whose focus was limited to the reaction of marginal consumers to price increases and did not consider, as Hirschman was trying to do, quality deterioration. Hirschman did not really discuss the fact that consumers who are primarily sensitive to prices may also be sensitive to quality, though they may find themselves unable to react to quality deterioration. In other words, there may well be poor "connoisseurs" who can appreciate connoisseur goods but cannot afford them. Hirschman was well aware of this fact, of course, but overlooked it as irrelevant to his discussion of how to move beyond the standard economics approach.

A second consequence has to do with the possibility that the quality of education at the private school may also eventually deteriorate. Will families move back to the public school? That choice is unlikely, for two interrelated reasons. First, the public school may not yet have improved its quality. Second, the public school would have to improve to a level above that of the private school, because if a better-quality alternative is not readily available, quality-sensitive customers will tend to exercise voice instead of exit. Once they have moved to a better-quality private school, if the quality then deteriorates, quality-driven parents will remain and exert voice for a long time before losing all hope. Their options are thus asymmetrical: when quality deteriorates and there is a better-quality alternative available, they will opt immediately for exit. If the alternative is not available, they will opt for voice. In the eyes of affluent and quality-driven parents, the public school risks quick deterioration and becomes competitive again only with great difficulty.[76]

Hirschman had in mind the gravely underfunded system of public schools in the United States (where his daughters, Katia and Lisa, received their postelementary education), as well as the many very expensive, high-quality private schools that exist there. In his example, the cumulative process of increasing deterioration and loss of voice as a repair mechanism for the public schools, conjoined to a more stubborn reaction of affluent parents to possible deterioration of private schools before moving back to the public system, resulted in an increasing bifurcation between the dismal fate of the public and the shining results of the private. Had the most quality-conscious parents been loyal to the public system, Hirschman observed, there might have been less tendency to exit and a higher incentive to use voice, thereby preventing the cumulative deterioration of public schools; in fact, however, the level of loyalty was low.[77]

The implications of Hirschman's analysis were momentous, for he showed that once voice enters the picture, competition in a market environment is not necessarily the best solution. At least for certain services characterized by a potentially universal reach, a regime of monopoly is essential to guarantee voice and strong pressure on management to maintain high quality—or, more precisely, to react efficiently and rapidly to potential lapses and deterioration. Monopoly, in this sense, can serve as a substitute for loyalty. Reviving a concept that was central in his previous *Development Projects Observed*, Hirschman also noted that loyalty, or monopolized loyalty, can help activate the resources of creativity necessary to discover new ways of exerting effective pressure to redress the lapse in performance.[78]

Moreover, unlike in standard economic theory, the presence of a small number of competitors against huge monopolists was not necessarily a better arrangement than no competition at all. By reducing the power of voice to the extent that quality-driven customers react to deterioration by exiting, the presence of even a few small competitors could do more harm than good to quasi-monopolists that have latitude for deterioration, because exit would result in a weakened voice without posing any serious threat to the survival of the large quasi-monopolist. In such a case, competition does not restrain monopoly and, at the same time, rids it of its more troublesome (or reformist) customers. Monopoly with a modicum of competition thus becomes, in Hirschman's words, "an oppression of the weak by the incompetent and an exploitation of the poor by the lazy which is the more durable and stifling as it is both *unambitious and escapable.*"[79]

This is frequently visible, for example, with unreliable electric power utilities in developing countries, whose more demanding customers decide at a certain point to install their own independent power generators. The United States Post Office is "another example of lazy monopolist": the presence of more efficient but more costly competitors serves the double goal of getting rid of its more fastidious and demanding customers and, at the same time, tyrannizing the customers for which exit to another service is either impractical or too costly. The same mechanism also works at the political level, as in the case of dictatorial regimes in Latin America that encouraged political opponents to go into voluntary exile—thereby saving their lives, but also disempowering voice at the local level.[80]

Finally, given that in all services that affect the quality of life of individuals and families, resistance to deterioration requires voice, and voice is often stronger and more articulated at upper socioeconomic levels than at lower ones, Hirschman concluded that "the cleavage between the quality of life at the top and at the middle or lower levels will tend to become more marked."[81] Asymmetrical options for exit and voice for different social groups, in other words, are a powerful mechanism enhancing social inequality.

Moreover, loss of voice at the lower levels could be expected more in societies characterized by strong upward social mobility than in more stratified societies, because attempts at private exit would have more chances to succeed in situations of strong social mobility, whereas recourse to voice would be more strongly motivated at every level of more stratified societies. This analysis posed some serious questions about the social sustainability of the so-called American Dream, because it showed that social mobility and social justice could work at cross-purposes. As Hirschman concluded, this "has not been an easy observation to make in a culture in which it had long been taken for granted that equality of opportunity combined with upward social mobility would assure both efficiency and social justice."[82]

Hirschman discussed the role of voice in a particularly perceptive chapter on the behavior of firms and political parties operating in a regime of duopoly. In this case, standard theory, based on an article published in the *Economic Journal* in 1929 by Harold Hotelling, predicted that, under certain assumptions such as zero elasticity of demand (and with some simplification in summarizing the story here), any two competing businesses would position themselves at the midpoints of the left and the right halves of a spatial distribution (as Hotelling proposed, "Main Street in a town or a transcontinental railroad"). This way, they would maximize social return as the distance of customers from either one of the two business would be minimized.[83] Hotelling was discussing an economic duopoly, but this model can be easily used for the analysis of electoral behaviors if, instead of businesses, we consider two political parties (here, distance or proximity to the political platform of a party corresponds to the distance or proximity of the customer to the business). Hotelling demonstrated that businesses (or parties), in order to maximize profits (or votes), would tend to move toward the center of the distribution, for they would be able to retain their customers (or voters) at the extreme of the distribution and also steal customers (or voters) from the competitor.[84]

The Hotelling model has been criticized and requalified on several occasions, but its framework has remained a fundamental theoretical description of the tendency of parties to move toward the center of the political spectrum, even though this model—when confronted with the facts—has often proven wrong. The concept of voice, Hirschman noticed, could explain many of the discrepancies between the Hotelling model and political events. The main error, Hirschman argued, was considering the captive consumer or voter as powerless and thus irremediably linked to the closer shop or party. This idea was based on the standard market behavior according to which consumers exert pressure on a firm by voting with their feet—that is, by exiting and buying the products of another firm. But in fact, voters who have "nowhere else to go" will use voice to the maximum (they have no alternative) and exert all sorts of influence to keep the party from changing position. Moving to the center, therefore, would not be immediately damaging in terms of votes (the voters have nowhere else to go, at least in the short term), but it would bring with it a political cost that might become important in the long run.

Moreover, it is usually the most convinced supporters who are also the most vocal and, by extension of the concept of voice, the most active in political proselytizing. This means that, for a party, it is more important to motivate its activists. Thus, Hirschman argued, "the adoption of a platform which is designed to gain votes at the center can be counter-productive."[85] Obviously, designing a credible, consistent, and appealing political platform is a complex endeavor: a weak party leadership could become excessively receptive to the demands of extremist activists, overshooting the mark and proposing a political platform that alienates all nonextremists; or demand may become very elastic at the extremes of the political spectrum, which means that one step further toward the center can cause party secession at the extreme.

What about the third element of the triad? Loyalty, in Hirschman's analysis, served two functions. First, it helped qualify certain mechanisms of exit and voice. For example, boycott often emerges as a specific by-product of loyalty, when one does not really want to exit but enacts strategies from within in order to achieve a change of policy. The element of loyalty can also help us understand different phases in the use of voice, which can be underutilized in certain cases and become particularly virulent in others, such as in organizations characterized by severe initiation or high fees for entry.[86]

Second, and more important, Hirschman uses the concept of loyalty to introduce a number of cases in which the social dimension is particularly important—for instance, a situation in which individual exit would produce a further deterioration of the product or service, and for this very reason the individual decides to avoid exit (and possibly use voice). Other examples are public goods, from which actual exit is in fact illusory. This treatment of loyalty as a qualification of the exit-voice dichotomy, however, was the one real weakness of the volume. Correctly, Adelman wrote that "loyalty was a blind spot in an otherwise enormously influential and illuminating book," as Hirschman had not actually managed to propose any real understanding of loyalty per se.[87] Episodes of censurable loyalty, as when officials of an administration are reluctant to resign even in the face of policies with which they utterly disagree, are cases in point. Hirschman had the recent example of many top officials in the Johnson administration who remained glued to their chairs despite the Vietnam escalation. He explained these cases as instances of postponed or denied exit and silenced voice, but was unable to discuss them from the perspective of loyalty.

The question of loyalty, however, remained important for Hirschman's thought, principally from the political perspective of citizens' loyalty to the national "community." If exit and voice epitomize different responses to the conflicting perspectives of the consumer and the firm, or the citizen and the government, loyalty apparently epitomizes the nonconflictual situation. But the more Hirschman reflected on the problem of democracy, the more he saw that, far from being dangerous to democracy, conflict was one of its fundamental functional modalities. How can one explain loyalty in a democratic framework frequently rife with conflicts? In a 1994 talk, Hirschman revived a long but often neglected tradition of thinkers who rejected the opposition between conflict and community spirit and instead emphasized that, especially in Western market societies, it is the repeated experience of muddling through conflict and negotiating compromise that produces the "social capital" that keeps society together. As Hirschman summarized that literature, "social conflicts produce themselves the valuable ties that hold modern democratic societies together and provide them with the strength and cohesion they need."[88] From this perspective, a lack of conflict, far from being a sign of cohesion and loyalty, may instead signal political and social apathy, a sort of deteriorated loyalty.

Of course, Hirschman was aware that social conflict can also be explosive and dissolve any form of national community and even civil habits. The civil war that erupted in 1991 Yugoslavia, fracturing the country and killing, in ten years of hostilities, about 140,000 people (more than 14,000 in the siege of Sarajevo alone, and more than 8,000 in the Srebrenica massacre), was a horrific example visible to all. The question of whether conflicts are conducive to disruption or instead strengthen social ties, Hirschman cautioned, "cannot be decided in general."[89] As he often remarked, only a careful contextual analysis of the specific cleavages within a society can help discern the potential outcome of conflicts.

But Hirschman also noted that the conflicts that appear with considerable frequency in pluralistic market societies often have to do with issues for which a compromise can be found; consequently, they are also open to renegotiation if conditions change. This kind of conflict is likely to become a supporting pillar of democratic societies, because it contributes decisively to forming the community spirit that a democratic market society needs. To invoke the need for community spirit in the face of conflicts, Hirschman concluded, is the wrong approach, like invoking a *deus ex machina*. As we have seen in other cases, if a solution to a problem exists, it resides in the process of looking for it: "What is actually required to make progress with the novel problems a society encounters on its road is political entrepreneurship, imagination, patience here, impatience there, and other varieties of *virtù* and *fortuna*."[90]

EXIT, VOICE, AND THE SOCIAL SCIENCES

By the late 1960s, Hirschman was a respected and well-known development economist. The publication of *Exit, Voice, and Loyalty* not only marked his emancipation from the field of development economics but catapulted him to an entirely different level of popularity. With this book, Hirschman created a new vocabulary with which economists and other social scientists could discuss questions that overlapped across different disciplinary fields.

Werner Baer, a development economist at the University of Illinois, among the first to review the book, described it as "an imaginative exploration of how modifications and extensions of our conceptual framework . . . can make the theory more relevant in explaining change and reactions to it."[91] Another reviewer claimed that the book offered "one of the most broad-gauged arguments" in the political economy literature of the last twenty years—that is, since the publication of Kenneth Arrow's *Social Choice and Individual Values*, a foundational text for the new field of modern social choice that intersected economic analysis and voting theory (and earned Arrow the Nobel Prize).[92] Harvard political scientist Karl W. Deutsch (like Hirschman, a political émigré from central Europe) mentioned the book as an example of how some leading economists were moving toward a more explicit consideration of political questions, and defined it as "an outstanding contribution also to political theory."[93] This was not Hirschman's first exercise in "trespassing" disciplinary borders, to use his own terminology, but certainly it was his highest interdisciplinary accomplishment, and one that promised to have an exhilaratingly broad reach.

In fact, the book was not only very favorably reviewed, but scholars from many different fields immediately appropriated it as a conceptual framework to be widely used and adapted to their needs (especially, as Barry noted, in the United States; much less in the UK). *Exit, Voice, and Loyalty* became a corpus of ideas commonly shared by professionals and insiders in relevant disciplines—that kind of knowledge that is considered "the badge that distinguishes the professionals and would-be professionals (advanced graduate students) from the dilettantes, the drop-outs and the inside-dopesters."[94] This is what Barry called the "in" book, characterized by the fact that "the theory can be stated in few words but at the same time has an unlimited range of application," that its fame travels more by word of mouth than via more institutionalized channels such as journal reviews, and that everybody feels that one must read it to "keep up with the field."[95]

In 1973, the International Social Science Council and the International Political Science Association organized a seminar on *Exit, Voice, and Loyalty* attended by scholars of the caliber of Mancur Olson, Oliver Williamson, Stein Rokkan, Giovanni Sartori, James Coleman, Shmuel Eisenstadt, and Jack Goody, presenting it as a "pathbreaking volume" at the "cutting-edges of social sciences."[96] In 1975, the economics community also recognized the centrality of Hirschman's essay, organizing a panel of its annual meeting around its implications, showing its applicability to union behavior in the labor market and urban governance, and highlighting the complementarity between Hirschman's book and the more recent work by Williamson on *Markets and Hierarchies*, which appeared in 1975.[97]

The exit-voice dichotomy was widely and instantaneously applied by scholars studying many different questions. The alternative between exit and voice might seem obvious now, but it had never been articulated explicitly enough to unleash its potential to address a wide range of disparate phenomena. In particular, the recognition that facilitating exit would weaken voice, or make it less likely, proved particularly fruitful. In the United States, this mechanism had already been highlighted, before publication of *Exit, Voice, and Loyalty*, with reference to the trade-off between black emigration from the southern United States and the possibilities for racial and political emancipation of the nonemigrating black population. As Donald R. Matthews and James W. Prothro argued in the mid-1960s, the southern black population was at risk of losing between a third and a half of its most highly trained members; as a consequence, those remaining behind would "not participate in politics as frequently or as effectively as they otherwise would," and their ability to fight for emancipation would thus be weakened.[98]

In 1972, the problem was reframed in terms of Hirschman's exit and voice. John Orbell and Toru Uno, two political scientists who had been studying urban neighborhood dynamics in Columbus, Ohio, when *Exit, Voice, and Loyalty* was published, redrafted their more recent research to incorporate the new and captivating terminology. They noted that Hirschman dealt with cities only in passing, but found his conceptual framework very useful for describing different attitudes toward political activism in urban settings. Their assumption was that voice, not exit, would be the mechanism most conducive to bringing about improvements in urban neighborhoods, but that the exit option would deplete problematic areas of their most needed tool for recuperation—namely, voice. Through a complex statistical study of the behavior of different groups (whites and blacks, people of high status and low status, urbanites and suburbanites, older generations and younger generations), Orbell and Uno were able to show how different groups would incline toward exit, voice, or a phased combination of the two. According to their sample, high-status whites would usually opt for voice more than for exit, and even more so in suburban areas than in urban ones, whereas low-status whites would usually feel disempowered in the first instance and thus opt for exit without considering voice. Compared to these groups, blacks would more likely use voice in response to problems than whites of a similar status living in similar areas.[99]

Exit and voice have also been used to analyze the changing composition of the Palestinian population and the dynamics of the political fight of Palestinians in Israel and in the occupied territories, and more generally in situations of conflict and refugee behavior around the world.[100] But the use of exit and voice has been wider still. A very basic online survey limited to recent literature shows the ubiquity of Hirschman's framework, from a study of doctors' working conditions in Ireland to one of housing renovation in Sweden, from the relationship between states and the International Criminal Court to why populations adversely affected by climate change stay put instead of migrating to more clement environments, from the market strategies of the Coca-Cola Company in the past hundred years to the reaction of fans at the takeover of Manchester United by an American businessman in the early 2000s.

A particularly ambitious application of Hirschman's tripartite framework was that of political scientist Stein Rokkan, who aimed at merging it with Talcott Parsons's paradigm of functional differentiation to examine the variations among political systems in the process of formation of modern Western European states. In this way, he was able to apply Hirschman's analysis not to bottom-up dynamics like those Hirschman had analyzed, such as the reaction of consumers or citizens to the deterioration of firms or public administrations, but rather to top-down mechanisms, such as how central authorities (in Rokkan's case, centers of power in modern Europe) affected exit and voice of lower-level actors (peripheral communities).[101]

The diffusion of the concepts of exit and voice to different topics also encouraged attempts at complicating the analytical framework. Scholars, for instance, elaborated on what Hirschman had mentioned only in passing—that whereas exit can be more easily seen as a binary choice (either one exits or one does not, though this also is a simplification), voice can be exercised in different gradations of volume and form. Similarly, the effects of different levels of voice can differ not only in terms of more or less responsiveness on the part of the receivers, but also in the "composition" of their response (e.g., a certain level of voice can produce a high probability of a mild response and a low probability of a more committed response, or the opposite; obviously, the possible combinations of different levels of response and their probability for any given level of voice varies on a case-by-case basis).

The dynamics of deterioration and reparation are also subject to possible complications. For example, deterioration does not necessarily imply that reparation is possible. Depending on this second phase in the deterioration-reparation process, voice may be stronger, weaker, or utterly nonexistent, and its absence may not necessarily be conducive to exit (recent studies on climate change and migratory behaviors of affected populations seem to show precisely this point).

Another complication of Hirschman's analytical framework can be found in the work of Barry, who discussed the mirror category of silence as opposed to voice, noticing how Hirschman conflated into voice two very different phenomena—namely, the social voice of group mobilization to secure a collective good, and the individual voice of one who is pursuing an individual benefit. By introducing this complication, Barry even suggested that Hirschman could have benefited from intertwining his analysis with Mancur Olson's *Logic of Collective Action*.[102] Interesting though this comment was, one imagines it did not really convince Hirschman, who had a partial and reductionist view of Olson's book. This was based on Hirschman's almost instinctive dislike for the figure of the free rider, as well as on Olson's admittedly unfortunate characterization of political groups, people committed to "lost causes," and even mass movements, which he considered not only "nonrational or irrational," but alienated, fanatically devoted to an ideology, and belonging to the "lunatic fringe" of society.[103]

Indeed, Hirschman's biased view had its roots in his personal predilection for the use of voice as a *collective* endeavor. In a later interview, asked about who had been his intellectual enemies, Hirschman observed: "one often writes against someone, even if unconsciously," and then he mentioned Mancur Olson and his concept of the free rider. Hirschman claimed, "I have spent several years arguing, particularly to economists, that collective action does exist and that people do take part in it."[104] For example, Hirschman differentiated his economic viewpoint on nonmarket mechanisms from that of public-choice theorists on the basis of public mobilization. Unsurprisingly, Gordon Tullock, one of the founders of public choice, was not convinced by Hirschman's analysis. Tullock argued that Hirschman's critique of exit was biased, as he discussed mainly cases in which exit would be unsuccessful in improving the efficiency of suppliers when they could rely on other sources of income such as government subsidies. Nor was Tullock convinced by Hirschman's starting point about the Nigerian railways. Even in the absence of relatively efficient truck ser-vices, Tullock claimed, the railways could have extorted more money from taxpayers to improve the service or just switched to other forms of inef-ficiency.[105] The observation of possible continuing inefficiency was a fair point, but the perspectives of Tullock and Hirschman were simply too dis-tant to form the basis of any fruitful dialogue: Tullock did not even address Hirschman's interest—namely, the mechanisms through which public mobilization occurs—while Hirschman put himself outside the perimeter of public-choice theory. As Mancur Olson, then president of the Public Choice Society, concluded, "the ideological gap was too wide to bridge."[106]

As Hirschman remarked, the costs of public goods such as public parks or police protection are sufficiently clear-cut. The same is not true, however, when one considers not public goods but public policies. The cost of striv-ing for policies that enhance "*the* 'public good' or *the* 'public happiness' " cannot be neatly separated from possessing these goods, for, as Hirschman put it, "striving for the public happiness will often be felt not so much as a cost, but as the closest available substitute for it."[107] Anticipating a theme he would address more fully about ten years later in his book *Shifting Involve-ments*, Hirschman insisted that, in the pursuit of the public good, costs turn in some mysterious way into benefits: "the sudden, historically so decisive outbursts of popular energies must be explained by precisely this change in sign, by the turning of what is normally sensed as a cost that is to be shirked into a benefit, a rewarding experience, and a 'happiness of pursuit' in which one simply must share. The possibility of this mutation is fundamental for the understanding of political change: achieving change often requires such a mutation."[108]

Hirschman himself would later return to his exit-voice dichotomy, using it for what must have been a particularly joyful reflection about the fall of the Berlin Wall in 1989 and the subsequent reunification of the two Ger-manys. As Hirschman noted, throughout the Cold War, exit and voice in East Germany worked as he had initially imagined in his 1970 book—that is, as alternative forces often working at cross-purposes. Political dissidence (voice) was not tolerated, and the only way for individuals to exercise their full independence from the regime was to exit, at first rather easily but then, after the Berlin Wall was built in 1961, at considerable personal risk. The events of 1989 showed an unexpected conjunction between the two mechanisms when, in the spring of that year, exit (via Hungary, Poland,

and Czechoslovakia) became unstoppable. The inability of the regime to react, in turn, made its weakness visible and opened new space for domestic protest—that is, voice.[109]

But this schematic explanation is not enough. Thanks to his many interviews with fleeing eastern Europeans (his last fieldwork), Hirschman noticed yet another, more direct and more compelling, mechanism of conjunction between exit and voice.[110] This was perhaps a more circumstantial but deeper explanation for the "real mystery of the 1989 events," as Hirschman put it, when a purely *private* act such as exit was transformed into a movement of *public* protest.[111] Even though those who intended to flee conceived of that action as a totally private affair, Hirschman conjectured, the sheer size of the flow could not help changing their perspective: "Too many people had the same idea, and . . . their moves were too successful to remain secret and private."[112] All of a sudden, the individuals trying to exit, converging at crossing points through the borders, railways stations, and embassies, understood that they were not alone, and that their private plans were in fact small pieces of a large public endeavor. Private exit turned into the new phenomenon of public exit, and this in turn generated and reinforced voice. For Hirschman, this was too good but also true. At seventy-five, he witnessed the pacific reunion of the two halves of his mother country that had resulted from Hitler's criminal and homicidal plans: "in some momentous constellations, so we have learned, exit can cooperate with voice, voice can emerge from exit, and exit can reinforce voice."[113]

Perhaps the most interesting variation on the theme of *Exit, Voice, and Loyalty* came from Guillermo O'Donnell, an Argentinian sociologist and democratic activist who worked in Argentina, Brazil, and the United States. O'Donnell made a very interesting distinction between the voice described by Hirschman, addressed by customers or citizens to managers or public officers, and another type of voice, used among peers. The former O'Donnell labeled "vertical voice," the latter "horizontal voice." As O'Donnell elaborated on this very simple but powerful distinction, he argued that group identity is shaped in important ways by horizontal voice, as mutual support or discussion of one's own views creates a bond among individuals. In fact, the possibility of using horizontal voice without restriction from government and without putting at stake one's own personal safety is a "constitutive feature" of democratic environments. As O'Donnell put it, "Horizontal voice is a necessary condition for the existence of the kind of collective vertical voice that is reasonably autonomous from those 'on top.' "[114]

In Argentina under dictator Jorge Rafael Videla, for example, with some risk and a small chance of success, it was still possible to address voice to the top, provided this was done in a respectful and nonpolitical manner, "but what meant almost certain death was any attempt to use horizontal voice. Individuals had to be isolated."[115] The obliteration of horizontal voice thus has crucial consequences for democracy, as it is a sufficient condition to severely curtail vertical voice; moreover, all voices that can only be expressed collectively are automatically silenced. This implies a further torsion of the type of voice that remains practicable, making things worse for individuals *and* social classes. When collective (horizontal) voice is condemned to silence, O'Donnell noted, "as we descend the ladder of social stratification a deeper silence is imposed. Thus, whatever vertical voice remains is not only drastically diminished, it is also inherently biased," for only members of the upper echelon of the social pyramid can exercise it (with caution).[116]

O'Donnell was an acute observer of the Argentinian regime and its deadly methods. But he never lost all hope. In a characteristically Hirschmanian twist, O'Donnell also added that horizontal voice cannot be totally silenced, for "oblique voice"—that is, voice that is meant to be heard by "others like me" but not by the repressive regime and its agents—continued to work to weaken the regime.[117]

Chapter Six

THE HISTORY AND THEORY OF MARKET SOCIETIES

In *A Contribution to the Critique of Political Economy*, Karl Marx wrote, "Mankind always takes up only such problems as it can solve," because, upon reflection, "the problem itself arises only when the material conditions necessary for its solution already exist or are at least in the process of formation."[1] This famous quote, Hirschman noted in the late 1970s, perfectly encapsulates the birth of development economics in the early postwar years.[2] Decolonization and the Cold War had made the conditions of Third World countries a central issue in both American and Soviet foreign relations with other nations, and, especially in the West, the powerful economic expansion of the United States and the improvement in the material well-being of its citizens seemed to show that escape from poverty and backwardness was a universally achievable goal. The postwar period, in other words, presented for the first time both a compelling reason for rich countries to intervene in foreign economies and a template on which to model action. As another pioneer of development put it in a very influential book, the most important item on the Western agenda was to "demonstrate that the underdeveloped nations—now the main focus of Communist hopes—can move successfully . . . into a well-established take-off within the orbit of the democratic world."[3]

During the 1970s, however, that early confidence was utterly shattered. Not only had the new field of development economics not delivered what it had promised, but the economic record was checkered at best, with some successes and many failures. More worrisome was that, irrespective of whether economic growth had occurred, many less developed countries were experiencing a series of military coups. Latin America, which Hirschman knew well, was undergoing a deep crisis. To mention only a few cases, Brazil and Bolivia in 1964, Argentina in 1966, Peru in 1968, Ecuador in 1972, Chile and Uruguay in 1973, and Argentina again in 1976 all witnessed democratic governments overthrown by military juntas.

Development economists were forced to face the crisis of their earlier convictions, according to which economic growth would have brought with it, almost as a by-product, improvements in the social and political life of developing countries. More generally, this wave of dictatorial regimes impugned the very nature of the political dimension of capitalism. A long tradition of Western thought had celebrated the civilizing virtues of trade and economic development. Even Marx, who had waged the strongest critique of the alienating effects of factory work and the exploitation of the working class, had conceded the progressive nature of the bourgeois era as opposed to the archaic feudal system.

Hirschman, deeply affected by the crisis that was unfolding before his eyes, began to pose searching questions about the relationship between economic growth and political developments. This led him to explore the debates of Western European political philosophers in the modern era, distant in time and yet so close in their relevance to contemporary issues.

ECONOMIC GROWTH AND POLITICAL CRISES

In the early 1970s, Irma Adelman (a Romanian émigrée who had fled the Nazi regime) and Cynthia Taft Morris, two quantitative development economists, attempted an investigation of the interactions among economic growth, income distribution, and political participation in a number of less developed countries. No novices to socioeconomic research, they were aware of the wide range of negative consequences of economic growth in the social, cultural, and ecological realms, yet they shared the prevailing view that economic growth was beneficial to all strata of a population and, most of all, that it would carry with it the spread of parliamentary democracy. The results of the analysis came "as a shock" to them.[4]

What they found was deeply disturbing. Not only, they wrote, were "increases in political participation . . . by no means automatic consequences of socioeconomic development," but economic growth systematically excluded the poorest strata of the population.[5] Kuznets's inverted-U hypothesis—that inequality grows with economic growth until it reaches a plateau and then starts to decrease while the economy continues to grow—emerged clearly from their study, but with one important qualification. Adelman and Morris noticed that at low levels of economic growth inequality grew only slowly, but that it remained at the high plateau level for a long period once higher levels of economic growth had been reached. Only at very high levels of economic development would inequality begin to decrease. The inverted-U curve was thus asymmetrical, suggesting that "the process of economic modernization shifts the income distribution in favour of the middle class and upper income groups and against lower income groups." They concluded that "the dynamics of economic development appear to work against the poor."[6] The implications were, in their words, "frightening": "hundreds of millions of desperately poor people throughout the world have been hurt rather than helped by economic development."[7]

In his first important study (the result of his doctoral research in political science at Yale University), Guillermo O'Donnell also argued that the studies from the 1950s that emphasized the correlation between economic growth and an increase in political liberty—as proposed, for example, in the work of Seymour Martin Lipset—had to be deeply revised. Economic growth led not to political democracy but to political pluralism. Whereas pluralism can be considered a crucial element of democracy, in O'Donnell's perspective it described a more segmented society, but not necessarily a more democratic one. In fact, O'Donnell considered the development of political pluralism in Latin America as *inversely* correlated with democracy. In O'Donnell's terms, "More socio-economic development = more likelihood of political democracy" should be recast as "More socio-economic development = more political pluralization ≠ more likelihood of political democracy."[8]

O'Donnell suggested that different phases of industrialization would produce different political outcomes, as they affected different class groups in different ways. The emergence of a first phase of industrialization based on the production of consumer goods, for example, explained the transition from a land-based oligarchic system to a populistic system. This early phase of industrialization would be characterized by tariff protection and state subsidies, and politically by a populist coalition based on the converging interests of industrialists and unions to expand internal consumption and increase wages in exchange for political support for the political elite. But when this phase of ISI policies reached the point of exhaustion, with the saturation of the domestic market and the emergence of balance-of-payments disequilibria as a consequence of new imports in intermediate and capital goods, conflict would irremediably emerge. The orthodox monetary policies that would presumably be implemented in response to macroeconomic disequilibria, and the compression of wages in favor of capitalist accumulation, would put the interests of the working class and the political elite mutually at variance.[9]

According to O'Donnell, high modernization requires a deeper penetration of technocratic roles into the centers of national governments. A technocratic network with strong problem-solving capabilities develops, permitting it to exert increasing control over crucial sectors and activities.[10] O'Donnell called "the political system that was implanted in Brazil in 1964 and in Argentina in 1966 'bureaucratic-authoritarian.'"[11] If the "authoritarian" side of the term includes nondemocratic political systems at low levels of modernization, the "bureaucratic" side refers to the "crucial features specific to authoritarian systems of high modernization: the growth of organizational strength of many social sectors, the governmental attempts at control by 'encapsulation,' the career patterns and power-bases of most incumbents of technocratic roles, and the pivotal role played by large (public and private) bureaucracies."[12] The bureaucratic-authoritarian state, in other words, is what more recent literature has been calling a high-modernist state.

In 1975, the Joint Committee on Latin American Studies of the American Council of Learned Societies and the Social Science Research Council, chaired by Hirschman, established a working group to study the crisis in Latin America. O'Donnell's concept of the bureaucratic-authoritarian state framed the discussion. Indiana University political scientist David Collier, who edited the volume that presented the results of the research, remarked that the resurgence of military rule in Argentina and Brazil, two countries that accounted for 65 percent of the population of Latin America and 75 percent of its industrial output, had occurred in the broader context of the erosion of the earlier expectation that economic growth and political democratization would proceed hand in hand. The 1970s saw a further deepening of bureaucratic-authoritarianism in these two countries and the emergence of similar regimes in Chile and Uruguay.[13]

As chair of the joint committee, an early supporter of the research, and unofficial coeditor of the final volume, Hirschman was an important member of the working group. In that capacity, he wrote perhaps the dourest assessment of the end of development economics:

"Economic development of underdeveloped areas" emerged as a new field of studies in the late 1940s and early 1950s. The task was truly formidable, but the promise of tackling it with success was held out by two concurrent developments. Theoretical advances . . . provided economists, so it was thought, with the tools they needed to give effective advice to governments . . . Secondly, the success of the Marshall Plan in Western Europe seemed to confirm the possibility of rapid economic transformation . . .

Some twenty-five years later, that early optimism has largely evaporated, for a number of reasons. Growth, while substantial, has by no means overcome the division of the world into the rich "north" and the underdeveloped "south." In the south itself, moreover, the fruits of growth have been divided more unevenly than had been anticipated. And there is another, often unacknowledged, reason for the disenchantment: it looks increasingly as though the effort to achieve growth, whether or not successful, brings with it calamitous side effects in the political realm, from the loss of democratic liberties at the hand of authoritarian, repressive regimes to the wholesale violation of elementary human rights.[14]

In a conversation with Clifford Geertz and others at the Institute for Advanced Study in Princeton, where Hirschman had been a visiting member in 1972–73 and which he had joined for good in 1974 (a perfect job for him, since it came with no teaching duties), Hirschman confessed his discouragement and bewilderment about "how it happened that economic development has an obvious correlation with the development of torture," adding, "there is some sort of close association here that leaves me tremendously appalled and puzzled."[15] Hirschman's own reassessment of *Journeys Toward Progress*, written a few months after the overthrow of Chile's democratic government, conveyed the same sense of dismay. Whereas the book, published in 1963, had a clearly optimistic tone, the tone of Hirschman's "Return Journey," a decade later, was much bleaker; the emphasis was not so much on the failure complex, or *fracasomania*, of Hirschman's Latin American colleagues as on the actual *fracaso* that had intervened. In particular, Hirschman argued, a new wave of "detailed studies of the determinants and consequences of public policies" was necessary for "the understanding of the singularly 'cold monster' that the State has become in a large number of Latin American countries."[16]

The reaction to the disillusionment took many forms. As Hirschman noted, many of his colleagues tried to recover the original correlation by attempting to show that political authoritarianism produced bad economic results. This, however, was more easily claimed than demonstrated. Hirschman's reaction took a more hands-on, multipronged course. For one, as we have seen, he organized a multidisciplinary collaboration to study the new forms of authoritarian politics. He also tried actively to provide practical assistance to institutions and individuals oppressed by the regime or directly in danger. Hirschman went several times to Santiago and Buenos Aires to speak at the Corporación de Estudios para Latinoamérica (CIEPLAN) and the Center for the Study of State and Society (CEDES), two think tanks founded in the mid-1970s whose positions were strongly antiauthoritarian. Finally, Hirschman helped scholars move to the United States, inviting them as research fellows at Harvard and the Institute for Advanced Study in Princeton. All of the members of the working group became fellows at the institute for at least one year thanks to Hirschman.[17] These included, among others, Fernando Henrique Cardoso, a Brazilian sociologist, and José Serra, an engineer and economist who was president of the União Nacional dos Estudantes, which strongly opposed the regime. Cardoso (then in his forties) and Serra (then in his thirties) belonged to a generation of intellectuals–political activists who would later play leading roles in Brazil's return to democracy. In the first half of the 1990s, Cardoso became minister of foreign affairs and minister of finance, and from 1995 to 2002, he was the president of Brazil. Serra was the minister of planning and budget and minister of health under Cardoso, then mayor of São Paulo, governor of the State of São Paulo, and eventually a senator.

Like many of his colleagues, Hirschman was particularly distressed that nobody had seen the crisis coming, let alone predicted its severity and amplitude—hence the deep feelings of failure and, perhaps even more upsetting, puzzlement that permeated the community of development scholars and practitioners. As a participant observer of the early phase of the development effort, Hirschman remembered well the enthusiasm and optimism that had characterized the field. In a 1973 article titled "The Changing Tolerance for Income Inequality in the Course of Economic Development," Hirschman tried to make sense of that early optimism, as well as "where we went wrong." This experience of optimism followed by utter failure prompted Hirschman to rephrase the Latin dictum *per aspera ad astra* (through hardship to the stars) as *per aspera ad disastra* (through hardship to disaster).[18]

Hirschman based his analysis of tolerance for income inequality on what he called the "tunnel effect" and its potential laws of motion. The tunnel effect took its name from a very simple and widely experienced situation. Suppose we are driving in a two-lane tunnel, with both lanes moving in the same direction, until a traffic jam stops us and the adjoining lane. When, after a while, we see the other lane move forward again, we usually feel relieved and hopeful: even if we are not moving yet, we assume the cause of the jam has been removed and we will soon move forward as well. Transposed to the social level, the tunnel effect explains why societies experiencing economic growth but also increasing inequality (the equivalent of only one line of cars moving forward in the jam) show a high tolerance for increasing inequality. Everybody thinks, the metaphor suggests, that the time for all to move ahead is approaching.

Back in the traffic jam, if we observe that the other line continues to move ahead while we remain stuck, early relief can abruptly turn into frustration and, ultimately, some sort of reaction (for example, voicing our discontent by honking, or illegally crossing the midline). At the social level, this occurs when a period of sustained economic growth produces, almost without warning, forms of protest by those who have remained behind. Anticipating a particular attention to semantic explorations that, though never absent from his interests, would become central in his next book, *The Passions and the Interests*, Hirschman found signs of these sudden turnarounds in the way the vocabulary of development changed terms and meanings across the decades: "in the fifties the term 'pole de croissance' (growth pole), coined by François Perroux, was widely used for the growing industrializing cities of the developing countries. At some point during the next decade, this expression, which suggested irradiation of growth, gave way to a new term, 'internal colonialism', which was now said to be practiced by these same cities with regard to their zones of economic influence."[19]

The metaphor of the tunnel effect is simple but, Hirschman noted, helps illuminate why in certain countries the experience of economic development suddenly turned into political crisis or worse. As Hirschman remarked, "The civil war in Nigeria and the bloody falling apart of Pakistan are only the most spectacular instances of such 'development disasters.' "[20] A combination of the tunnel effect, which helps people tolerate increasing inequality in times of economic growth, and the presence of enlightened elites endowed with the necessary antennae to anticipate the explosion of discontent when inequality is sudden perceived to be too much or unfair, is ideal for overcoming the political crises inherent in economic development. But, Hirschman argued, the presence and strength of the tunnel effect depends heavily on the specific social structure of different countries.

In particular, populations highly segmented along ethnic lines will likely be less equipped to develop the hopeful sentiments that fuel the tunnel effect. If the group moving ahead consists of people belonging to a separate and highly recognizable ethnic group, individuals from other groups, far from feeling on the verge of advancement as well, will feel hopelessly cut out of the development process. Similar negative feedback loops develop in countries characterized by centralistic clientelism as opposed to decentralized political systems.

Hirschman, in sum, was trying to address the crisis of the late 1960s and early 1970s by building an interpretative frame in which, in contrast with most conventional representations, the development process is inherently "exposed to crisis, and perhaps disaster, even after lengthy periods of forward movement." Not unexpectedly, given his style of thought, he concluded that "the view here proposed necessarily allocates a decisive role to politics."[21] Likewise, Hirschman's interpretative frame might help elucidate the functioning of certain social dynamics, but it is unable to forecast the course of social conflict with any precision. Only detailed historical analysis of the characteristics and developments of a specific country would be able to help, if at all, in this respect. Hirschman concluded that "it may be impossible to tell in advance whether a given country is or is not adequately supplied with the tunnel effect . . . it is conceivable that only development itself will tell."[22]

The essay on the tunnel effect was enormously influential, but it also upset scholars on the left who found it excessively conciliatory toward existing inequalities in less developed countries, especially in Latin America.[23] This was, by then, a well-known response to Hirschman's reformism from increasingly radicalized pulpits.

But Hirschman's attempt at facing the crisis head-on also had an apparently serendipitous counterpoint. As Hirschman himself put it, he "withdrew" into the history of ideas to study how political philosophers of the early modern era and the Enlightenment had commented on the economic growth of their times and its possible political consequences. The result of this effort was Hirschman's 1977 book, *The Passions and the Interests*.

THE POLITICAL CONSEQUENCES OF ECONOMIC GROWTH:
THE PASSIONS AND THE INTERESTS

Hirschman took great interest in how the moral philosophers of the seventeenth and eighteenth centuries, facing a period of strong economic expansion, discussed its political consequences. Convinced that contemporary social science had proven incapable of shedding light on this nexus, he conjectured that an age in which political philosophy was devoid of disciplinary barriers and thus could stretch its interests from economic to political issues, might have been more effective in exploring how commercial and industrial expansion affected international peace and political and individual liberty.[24]

The age of industry and commerce has often been described as a rationalist civilization, in marked contrast to previous periods in which passions reigned unchecked. "Capitalist civilization," Joseph Schumpeter wrote, "is rationalistic and 'anti-heroic' . . . no flourishing of swords about it, not much physical prowess, no chance to gallop the armored horse into the enemy."[25] This juxtaposition implied a deep fracture between the two ages. Paul Hazard described the transformation of the European culture between the seventeenth and eighteenth centuries as a sudden and total change. "Never was a greater contrast, never a more sudden transition than this!" began his 1952 book. "One day," he wrote a few lines later, "the French people, almost to a man, were thinking like Bossuet. The day after, they were thinking like Voltaire. No ordinary swing of the pendulum, that. It was a revolution."[26]

In his inquiry, Hirschman adopted a very different perspective. Instead of emphasizing the opposition between two altogether different epochs, he reconstructed the story of a long transformation of ideas on commerce, government, and individual morality in which one small step led to the next. The overall change in perspective at the end of this process was indeed formidable, but the process of transformation was anything but clamorous—it was slow, piecemeal, and mostly unacknowledged by contemporaries. Contrary to the usual depiction of the bourgeois commercial era of the eighteenth century as totally opposed in character to a previous aristocratic era, Hirschman underscored how the former was born out of the latter, and how central elements of bourgeois ideology predated the full affirmation of this new industrious class. In a long transition stretching from the Renaissance to the eighteenth century, major ideas and attitudes on virtues and power slowly, and apparently inadvertently, changed into something quite distant from their original roots. This discovery was entirely unexpected to Hirschman; he called it an "intriguing by-product" of his inquiry. The "spirit" of capitalism, Hirschman argued, was not a new ideology that superseded an antiquated and outdated one. Instead, it emerged serendipitously from a long process of transformation of ideas that were initially far removed from any possible bourgeois horizon.[27] Indeed, most of *The Passions and the Interests* is dedicated to this "intriguing by-product."

Hirschman's starting point is squarely in the political realm, but what were initially strictly political reflections would expand to include the broader territory of human nature. In the Renaissance, Hirschman notes, a new attention to "real" political processes based on "the effective truth of things," as Machiavelli put it, emerged. This new attitude was in contrast with the previous focus of political philosophers on how imaginary forms of government ought to be informed by moral precepts.[28] In subsequent centuries, from Thomas Hobbes to Giambattista Vico and Baruch Spinoza, this interest in the truth of things extended from the study of the state to the study of human nature, and in particular how man's pernicious and destructive passions could be restrained. "Philosophy," Vico wrote, "considers man as he ought to be. . . . Legislation considers man as he is."[29] But once man-as-he-is became the focus of inquiry, the disruptive power of passions became an inescapable question. Surely, coercion and repression were ineffective, for how could the sovereign be exempt from the very passions that characterized human nature? In fact, the sovereign's power permitted his passions to go unchecked and thus become more dangerous.

Literature of the era discussed at length the possibility that unintended positive outcomes at the social level could emerge from the manifestation of negative passions at the individual level. Though with very different emphases, Pascal, Vico, and Bernard Mandeville all entertained the idea that the organization of society, Providence, or some dexterous politician could turn private vices into public benefits. As Vico put it, "Out of ferocity, avarice, and ambition . . . [society] makes national defense, commerce, and politics."[30] These were, in some sense, anticipations of Adam Smith's concept of the Invisible Hand—though on a broader spectrum of activities than just commerce (but, at least in the case of Mandeville, with a narrower focus on the exclusive role of vices). Borrowing from Thomas Schelling's vocabulary, one could say that all those authors argued that pernicious "micromotives" would somehow result in beneficial "macrobehaviors."[31]

But another attempt at explaining how a well-ordered society could emerge from a world of individual passions held more promise. If passions are a fundamental human attribute, then only passions can counterbalance passions. Praising virtue against vice, as old moral philosophers did, was useless if one was unable to explain the very process through which passions unfold, develop, diversify, become intertwined, and enter into conflict.

During the eighteenth century, this idea of countervailing passions became widespread; it was embodied in the principles of the division of powers and the check and balances that informed the constitutional debate in the United States. As Hirschman summarized, the train of thought developed thus far returned to its point of departure: "it had started with the state, whence it turned to consider problems of individual conduct, and in due course the insights yielded by this phase were imported back into the theory of politics."[32] But another step also took place in the eighteenth century— namely, "interest" emerged as *the* passion best suited to tame the others. Why was that? Basically, it was because of its capacity to defuse aggressiveness and drive individuals as well as states to develop peaceful relations.

The term *interest* was initially difficult to define. All human aspirations could be part of someone's—or the sovereign's—interest. But interest also denoted a specific element of calculation and rationality that was immune from—or at least tempered by—unruly passions and disorderly appetites. As Hirschman put it later, at a conference at the Collège de France, calculation was "the dominant or fundamental element"; indeed, "it was probably this stress on rational calculation that accounts for the high marks that interest (interest-governed behaviour) received" between the late sixteenth and early seventeenth centuries.[33] When referring to statecraft, the concept was instrumental on two fronts. First, it made it possible to discuss in a secular and detached manner the morally questionable actions that a sovereign must undertake to reach certain political ends. In other words, interest or interests worked as a euphemism for the Machiavellian approach to statecraft.

The calculating dimension of interest, however, also implied a restraint from imprudent, wild, and destructive passions. If the prince was allowed, in name of his interest (or "reason of state") to act viciously, he should act so only in a calculated way—that is, only insofar as cruelty, violence, and treason were instrumental to the interests of state, not driven by blind passions.

At the same time that the concept of interests grew in opposition to the passions, it also increasingly narrowed its focus on the material or economic. There are multiple reasons for this: from the use of the term *interest* in the practice of moneylending, to the nature of rational calculation that belongs both to the concept of interest and to commercial practices, to the increasing importance of economic growth in the second half of the eighteenth century. Whatever the reason, especially at the individual level, the term *interest* conflated the idea of the pursuit of wealth as a passion able to exercise a countervailing role against more vicious passions (as euphemism for more morally connotated "avarice" or "love of lucre," for example) with the idea of rational calculation as an attitude that was in itself opposed to passions.[34]

Interest meant most of all predictability and constancy—not heroic virtues, to be sure, but decisive for the expansion of commerce among individuals. As Hirschman pointed out, it was this mediocrity that was, only somewhat paradoxically, widely praised: "commercial and economic activities were . . . looked upon more kindly not because of any rise in the esteem in which they were held; on the contrary, any preference for them expressed a desire for a vacation from (disastrous) greatness."[35] Commerce, in other words, was *doux*, a word not easily translated in English that conveys the idea of "sweetness, softness, calm, and gentleness and is the antonym of violence."[36] The most eloquent characterization of this idea was probably that of Montesquieu in his *Esprit des lois*: "wherever the ways of man are gentle (*mœurs douces*) there is commerce; and wherever there is commerce, there the ways of men are gentle."[37]

In this gentleness, in this *douceur*, lay the solution to the question that had originally prompted the train of thought that Hirschman followed—the problem of statecraft. The analysis of passions was prompted by Machiavelli's attempt to provide guidance for the prince by discussing the "effective truth of things" as opposed to the "imaginary republics and monarchies that have never been seen nor have been known to exist."[38] Two centuries later, the concept of *doux commerce*—a late heir of Machiavelli's initial impulse—would provide a powerful principle to explain how the prince (or the state) can prosper, and its subjects (or citizens) with him. First of all, commerce makes the exercise of arbitrary power by the prince impractical, if not outright ineffectual. At the national level, the intricate and delicate web of commercial relations makes it impossible for the monarch to exercise brutal and capricious authority without deeply damaging the country's economy. Moreover, any attempt to debase coinage or to confiscate wealth would probably produce a flow of resources and wealth abroad. And at the international level, warfare is the perfect way to ruin commerce.

True to form, Hirschman particularly appreciated the unexpected consequences of commerce that his favored authors highlighted. As Sir James Steuart noted, it was often the prince's desire for self-aggrandizement and self-enrichment that initially prompted international trade and the establishment of national industry. But trade and industry caused the growth of a commercial class most interested in peace. The increasing complexity of the economy would make any act of arbitrary and despotic intervention on the part of the prince hugely disruptive. Steuart summarized:

The power of a modern prince . . . immediately becomes limited so soon as he establishes the plan of œconomy which we are endeavouring to explain [that is, trade and industry]. If his authority formerly resembled the solidity and force of the wedge . . . it will at length come to resemble the delicacy of the watch. . . . A modern œconomy, therefore, is the most effectual bridle ever was invented against the folly of the despotism.[39]

This line of thought petered out with the work of the Physiocrats and Adam Smith. The Physiocrats abandoned the idea of interests as a constraint on the absolutist and unpredictable passions of the sovereign. In a more grandiose (and more naïve) approach, they imagined that the sovereign would promote the public interest for reasons of self-interest. In a system that they called "legal despotism," the monarch would be co-owner of all the productive resources of his reign, thereby making him sensitive to their orderly growth, while a judicial order would assure that the sovereign promulgated laws that were not in conflict with the nation's general interests.

Adam Smith's analysis moved in the opposite direction. Instead of imagining a broad system that subsumed the political and the economic, Hirschman emphasized Smith's focus on the economic rationale for the pursuit of individual self-interest. This is an inevitable simplification of Hirschman's discussion of Smith's *Wealth of Nations*, but Hirschman, in turn, oversimplified Smith. Hirschman's inquiry started from the relationship between economic growth and political development, and from this perspective he found little of interest in Smith. "With respect to arbitrary decisions and harmful policies of the *central* government," Hirschman argued, "Smith does not hold out much hope that economic development itself will bring improvements."[40] Yet, in an important reference to his friend David Hume, Smith argued that "by far the most important of all [the] effects" of commerce and manufactures was that they "gradually introduced order and good government, and with them, the liberty and security of individuals . . . from the sovereign down to the smallest baron."[41]

Smith's work was more important to Hirschman because it provided the final *coup de grâce* to the Montesquieu-Steuart thesis of the capitalist spirit as an agent of political improvement through the control of formerly unbridled passions. This is not because Smith believed that only economic interests existed (as caricatures of his thought emphasize). In *The Theory of Moral Sentiments*, Smith discussed at great length the noneconomic reasons behind the pursuit of economic advancement. As he put it in a famous passage, "it is chiefly from [the] regard to the sentiments of mankind that we pursue riches and avoid poverty."[42] But, according to Hirschman, this reflection had momentous consequences. By reducing economic interest to a mere vehicle for other, more fundamental, passions, Smith in fact undercut the idea that an opposition among mutually counterbalancing passions, or between interests and passions, formed the basis of any social order. Either the common man had no passions, according to Smith, or his passions could be subsumed under the concept of interests. *The Wealth of Nations*, Hirschman thus concluded, "marks an end to the speculations about the effects of interest-motivated on passionate behaviour that had exercised the minds of some of Smith's more illustrious predecessors."[43]

As we saw at the end of the previous section, Hirschman's interest in the history of ideas about the political consequences of economic growth in the seventeenth and eighteenth centuries originated from his disillusionment in the face of the disastrous political consequences that development policies in many underdeveloped countries directly triggered. Hirschman, a major protagonist of that first era of development economics, was deeply disturbed by this record. As he conceived it, his study was an act of withdrawal from the present predicament in order to look into past debates for some sort of interpretative lens for postwar development discourse.

One might wonder whether this retreat into the history of ideas was not also an act of denial. After the first sentence of the book describing the essay's origin in "the incapacity of contemporary social science to shed light on the political consequences of economic growth and, perhaps even more, in the so frequently calamitous political correlates of economic growth," it is surprising to find no reference whatsoever to these calamitous political correlations: Hirschman's focus was entirely on the positive consequences of *doux commerce*. Only in one instance does he mention its negative aspects. "The persistent use of the term *le doux commerce*," he wrote, "strikes us as a strange aberration for an age when the slave trade was at its peak and when trade in general was still a hazardous, adventurous, and often violent business." In fact, Marx would scornfully notice, "Das ist der *doux commerce!*"[44]

Clearly, Hirschman was still committed to finding the positive dimension of economic development. In an important article published a couple of years after *The Passions and the Interests*, Hirschman once again summarized the book as an analysis of how past political philosophers had speculated that the expansion of commerce and industry would restrain the passions of the sovereign, resulting therefore "in less arbitrary and more human government." Economic growth appeared to be a natural constraint to arbitrariness and despotism. In positive terms, "a thriving market economy would be the basis for a political order in which the exercise of individual rights and freedoms would be insured."[45] Reviewers of the book, too, ignored the disturbing question that prompted it in the first instance, captured as they were by this tour de force of political arguments in favor of capitalism, to paraphrase the book's subtitle. Virtually no book review even mentioned the unhappy correlation between economic expansion and the deterioration, or worse, of the political landscape.

But this may have had more to do with Hirschman's penchant for highlighting possible, though perhaps improbable, positive sequences of economic and political processes than with any real act of denial on his part. After all, since the political catastrophe of many developing countries was there before everybody's eyes, why not making the best of a past debate on how economic growth might have positive political consequence? And in fact, in the third part of *The Passions and the Interests*—almost an epilogue for its brevity and separateness from the core of the essay—Hirschman returned to his initial question, though the words he used reveal his propensity for positive bias: "The Montesquieu-Steuart speculations about the salutary political consequences of economic expansion were a feat of imagination in the realm of political economy, a feat that remains magnificent even though history may have proven wrong the substance of those speculations."[46]

Yet the question of the political damages of economic growth could not be avoided. An exponent of Scottish Enlightenment such as Adam Ferguson, for example, offered many examples of how the preoccupation with individual enrichment can lead to political despotism, including the corruption of values through excessive luxury and consumption, the fear of downward mobility, and the growing conviction that only undisturbed government can guarantee continuing prosperity. As Hirschman noted, Sir James Steuart's metaphor of the economy as a delicate mechanism like a watch could trigger precisely this kind of authoritarian reaction, in fact the opposite of Steuart's original idea: "The need to keep it working—to insure tranquillity, regularity, and efficiency—is not just a bar to princely caprice. Ferguson perceives correctly that it can be invoked as a key argument for authoritarian rule."[47] Hirschman found the same concerns in Tocqueville: "A nation that demands from its government nothing but the maintenance of order is already a slave in the bottom of its heart."[48] Surprisingly, the vast majority of reviewers completely ignored these perceptive pages, despite the important questions they raised.

Though he enjoyed the highly favorable reactions to the book, Hirschman must have regretted this blindness on the part of his readers. Indeed, the issues of participation and of the good health of civic spirit were particularly dear to him. It is not strange, then, that he approached the conclusion of his essay with a number of reflections on the dangers of the atrophy of civic spirit, in particular that of opening the door to tyranny. Hirschman, ever alert to that possibility, had seen it at work in prewar Germany and Europe, in Latin America in the postwar years, and in many other countries around the world. As Hirschman remarked in 1979, Tocqueville had summarized the prevailing doctrine of his times as follows: "A close tie and a necessary relation exist between these two things: freedom and industry."[49] To this, Hirschman added: "Yesterday's hopeful doctrine and today's dismal reality could not be farther apart and Tocqueville's sentence would seem to be more applicable to the current Latin American experience if it read instead: 'A close tie and a necessary relation exist between these two things: torture and industry.' "[50]

THE HISTORY OF POLITICAL THEORY AS HISTORY OF POLITICAL DISCOURSE

The Passions and the Interests was immediately hailed as a great accomplishment, reaching a wide audience. It was reviewed in all the major journals of political science, economics, sociology, history, economic history, development economics, and philosophy, confirming its author's interdisciplinary intellectual status. Alan Ryan, in *Political Theory*, described it as "an extraordinarily agreeable essay in the history of ideas."[51] Other reviewers labeled it "a gem of intellectual historiography," an "intellectual treat," a "superb contribution," and so on.[52] In a matter of months, *The Passions and the Interests* became an "in" book like its predecessor, and a standard reference not only in studies of modern political philosophy but also in a variety of other fields, from sociological epistemology to the intersection of juridical and financial studies to theories of spontaneous disorder in international political economy.[53]

The success of the book lay partly in its ability to interest scholars from many different fields with its elegant, witty, and lucid style—what one reviewer has described as the feeling that "we are part of an exhilarating common room conversation."[54] Most important, commentators valued the methodological complexity of Hirschman's essay. Combining elements from many obscure and rarely examined treatises with an imaginative rereading of more established philosophers, Hirschman put together a persuasive argument about how the "tacit dimension" of a set of assumptions about trade and industry developed throughout modern preindustrial centuries.

The study of tacit knowledge—a concept famously developed by Michael Polanyi—is not an easy task, and Hirschman's historical analysis was considered a piece of virtuosity. Economic historian Jan de Vries, for example, described the study as "a masterly performance of piecing together an intellectual jigsaw puzzle that begins with Machiavelli and ends with the Scottish political economists."[55] One reviewer, however, also noted that this tacit dimension, presented in the first part of the essay as a unified intellectual development covering two centuries, was in the subsequent part discussed as though it consisted of many different *explicit* views. The two parts, however, seemed to remain mutually uncoordinated.[56]

Hirschman's book also discussed in a novel way the mechanisms typical of processes of social change. Scholars had long been conversant with the concept of unintended consequences—that is, the unexpected outcomes of human action. In his book, by examining what trade and industry were expected to but ultimately did not accomplish, Hirschman pointed to the obverse of this—that is, "the intended but unrealized effects of social decisions."[57] Perhaps reminiscent of the Principle of the Hiding Hand, Hirschman highlighted why this obverse phenomenon is of interest to the social scientist: "the expectation of large, if unrealistic, benefits obviously serves to facilitate certain social decisions."[58]

More particularly, Hirschman's essay was considered an important contribution to understanding the evolution of legitimating beliefs of the market society. Of course, as Hirschman was well aware, this kind of inquiry goes back at least to Max Weber's *Protestant Ethic and the Spirit of Capitalism*. In the last pages of the essay, he tried to articulate the differences between Weber's and his own approach. Whereas Weber found that capitalistic behavior was the unintended and counterintuitive psychological response of individuals to Calvin's doctrine of predestination, Hirschman emphasized instead the more conscious reflections of intellectuals who recognized the beneficial side effects of moneymaking activities. Weber, in other words, explained the diffusion of capitalism as "the result of a desperate *search for individual salvation*," whereas Hirschman submitted that it resulted from "an equally desperate search for a way of *avoiding society's ruin*."[59] Both perspectives could be valid; they were not mutually exclusive. But Hirschman argued that the great popularity of Weber's thesis had in fact overshadowed the other one. As a consequence, scholars had de facto ignored the core of Hirschman's inquiry—namely, how the discourse on

capitalism had emerged from a preoccupation not with individual salvation but with collective prosperity.

Interestingly, criticisms of the book often came from the same scholars
who had greatly praised it. *The Passions and the Interests*, in other words,
was for many as stimulating as it was problematic, in particular from a
methodological point of view. Moreover, even the strongest criticisms were
particularly constructive, showing further directions for inquiries and thus
implicitly offering yet another insight into how the scholarly community had
received Hirschman's new effort. The two major criticisms focused on a sort
of one-sidedness on Hirschman's part and on his endogenous perspective.

As for the first point, reviewers otherwise enthusiastic, such as Nannerl
Keohane, found Hirschman's treatment of the thought of many political philosophers excessively simplistic (in particular, Keohane had in mind Adam
Smith and Montesquieu). This simplification made it easier for Hirschman
to bring his points home, but at the price of sacrificing the complexity of
their thought. Barry Supple highlighted the lack of a firm chronological
pattern that worked to the same effect, and in a similar vein, Louis Schneider wrote that Hirschman had been excessively selective: "Sometimes one
has the impression that Hirschman is not far from wanting simply to give
attention to the development of ideas that interest him." Peter G. Stillman
lamented the relegation of Ferguson to the epilogue "because he does not
fit Hirschman's developmental sequence."[60]

The question of how selective Hirschman had been raised the problem
not only of the excessive simplification of modern debates on political
philosophy but also, more importantly, of their significance. Some sort of
selection, after all, is intrinsic to every historical reconstruction, and even
great concision is legitimate if in the end the analysis works. In fact, the
book was exhilarating, as many pointed out, precisely because it was able
to master a vast body of material and a huge historical horizon in little
more than a hundred pages. The problem of significance, instead, called
into question whether Hirschman had actually unveiled an important train
of thought in the history of ideas, or only a marginal issue.

Thomas Kaiser, for instance, argued that Hirschman was unable to make
clear

how pervasive and strongly held the view that economic expansion would produce benign political effects really was in the early modern period. He does find

evidence of this 'doctrine' in the works of Montesquieu, Steuart, and Millar; and yet even these individuals, as Hirschman admits, continued to harbor serious reservations about the impact of expanded commercial activity. If their political apologies for economic expansion, which represent, presumably, the strongest and most influential Hirschman can find, turn out to be so lukewarm, then, it is fair to ask, how important a 'doctrine' generally could this have been?[61]

In other words, was the doctrine discussed by Hirschman really historically relevant? The extent to which those ideas actually shaped the intellectual framework of their epoch remained a matter of dispute.[62]

The second line of criticisms was based on what sociologist Gianfranco Poggi considered important missing pieces in Hirschman's reconstruction— namely, the many and diversified contributions that legal studies had made in the elaboration of restraints for the passions (*and* the interests) of both individuals and sovereigns. Legal studies, Poggi argued, constituted a "monumental intellectual tradition which developed continuously and creatively over the centuries of Hirschman's story (as well as before and after) and had a direct and material bearing upon his topic."[63] Roman law, the absolutist codifications, secular, natural law, public law, and constitutionalism were very important in the cultural life of modern Europe, and the interpenetration of juridical and philosophical thought in the authors that Hirschman discusses was in fact of paramount importance.

In particular, Poggi criticized what he saw as methodological flaws produced by this oversight. Hirschman adopted a remarkably consistent endogenous approach to intellectual history—that is, he discussed each new argument as a response to, or a qualification of, a previous argument. But an endogenous approach would not consider the social context of the scholars examined, or the political, institutional, and economic developments of the period under consideration. According to Poggi, a serious analysis of the European legal tradition would have helped avoid the excesses of this endogenous bias, or at least mitigate them. As he concluded,

it sometimes appears nearly pointless to seek to make sense of an intellectual story of such duration and significance exclusively in endogenous terms, when massive contextual factors simply (but vainly) cry out for consideration. In the name of his approach Hirschman forces himself to keep out of his argument those cataclismic contextual developments we label with such terms as secularization, commercialization, individualization, separation between state and society and between public and private realm, transition from hierarchical to functional differentiation, or from the primacy of the polity to that of the economy.[64]

Supple advanced a similar criticism: without any need to fall into a materialistic explanation of intellectual history, the history of ideas so intimately concerned with the real world of political economy would have benefited from a less strictly endogenous approach.[65]

Louis Schneider highlighted another two missing traditions—namely, the humanist and the Marxist traditions, which counterbalance the Montesquieu-Steuart line of argument by throwing doubt on the very idea that the market can be a sufficiently solid foundation for the life of an entire society, including its moral, cultural, and psychological dimensions. Schneider recognized that these stood outside the temporal framework of Hirschman's book but concluded, "some meticulous analysis of the sheer ideological element in pro- and anti-market views of past and present, some analysis of pertinent romantic notions as such, would have enriched the account he affords us."[66]

Wuthnow offered a possible way out of what looked like an impasse in the eyes of critics of Hirschman's endogenous perspective. That Hirschman's history-of-ideas approach failed to show the complex changes occurring in the world economy was actually a given, not really a point of criticism. Indeed, correspondence with Quentin Skinner and Michael Walzer while Hirschman was preparing the manuscript shows that Hirschman had adopted this specifically endogenous perspective consciously, aware of its advantages as well as its limits.[67] More fruitfully, Hirschman's analysis could be appreciated from the perspective of the sociology of knowledge, for it revealed "an interesting intellectual progression that roughly parallels the transition from mercantilism to the free-market system."[68] The succession of analyses by political philosophers on human nature and the increasing emphasis on the idea of countervailing passions that Hirschman traces throughout the modern era became "a miniature reflection of the picture of opposing political forces that constitute the larger world order. . . . In its original formulation [this idea] remained a reflection of the mercantile thinking of the day." Later, the transition from mercantilism to free-market capitalism found a parallel in the political projects of the Physiocrats and Smith. Though very different one from the other, they were both examples of the new idea of "using political means in the service of economic interests."[69]

Hirschman's analysis, in other words, mirrored, in the history of ideas, the shift from mercantilism to free-market capitalism in the history of the world economy. Wuthnow's words are particularly clear:

There is, in short, a subtle shift in the passions-interests argument between the 17th century and the end of the 18th that corresponds generally with changes in the structure of the world economy over the same period. The passions are depicted first as being in conflict with one another, then in conflict with the interests, and finally united with the interests. During the same period, the world economy is dominated first by conflict among the core powers, then by domestic conflict between political and commercial interest groups, and finally by a reintegration of political and economic interests along laissez-faire and free-trade principles. The similarities may have been unconscious or unintended, but the explicit identification of the passions with men of power and the interests with men of commerce in many of the writings makes the connection more immediate and apparent.[70]

Both critics and supporters of Hirschman's endogenous perspective highlighted one particularly innovative feature of Hirschman's study: Hirschman paid great attention to the specific language used by the authors he studied. He was not parsimonious with direct quotations, and he built his analysis on the semantic transformations of words as fundamental indicators of the transformation of mentalities and political theories throughout the first three centuries of the modern era.

This was an approach that J. G. A. Pocock and Quentin Skinner were introducing in those very years and that revolutionized the study of political thought. Hirschman was well acquainted with Skinner's work, as the latter was a scholar in residence at the Institute for Advanced Study in Princeton in 1974–75 and then again for three years from 1976 to 1979. Pocock and Skinner were considered the forerunners of a new program in the history of political thought as "the history of political language and discourse." As Pocock himself put it, "it seems to us that history in this field can better be written if we focus our attention on the acts of articulation and conceptualization performed by thinkers as agents in the world of speech."[71] Traditional history of ideas would thus give way to a history of languages, vocabularies, ideologies, and paradigms, and it is not by chance that Hirschman also treated specific constellations of meaning that solidi-fied into a language as paradigms à la Kuhn.[72]

Just as Pocock had written his important study of *The Machiavellian Moment* as a "tunnel history," pursuing one specific theme (the virtues of *vivere civile* in Florentine republicanism) as a "problem in historical self-understanding," Hirschman too had studied how the broad concepts of passions and interests appeared and reappeared in successive texts and contexts, changing meaning and roles in the process and contributing, in turn, to the shaping of new worldviews.[73] Indeed, Pocock and Hirschman seemed to be subjected to the same kind of criticism. As Pocock wrote, "all critics, both those who accuse me of making too much of history and those who accuse me of making too little, unite to accuse me of unhistorically abstracting from the texture of history those languages and thought-pat-terns whose history I aim to write."[74] Although this accusation was clearly misguided with reference to Pocock and Skinner, as we have seen, it was not unfounded when directed at Hirschman.

In any case, and in spite of the critiques, the novelty of the inquiry was momentous. Hirschman offered a very fertile analysis of a crucial period in the history of modern political thought, "lurking in the wildernesses between disciplinary territories."[75] Scholars adopted the dichotomy of pas-sions and interests as an interpretative lens to discuss contemporary forms of power and the sources of tyranny. For example, because of their com-mand of complex planning techniques, Wuthnow regarded "the experts" and technicians as the new forces allegedly able to restrain what was con-sidered the arbitrary power of the middle classes. "Like the market in an earlier day," Wuthnow concluded, "the technology upon which much of the present world economy depends is justified in the name of liberation, inevitability, rationality, peace, and pleasure" against the unpredictability of behaviors driven by irrational passions and antidemocratic temptations.[76]

But if one looked at the Soviet Union, it did not seem that the passions of the rulers were the driving force of tyranny. As philosopher, anthropologist, and historian Ernest Gellner (an émigré from Czechoslovakia to London in 1939) wrote, "it is not some uncontrollable Dostoevskian passion in the hearts of Soviet bureaucrats which inhibits the softening of central rule. In the Brezhnev era, those apparatchiks look sober, not to say dreary men, and rather unpromising material for the *Possessed* or *Brothers Karamazov*."[77] Neither the market nor technology would have made them more *douces*.

According to Gellner, in ideal agreement with O'Donnell's analysis, "modern authoritarianism is not primarily rooted in the passions of men."[78]

Hirschman also participated in the discussion about the interactions between ideologies of economic growth and forms of political authoritarianism in the contemporary world. As mentioned, he principally focused on Latin America, chairing the joint committee that would produce the 1979 volume edited by Collier. That was also an opportunity for Hirschman to take up his analysis where it had left off at the end of his 1977 book.

RIVAL VIEWS OF INDUSTRIALIZATION AND POLITICS

The third and final part of *The Passions and the Interests*, dedicated to the potentially authoritarian interpretations of the analysis of Montesquieu and Steuart, was the original core of Hirschman's inquiry. As we saw, however, he left the argument only barely sketched—as though, as one perceptive reviewer put it, "just at the point that he strikes pay dirt, he puts down his shovel."[79]

In the second half of the 1970s and the early 1980s, however, Hirschman would further elaborate on these themes in two long and important articles. In his study on the authoritarian turn in Latin America, Hirschman argued that the two mutually opposed consequences of economic growth that had characterized the European political discourse in the modern era—economic growth first as a restraint to irrational behaviors and passions, then as the basis for authoritarian rule—could also be easily discerned in Latin American debates of the twentieth century. In the 1950s, observers emphasized that development reduced political infighting and that the production of staples for export needed political maturity—"coffee is incompatible with anarchy," one scholar wrote—but with the concomitant appearance of economic and political crises in the 1960s and 1970s, many concluded that a causal relationship linked the authoritarian turn to the economic crisis.[80]

As we saw in the previous chapter, in the late 1960s Hirschman had tried to mitigate the defeatist interpretation of postwar industrialization policies in Latin America, questioning in particular the alleged "exhaustion" of ISI policies. Looking back, however, Hirschman realized that his complex analysis might somehow have conveyed the wrong message. In his 1968 article, he had highlighted that ISI policies developed in a phased sequence, that early phases were easier, and that the shift from consumer goods to intermediate and capital goods presented important difficulties. In sum, Hirschman felt he had contributed to the idea that a specific threshold exists after all, and thus to the conclusion of O'Donnell and others that at that specific threshold moment, a political reaction to the economic difficulties in the form of an authoritarian coup might occur.

Hirschman advanced two arguments to counter this reading. The first was a historical refutation of O'Donnell's interpretation. More than an exhaustion of the early phase of ISI policies, other changes in economic policies might account for a change of phase, such as the introduction of more orthodox, market-oriented policies or of policies that would finance continuing domestic industrialization through an uneven expansion of consumption by different social groups. In both these cases—and, according to Hirschman, more persuasively than in the hypothesis of an exhaustion of ISI policies—an authoritarian turn was plausible, in principle, as a way to force unpleasant economic policies on the population (or a large part of it). Yet, though this was theoretically possible, Hirschman also highlighted that those policies had been adopted in many Latin American countries not necessarily concomitantly with the establishment of authoritarian regimes, but before, after, or in their total absence. The historical record, in sum, offered only a selective number of cases of the simultaneous presence of authoritarian policy making and a move away from ISI policies, but did not prove any causal relationship.

Unsurprisingly, Hirschman wondered whether the ideological dimension could shed light on the political processes of Latin American countries. Latin American ideology was one of Hirschman's long-lasting passions, and he had written on it on various occasions—for example, in his 1961 article on "Ideologies of Economic Development in Latin America" and his 1963 book, *Journeys Toward Progress*. This time, Hirschman stressed the possibility that the relationship between economic difficulties and an authoritarian turn was not direct, as the theories discussed above implied, but indirect, via the amplifying and distorting dynamics of ideological debates. In other words, the reaction of intellectuals, policy makers, and other influential voices in Latin American societies were disproportionate to the nature and gravity of the problems, eventually twisting the political debate. As Hirschman put it, "it is as though the inflation of the price level has produced in the ideological realm an inflation in the generation of 'fundamental remedies.' When the policies that are thus proposed are considerably beyond the capabilities of a society, a pervasive feeling of frustration is easily generated."[81] In particular, when the "fundamental remedies" for the ills of Latin American economies were of an antagonistic nature, such as domestic wealth or income redistribution or a deep reconsideration of international economic relations (solutions that are felt to "rob Peter to pay Paul"), the possibility of conflict among different groups and eventually of an authoritarian coup increased.

Hirschman was clearly not advocating any reactionary solution such as self-restraint on the part of protesters against the status quo and of intellectuals who denounced unpleasant realities. Indeed, he discussed this ideological dimension with "some reluctance," aware he could be misunderstood; nor did he intend to claim that purely ideological explanations sufficed. But he claimed nonetheless that "this strange process of ideological escalation may well have contributed to that pervasive sense of being in a desperate predicament which is a precondition for radical regime change."[82]

More generally, Hirschman tentatively proposed that a common characteristic of the various paths followed by Latin American countries was that the two basic functions that are activated through a process of economic growth and that follow one another in a growing spiral—an accumulation function that unbalances society, and a reform function that rebalances social disequilibria—have historically succeeded one another in very short phases and been supported by the same groups of intellectuals. Whereas in Europe the accumulation function performed by entrepreneurs had its own intellectual constituency and was still vigorous when the reform function appeared, in Latin America the same intellectual constituency, according to Hirschman, first supported development policies and industrialization and then, a mere ten to twenty years later, changed camp by questioning the effects of industrialization and calling loudly for reformist and redistributional policies.

As he did earlier in *The Passions and the Interests*, here too Hirschman resorted to the category of language to discuss the political consequences of ideological shifts. This "ideological mutation," Hirschman posited, enhanced the readiness of the entrepreneurial class to "use force . . . [and] served to make up, as it were, for the lost ideological support. For, as Rousseau pointed out long ago in his *Essay on the Origin of Languages*, force is a substitute for 'eloquence' and 'persuasion.' "[83] Once again, the history of economic and political developments, Hirschman implied, could be interpreted through the lenses of the history of economic and political discourse and the history of ideology. In Hirschman's vision, both structural and ideological factors had equal standing. "I would rather be eclectic than reductionist," he claimed.[84]

The policy conclusions were yet another demonstration of Hirschman's total lack of trust in precooked recipes. The fundamental issue was how to pace the different phases corresponding to the accumulation function and the reform function. The untimely appearance of pressures toward reform after the phase of accumulation had an important role in the breakdown of democratic regimes; that is,

if reform appears "too early," it will paralyze the entrepreneurial forces . . . and this will lead to stagnation, discontent—and an attempt to secure the process of accumulation and growth by means of an authoritarian regime. If reform appears "too late," the pressures for it, long held back, will explode with violence, and in its wake the identical political configuration is to be expected unless a successful revolution (presumably with its own authoritarian stamp) has been able to take over.[85]

But during the 1970s, the problem was not just one of finding the right relation between the accumulation function and the reform function. The problem started to take a completely new shape during the momentous slowdowns of growth in many countries in the presence of persistently high levels of inflation. This combination of the two phenomena—stagnation *and* inflation—was unprecedented. Historically, they had been mutually exclusive; in fact, in the 1970s, their concomitant emergence marked the birth of a new term, *stagflation*.

When the Brookings Institution asked political scientist Leon N. Lindberg and historian Charles S. Maier to organize a working group on this problem, Hirschman was invited to contribute on Latin America, one of the regions most deeply affected by it. As Maier and Lindberg emphasized, the aim was to understand the institutional structures of these phenomena, treating the causes of inflation and stagnation as endogenous factors (that is, as effects of changes in political power and social organization, in the expectations of political and economic actors, and in the interaction among these actors), rather than as external shocks, as conventional economic analysis would have considered them.[86]

The macroeconomic landscape was changing quickly, for stagnation meant, in Hirschman's terminology, a weakening of the accumulation phase, and inflation implied an impoverishment of wages and a hidden redistribution of income. True to his recent analysis, Hirschman paid attention to the underlying value changes that influenced the behavior of class groups, interpreting inflation as the result of a continuing tug-of-war among interest groups, in a sort of escalation of rival claims by different groups to a larger share of national income. But if this process could be seen as spiraling out of control, Hirschman also drew attention to an unexpected and important positive side effect of this tug-of-war—namely, that it acted out a conflict in a relatively bloodless manner in societies characterized by deep social fractures.[87]

Hirschman's articles on the rise of authoritarianism in Latin America and the political economy of inflation responded to the need he had long felt to extend the analysis in *The Passions and the Interests* to the political consequences of industrial growth, moving beyond the end of the eighteenth century. As Hirschman had written to Michael Walzer in 1973, "a parallel essay should probably be written about the speculations on the political consequences of the rise of *industry*—mine, so far at least, is primarily on the expansion of commerce."[88] It is worth remembering here that the subtitle of the book was "Political Arguments for Capitalism *Before* Its Triumph" (my italics). Yet to be seen were the political arguments for capitalism when it eventually triumphed.

Hirschman elaborated on this question in his Marc Bloch Lecture at the École des Hautes Études en Sciences Sociales in Paris on May 27, 1982, in which he aimed at extending the kind of analysis he had pursued in *The Passions and the Interests* to the period from Adam Smith to the second half of the twentieth century. The lecture was published later that year in the *Journal of Economic Literature* as "Rival Interpretations of Market Society: Civilizing, Destructive, or Feeble?"[89]

An "extended tour d'horizon of interpretations of capitalist development," the lecture was a masterpiece of rhetorical elegance and insightful contents.[90] In it, Hirschman examined several critiques of the capitalist social and economic order and their interrelations. The sequence of theories was built as if each successive theory emerged as the antithesis to the preceding one. Hirschman apparently set the stage again for a strictly endogenous history of ideas. But this is in fact only a superficial impression, for there is no historical necessity in this sequence; if anything, Hirschman shows that each thesis had its own historical evolution. In all the cases he discussed, "there was an almost total lack of communication between the conflicting theses. Intimately related intellectual formations unfolded at great length, without ever taking cognizance of each other."[91]

Hirschman's starting point is the *doux commerce* thesis he had discussed in *The Passions and the Interests*, which he introduced by claiming that its full maturation in the eighteenth century marked the affirmation, for the first time in human history, of the idea that the social order is an important cause of human unhappiness—hence the idea that a social order whose fabric is deeply intertwined with commerce will produce a number of virtues such as industriousness, frugality, punctuality, probity, and so on, able to restrain disruptive and otherwise socially dangerous passions. Hirschman added in passing that "the idea of a perfectible social order arose at about the same time as that of human actions and decisions having unintended effects"; it looked as though the latter idea had emerged as a way to neutralize the former, by arguing that even the best intentioned institutional reforms might be conducive, "via those unforeseen consequences or 'perverse effects,' to all kinds of disastrous results."[92]

Hirschman did not elaborate further in this article on the momentous appearance of the idea of unintended consequences, but the point stuck with him. This perverse effect would become one of the three ordering principles of his 1991 book, *The Rhetoric of Reaction*, which insisted on the unintended negative consequences of human action and thus mounted a powerful argument against attempts at social reform. It is a particularly striking example of the process of generation of ideas in Hirschman's thought—of the way early intuitions and *petites idées* would appear first as small asides or passing comments, stay (sometimes for a long time) on the back burner, and eventually reemerge as central pieces of subsequent reflections.

The *doux commerce* thesis, according to Hirschman, was an early victim of the industrial revolution. That trade expansion had helped shape, almost as a by-product, a less violent environment and more disciplined bourgeois order was a truth applicable only to European countries, since the expansion of commerce in the rest of the world was often accompanied by violence and human and social havoc. The industrial revolution, Hirschman posited, meant that "a new revolutionary force had arisen in the very center of capitalist expansion," in fact bringing havoc home. This force was usually characterized as "wild, blind, relentless, unbridled—hence anything but *doux*."[93] A number of theories thus emerged to show how industrial society produced within itself destructive forces that undermined its existence in the long run. Hirschman grouped these theories under the label of the self-destruction thesis.

One of the most famous statements in this sense is Marx and Engels's 1850 address to the Communist League, in which they urged that proletarian forces take advantage of the contradictions of capitalist society so that "the rule of the bourgeois democrats, from the very first, will carry within it the seeds of its own destruction."[94] In that instance, Marx and Engels emphasized the material contradiction of the capitalistic socioeconomic order. Another line of thought was perhaps stronger and definitely more catholic, including both Marx and Engels and liberal scholars such as Joseph Schumpeter. This second line of thought viewed the seeds of self-destruction in the moral corruption that a capitalist society produces.

Each author put this in his own way. Marx and Engels, in *The Communist Manifesto*, wrote:

The bourgeoisie, wherever it has got the upper hand, has . . . pitilessly torn asunder the motley feudal ties that bound man to his 'natural superiors,' and has left remaining no other nexus between man and man than naked self-interest, than callous 'cash payment.' . . . It has resolved personal worth into exchange value, and in place of the numberless indefeasible chartered freedoms, has set up that single, unconscionable freedom—Free Trade.[95]

Commerce destroyed the traditional bonds among individuals, substituting money relations for all other types of relationships. The self-destruction thesis, in other words, is the obverse of the *doux commerce* thesis.

Joseph Schumpeter focused on the new rationalist spirit that comes with capitalism, highlighting that, after having destroyed past and outdated institutions, this rationalist attitude would eventually turn against itself and attack the very pillars of capitalist society, such as "private property and the whole scheme of bourgeois values."[96] This version rested more on an ideological explanation than did other versions of the self-destruction thesis.

Interestingly, Hirschman noticed an ideological limit on the part of contemporary economists to find arguments in favor of capitalism. Between the end of the nineteenth and the beginning of the twentieth century, sociologists such as Emile Durkheim and Georg Simmel had tried to react to the eclipse of the *doux commerce* thesis by emphasizing that, while capitalism destroys traditional bonds, it is somehow able to create new interpersonal bonds. Economists, however, showed themselves completely unable to explain how markets can strengthen social integration. Having theorized an ideal market characterized by perfect competition, in which large numbers of economic actors participate under conditions of perfect information, economists have in fact excluded all possibilities for any "prolonged human or social contact among or between the parties."[97] Having succeeded in building a watertight *economic* legitimacy for the market system, "they have sacrificed the *sociological* legitimacy that could rightfully have been claimed for the way, so unlike the perfect-competition model, most markets function in the real world."[98]

But there is a third thesis, paradoxically related to the two preceding ones. Whereas the self-destruction thesis insisted on the violence and havoc caused by capitalist transformation, several observers emphasized that many societies had instead experienced difficulties resulting from the weakness of the capitalist revolution. According to these critics, capitalistic institutions and ideology were unable to destroy once and for all the remnants of the feudal past. National bourgeoisies and their worldviews had thus remained subservient to the powerful values and social structure of the *ancien régime*, failing to bring their countries into modernity. Hirschman called this the feudal-shackles thesis.

Interestingly, authors who have articulated the self-destruction thesis have also often been eloquent representatives of the feudal-shackles thesis. As is well known, Marxist thought sees in the bourgeois revolution an important way station on the path to a communist society. Capitalist societies, in this perspective, have undoubtedly brought havoc at home but have also managed to overcome the feudal mode of production, at least in the capitalist core. What is worse is for countries to undergo only a limited capitalist transformation, and it is not by chance that scholars who have most forcefully articulated this thesis are from late or late-late industrializing countries. In Italy, both Antonio Gramsci and Emilio Sereni (a cousin of Colorni) discussed the problem of Italian unification in terms of a failed bourgeois revolution that left the southern feudal *latifundio* in place, thus reinforcing Italian social and economic dualism. In Central Europe, George Lukács emphasized the weakness of the local bourgeoisie before the vested interests of feudal landlords (and as we saw in chapter 2, Alexander Gerschenkron, though not a Marxist, had a very similar reading of the role of the Junkers in German history). In non-European societies, scholars have focused on the weakness of the local bourgeoisie and its economic, social, and ideological subservience to the interests and values of landed classes. Andre Gunder Frank, for example, wrote about the "development of underdevelopment" in Latin America as a specific condition of social and economic minority due to a weak liberal bourgeoisie, as opposed to the original undevelopment of core industrial countries that succeeded in transitioning from a feudal to a fully capitalist social order.[99]

But if the feudal-shackles thesis is the antithesis of the self-destruction thesis, it must also be qualified with respect to the *doux commerce* thesis. In a sense, the feudal-shackles thesis can be seen as a *doux commerce* thesis that did not come to fruition. The idea is that if only the *doux commerce* thesis had become true, it would have been possible to avoid the feudal shackles that keep a country from modernizing. The United States offers the best example of this intuition by providing a testimony of powerful modernization in the absence of any feudal shackles.

Yet, Hirschman noted, there is a tradition of thought that sees a curse in this apparent blessing of the absence of a feudal past. As Louis Hartz wrote in the mid-twentieth century, the lack of a feudal past deprived America of social and ideological diversity, which is, according to Hartz, one of the main ingredients of genuine liberty—hence America's "liberal absolutism," its tendency toward a "tyranny of the majority," and the inability of American politics to elaborate a strong and durable consensus for a developed welfare system.[100] Hirschman labeled this line of thought the feudal-blessings thesis.

As this discussion has shown, Hirschman presented each thesis as the negation of the preceding one. The self-destruction thesis is the obverse of the *doux commerce* thesis; the feudal-shackles thesis posits that the capitalist revolution has been not violent and forceful but weak and limited. Finally, the feudal-blessings thesis negates the feudal-shackles thesis by claiming that the very lack of a feudal past, apparently so liberating for American history, has also meant the lack of a truly pluralistic liberal

FIGURE 6.1 Albert O. Hirschman, Marc Bloch Lecture at the École des Hautes Études en Sciences Socia-les, Paris, May 27, 1982. Courtesy of Katia Salomon

tradition. However, Hirschman chose this sequential presentation purely as an expositive device and not because he saw in it any actual historical law or correspondence between different phases in the history of ideas and different historical periods.

The only sequence of theories that can perhaps be explained more cred-ibly as a real counterpoint to the succession of actual historical phases is that between the apex of the *doux commerce* thesis in the eighteenth cen-tury (that is, during a period of thriving trade but before the industrial revolution) and the self-destruction thesis in the nineteenth century (when the consequences of the factory system for workers' lives and the accom-panying Dickensian repertoire of misery and destitution became evident). Yet even this specific sequence does not exhaust the complexity of each of these theses when considered independently. Hirschman made this point clearly. His schematic presentation, or mapping of the different theses, helped clarify their mutual relationships and "establish contact between a number of ideological formations that are in fact closely related *but have evolved in total isolation from one another.*"[101]

But Hirschman's goal was not simply to build a sequential map of dif-ferent ideologies and theses. More than just a spectator and chronicler of ideological theories, Hirschman confessed his interest in the question "as to which one is *right*."[102] Here Hirschman's love for nuances and immeasurable combinations of different and apparently opposed elements reappears in full. Although the different theses have been presented as if each were in some respect the opposite or the negation of the preceding one, it is more than probable that, in real life, elements from more than one thesis often coexist. To be sure, this is not true of all possible combinations—for instance, the *doux commerce* and the feudal-blessings theses add up to a real contradiction—but it has often been noted that capitalist and precapitalist values and norms can exist within the same society, and the amalgam among different elements is not necessarily negative.

This conclusion applies even more solidly to the contextual presence of elements pertaining to the *doux commerce* and the self-destruction theses. Commercial transactions, for example, contribute to develop norms of trust and reliability, on the one hand, and a pervasive "element of calculation and instrumental reason," on the other. From this perspective, Hirschman argued, the moral basis of capitalist society can be seen as "constantly depleted and replenished at the same time," and the right balance a movable and unstable target.[103] Of course, this analysis makes it much more difficult for the social scientist to reach any "ironclad" conclusion about the direction and outcome of processes of social change. Indeed, this indeterminacy was another important by-product of Hirschman's analysis: "after so many failed prophecies, is it not in the interest of social science to embrace complexity, be it at some sacrifice of its claim to predictive power?"[104]

Chapter Seven

THE WORKING OF DEMOCRACY

When, in the spring of 1978, Hirschman was invited to deliver the 1979 Eliot Janeway Lectures in Historical Economics at Princeton University, the press and bookshops were filled with articles and books on the tenth anniversary of 1968—its spirit, the street demonstrations, the widespread engagement with public issues, the revolution in social norms, the rejection of past conventions. Commentators remarked upon the abrupt emergence and strength of social consciousness in place of the individualism of the previous decade. The slogan "The personal is political," meaning the inextricable link between individual experience and the larger social context, epitomized this new sensitivity.

If the 1950s and early 1960s had been a decade of solid economic growth, mass consumption, and access to durable goods for increasingly broad strata of the population, especially in North America and Western Europe—the dream of family prosperity closer than ever before—the late 1960s marked a rejection of the values of personal gain in favor of the centrality of public issues and the social dimension, the refusal of the household in favor of the street. Then, in the 1970s, the so-called reflux intervened. The tide changed direction, and people turned again to care primarily for their private interests. But it was not a simple swing of the pendulum, a return to the private perspective of the optimistic 1950s. Princeton historian Daniel T. Rodgers has masterfully described the 1970s as characterized by fundamental reformulations of ideas about society—its "character," its institutions and cultural debates, and its fundamental economic structures. As he put it,

conceptions of human nature that in the post–World War II era had been thick with context, social circumstance, institutions, and history gave way to conceptions of human nature that stressed choice, agency, performance, and desire. Strong metaphors of society were supplanted by weaker ones. Imagined collectivities shrank; notions of structure and power thinned out. Viewed by its acts of mind, the last quarter of the century was an era of disaggregation, a great age of fracture.[1]

Intellectual landscapes altered on all sides of the political spectrum, and both the left and the right had to reassess their roles in relation to fundamental changes in international economic relations, the crisis of the welfare state, the early instances of globalization, the end of sustained postwar growth, and the beginning of a surge in inequality that continues today. Only one decade after 1968, everybody agreed that it was as though an entire geological era had passed.[2]

After his explorations in the history of ideas of the modern era that culminated in the book *The Passions and the Interests* (1977) and the lecture "Rival Interpretations of Market Society" (1982), Hirschman returned to the study of democracies in the second half of the twentieth century. The topic was not new to him. The question of how democracies developed, thrived, or collapsed had been a core issue not only of his life as a scholar but of his experience as an individual since adolescence. The question of democracy emerged explicitly at times (as in *Journeys Toward Progress*, 1963; "Foreign Aid: A Critique and a Proposal," 1968; *Exit, Voice, and Loyalty*, 1970; and "The Turn to Authoritarianism in Latin America," 1979, among others), and at other times remained in the background, though as a powerful stimulus for research (as in *National Power and the Structure of Foreign Trade*, 1945; *The Strategy of Economic Development*, 1958; and "The Political Economy of Import-Substituting Industrialization in Latin America," 1968).

But, as we have briefly sketched, the cultural landscape had profoundly changed, a fact that obviously did not pass unobserved by Hirschman. The invitation to give the Eliot Janeway Lectures at Princeton gave him the opportunity to reflect on the deep social changes he was witnessing and to explore the question of whether a private-public cycle could be not only detected but explained. Hirschman delivered the Janeway Lectures in December 1979. The resulting manuscript, he wrote, perhaps fell short of offering a comprehensive, watertight interpretation of the topic he had chosen to address. Nonetheless, the inquiry opened new vistas on some of the fundamental processes of social change in the postwar period. As Hirschman admitted, tongue in cheek, he was not even sure he could claim that his book, published in 1982 as *Shifting Involvements: Private Interest and Public Action*, qualified as a work of social science; if anything, it was "so directly concerned with change and upheaval, both individual and social, that at times I had the feeling that I was writing a conceptual outline of a *Bildungsroman*."[3]

PUBLIC PARTICIPATION AND PRIVATE INTERESTS IN WESTERN DEMOCRACIES: *SHIFTING INVOLVEMENTS*

The shifts in spirit from the 1950s and the 1960s, Hirschman noted, raised the question of whether "our societies are in some way predisposed toward oscillations between periods of intense preoccupation with public issues and of almost total concentration on individual improvement and private welfare goals."[4] Oscillations was a milder way of referring to cycles—a notoriously challenging word, as the history of economics is full of attempts at describing regular cycles of economic activity. But Hirschman was not so much interested in finding any iron law of cyclical social change as he was in explaining how specific characteristics of a certain phase triggered a process conducive to a shift in priorities and general attitude—from private-centered to participation-driven, or the other way around. Once again, Hirschman aimed at unfolding the endogenous mechanisms that could explain the shift—that is, how a phase was rooted in certain specific characteristics of the one that preceded it. In particular, Hirschman wanted to focus on the specific aspects of "economic structure and development" that could account for the shift.[5]

But if Hirschman framed his analysis in economic terms and apparently addressed standard microeconomic concepts such as consumer preference, his approach—as by now we have come to know—was far from orthodox. First, Hirschman was interested in unraveling the mechanisms behind shifting preferences, whereas mainstream economics considers preferences as given. The economist is not interested in *why* one buys (prefers) this or that. Second, Hirschman intended in particular to examine how the disappointment of the consumer-citizen, which is at the root of shifting preferences, works. For this, he relied on the work of Herbert Simon, Richard Cyert, Charles Lindblom, and others, who had highlighted the conditions of "bounded rationality," ignorance, and contextual uncertainty of economic actors.[6] Though this was a relevant and well-respected line of inquiry, it was decidedly not mainstream.

How did Hirschman proceed in his quest for the shifting involvements of the consumer-citizen? His basic premise was that "acts of consumption, as well as acts of participation in public affairs, which are undertaken because they are expected to yield satisfaction, also yield disappointment and dissatisfaction. . . . To the extent that the disappointment is not wholly eliminated by an instantaneous downward adjustment of expectations, any pattern of consumption or of time use carries within itself, to use the hallowed metaphor, 'the seeds of its own destruction.' "[7]

Using as a starting point of analysis Tibor Scitovsky's 1976 book *The Joyless Economy*, Hirschman first offered a catalog of possible consumer disappointments. In his book, Scitovsky aimed at incorporating contributions from physiology and psychology to explain the microfoundations of consumer behavior. In a nutshell, individuals feel discomfort whenever their basic needs (thirst, hunger, protection from bad weather and extreme temperatures) are unfulfilled, or when they experience boredom after having fulfilled their needs (the latter case is the condition of affluent societies). Discomfort requires new stimulations, in the form of additional consumption. The process through which these new stimuli are pursued produces pleasure and, at the end of it, comfort. Pleasure and comfort, however, though deeply connected, are functionally opposed. Pleasure is experienced while pursuing comfort, and comfort is achieved only when the process of overcoming discomfort—the very process that produces pleasure—comes to an end.[8]

Hirschman argued that the durable goods characteristic of a mass consumption society are particularly apt to create comfort but little pleasure. Whereas the consumption of truly nondurable goods such as food, sex and sleep provides mainly pleasure but only very temporary comfort, durable goods such as refrigerators and air-conditioning yield a comparatively small amount of pleasure, though they make life much more comfortable. This preponderance of comfort over pleasure requires further stimulations. Indeed, durable goods (which Hirschman divides into different subcategories) are disappointment prone: they age, go out of fashion, become less reliable, and most of all, do not yield "pleasure." Moreover, Hirschman noted, this disappointment risks being particularly strong for the first generation experiencing the new durables, for this generation probably nurtured excessively high expectations of the magic of mass consumption.

The physiopsychological approach on which this discussion is based was a novel effort for the economics discipline in the mid-1970s. For the subfield of the economics of happiness, as well as for certain strands of behavioral economics, Scitovsky's book remains a classic. To the noneconomist, however, this discussion sounds pretty limited and naïve. Robert E. Lane, a political scientist at Yale and the former president of the International Society of Political Psychology, effectively summarized the criticisms against the deficiencies of economic theories attempting to model consumer satisfaction. First, those models employ a theory of human choice incompatible with the research findings of psychologists and behavioralists. Second, they do not mutually relate different kinds of human needs, thus offering a disaggregated and unrealistic model of human behavior. Finally, and more important, market mechanisms and goods "are only weakly related to the things that make people happy: autonomy, self-esteem, family felicity, tension-free leisure, friendship."[9] Moreover, as Hirschman also recognized, the private-public dichotomy was only one among many. What about the dichotomy of materialistic versus spiritual life, for instance? Both refer to the private sphere but relate very differently to the stimulation-pleasure-comfort mechanism that is so central in Scitovsky's and Hirschman's analyses. Hirschman simply dodged the criticism: "a beginning had to be made somewhere," he wrote. More convincingly, he added that the private-public shift is of particular relevance to the mechanisms of social change witnessed in the postwar decades.

Hirschman's analysis becomes more interesting in the observations that he managed to extract from the model itself. Relatively backward societies are not necessarily more prone to social discontent, he claimed, with implicit reference to the progressively teleological view of modernization theory. On the contrary, "disappointment could be especially widespread in a society in which mass diffusion of durables first occurs. This is of course quite paradoxical, since one might expect a population to be in a fine mood when large parts of it accede for the first time to the much celebrated, Rostovian blessings of 'high mass consumption.'"[10] Moreover, both a fine mood and disappointment, Hirschman added, may exist at the same time, with the older generation proud of the progress it has achieved and the younger generation dissatisfied with the materialistic and apparently "empty" lifestyle of the parents. "As a result of these contrasting moods," Hirschman concluded, "the period of transition to 'high mass consumption' could be politically quite volatile."[11]

Hirschman's most convincing analysis has to do with the consequences of the increasing diffusion of public services, such as education and health, and the potential disappointment of the consumer-citizens. As economic prosperity increases, these services undergo a major transformation, from elite realities, often private in nature, to widespread public services. But during this transition, the reliability and quality of these services, subject to an unprecedented expansion, become visibly worse. Again, the paradoxical relation between social needs and the supply and quality of services becomes apparent: it is "precisely when a society makes a determined effort to widen access to certain services that the quality of these services will decline."[12]

This analysis addressed, in typical Hirschmanesque fashion, the then widely debated crisis of the welfare state, against which strong criticisms were leveled by both the left and the right. Leftist authors underscored the inner contradiction of a state machinery that must guarantee capital accumulation but at the same time legitimate itself through the provision of social services. James O'Connor's *The Fiscal Crisis of the State*, published in 1973, was a prime example of this perspective. Conservative scholars, ideologically hostile to big government, denounced the excessive burden of social services on governmental resources, their ineffectiveness, or worse, their perverse effects. Perhaps the most famous example of this perspective is Charles Murray's *Losing Ground*; it would appear only in 1984, but the argument was well entrenched in the public debate by the time Hirschman published *Shifting Involvements* in 1982. From yet another perspective, in 1976 Fred Hirsch highlighted the problem of *The Social Limits to Growth*— that is, the impossibility for increasing numbers of people to get access to finite resources and "positional goods," such as an exclusive diploma or an uncrowded beach.[13]

In a panel at the American Economic Association (AEA) in December 1979 (that is, around the time of the Janeway Lectures), Hirschman bundled all these criticisms under the rubric of the "structuralist (or fundamentalist) fallacy"—that is, an unjustified tendency to diagnose fundamental disorders and prescribe radical cures.[14] In a less definitive way, and with a more reformist attitude, Hirschman proposed to consider the crisis as a temporary, perhaps counterintuitive, but natural effect of economic and social advancement. No doubt, the decade's economic malaise of stagflation and the ineffectiveness of established Keynesian recipes seemed to support the criticisms of the O'Connors and the Murrays.[15] Yet, Hirschman argued, the welfare state was not suffering from a "systemic crisis," but rather from more benign "growing pains."[16]

In an attempt to reach out to his colleagues, at the AEA Hirschman described the deterioration of the quality of services in terms of "output elasticity of quality." If in *Exit, Voice, and Loyalty*, Hirschman had focused on citizens' reaction to the deterioration of public services, at the AEA he examined in greater detail the mechanism of organizational deterioration. Again, a prominent example was public schools, which Hirschman had previously discussed in *Exit, Voice, and Loyalty*. The rapid expansion of public education, he argued, was clearly experiencing visible deterioration, especially because the service continued to be offered in spite of evident shortages and bottlenecks in its inputs. Because of the growing needs for teachers, high-quality teachers were supplemented with mediocre ones, schoolrooms were in short supply and overcrowded, library facilities were undersized, and so on. The substitutability of inputs made this process viable, though characterized by deteriorating quality.

But this, Hirschman suggested, raised a question about the limiting assumptions of standard economic theory: "Since substitutability is the rule in the world of neoclassical economics," he quipped, "it may be surprising that changes in the quality of output have not been given more attention."[17] Yet it was not inexplicable, if one considered that perfect information in a competitive market was a pervasive assumption of mainstream economics. Under this assumption, economic actors would immediately adjust their behavior to the deteriorating quality of services. In fact, as the real world shows, the educational system is a much more inertial and complex mechanism, consumers do not have perfect knowledge and are ignorant of crucial information, and input shifts often happen in noncompetitive markets.[18]

All of this discussion was directly relevant to the inquiry that Hirschman was conducting in *Shifting Involvements*. The disappointment experienced by the consumer-citizen, Hirschman claimed, opened the door to altogether diverse forms of pursuit of happiness. In affluent democratic societies, he noted, this often proved to be social engagement and political action.

The shift cannot be explained by standard economic theory. It is not simply a shift in tastes, a new set of preferences resulting from past experiences. In fact, Hirschman argued that mainstream economic theory of revealed preferences, if perhaps able to explain a shift in tastes (apples versus pears), is conspicuously unable to explain changes in lifestyle and values. To address these questions, one must refer to extra-economic concepts, such as the role of ideologies or the philosophical concept, introduced by Harry G. Frankfurt, of "second-order desires"—that is, the individual volitions that contribute to define "our concept of ourselves as persons."[19] Frankfurt explained:

Besides wanting and choosing and being moved to do this or that, men may also want to have (or not to have) certain desires and motives. They are capable of wanting to be different, in their preferences and purposes, from what they are. Many animals appear to have the capacity . . . to do or not to do one thing or another. No animal other than man, however, appears to have the capacity for reflective self-evaluation.[20]

Amartya Sen also criticized the revealed preference approach insofar as it considered exclusively "isolated act[s] of choice."[21] Concepts such as sympathy and, more important, commitment and morality, Sen added, are crucial in determining a person's behavior, and it is difficult to define them simply as preferences when they may actually go against one's own advantage. The shifts in what Sen called "meta-ranking" of preferences, or "ordering the orderings," involve a general change of perspective that standard economics is unable to explain.[22] As Hirschman put it, in an article that is an elaboration of some points first addressed in *Shifting Involvements*, "A taste is almost defined as a preference about which you do not argue—*de gustibus non est disputandum*. A taste about which you argue, with others or yourself*, ceases ipso facto being a taste—it turns into a *value*."[23]

This complex discussion and multiple references to concepts developed by philosophers like Frankfurt or heterodox economists like Sen served Hirschman to move to the next phase in his analysis. The experience of repeated disappointments can be seen as an accumulation of reasons to exit the consumerist lifestyle and adopt voice in the public arena as the new guiding attitude. In an unexpected twist on his famous exit-voice dichotomy, Hirschman recognized that in this case exit and voice are not opposed concepts, but rather two complementary phases of a single process. Voice becomes a positive response to the need to exit.[24]

The absence of this process of personal transformation is what Hirschman considered flawed in the analyses of Mancur Olson and Tibor Scitovsky: their actors, in Hirschman's view, seem to lack any history, or are compelled to find satisfaction by looking for more of the same (i.e., higher levels of consumption), and thus are constitutionally unable to commit to a specific vision of life, or to have specific value biases.[25] In a word, Hirschman found Olson's and Scitovsky's analyses unable to explain *political* action. In fact, Hirschman's model presupposes in its central phase that citizens are heavily involved in the public arena, "spurning, *pace* Olson, any temptation to sit back in the hope to get a free ride."[26] Hirschman's criticism of Olson's work was actually misplaced, for Olson had not offered any iron law, but a more modest (though powerful) model that tried to explain why collective action might, under certain conditions, not take place, adding furthermore that he was discussing a possibility, not a necessity.[27]

In any case, Hirschman continued, eventually disappointment from public engagement also increases. Why? All possible outcomes of public engagement, in Hirschman's account, can potentially push the citizen away from public life: failure to reach important goals is of course disappointing and may lead to disenchantment and retirement to private life, but also success may drain motivation, or transform the original goal. In any case, two basic mechanisms are at work here: overcommitment and underinvolvement. Overcommitment refers to the passion that the pursuit of public goals often produces, transforming participation and the time dedicated to the cause into a benefit instead of a cost—until activism fatigue breaks the spell. Underinvolvement refers to the opposing idea that, especially in a democracy, institutional arrangements have been conceived to cool down excessively passionate behaviors. Even the voting system and its ability to transform different degrees of political passion of the individual citizen into a uniform political outcome—the ballot—may account for the growing apathy of many mature democracies.[28]

Yet if disappointment is not inherent to facts but rather a feeling of the citizen-activist, then what produces it? According to Hirschman, the reformist's retreat into the private is due to an inability to have realistic expectations and to visualize "intermediate outcomes and halfway houses."[29] The true visionary act, Hirschman implied, is not to prefigure outright revolution—often a simplistic and schematic act of imagination—but to conceive the possibility of even modest advancements, and to build political resilience. "It is the poverty of our imagination that paradoxically produces images of 'total' change in lieu of more modest expectations," he writes.[30] Hirschman's reformism also emerged from another consideration. The oscillation between the private and public dimensions is not, per se, cause for concern. If Hirschman saw a problem, it was in excessive oscillations, and especially in the pattern of Western societies, characterized by long periods of preeminence of the private dotted with sudden and violent outburst of public commitment, which are "hardly likely to be constructive."[31]

In the end, the consumer-citizen described by Hirschman, with his story of successive phases of enthusiasm and disappointment, is a very different animal from the "rational actor" who populates standard economic theory. But far from being a flaw, this is in fact a richness. The consumer-citizens in Hirschman's story are "*superior* to the 'rational actor' inasmuch as they can conceive of *various* states of happiness, and are able to transcend one in order to achieve the other."[32] This more complex behavior is clearly a result of the many disappointments experienced in the shifts from private to public life and vice versa. Hirschman's younger colleague, Guillermo O'Donnell, emphasized the importance of Hirschman's new book in presenting a "cogent critique of the usual assumptions of economic theory about stable and transitive individual preferences."[33] As he wrote, highlighting the principle of disappointment in Hirschman's analysis, "*Angst*, omnipotence, denial of death, *hubris* and innumerable related terms point to a much more inherently dissatisfied and tense animal than the chooser between two or more preferences that mainstream economics—and, to a large extent, political science—present to us."[34]

In general, *Shifting Involvements* had a mildly positive reception. It was considered by many to be insightful, provocative, characterized by refreshing argument and deep erudition. New publications by Hirschman raised widespread expectations of remarkably readable, elegant, witty, and though-provoking prose.[35] But if reviewers were not disappointed on this count, the book nonetheless left many perplexed. Two main lines of criticism are recognizable. One focused on Hirschman's theory of cycles, which many found substantially weak. Raymond Boudon called it a "shaky theory."[36]

True enough, Hirschman himself raised flags at the very beginning of the volume, recognizing the "tentative and speculative character of the whole undertaking."[37] He acknowledged he would not be able to "prove" the existence of regular cycles in any straightforward way; at best, his enterprise was similar to Kondratieff's attempt to individuate very long cycles—so long, in fact, that one cannot be really sure they actually exist. His only goal, he remarked, was to provide a "phenomenology" of disappointments and shifting involvements.[38] Yet the entire book describes what Hirschman identified as a private-public cycle, and reviewers, not unexpectedly, took him seriously.

In particular, many commentators questioned the link between the experience of disappointment and the shift in lifestyle and values. Disappointment is not necessarily conducive to such change, as Hirschman seemed to imply. If the causal relationship between disappointment and shift is left undemonstrated, one reviewer noted, the risk of a *post hoc* fallacy—the claim that if disappointment precedes a change, it is because the former causes the latter—is just around the corner.[39] As some argued, other mechanisms can work as plausible explanations for the emergence of public activism in the 1960s: the Vietnam War, for example, may have seemed to public opinion more preposterous than the Korean War, thus triggering a peace movement that did not take off in the 1950s. Historical realities, in this example, would explain public commitment better than shifting preferences. Also, as sociologist Arthur Stinchcombe observed in one of the most articulate reviews of the book, participation in the public arena can arise not necessarily because of changes in individual preferences, but because people see new political possibilities that were previously out of view. As Stinchcombe noted, "recent fashion in sociology, the Oberschall, Tilly, and Skocpol fashion, is to interpret social movements by changes in resources (possibilities) rather than changes in people's minds."[40]

Similarly undemonstrated, for a number of reviewers, was the link between the individual experience and the process of collective change. Was it actually possible to demonstrate that individual cycles are synchronized into broader, societal cycles? One otherwise very positive review described the essay as "stubbornly grounded in methodological individualism."[41] More recently, historian Charles S. Maier argued about the book that "the discussion is resolutely atomistic. Although Hirschman must have had large-scale public swings of mood in mind, he discusses individual choice throughout."[42]

Hirschman tried to link the private with the collective through the example of societies that reach the stage of mass consumption for the first time. In such a case, the experience of increasing disappointment would be felt by the society at large, or at least by a relevant subgroup of it, such as the younger generations. But beyond this, Hirschman did not really offer a historical interpretation that could substantiate his claim. As one sociologist lamented, historical data were necessary to test Hirschman's model of social change.[43] But historical analysis is conspicuously missing from Hirschman's essay. *Shifting Involvements*, Maier has argued, "takes for granted the aggregation of cyclical behavior. For the historian, however, it is the aggregation that must be explained; the individual's scurrying back and forth is only half the story."[44]

A second line of criticisms questioned the historical record and can be divided into two subquestions. The first has to do with the reality of what we call the historical record: did Hirschman's oscillations actually take place? Unless we take for granted the stereotypes of the private-oriented 1950s and 1970s and public-oriented 1960s, scholarly research has shown a much more complex picture. Stinchcombe noted that from many important perspectives, such as public support for an expansion of civil rights for black citizens, the oscillations were nowhere to be seen. The development was remarkably linear throughout the 1950s, 1960s, and 1970s, despite the ups and downs of the civil rights movement. The same could be said for the constant increase in public expenditures throughout the 1950s and 1960s. Stinchcombe questioned the general applicability of Hirschman's scheme, though he suggested that it helped understand the specific case of youth protest in late 1960s American colleges, in particular "why students of the sixties differed from those of the fifties and seventies."[45] Others criticized the existence of Hirschman's cycle starting from the private-public dichotomy, specifically within the context of the debate on the crisis of the welfare state. For example, if one considers the growth of a voluntary not-for-profit sector capable of offering services similar to the public sector, then the dichotomic approach inherent in the private-public oscillations loses at least some of its explanatory force.[46]

The second subquestion has to do with the endogeneity of Hirschman's analysis. As he argued, an endogenous theory was necessary to make his case for shifting involvements based on periodic collective experiences of disappointment. Yet exogenous events—historical events—remain fundamental to explain collective behavior. Hirschman himself recognized this, claiming that his essay aimed only at "correcting" the exogenous bias; "there is no denying," he conceded, that wars and revolutions play a crucial role in enhancing people's participation in the public life, or, on the contrary, that rapid economic growth makes people retreat into the private sphere.[47] But it was not clear exactly what he was trying to demonstrate, a problem that did not escape the notice of several commentators. Massimo Paci, for instance, wrote that even a superficial look at the evolution of national welfare systems confirms the importance of exogenous factors, concluding that Hirschman's attempt to build an endogenous model of shifting involvements was premature if not impossible, at least as far as public commitment to the welfare state is concerned.[48] Others pointed out the blurred borders between endogenous and exogenous causes.[49]

In the end, to most readers the book appealed not for its theoretical construct or for its "sometimes true theory," as Stinchcombe put it, but for the new vistas it helped to open in the social sciences.[50] The assumption that preferences are given and stable was common to economics, sociology, and psychology. Cyclical changes in values, though not a new phenomenon to social scientists, was nonetheless a marginal notion in neoclassical economics and in Parsonian sociology. Social theory, lamented Stinchcombe, "has absolutely zero to say about why masses of people change their minds on a major social value."[51] Hirschman's work, with all its limits—even the most sympathetic reviewers noticed its lack of rigor—was instrumental in opening the eyes of social scientists to the processes of cultural change.[52]

As in *Exit, Voice, and Loyalty*, Hirschman showed that a purely economistic approach produced very limited understanding of social change. Once again, he took as his preferred target economic imperialism à la Becker, according to which "the economic approach provides a useful framework for understanding all human behavior." Rational actors with stable preferences were the least useful concept to explain human behavior, Hirschman retorted. As he put it (in italics in the original): *"The world I am trying to understand . . . is one in which men think they want one thing and then upon getting it, find out to their dismay that they don't want it nearly as much as they thought or don't want it at all and that something else, of which they were hardly aware, is what they really want."*[53] Hirschman's analysis turned the tables: by insisting on values and unpredictability, he offered, in the words of Sidney Tarrow, "a stimulating alternative to rational choice theory."[54]

In conclusion, as Stinchcombe put it, "the question of Hirschman's essay can be formulated as: 'Is it sometimes useful to think of humans as the kinds of animals who change their mind a lot, often jointly, about what is good, true, beautiful, just, and preferable?' "[55] Despite their reservations, many scholars answered in the affirmative.

DEMOCRACY AND DEVELOPMENT:
GETTING AHEAD COLLECTIVELY

In early 1983, Albert and Sarah Hirschman were back to Colombia, driving along large haciendas in the northern Department of Córdoba. On the Caribbean coast, they arrived at a small village of fishermen, Cristo Rey. To the eyes of people with European backgrounds like the Hirschmans, fishermen have been doing the job of their ancestors for generations, but Albert and Sarah soon discovered that that was not true for the inhabitants of Cristo Rey. Until a few years before, they had been working the land, each family dividing their time between their own small plot for self-consumption and wage labor for nearby haciendas. In 1975, a group of villagers seized a piece of land that belonged to a hacienda but had remained uncultivated for years. Land seizures had been quite common throughout the 1960s in Colombia, and they had often proved successful. By the mid-1970s, however, the wind had changed, and the Cristo Rey peasants were soon ejected.

That early experience, though itself a failure, planted the seeds for a subsequent, more successful enterprise. The bond that developed among peasants during the fight for land did not dissolve, and, very practically, they decided that if they could not take the land, they would take the sea. They established a cooperative, secured financial help and vocational training from a number of private and public associations, and in a few years the peasants-turned-fishermen had become a remarkable success story. Hirschman noted blissfully that "a fish restaurant and a small hotel are in the planning stage!"[56]

The story, though perhaps banal in its simplicity, is interesting. From it, Hirschman extracted a series of considerations on one particular sub-category of dynamics of social change: the power of social activism to transform apparently irreformable situations (such as the Cristo Rey peasants' lack of access to adequate resources and means of production) and improve the living conditions of groups and individuals.

The cooperative of fishermen in Cristo Rey was only one of some forty-five grassroots development projects that Albert and Sarah visited in early 1983 in six Latin American countries (the Dominican Republic, Colombia, Peru, Chile, Argentina, and Uruguay). As we know, field research was a well-known method of inquiry for them. *Journeys Toward Progress* and *Development Projects Observed* could not have been written without similar direct experiences, and as Adelman shows, Hirschman had been visiting Latin American countries regularly throughout the decades. As in previous exercises, the Hirschmans' goal was to extract insights from the specific set of projects they visited and their practice of "thick observation" (as on previous trips, Sarah accompanied Albert, participated in the interviews, and wrote the field notes).

Of course, collective mobilization had been amply studied. In 1978, Charles Tilly had published an entire book on collective action and the different forms of mobilization that characterize social movements. In particular, "defensive mobilization" could be often observed as a quasi-spontaneous initiative to gather forces against an external threat. Food riots, tax rebellions, and draft resistance could be explained this way, challenging, in Tilly's words, "the common assumption . . . that mobilization is always a top-down phenomenon, organized by leaders and agitators," as in the cases of "preparatory" and "offensive" mobilization.[57] Ten years earlier, Barrington Moore, Jr. and Eric Wolf had offered numerous examples of how this defensive response was at the root of peasant revolts.[58] These were all solidly structured studies (some of them, according to Hirschman, even *excessively* structured and not very convincing, such as Moore's work). To a greater degree than in the past, however, this time the plan was to write an essay that would retain the vividness of fresh impressions—Hirschman later described the resulting essay as more of a "reasoned travelogue" than a "scholarly treatise."[59]

Not unexpectedly, Albert and Sarah picked as their research area a continent that they knew well and with whose language they were well acquainted. To reduce logistical issues to a minimum, they secured the support of the Inter-American Foundation (IAF), a U.S. government organization established in 1969 to fund grassroots development projects undertaken by local communities in Latin America and the Caribbean as an alternative to traditional foreign aid that operated at the intergovernmental level.[60]

The trip was an opportunity for Albert to reflect on some ideas he had developed in previous books, such as how cooperatives play a supporting role for voice and a symmetrical protecting role against forced exit; how responses to pressing social, political, and economic problems can anticipate, instead of exclusively follow, "structural," all-encompassing reforms (a question discussed at length in *Journeys*); how apparently failed endeavors trigger unexpected and creative responses (a theme of both *Development Projects Observed* and *Journeys*); and how unknown and hidden resources exist in the social body that come to hand to overcome a difficult predicament (a question discussed in *The Strategy of Economic Development* and *Development Projects Observed*).

Most of all, the trip and the book that was based on it, *Getting Ahead Collectively*, offered Hirschman an opportunity to observe development projects from a perspective opposite to that adopted in *Development Projects Observed* (the donor's perspective of the World Bank). Even though the IAF financed the inquiry, Hirschman was not interested here in donor-recipient relations. The view, in fact, was neither top-down nor bottom-up. More precisely, it was at the level of those who initiated development projects on their own behalf. Hirschman, in other words, was interested in the participatory dimension of grassroots development projects—that is, how social activism emerges, and how people join forces for a common objective. He was curious to investigate the specific features of development projects characterized by strong, popular, local ownership and develop a comparative analysis of the various experiences.

Moreover, he was interested in exploring the potential of grassroots development projects to strengthen political pluralism and erode the foundations of authoritarian regimes. Crucial though the process of social aggregation was for the relationship between private and public interest, Hirschman had failed to address it in his previous book, *Shifting Involvements*. It was instead the very core of *Getting Ahead Collectively*.

Indeed, as Hirschman noted, Adam Smith had famously argued that "the desire of bettering our condition . . . though generally calm and dispassionate, comes with us from the womb and never leaves us till we go into the grave."[61] In Smith's argument, this reflection pertained primarily to individuals. But what about the collective dimension of improving living conditions? After all, Hirschman considered, "there is in fact a continuum of actions—from the wholly private to the most outspokenly public, with many intermediate and hybrid varieties in between—that . . . are all conceived and intended by the participants as means to the end of 'bettering their conditions.'"[62]

In *Getting Ahead*, Hirschman's attention is entirely captured by collective action—what triggers it and what its consequences are. In particular, Hirschman was interested in bringing to light the unexpected mechanisms and inverted sequences that grassroots collective action puts in motion. Of equal interest was which processes are conducive to the emergence of collective endeavors in the first place.

One easy answer is that adversities pressure individuals to join forces. Changing conditions of the natural landscape, such as a rising river that suddenly begins to threaten a nearby settlement, are an obvious example. Hirschman noted how the dislocation of a few peasant families who lived close to a river in the region of Córdoba, Argentina, had put in motion an entire process that deeply transformed not only the lives of the families singularly taken, but the social context in which they were embedded. In their new location, far removed from the river, those few families, which had always had access to potable water, soon faced the distressing situation of a chronic lack of water; as a reaction, they collaborated to build a communal water supply system. But the consequences went further. The success in building the water distribution network and the reliability of the system, in turn, made it possible to accept new families and broaden the community. As a result of a cooperative endeavor to evacuate a dangerous area, an anonymous settlement of poor houses became in a few years a small village with its own name: La Merced.

More than aggression by nature, however, Hirschman was interested in how groups would react to aggression by others. Unsurprisingly, land ownership was a crucial question in Latin America, and fraud and litigation about title to ownership have never been in short supply. Hirschman highlighted how the common fight for land ownership often triggered a number of other communal endeavors that would not otherwise have been undertaken, such as the improvement of public utilities, the construction of a communal meeting place, and cultural and educational activities.

Notably, Hirschman did not explain these developments in terms of the theory according to which ownership title changes the economic incentives of peasants, who now have a direct interest in improving the capital endowment of their own land. Hirschman showed instead the sequence of additional and unexpected social benefits that an initial cooperative action was able to trigger. The very act of cooperating brought to the surface initiatives and forces that had hitherto remained dormant. It is not by chance that Hirschman highlighted how many communal activities besides the common fight for ownership began *before* ownership was secured, as a direct consequence of the bond construed by the struggle itself. They were, in other words, the outcome of a social experience, not an economic one. Besides reorganization of land plots, the construction of a small dam, and the planning of a consumer store, Hirschman noted, "the art of discussion and joint decision-making was being slowly acquired."[63] Describing the aggressive attempt by the Chilean military regime to dismantle the communal property and working of the land by the Mapuche population in the south of the country, Hirschman highlighted the "new feeling of solidarity and desire for collective advance" that the policies of the military government had inadvertently aroused.[64]

Throughout the book, Hirschman remarked on the limitations of economic reasoning to explain the logic and functioning of grassroots activism. A strictly economic explanation for the birth of cooperative enterprises would probably have focused on the need to mobilize a minimal amount of capital. Yet Hirschman's examples suggested that "a more fundamental need is . . . some experience dispelling isolation and mutual distrust."[65] Indeed, in his view, grassroots development arose from "a revulsion against the worship of the 'gross national product' and of the 'rate of growth' as unique arbiters of economic and human progress."[66]

Against these macroeconomic measures, grassroots development was in fact a reaffirmation of the need for social interaction and cooperation at the micro level. Not for the first time, Hirschman was on the same wavelength as O'Donnell, who only one year before had argued that "besides the crucial importance of 'grand politics', that takes place on the grand scenarios of national life," it was also important to "explore the feedback loop mechanisms that the spreading of democratic values and practices at both levels—*macro* and *micro*—could generate."[67]

As an addendum to the critique of cost-benefit analysis that he had been articulating since the mid-1960s, in particular in *Development Projects Observed*, Hirschman underlined the importance of "intangible" costs and benefits of cooperative endeavors, which were, in his view, at least as relevant as direct economic costs and benefits. Among the costs, for example, one should consider a certain loss of freedom for the participants, whose power to buy and sell in the market would necessarily be limited. But on the other side of the coin were intangible benefits. If successful, a cooperative not only would improve the material life of its members and make them stronger against aggression from more powerful forces, but it would also carry a "symbolic value"; it would be "an act of self-affirmation that fills people with pride" and could represent "a beginning of liberation [for] long-suffering and long-oppressed groups."[68]

Clearly, Hirschman took particular pleasure in the cooperative response to fraudulent schemes to dispossess peasants of their land, or aggressive policies to change or obliterate their culture. "Occasionally it happens that the common experience of having been taken advantage of, swindled or

FIGURE 7.1 Albert and Sarah Hirschman, Dominican Republic, during their field trip for *Getting Ahead Collectively*, 1983. Courtesy of Katia Salomon

otherwise hurt," he wrote, "will lead to some collective reaction that takes the perpetrators by surprise."[69] There is an echo here of Hirschman's definition of the reform monger, penned twenty years before in *Journeys*: "the chessplayer who exasperatingly fights on when 'objectively' he has already lost—and occasionally goes on to win!"[70] The dignity intrinsic in the reaction and the surplus of satisfaction if the reaction is successful were very important elements to Hirschman's sensibility: "The poor are used to their poverty which they bear in silence and isolation, but the fact of being treated with *injustice* can bring out unsuspected capacities for indignation, resistance and common action."[71]

Yet the unexpected mobilization of hidden social resources and the unsuspected capacity for communal resistance probably were not Hirschman's most important discoveries from the trip. Perhaps the more striking characteristic that emerged from Albert and Sarah's conversations with participants in grassroots development projects was that, in one way or another, they had all had previous experiences of social activism. This did not necessarily mean previous experience in cooperatives or struggles. Indeed, Hirschman noted that many people with whom he and Sarah spoke had stressed the importance of soccer for their socialization, and how participation in the planning and joint construction of a soccer field for the community was often their first experience of activism, providing them with the ability and confidence to address more difficult projects.[72]

Whatever the original experience, as Hirschman put it, "it is as though the protagonists' earlier aspiration for social change, their bent for collective action, had not really left them."[73] The interesting thing to Hirschman was that this "social energy" would probably reappear later in different forms, thus making it difficult to relate the latter experience to the former. "It may therefore be quite difficult to notice," Hirschman concluded, "that we have here a special kind of sequence, a *renewal* of energy rather than a wholly new outbreak."[74] Out of apparently disconnected episodes of social discontent and reaction against unbearable or unjust conditions, Hirschman saw a pattern emerging that resonated particularly well with his reformist vision and possibilist attitude. He called it the Principle of Conservation and Mutation of Social Energy.

As he had already showed with the Principle of the Hiding Hand that opened his 1967 book, *Development Projects Observed*, Hirschman's enunciation of principles of social change affirmed as much as debased the existence of rules of conduct in social behavior. As mentioned, in his 1994 preface to the new edition of *Development Projects Observed*, Hirschman confessed that giving pride of place as first chapter of the book to the Principle of the Hiding Hand was "close to a provocation."[75] In a similar move, Hirschman immediately disclaimed any universal validity for this newly baptized Principle of Conservation and Mutation of Social Energy. Yet it was rhetorically effective, as Hirschman's point was to direct the reader's attention to the persistence (or, as he put it, conservation) of an attitude of social activism in the life of individuals, and to their ability to socialize this attitude.

This does not necessarily contradict Hirschman's earlier observation that often an aggressive episode, whether from nature or people, would trigger a communal response from individuals who were previously separated. Hirschman's principle, after all, was as much about the mutation of social energy as about its conservation. The experience of social activism and mobilization was thus like a karst river, at times visible and strong, at times hidden underground, only to reappear unexpectedly, often after a tortuous and unpredictable course.

Going back to the story of the Cristo Rey fishermen, for example, Hirschman wondered, "could it have happened without that first step, the failed attempt to seize the land?"[76] Seizing land required perhaps more courage, as it implied a direct confrontation with the landowner and the police or militias. Starting a fishing cooperative, however, was a far more complicated affair. Past experience, in a sense, had served to build a connection and a vision, even if the specific attempt had failed. Then, "having . . . created a *vision of change*, [the Cristo Rey peasants] were now ready for joint endeavours that required much greater sophistication and persistence."[77]

The same mechanism accounted for numerous other cases that the Hirschmans encountered. Moreover, Hirschman noticed that this principle was a fitting argument against what he had once dubbed *fracasomania*. Clearly, postulating a connection between failed attempts at social reform or mobilization and the creation of social energy that would later prompt a successful endeavor eroded the very foundations of that gloomy failure complex.

At the aggregate level, too, Hirschman individuated the contours of a process of formation and diffusion of welfare services that, though not particularly linear, was far from ineffective. If in more advanced countries local private efforts at social promotion had often played a bellwether role for subsequent comprehensive government initiatives, in Latin American countries the path to social welfare followed a more oscillatory trajectory. In the absence of a strong middle class, usually this process began with some state-led reformist initiatives, which created a bureaucracy specialized in the new sector of welfare promotion. Later on, when the reformist phase came to an end, the welfare bureaucracy and state agencies would try to continue their work in a private capacity. A new network of associations and cooperatives—often connected in a continuum of corporate relations, funding, and policy making to a broader international network—would thus emerge, complementing or, more often, substituting for the national government in the supply of welfare services.[78] This is another example of Hirschman's eye for "inverted sequences," or an adaptation of Gerschenkron's "substitute factors" in late-industrializing countries. As in other cases—most notably in *Journeys*—Hirschman rejected the failure narrative to embrace instead the idea of a Latin American way to welfare promotion.

Things could also go sour, however. As Judith Tendler showed in a very lucid report just before Hirschman's book appeared, it can happen that the government later reenters the social sector previously occupied by local activist organizations. In these cases, tensions are likely to arise: "When governments suddenly move into areas previously occupied peacefully by PVOs [private voluntary organizations]," Tendler wrote, "they sometimes find it difficult to tolerate the power or prestige that the PVO has come to hold in that area. Bad relations may ensue."[79] To complicate things further, the return to a pluralist regime and the substitution of a reformist for a repressive government could abruptly change the political significance of the local activist endeavor: "Whereas under the repressive government the PVO may be considered reformist, a sole defender of the poor, it may suddenly look reactionary under the new government."[80]

Two additional comments are in order. First, it should be noted that Hirschman's interest in the subject of welfare services overlapped to a considerable extent with the recent emergence of a "basic needs" approach in the development discourse, as well as with the new focus on human rights as global discourse. Both emerged (or at least acquired new visibility) in the second half of the 1970s.[81] In Hirschman's synthesis, a "new set of human rights"—food, access to potable water, shelter, education, health care, and participation in decision making—now complemented the widely accepted rights to religion, expression, and personal freedom. "The wide distance separating the actual conditions of life of countless Latin Americans from what is increasingly felt as the conditions to which they have a *right*," Hirschman concluded, "is the source of the enormous tensions in that continent."[82] Perceptive though this comment on the intersection of the development discourse and the more recent human rights discourse was, Hirschman did not elaborate further.

More relevant to Albert and Sarah's analysis was instead the issue of democracy. A central question underlying their recent trip to Latin America was whether grassroots development projects were affecting in any way the broader political landscape of Latin American countries. The answer was decisively in the positive. In particular, Hirschman noted the highly private dimension of many (though by no means all) Latin American authoritarian regimes between the 1960s and the 1970s, which depended for their stability on the "thorough *privatization* of their citizens' lives."[83] Unlike totalitarian regimes, in which the masses were on permanent mobilization, Latin American regimes tended to demobilize masses and to push the individual into the private sphere. Often regimes accepted initiatives of social promotion as diversionary, apolitical endeavors that would therefore distract citizens from political participation. As Tendler put it, "PVOs may be the only tolerated form of assistance to and organization among the poor."[84] Governments, however, might not realize that the very act of associating into a cooperative, even though within the limits of an exclusive focus on social issues and with no direct political demands, would help the diffusion of a "*more caring* and *less private*" set of social relations, intrinsically at odds with the "very structural requirements of those regimes."[85] Grassroots activism, in other words, had become a "dangerous Trojan Horse" for democratic values in authoritarian regimes.[86]

In this perspective, Hirschman's book filled a void in the literature. The focus of social scientists working on rural Latin America was preponderantly on the most visible and dramatic expressions of agrarian discontent, such as revolts, land occupations, and rural violence. The study of rural grassroots movements that aimed at implementing viable reforms of the economic, social, and political practices without depending on government initiatives was much less cultivated. Hirschman's 1984 essay was a contribution to redirecting attention to these less dramatic but nonetheless crucial initiatives.[87]

Once again, it is worth mentioning Hirschman's penchant for analyses that unfold as a search for potential mechanisms of change and grassroots reforms. Consider, as a comparison, Tendler's gloomier rendition of social cooperatives in Latin America, published in 1983 by the same IAF that supported Hirschman's trip:

Coops, if successful, can turn into the very monster that they are supposed to slay. They may preach the rhetoric of participation and community mindedness, while in truth catering to a small and better-off portion of the population they say they represent. . . . Though the good qualities may seem to inhere in an activity, they will often be present only at certain stages of a coop's history, and only in certain social and economic environments.[88]

The difference in tone and prospects could not be more startling, and there is no doubt that critics could easily prove Hirschman's sample biased by an excess of optimism, or more technically by the error of having built his sample on the dependent variable—that is, of having cherry-picked grassroots cooperatives that had proved successful in order to demonstrate that successful grassroots activism in Latin America is a reality.

Indeed, this criticism would not be off the mark, but it does not mean that Hirschman's study is therefore devoid of any value (as critics of *Development Projects Observed* claimed on very similar bases). More simply, Hirschman's interest resided in what might work—losing in comprehensiveness, perhaps, but gaining in reformist insight.

Tendler and Hirschman had a very similar approach to the study of development sequences, and a very consonant view about the importance of the relationship between economic and political dynamics. They shared the same liberal values, and it is worth remembering here that Tendler—by the early 1980s an accomplished scholar—had written her PhD dissertation in the mid-1960s under Hirschman's supervision. The point here is not that their analyses were mutually at variance; in fact, they were not. Tendler's report held that most cooperative enterprises ultimately had a positive social impact, even though they did not apply the cooperative principles they proclaimed.

The specificity of Hirschman's analysis (both its uniqueness and its limit) resided in a conscious choice to emphasize what worked or might have worked, sacrificing other perspectives. Indeed, only a few months after the publication of *Getting Ahead Collectively*, at a conference in São Paulo, Hirschman made explicit what had remained implicit, though quite apparent, in the book—that he was "think[ing] of the possible rather than of the probable."[89]

In the end, Hirschman remained somewhat ambivalent with regard to the possibilities of actual democratization in Latin America. Despite the recent demise of apparently solid authoritarian regimes in Ecuador (1977–1979), Peru (1978–1980), Bolivia (1982), Argentina (1983), Uruguay (1984), and Brazil (1984), Hirschman felt obliged to open his remarks at the São Paulo conference by saying, "The point of departure of any serious thought about the chances for the consolidation of democracy in Latin America must surely be pessimism."[90] As the most important characteristic of Latin American politics was instability, there was no guarantee that this new "democratic wave" (to borrow a later expression of Samuel Huntington) would not quickly and unexpectedly recede. Previous waves, after all, had been followed by authoritarian backlashes in a cyclical pattern particularly characteristic of Latin American countries. Huntington described this pattern as an oscillation between populist democratic governments and conservative military regimes. "In these countries," as Huntington put it with a distinct taste for paradox, "the change of regime thus performs the same function as the change of parties in a stable democratic system. The country does not alternate between democratic and authoritarian political systems; the alternation of democracy and authoritarianism *is* the country's political system."[91]

Yet, despite his cautious position, Hirschman could not help looking for those "narrow paths" and "partial advances" that might strengthen the process of democratization.[92] In particular, in São Paulo he emphasized the importance of uncertainty, with two different but complementary inflections. First, uncertainty of outcomes is a normal and unavoidable feature of democratic policy making, because pluralist elections can steer the country in one direction or an altogether different one. Only authoritarian regimes know (or pretend to know) where they are going. Second, and even more important, a truly democratic process of decision making entails that ideas are formed through the deliberative process itself. Following French political scientist Bernard Manin, Hirschman thus highlighted the importance, on the part of citizens and politicians, of recognizing that uncertainty about the proper course to take is a fundamental element of democratic deliberation. Again, only authoritarian regimes pretend to know better. As Hirschman put it, "the total absence of this sort of uncertainty, the lack of openness to new information and to the opinion of others, is a real danger to the functioning of democratic society."[93]

This aversion to the intrinsically open paths of democratic politics and the new possibilities that may appear through a free exchange of ideas and the deliberative process—in other words, this intransigent attitude— remained a central question for Hirschman in the years to come. While he continued to work on Latin American issues and other occasional writings, the deterioration of democratic discourse as a result of intransigent, closed, nondialogic attitudes became a central issue in his reflections.[94] Exhilarating though the fall of the Berlin Wall was, Hirschman saw other, less visible, but nonetheless dangerous walls rise between different parts of the body politic. His subsequent book was thus entirely devoted to dissecting and unveiling the rhetorical mechanisms of intransigent political discourse.

ARGUMENTS AGAINST INTRANSIGENT POLITICS:
THE RHETORIC OF REACTION

The election of Ronald Reagan as the fortieth president of the United States on November 4, 1980, marked a significant shift away from social welfare policies that had been in place since the years of the New Deal. In particular, legislative and budgetary changes in 1981 and 1982 significantly cut resources for the programs targeting the poorest strata of the population. As far as the future of the American welfare state was concerned, Reagan's reelection in November 1984 did not bode well.

Disenchantment with social welfare policies, which had started in the 1970s, intensified throughout the 1980s. Many saw the Great Society and the War on Poverty, as two observers put it toward the end of the 1980s, as "well-intentioned failures" at best, characterized by "ivory tower naïveté in program design, bureaucratic lethargy and cooptation by special interests in program implementation, and trivial achievements, unintended consequences, and reinforced pathologies in program outcomes."[95] Policy studies critical of social welfare programs far outnumbered positive assessments, and this attitude spanned the entire political spectrum: "Conservatives perceive vindication of the folly of government intervention; radicals see repressive social control and cooptation; and increasingly, liberals have shifted from an upbeat vision of muddling through to a diagnosis of mucking up and have distanced themselves from past optimism by rechristening themselves 'progressives.' "[96]

To be sure, defendants of the American welfare system existed, but they also felt that it had been, if anything, a "hidden success," as the title of one book put it.[97] The most popular analysis of the issue, however, was the highly critical book by Charles Murray, *Losing Ground*, published in 1984. In it, Murray argued that in the 1960s, basic indicators of the well-being of individuals in the United States took a turn for the worse, and this happened "most consistently and most drastically for the poor."[98] The reason, he claimed, was that welfare programs had changed "the rules of the game" and thus the incentives for making a living, raising a family, and shaping one's own life. "The error was strategic," he wrote, as the poor now had an incentive to behave in the short term in ways that would be destructive in the long term; to add insult to injury, the provision of welfare benefits hid this fundamental mistake from sight. Murray concluded, "We tried to provide more for the poor and produced more poor instead. We tried to remove the barriers to escape from poverty, and inadvertently built a trap."[99]

The Ford Foundation reacted to this growing feeling of disillusionment and frustration by launching, in 1985, a special initiative called the Project on Social Welfare and the American Future. A panel of experts from academia and the private sector was established to produce policy recommendations on how to improve the welfare system in the United States; Hirschman was invited to join. The panel recognized the many shortcomings in the welfare system. The final report stated, "Gaps in health insurance coverage, the lack of coordinated skill-development efforts to meet the needs of a changing work force, and the high costs of long-term care suggest the need to review the appropriateness of our social welfare system."[100] The question, however, was how the system could be reformed and improved, not torn apart, as the conservatives suggested.

As the drafter of the final report put it, the United States was facing a "social deficit" that called for a holistic look at welfare policies instead of piecemeal discussions about different welfare jurisdictions: "We feel that social problems are interrelated, and that we all need the social welfare system at some point in our lives. It isn't something for someone else . . . a good investment in children helps adults, and a good investment in senior citizens helps all of us who are their children and grandchildren." According to the panel, the programs created between the 1930s and the 1960s were well conceived but belonged to a different epoch. The system should not be dismantled, but it needed to be thoroughly modernized.[101]

In addition to the collective work of the panel of experts, the Ford Foundation supported a number of independent studies to contribute specific policy proposals. Political scientist and historian Ira Katznelson, for example, explored critical junctures in the history of state building in the United States, while sociologist Theda Skocpol worked on "The Politics of Social Provision in the United States." They both published a number of works related to these subjects throughout the 1990s.[102]

The reflection initiated by the Ford Foundation became for Hirschman an opportunity to study the rhetorical structure of the arguments against the welfare system. This analysis would become the subject of his 1991 book, *The Rhetoric of Reaction*. As a liberal in the United States, Hirschman recounted in the preface to the book, he was concerned by the virulent neoconservative attacks on social welfare policies. Beyond different opinions about specific policies, Hirschman was puzzled by what looked like a deeper and apparently irreparable cleavage between liberal and conservative views on some basic elements of society. Hirschman, however, purposefully avoided trying to "inquire into the conservative mind," choosing instead to focus on the surface, the rhetorical phenomena that characterized conservative discourse—and, as we will see, progressive rhetoric as well—in the hope of enhancing communication between opposed camps.[103]

In a sense, *The Rhetoric of Reaction* is an essay on the political misuses of a fundamental concept in the social sciences—the unintended consequences of social action. In 1936, sociologist Robert K. Merton had written a short article on "The Unanticipated Consequences of Purposive Social Action" that immediately became a classic; he was the first to recognize that, though in different contexts and using different terms, "the problem of the unanticipated consequences of purposive action has been treated by virtually every substantial contributor to the long history of social thought."[104] Hirschman's book is a learned and sophisticated analysis of the many variations of unintended consequences, and the differences and logical incompatibilities that exist among them.

The structure of the book is very simple. Hirschman's starting point is a 1949 lecture by British sociologist Thomas H. Marshall on the progression of citizenship rights in England. Marshall identified three different dimensions of citizenship—the civil, the political, and the social. Each dimension gained center stage and became a matter of contention between progressives and conservatives in different epochs. Civil citizenship was conquered in the eighteenth century with the end of the absolutist age, establishing new values and freedoms. Political citizenship—that is, the right to vote—expanded enormously throughout the nineteenth century. Finally, the twentieth century witnessed the blossoming of a new idea of social citizenship, embodied in the institutions of the welfare state. Marshall delivered his lecture in the aftermath of World War II, precisely when the welfare state was taking off in Britain thanks to the work of Lord Beveridge and the Labour Party cabinet, but the 1970s and the 1980s showed all the difficulties of preserving and improving this third element of citizenship. Moreover, Hirschman noted, this backlash was not exclusive to the third phase. In fact, one could easily argue that each step forward in the extension of citizenship had faced a barrage of conservative reaction.

Hirschman discerned three different formal types of reactionary theses. He explained, tongue in cheek, "I must have an inbred urge toward symmetry. In canvassing for the principal ways of criticizing, assaulting, and ridiculing the three successive 'progressive' thrusts of Marshall's story, I have come up with another triad."[105] These three reactionary theses Hirschman labeled the *perversity thesis*, the *futility thesis*, and the *jeopardy thesis*. Though they shared a certain family resemblance, the three theses were clearly different:

According to the *perversity* thesis, any purposive action to improve some feature of the political, social, or economic order only serves to exacerbate the condition one wishes to remedy. The *futility* thesis holds that attempts at social transformation will be unavailing, that they will simply fail to "make a dent." Finally, the *jeopardy* thesis argues that the cost of the proposed change or reform is too high as it endangers some previous, precious accomplishment.[106]

Having set the stage of three phases of civil, political, and social advancement (as proposed by Marshall) and three reactionary arguments against each of these advancements, Hirschman proceeded in the central chapters of the book to explore how each argument had unfolded in the three historical phases. Hirschman's intention was not to reject the possibility that unintended negative consequences could follow social and political initiatives; his point was to expose the "systematic biases" of a certain political rhetoric.[107]

Along with *The Passions and the Interests*, *The Rhetoric of Reaction* is one of Hirschman's most accessible books. Both center on the history of ideas and a literature strongly rooted in modern European thought; even though they appeared fifteen years apart, they are strongly related and appeal to readers with many different interests. A few elements stand out in Hirschman's discussion that complicate the seemingly neat three-phases-by-three-theses matrix.

Discussing the perversity thesis, Hirschman noted that it stemmed from an important turnaround in the historical development of the more catholic concept of "unintended consequences." During the seventeenth and a large part of the eighteenth century, the most common discussions of unintended consequences highlighted how selfish and morally deplorable passions could in many cases produce positive social outcomes. One of the most famous examples is Adam Smith's often quoted passage from the early chapters of his *Wealth of Nations*: "It is not from the benevolence of the butcher, the brewer, or the baker that we expect our dinner, but from their regard to their own interest. We address ourselves, not to their humanity but to their self-love, and never talk to them of our own necessities but of their advantages."[108]

But Smith was one of the last to use this concept from this positive perspective. The political and social revolutions of the late eighteenth century turned the principal meaning of unintended consequences from a mainly benign to a decisively negative connotation. This shift in meaning, Hirschman claimed, was not a mere variant of basically the same idea, but a fundamental transformation of it, indeed "its denial and betrayal." As Hirschman put it, "the concept of unintended consequences originally introduced uncertainty and open-endedness into social thought," whereas those who consider it the source of a mainly perverse effect "retreat to viewing the social universe as once again wholly predictable."[109]

In his book, Hirschman noted how the perversity thesis drew strength from its affinity to the plots of old myths, such as the story of Oedipus, or the sequence hubris-nemesis (haughtiness that leads to punishment); at about the same time, his colleague Amartya Sen, at Darwin College in Cambridge, proposed an interesting development of the concept, stemming from the influence of the Darwinian theory of natural selection on contemporary social and political thought. The idea of natural selection shows how the progress of species emerges as a by-product of the struggle for survival. By focusing on "adapting the species" instead of "adjusting the environment" in which the species lives, this theory also invites social Darwinists to consider any attempt at purposive social change as an undue interference of the "natural" mechanisms of social coordination—and as such bound to produce perverse effects.[110]

One possible unintended consequence of social action is the outright lack of consequences. This is Hirschman's futility thesis, and, in this sense, it could be considered simply a variation on the broader theme of unintended effects. If we juxtapose it to the perverse effect, however, we discover a sharp distinction: they are two basically opposed ways of thinking about how human actions affect the social order. The perversity effect implies a highly volatile social order, which reacts unexpectedly and perversely to any attempt to change it. On the contrary, the futility effect implies a social order that is stable and apparently immutable; no matter how strongly one tries to change it, the effects will be null. In the former case, human action triggers all possible negative effects; in the latter, human action is simply impotent to produce any effect at all—which, Hirschman adds, may explain why the futility thesis is so insulting to the advocates of change.[111]

Though Hirschman discussed all three of his theses across different historical phases, the jeopardy effect is unquestionably the most complex from a historical perspective. In *The Rhetoric of Reaction*, Hirschman discussed in great detail the Reform Bills adopted in England in 1832 and 1867 that deeply transformed that country's electoral system, showing that the argument according to which the democratization of the English political system would jeopardize the preservation of individual liberties was indeed pervasive—and ultimately wrong. On the same basis, Hirschman denounced the conservative rhetoric against the welfare state in the mid-twentieth century, according to which the welfare state would endanger individual liberties and indeed democratic governance. It was easy for Hirschman to list a number of other events as more credible causes of the political instability or "malaise" that hit Western democracies in the 1970s: the Watergate scandal, the weakness of both Conservative and Labour cabinets in Great Britain, or political terrorism in West Germany and Italy.[112] The historical dimension of this chapter later prompted Hirschman to explore further variations of the jeopardy thesis, such as when sequences of political and economic reforms risk "getting stuck" because of the very characteristics that were instrumental to advancing reform at an earlier phase.[113]

But the analysis of the jeopardy thesis is particularly interesting for yet another reason—namely, the surprising new perspective that it revealed to Hirschman himself about the fundamental thesis of his book. Writing the chapter on the jeopardy thesis, Hirschman recognized that the thesis is not simply an element of reactionary rhetoric but a broader rhetorical posture that also applied to progressive discourse. The reactionary version states that a new reform would jeopardize an older and more important accomplishment; the progressive version claims that the new reform is necessary to solidify the previous one.

This new—and unanticipated—twist in Hirschman's reflection opened the door to a full reassessment of his analysis: besides the jeopardy thesis, the perversity and futility theses also have their progressive counterparts. Against the perversity thesis of the reactionaries, progressives would claim that change is imperative to prevent the total ruin of the social and political order. Against the futility thesis, progressives would claim that change is unavoidable because the "laws" of history demand it, and it would be futile to oppose them. This was a particularly clear instance of what Hirschman would call, only one year after the publication of *The Rhetoric of Reaction*, his propensity for self-subversion—that is, his tendency substantially to reconsider his own analysis to reveal previously unseen elements that go in unexpected and indeed sometimes opposite directions with respect to the original analysis (as this is a central element of Hirschman's style as a social scientist, more will be said about it in the next chapter).

The discovery of a "progressive" rhetoric of reaction had direct implications for the debate within the reformist camp. Hirschman's message for a reformist, progressive agenda was essentially to highlight the importance of self-restraint in the use of rhetorical arguments. Impeding disaster (the anti-perversity thesis) is not a positive argument for change. Much more enticing would be to focus on the beneficial effects of a proposed reform rather than on an assessment of least damage. By the time the book appeared, moreover, the allegedly ironclad "laws" of history (the anti-futility thesis) had been discredited by the sudden fall of the Communist world. "With the latest upheavals and *pace* Francis Fukuyama," quipped Hirschman, "the tide of history appears to run quite strongly against the tide-of-history view of history!"[114] The solidification-of-previous-reforms argument (the anti-jeopardy thesis) is, in fact, not unreasonable; we can find several applications of it in Hirschman's previous works (such as his analysis of reformist policies in Latin America in *Journeys Toward Progress*). Yet even this rhetorical thesis must be handled with caution, Hirschman insisted, as possible conflicts can easily arise between different policies that, though belonging to the reformist agenda, nonetheless show important trade-offs. It would be disingenuous and naïve, for instance, to pretend that conflicts or frictions cannot arise between the goals of stimulating growth and correcting inequality.

But worse than political disingenuity, for Hirschman, was the danger that progressive politics might turn into some sort of authoritarian attitude. He explained, "The conviction, born from the mutual benefit thesis, that a given reform carries no conceivable cost and that therefore nothing stands in its way can easily shade over the feeling that nothing *should* stand in its way."[115] As a consequence, if a conflict between different goals arises, single-minded reformists might consider other policies as obstacles to be removed, whatever the cost. "The advocates of that change will then be tempted to act in accordance with the maxim 'the end justifies the means' and may well *prove the jeopardy thesis right* by their willingness to sacrifice positive accomplishments of their society for the sake of the specific forward step on which they have set their hearts."[116] This attitude runs counter to the very core of democratic deliberation, whose essence, Hirschman insisted, is compromise. In the end, Hirschman's book had changed its nature, from an essay on reactionary rhetoric to a broader study of "the rhetoric of intransigence."[117] Harvard University Press objected to this proposed new title (*intransigence* was considered too difficult a word for the American public), but the Brazilian, Italian, and Mexican translations appeared with the (plural) title *Rhetorics of Intransigence*.

Hirschman's triad, not unexpectedly, gained some currency, and has since been used in many different fields, not only in analyses of debates about welfare policies in the United States and elsewhere, but also in discussions of economic restructuring in South Africa and about the enduring relevance of Marxist thought.[118]

Several readers considered the book and its style "vintage Hirschman . . . learned, elegant, insightful" and "big-think intellectual stimulation."[119] The focus on the rhetorical dimension was also appreciated, not only because of the learned discussion of rhetorical *topoi*, but also because Hirschman tied his classification to a compelling discussion of what a commentator described as "the typical rhetorical situation for the reactionary, that of being unable to oppose some change in principle, yet wanting to oppose it anyway."[120]

But precisely on this point—that is, his rhetorical strategy—opinions varied. Even sympathetic reviewers were unconvinced by Hirschman's decision to focus exclusively on rhetoric. John DiIulio, Jr., for example, a professor of politics and public affairs and director of the Center of Domestic and Comparative Policy Studies at Princeton University, noted that this tight focus implied that the choice between reactionary and progressive arguments was mainly ideological in nature and that "the facts about the efficacy of public policies can rarely, if ever, speak clearly for themselves." But, he concluded, "except for dyed-in-the-wool ideologues . . . that is simply not the case."[121] The *Harvard Law Review* published a similar criticism. The sole focus on the rhetorical aspect of political debate was an exercise in labeling, but "such a label does not tell us, however, whether the argument is a persuasive one—that is, whether the negative effects do in fact outweigh the positive one."[122]

Others questioned the very foundations of Hirschman's project. As Hirschman wrote in the preface, his was an attempt at exposing how political discourse is often shaped "not so much by fundamental personality traits, but simply by the imperatives of argument." He hoped that "exposing these servitudes might actually help to loosen them and thus modify the discourse and restore communication" between opposing political factions.[123] But many wondered whether it was at all possible to distinguish the rhetorical dimension from the substantive "core" of a political argument. One reviewer wrote:

To counsel . . . that public deliberations should be technically sophisticated and rhetorically fair is to miss an important point about democracy. In permitting a vigorous contest by partisans for citizens' hearts and minds, democratic institutions invite rhetorical excesses and abuses of all kinds, the more so as information and patterns of communication become richer and more complex. . . . The task, as always, is to sharpen the persuasive power of rational argument.[124]

Another asked, "Isn't conflict over single issues and a basic ideological bipartisanship the norm?"[125] Hirschman, in other words, was accused of being either naïve, in his hope that a call for more rhetorical self-consciousness could somehow elevate the political discourse, or disingenuous, in that exposing reactionary rhetoric was per se a rhetorical move.

Cambridge political theorist John Dunn, sympathetic to Hirschman and the book, also highlighted this problem. Dunn noted that, as in the case of *The Passions and the Interests*, Hirschman's use of historical sources was aimed not so much at recapturing old debates as at finding shapes of argument that might be useful for his specific analytical project. This "serenely opportunistic exploitation" of the cherished preserves of historians of ideas, Dunn wrote, had been particularly successful in the 1977 book, but in *The Rhetoric of Reaction* it seemed less convincing and not entirely free from the suspicion of being self-serving. The focus on rhetoric, Dunn wrote, "serves admirably to sharpen sensitivity to the fallacies of political opponents. But it also serves to broaden sensitivity to the ease with which it is possible for one's political friends (or indeed oneself) to err in the same fashion."[126]

In sum, readers pointed out a potentially ambiguous position on the part of Hirschman. While his stated project was to deflate the rhetoric of intransigence and build a bridge between opposing factions, it seemed that he had not been immune from using his analysis of rhetoric to attack and ridicule conservative positions, debasing their legitimacy irrespective of the specific contents of their argument.

One particularly harsh rebuttal came from Raymond Boudon, who was in total disagreement with Hirschman's book. He wrote, "We must of course recognize that the three rhetorical themes which hold the attention of our author . . . are of frequent use. But my agreement with Hirschman ends here."[127] A long list of criticisms followed. Not only did Boudon find Hirschman's choice of rhetorical principles arbitrarily limited to a small sample of figures, but the very goal of discussing "reactionary" rhetoric seemed to Boudon misplaced: rhetoric, like language, is inseparable from political discourse, and actors at every conceivable position on the political spectrum use it. As Boudon put it, "there is not 'reactionary' rhetoric and 'progressive' rhetoric, but only rhetoric *tout court*."[128]

Boudon also accused Hirschman of confounding rhetorical figures and substantive analysis. Tocqueville, he argued, could reconcile the good intentions of the French revolutionaries with the atrocities that were perpetrated in the name of the Revolution only by referring to the concept of perverse effect. But was this a rhetorical device or a more substantive interpretative category? According to Boudon, the subtleties of the relationship between rhetorical and cognitive arguments seemed to "elude" Hirschman.[129] Moreover, he charged Hirschman with having conflated in the same category of reactionary thinkers figures as different as Joseph De Maistre (an actual reactionary) and Tocqueville (a conservative).

Boudon verged on accusing Hirschman not simply of naïveté or weak scholarship but, more disturbingly, of bad faith, writing: "Every sociologist knows . . . that whatever the position of political discourse on the ideological continuum, it cannot do without ideology or rhetoric. He also knows that the most common rhetorical method is to suggest that rhetoric is the work of others."[130] Boudon concluded:

What is clear from his book . . . is that Albert Hirschman does not like either the American conservatives or the conservatives in general. This feeling is as legitimate as any other and he is not the only one to experience it. But why the hell (*pourquoi diable*) not to have led a critical discussion or a frank attack against them, rather than resort to the oblique methods of what one is entitled to call— *horresco referens*—the "rhetoric" of suspicion?[131]

It is unclear why Boudon decided to attack Hirschman head-on. He had found *Shifting Involvements* weak, and perhaps this second disappointment was more than he could bear. Adelman mentions envy and resentment, as Hirschman had apparently failed to make the "proper genuflections" and pay respect to Boudon's own discussion of perverse effects and unintended consequences.[132] It is evident, in any case, that the clash was loud and unpleasant. In his reply, Hirschman wrote that "the vindictive tone of Boudon's article prevents me from dodging polemics."[133] Hirschman felt accused both of having said things that he never said, and, even more unusually, of having failed to say things that in fact he did say, and proceeded to counter the many accusation with equal harshness. He rejected, for example, the suggestion that he failed to notice the profound difference between reactionary and conservative thought, as Boudon alleged. Maistre, Hirschman noted, had been discussed in *Rhetoric of Reaction* as perhaps the purest representative of the thesis of the perverse effect, while Tocqueville was a representative of the futility thesis. "The difference between these two theses seems fundamental to me," Hirschman added, but "Boudon can invoke an attenuating circumstance: he does not seem to have understood this difference."[134]

Historian Jerry Muller, a deeply learned scholar of capitalism and the history of ideas and a longtime admirer of Hirschman, rejected outright the idea that Hirschman might have been moved by bad faith or disingenuousness. Nonetheless, he found the book particularly disappointing because of the confusion it created between an apparently detached analysis of rhetorical figures and Hirschman's attacks on conservative positions throughout the book. Muller lamented, in particular, the huge gap between Hirschman's presentation of the arguments offered by reactionary authors and their actual claims; this was, he wrote, "among the most disturbing features" of the book.[135] In the end, Muller argued, if Hirschman's goal was to contribute to a more respectful and constructive public debate, the outcome was a failure. *The Rhetoric of Reaction*, he wrote, "explains to progressives why they need not deal with conservatives at all, indeed why conservatives should be excluded from serious intellectual debate. . . . Hirschman's negative psychological characterization of 'reactionaries' reinforces the stigmatization of conservatives, and this in turn makes those who regard themselves as liberals less likely to question viewpoints presented as progressive, for fear of being called conservative, neoconservative, or reactionary."[136]

Muller explained the failure of the book as what economic historian David Landes termed "the echo-chamber effect"—a feedback loop mechanism in which one's own perceptions about the world are "consistently reinforced by communicating exclusively with others who share their basic assumptions."[137] Judging from the information available in the preface and the acknowledgments, Hirschman does not seem to have discussed his draft with conservative colleagues or audiences. At the beginning of *Rhetoric*, Hirschman borrows a sentence from a short story by Jamaica Kincaid he had read in the *New Yorker*: "How does a person get to be that way?" Not without disarming irony, Muller suggested that "the obvious solution would seem to be to ask them."[138]

Albert Hirschman retired as an active member of the Institute for Advanced Study in 1985, when he turned seventy. Clifford Geertz, his colleague and friend at IAS, said at the retirement party, "I have never had a closer friend, or one who has had more impact, both personally and in scholarly terms, upon me than Albert."[139] Hirschman maintained his office, administrative assistance, and a generous research fund, and, as we have seen, he continued to work and publish important analyses. These included a number of interventions on economic and political developments in Latin America and the Third World, some major methodological pieces, articles on democracy and public discourse, and his last book-length essay, *The Rhetoric of Reaction*. Other volumes appeared as well: collections of talks, lectures, articles previously published in journals, and a long interview that had been originally published in Italian as a stand-alone book.[140]

For the institute, it was no easy task to replace Hirschman. Clifford Geertz, Michael Walzer (who had joined in 1980), and Hirschman "had made the IAS a haven for interpretive social science," and it was impossible to reconstitute that special alchemy.[141] An Albert O. Hirschman Chair in Economics was eventually established, and Eric S. Maskin was its first holder (2000–2012), followed for only two years by Dani Rodrik (2013–2015). The chair has either been suspended or canceled since 2015.

Retirement was much easier for Hirschman himself, for it "coincided with international fame." According to Adelman, "it would be hard to imagine a social scientist enjoying more respect in so many corners of the world than Hirschman."[142] He started to collect honorary degrees and other honorifics, and his name circulated as one of the next Nobel laureates in economics. By the late 1980s, Adelman reports, "rumors of Hirschman's nomination for the Nobel were flying fast and furious."[143] Yet the Nobel Prize eluded him. Adelman writes that "no question came up more often in the course of a decade's research" for his biography, and lists several possible explanations advanced by insiders: Hirschman was admired and influential but had no "school" behind him, he was not mathematical, and he was excessively interdisciplinary.[144] One further explanation can be added: it is possible that Hirschman's admirers thought he stood no real chance of winning, so when the time for nominations came, they opted for those second or third choices who seemed to promise a wider consensus.[145] In other words, Hirschman's potential supporters chose the more probable candidate over the just possible Hirschman. By those lights, the Nobel Prize did not arrive because it was a self-fulfilling prophecy: Hirschman's supporters were not as "possibilist" as their dream candidate.

FIGURE 7.2 Albert O. Hirschman in the French Alps, 1991. Courtesy of Katia Salomon

The Hirschmans returned ever more frequently to Germany and in particular Berlin, where Hirschman was a de facto member of the Wissenschaftskolleg directed by his dear friend, the prominent sociologist Wolf Lepenies. They enjoyed moments of great exhilaration at seeing Chile return to democracy in 1990 and Brazil elect Fernando Henrique Cardoso as president in 1994. They also had built a tradition, from the early 1970s, of visiting their daughter Katia and her husband, Alain Salomon, in France. Hiking in the Alps was a family passion.

In June 1996, during an excursion, Hirschman fell and struck his head against a rock, causing a cerebral hematoma that affected his speech, gait, and sense of balance. Thereafter, Adelman writes, "there was little to arrest the steady, ineluctable decline, the deteriorating hearing and speaking, his tortuous difficulty writing, and the loss of affect or expression."[146] The loss of his daughter Lisa, an accomplished psychologist in California who died of brain cancer in 1999 at the age of fifty-two, was a dreadful blow. By the early 2000s, Adelman recalls, Hirschman was still lucid but unable to write or read very much, though he took to painting.

Albert Hirschman lived for many more years, increasingly withdrawn from the world. He survived Sarah, who died in January 2012 of cancer, following her on December 10, 2012.

Chapter Eight

THE LEGACY OF ALBERT HIRSCHMAN

When Albert Hirschman died in December 2012 at the age of ninety-seven, he was saluted as one of the most prominent social scientists of the twentieth century. His intuitions and the concepts that he shaped had long entered the standard vocabulary of many disciplines. "Exit Albert Hirschman," wrote the *Economist*, one word sufficing to pay homage to the man and his legacy. His independence of thought and originality were praised by all; he was described as a "lateral thinker," as an "unusual thinker," as "heretical."[1] Indeed, he had earned those stripes thanks to a number of beautiful breakthrough analyses and an uncommon writing style—as the *Economist* quipped, "Mr. Hirschman wrote better in his third language than most economists do in their first," though in fact English was his fourth or fifth language—but at the price of risking (and, at times, experiencing) professional marginalization.[2] Yet he made it to the pinnacle of his profession, as a faculty member of the Institute for Advanced Study at Princeton, and was unanimously considered by colleagues and students to be in a league of his own. In 2007, the U.S.-based Social Science Research Council instituted as its highest honor the Albert O. Hirschman Prize.

Despite the virtually unanimous agreement about his importance, describing Hirschman's legacy and influence on others is not an easy task—arguably because he was indeed in a league of his own. His search for fresh perspectives was so eclectic that, as many have noted, no recognizable school has ever developed in his footsteps (although there were many "fellow travelers," such as Charles Lindblom, Burton Klein, Judith Tendler, Paul Streeten, and Donald Schön, to name a few). As Michael McPherson wrote in a beautiful piece on Hirschman's "method," this is not surprising: "A school which numbered among its prime doctrines that of searching out what the doctrines overlooked would have something in common with an anarchists' convention."[3] One could also add, paraphrasing one Marx, that no true Hirschmanian would ever care to belong to a school of thought that accepted her as a member.[4]

This said, it is possible to make a few observations about Hirschman's work and method, as well as his influence on the development of social science thought, that may help give a sense of the vastness of his legacy.

The first and easiest point to be made is Hirschman's resistance to pre-cooked recipes and standard explanations. This does not mean that he was necessarily a "contrarian," the fellow who claims to know better than the others. Often he simply removed himself from the debate and followed his own line of reasoning. We noted this, following Adelman, in Hirschman's disinterest in the fight between Keynesian and orthodox economists in 1936 London. But we also emphasized this, proposing a somewhat different reading than Adelman's, in Hirschman's analysis of monetary policies in Europe after World War II. In that case, Hirschman was not simply a dissenter against the orthodox positions of deflationist economists à la Gide (in France) or Einaudi (in Italy). On the contrary, he approved those policies and found them useful, to the extent that they could be considered dynamically—that is, as specific policies adapted to address a specific situation and destined to be changed in due course.

Hirschman, in other words, was not so much a heterodox as a frequent "dissenter," as he defined himself. Of course, in practice this also meant being often at odds with the current orthodoxy. The principal characteristic of orthodoxy to which Hirschman objected was its static nature, its tendency "to use the same recipe, administer the same therapy, to resolve the most various types of problems; never to admit complexity and try to reduce it as much as possible, while ignoring that things are always more complicated in reality."[5]

In the same vein, Hirschman described the new field of development economics that was taking shape in the 1950s as a direct, heterodox challenge to mainstream economics. But he also noted, as we saw in chapter 3, that this heterodox approach was becoming a new orthodoxy. Hirschman became the dissenter to the heterodox challengers of mainstream economics.

PROVING HAMLET WRONG

As an elderly man, Albert Hirschman recollected his stupor of many years before, when he was twelve or thirteen and his father told him that he had no clear answer to something that young Albert had just asked him. Albert ran to his sister to communicate the inexplicable discovery that their father had no *Weltanschauung*.[6] If Hirschman remembered that small and not particularly brilliant comment so many years later, it is because, as he wrote, with his German upbringing he considered it important to have a full-fledged *Weltanschauung*.[7] Yet during his adolescence and in his early twenties, he experienced plenty of occasions to lose those early certainties. Doubt, in fact, became a fundamental element of his way of looking at the world.

Particularly influential in this respect was Hirschman's brother-in-law and dear friend, Eugenio Colorni. As Hirschman wrote, Colorni and his friends were "strongly-committed anti-Fascists. Yet they were not rigidly tied to any ideology and were far from professing to have all the answers to the economic, social, and political issues of the time. Moreover, they did not seem to be particularly unhappy or bothered by this situation."[8] Colorni, six years older than Hirschman, "seemed . . . to cultivate and relish an intellectual style that took nothing for granted except his doubts."[9]

Manlio Rossi-Doria noticed this aspect of his character as well. In a letter to his wife, Rossi-Doria emphasized how Colorni "rid himself . . . of any rigid thought constructions."[10] Albert's sister Ursula, too, remembered Eugenio's intellectual freedom. Unlike her brother, Ursula, briefly a Communist in Paris, was fascinated by the strength orthodox comrades derived from ideological certainty, but she found in Eugenio a liberating energy: "I fell in love with his happy and irreverent approach to all manner of taboos, and the way he brought all of the freedom of culture into the question of politics. In doing so, his political commitment did not diminish but, on the contrary, became more robust, losing in dogmatic certainty and gaining immensely in vitality and imagination."[11]

Hirschman was deeply influenced by this "intimate connection" between intellectual openness and commitment to political antifascist activism. As he adroitly put it, it seemed that Colorni and his friends had set out to "prove Hamlet wrong: they were intent on showing that doubt could *motivate* action instead of undermining and enervating it."[12]

Hirschman's recollection of Colorni's attitude and Hirschman's assessment of his own work add up to very much the same thing. If we think about his work as a young "freelance researcher" in Italy and France in the late 1930s, as a postdoc at Berkeley, at the Fed after the war, in Colombia in the 1950s, and in academia after that, we can easily use the concept of doubt as a unifying theme across those different endeavours. The same is true of his writings. As McPherson wrote, Hirschman's work is characterized by "unity and diversity" at the same time. We have seen the wide variety of topics and different structures of argumentation that Hirschman's work displays. Yet, McPherson notes, all Hirschman's writings share "a highly distinctive, almost unmistakable, style of thought."[13] McPherson individuates this distinctive style in the "contrapuntal" or "reactive" character of Hirschman's work—his tendency to look for what the main disciplinary strand has neglected or overlooked, "and discover the hidden features of reality it reveals."[14]

While true, this is an excessively narrow definition of Hirschman's "style." Hirschman distanced himself from it, though he had to admit to "having frequently a reaction, perhaps something approaching a reflex . . . of the 'it ain't necessarily so' kind."[15] But it is a useful definition to the extent that it highlights the major symptoms of a doubting mind, not satisfied by the apparent solidity of any highly praised and respected theoretical proposition, and curious to explore a broader territory and paths not taken by others.

The idea of proving Hamlet wrong is important, for it describes not only Hirschman's doubting attitude but also his tendency to use the new spaces opened through doubt to elaborate theories that can explain processes of social change in a more realistic and sophisticated way than mainstream approaches, and to imagine paths of reform and steps toward more satisfying arrangements of social interrelationships that "standard" theories left unseen. For Hirschman, as for Colorni, doubting is not a force conducive to abstraction and paralysis, but rather the foundation for commitment to action.

POLITICS IN TURBULENT TIMES

Proving Hamlet wrong, in other words, was for Hirschman the foundation of his deeply reformist convictions. As Hirschman wrote, again reflecting on the attitude of Colorni and his antifascist friends, "this sort of combination of participation in public affairs with intellectual openness seems to me the ideal micro-foundation of a democratic politics."[16]

In the late 1980s, for example, several theorists of democracy high-lighted the fundamental importance of *deliberation* for the proper working of democracy. As Hirschman argued, "for a democracy to function well and to endure, it is essential . . . that opinions *not* be fully formed *in advance* of the process of deliberation."[17] Participants in the deliberation process should thus maintain a degree of tentativeness about their own opinions and openness to their possible modification in light of new information. In sum, they should be open to doubt.

This attitude, Hirschman argued, was somewhat orthogonal to the importance usually given, in our culture, to having well-formed opinions. Although forming strong opinions may be beneficial to the self-esteem and social approval of the individual, it brings with it potentially dangerous side effects at the social level, in the form of a deterioration of the delib-erative process, a central pillar of the democratic process. Hirschman thus concluded, "Social scientists and psychologists who hold forth so volubly on the virtues of individuality, personality, and identity might therefore do well to explore how to combine these desiderata with such democratic qualities as intellectual openness, flexibility, and readiness to appreciate a new argument, perhaps even pleasure in embracing it."[18]

Hirschman's focus on processes of policy making, despite the diverse arguments and methodological approaches of his various books (from the very historically grounded analysis in *Journeys Toward Progress* to the much more abstract approach of *Exit, Voice, and Loyalty*), rests on this vision, deeply embedded in Hirschman's thought, of open-minded delib-eration, wide participation, and intellectual openness. One could recapitu-late Hirschman's entire intellectual trajectory as an attempt to understand processes of deliberative decision making and explore ways to find and activate the social resources that fuel these processes.

Hirschman's emphasis on the concept of possibilism is arguably the most explicit statement of what he thought was his contribution to the deliberative process as reformist activism, and to the study of it as social science. Most social scientists, Hirschman noted, focus on explaining the regularities of social dynamics, and this is obviously an important task. But Hirschman emphasized the opposite type of endeavour: "to underline the multiplicity and creative disorder of the human adventure, to bring out the uniqueness of a certain occurrence, and to perceive an entirely new way of turning a historical corner."[19] This was particularly promising in seeking to explain the process of social change, for, he added, unless "novelty, creativity, and uniqueness" take place, large-scale social change cannot occur. In the first place, if all elements of social dynamics were already known, reactionary forces could easily foresee and preempt them. Second, he wrote, "radical reformers are unlikely to generate the extraordinary social energy they need to achieve change unless they are exhilaratingly conscious of writing an entirely new page of human history."[20]

This passage is not just an aside to Hirschman's "passion for the possible"—an expression coined by nineteenth-century Danish philosopher Søren Kierkegaard, whom Hirschman read in 1944 in Italy. In fact, it shows the centrality that Hirschman gave to the sources of social and political activism. Hirschman conceived even his seemingly most naïve policy proposals (for example, the plan for an Inter-American Divestment Corporation and the reorganization of foreign aid policies, discussed in chapter 5) as exercises in de-emphasizing sociopolitical realities that may appear to be excessively constraining to political actors. As he put it,

the reason for this agnosticism is . . . the observation that the constraints on policy makers are far less binding in a number of conceivable historical constellations than at "normal" times. Moreover, one important condition for such constellations to yield real change is the prior availability and discussion (followed then, of course, by contemptuous dismissal) of "radical reform" ideas that can be readily picked up when times suddenly cease to be normal.[21]

Again, Hirschman shows that the analytical tools he frequently used, such as the notions of blessing (or curse) in disguise, cognitive dissonance (according to which changes in beliefs and attitudes are not necessarily prerequisites to social change, but can follow it), and unintended consequences of human action, all serve the purpose of escaping the straitjacket of predictability and regularity in social dynamics in favor of "an approach to the social world that would stress the unique rather than the general, the unexpected rather than the expected, and the possible rather than the probable."[22]

This idea had profound roots in Hirschman's thought. Even before reading Kierkegaard, Hirschman knew Paul Valéry and appreciated his aphorism about the fragility of peace before the aggressive power politics of national states. As we saw in chapter 2, Hirschman quoted it in *National Power*: "Peace," Valéry wrote, is a "virtual mute, continuous victory of the possible forces over the probable appetites."[23]

Hirschman's attention to the possible over the probable, to the conjunctural over the structural, is the basis of yet another of his deep-rooted predilections and a fundamental element of his cognitive style—that is, the importance of history. In diametric opposition to the standards of social analysis that took shape after World War II, Hirschman considered the study of history an enormously rich and ineluctable source for understanding social change. We have highlighted this in many cases throughout this book, most explicitly perhaps in our discussion of *Journeys Toward Progress* and *Development Projects Observed*, two studies whose epistemological *raison d'etre* is in the decades-long historical trajectory of policy debates and development projects. This attention to history was not just one particular methodological predilection of the early 1960s; it informs in depth Hirschman's analytical style. Hirschman highlighted his profound "respect for the autonomy of the actors." As he argued, "the unfolding of social events . . . makes prediction exceedingly difficult and contributes to that peculiar open-endedness of history that is the despair of the paradigm-obsessed social scientist."[24]

What he called the "many might-have-beens of history" are necessary to maintain an openness to the basic unpredictability of human action.[25] In the aftermath of the 1989 Eastern European revolutions, for example, Hirschman pointed out that "no one foresaw them." The end of the Cold War was a huge surprise to experts, politicians, and ordinary people, suggesting that "the utmost modesty is in order when it comes to pronouncements about the future of human societies."[26] Indeed, the "inventiveness of history" is the foundational ground of Hirschman's "passion for the possible."[27]

As we have seen throughout this book, Hirschman's contributions to development economics and the social sciences have had varying degrees of success. If linkages and the exit-voice dichotomy have been immediately adopted by the scholarly community, the Hiding Hand puzzled many people and was harshly criticized. Policy proposals like the divestment corporation were de facto ignored. The same fate seems to have characterized also Hirschman's methodological stance, his "possibilism."[28] Recently, however, more than any of his other insights, it is his philosophy of history and social science, his possibilism, that has become a source of inspiration. Two recent books, very different one from the other, show how Hirschman's possibilism is not only built on interdisciplinary grounds but also adopted as a central methodological stance in different studies—a unifying perspective, so to speak, among different disciplines.

In a pathbreaking 2017 analysis of how the global financial crisis has engendered inchoate discontinuities across several aspects of the international financial architecture that are of particular importance to emerging markets and developing economies, international political economist Ilene Grabel claimed that "we are today immersed in a Hirschmanian moment"— that is, a period characterized by basic (though productive) incoherence in global financial governance.[29] Moreover, she added, another feature of the Hirschmanian moment is that, though inherently potentially dangerous, an unstable and evolving institutional landscape also offers unexpected possibilities for change and new opportunities for emerging markets to engage in ideational, policy, and institutional experimentation in the realm of global financial governance. As Grabel put it, "the emergent Hirschmanian world is a good world to inhabit—one far better attuned to development than a fully coherent system."[30]

Coining a new oxymoron in the Hirschmanian tradition, Grabel presented her "productive incoherence thesis" as the analysis of an "emerging constellation" (a term dear to Hirschman) of financial governance institutions and policies characterized by "inconsistent, contradictory, redundant, ad hoc, and meagre" changes, as well as by only "tentative" reactions to the disruption of the institutional landscape. This incoherence, however, is "a welcome rupture, a break from totalizing visions," because "for the first time in a generation, many emerging markets and developing economies have escaped the straitjacket of a commanding theoretical orthodoxy and the associated straitjacket of a narrowly prescribed menu of appropriate institutional forms and policy practices."[31] When things don't fall apart (as Grabel aptly titled her book), new spaces open for inventive reformist agendas.[32]

Also in 2017, political scientist Kathryn Sikkink published a book titled *Evidence for Hope*, on human rights in the twenty-first century. Sikkink pointed out that the dominant note in the current discourse about human rights is pessimism. Governments, academics, the general public, and even human rights activists all seem to agree that human rights have failed, either because they have incurred a crisis of legitimacy (they are the wrong battle because they do not address, say, the problem of inequality, or worse, with their emphasis on the individual, they have been instrumental to the rise of neoliberalism) or because they have proved ineffective. According to Sikkink, however, this pessimism is both inaccurate—progress *has* taken place—and unhelpful. "I am more hopeful than others," she writes, referring explicitly to Hirschman's possibilism.[33]

Like Hirschman, Sikkink devotes considerable attention not only to debasing the positions of her more pessimistic colleagues on factual terms, but also to discussing their ideological attitude. Sikkink argues that if human rights have progressed (though not everywhere and not in all ways), but the belief is widespread that human rights violations are getting worse, this is due to an erroneous comparison that scholars and activists make between the ideal goals and the real achievements.[34] Emphasis on the gap between limited accomplishments and the unrestrained ideal is, according to Sikkink, an ideological mistake, like the failure complex, or *fracasomania*, that Hirschman described as a trait typical of Latin American intellectuals. *Fracasomania* is not just a witty description of moody intellectuals but a concept that helps make sense of the difficulties that reformers face. Sikkink quotes, for example, a South African jurist: "the criticism made by an academic that nothing is working is taken up by those who have an interest in seeing that they are not held accountable."[35]

If the goal of social analysis is not only to provide "neutral" observations but also to build more solid foundations for policy making, reforms, and social activism, as Hirschman showed throughout his life, clearly morality cannot be expunged from the social sciences. Values do not intervene only at a later moment, after allegedly scientific analysis has been carried out; they inform research questions, methodology, myriads of propositions, and even elements of style. The point should not be unduly simplified. Because of his long acquaintance with the writings of his predilected philosophers of the modern era, Hirschman was well aware that modern social science had emerged from the very separation between moral reflections and political analysis.

Modern social science, Hirschman wrote in 1980, "arose to a considerable extent in the process of *emancipating* itself from traditional moral teachings."[36] As Hirschman had already noted in *The Passions and the Interests*, a crucial step in this direction was made by Machiavelli, who proclaimed that he would write about political institutions as they really existed, not about imaginary states governed by moral precepts. Pascal in the seventeenth century and Montesquieu in the eighteenth also emphasized the uselessness of discussing politics with arguments about morality, reason, and justice. Marx too considered moral arguments weak next to his scientific socialism, which scientifically demonstrated the laws of history, though he was perhaps least convincing in this respect and, at the same time, all the more persuasive: "In effect, Marx mixed, uncannily, these 'cold' scientific propositions with 'hot' moral outrage and it was perhaps this odd amalgam, with all of its inner tensions unresolved, that was (and is) responsible for the extraordinary appeal of his work in an age both addicted to science and starved of moral values."[37]

Hirschman saw the importance of that effort at separating the "ought" from the "is" in the history of European thought in the modern era. In fact, his essay on morality and the social sciences—which focuses primarily on morality and economics—offers many reflections on the difficulty of bringing the two dimensions together. As a French saying goes, "with beautiful sentiments one makes bad literature."[38] But Hirschman was also sympathetic to the lack of rigid compartmentalization that characterized those modern thinkers of the sixteenth to the eighteenth century who, tellingly, were called moral philosophers. Moreover, by the last quarter of the twentieth century, studies about the unavoidable role of morality in explaining market behaviors (such as Solow's studies on the labor market and the role that "principles of appropriate behavior" have for workers during salary negotiations) were proliferating.[39] The reintroduction of morality in the social sciences, though tentative and piecemeal, was undeniable. Morality, Hirschman wrote, "belongs into [sic] the center of our work."[40] What he hoped was that those early instances of reintegration of morality and social science might grow into a powerful movement.

Down the road, it is then possible to visualize a kind of social science that would be very different from the one most of us have been practicing: a moral social science where moral considerations are not repressed or kept apart, but are systematically commingled with analytical argument . . .; where the transition from preaching to proving and back again is performed frequently and with ease; and where moral considerations need no longer be smuggled in surreptitiously, nor expressed unconsciously, but are displayed openly and disarmingly.[41]

Hirschman concluded his essay, paraphrasing Keynes, by declaring that such was his dream for a "social science for our grandchildren."[42]

THE REBIRTH OF DEVELOPMENT ECONOMICS

After his early work on European economies and international economic relations at Berkeley and the Fed, Hirschman's first major field of specialization was development economics. The development question was the basis of three important books in a decade and many significant articles throughout Hirschman's scholarly career. Even when he delved into other issues, such as the ideologies of capitalism or the transformations of democracies and democratic debate, Hirschman never abandoned the development question. What remains of that work requires some elaboration, as we must discuss both the legacy of Hirschman's intellectual project—that is, his vision of development economics—and the legacy of his specific contributions to the development question, in terms of both contents and methodology. Let's start with the analysis of Hirschman's intellectual project with regard to development economics.

Hirschman once defined development economics as characterized by two major postures: "the rejection of the *monoeconomics claim* and the assertion of the *mutual-benefit claim*."[43] By the first, Hirschman meant that the economies of underdeveloped countries are fundamentally different from those of advanced industrial countries, so that "traditional economic analysis, which has concentrated on the industrial countries, must therefore be recast in significant respects when dealing with underdeveloped countries."[44] Development economists, in other words, rejected the idea that a single theoretical edifice was sufficient to analyze both developed and less developed economies. By the second, Hirschman meant that economic relations between the two groups can be shaped in such a way as to benefit both; they are not necessarily beneficial, but mutual benefits are not ruled out. The four combinations resulting from the rejection or assertion of each claim served to describe "a comprehensive typology" of the major theoretical approaches to studying the development of less developed countries (table 8.1).[45]

TABLE 8.1
Types of development theories

		Monoeconomics claim	
		Asserted	*Rejected*
Mutual-benefit claim	*Asserted*	Orthodox economics	Development economics
	Rejected	Marx?	Neo-Marxist theories

Source: Hirschman 1981b, 3.

Orthodox economics asserted both claims—that is, a theoretical edifice able to deal with both advanced and less developed countries and a theory of international economic relations that assumed benefits for both groups of countries. In particular, the orthodox position would hold that "economics consists of a number of simple, yet 'powerful' theorems of universal validity: there is only one economics ('just as there is one physics')."[46]

The question mark next to Marx indicates the difficulty in confining him to one cell, as his description of the spoliation of backward regions by capitalist regions (a rejection of the mutual-benefit claim) and his view about the objectively progressive role of British capitalism in India (an assertion of the mutual-benefit claim) demonstrate. But the surprising result of Hirschman's exercise is the exclusion of what he defines as neo-Marxist theories—that is, structuralism and dependency theory—from the boundaries of development economics. This is indeed a very narrow definition of the discipline and one with which it is difficult to agree. But Hirschman's point can be explained if we look at the political stance behind these analytical propositions.

Hirschman's approach had always been deeply reformist. He defined his 1963 study of policy making in Latin America, *Journeys Toward Progress*, as sort of a "reform monger's manual," conceived not only as an instrument against conservative right-wing policies but also, and most important, as a book in direct "competition to the many handbooks on the techniques of revolutions, coups d'état, and guerrilla warfare" that the revolutionary spirit of those years produced in great quantity.[47]

Hirschman's view of development economics thus coincided with his reformist attitude: a quest for pressure mechanisms, investment sequences, and policy-making processes that could advance development, no matter how disorderly. The revolutionary view was to Hirschman's eyes the negation of this effort. If his study of development mechanisms was trying to understand how one thing leads to another, the idea of revolution had nothing to say in this respect, for it simply promised to wipe out the wrong socioeconomic structure and replace it with the right one. In fact, Hirschman shared many analyses with structuralist scholars and deeply respected many founders of dependency theory and their work. But he also posited that the revolutionary drift of many analyses corresponded to a progressive withering of their analytical power. An example was Andre Gunder Frank, whose rich historical analyses were much deeper and more convincing than the more schematic analyses of his essays on revolution.[48]

In retrospect, Hirschman's intellectual project for a development economics as theoretically distinct from orthodox economics has completely failed. Starting in the 1970s and increasingly in subsequent decades, development economics has disappeared as a distinct theoretical construct and has become one of the many applied fields under the ever larger umbrella of neoclassical economics. As Roger Backhouse and Béatrice Cherrier have convincingly argued, this centripetal phenomenon has characterized virtually all economics subdisciplines, which have become theoretically more homogeneous while maintaining their own characterization as applied subfields of the same theoretical apparatus. This is what happened to development economics.[49]

Even a cursory look at textbooks in development economics from the 1980s on clearly reveals the trend toward using neoclassical methods. For example, the 1983 *Economics of Development* states that "this text makes extensive use of theoretical tools of classical and neoclassical economics in the belief that these tools contribute substantially to our understanding of development problems and their solution."[50] In the mid-1990s, Pierre-Richard Agénor and Peter J. Montiel introduced their *Development Macroeconomics* textbook by claiming that they were adapting "standard macroeconomic analysis" to the conditions of developing countries, while Rudiger Dornbusch argued that "in some deep ways the problems are about the same everywhere," and "the battle cry 'this country is different' " was nothing more than "a scoundrel's plea for protecting outdated interpretations or politicized policy advice from intellectual import competition."[51]

In 2007, Dani Rodrik published *One Economics, Many Recipes*, which, as he wrote in a section titled "A Credo of Sorts," was "strictly grounded in neoclassical economic analysis."[52] Starting with the very title of his book, Rodrik seemed to refer directly to Hirschman's monoeconomics claim. In that sense, it might perhaps seem ironic that the Social Science Research Council awarded its inaugural 2007 Albert O. Hirschman Prize—as mentioned, the SSRC highest honor—to Dani Rodrik.

In fact, however, it is a decision that makes complete sense, given the distinctly Hirschmanian flavor of Rodrik's work. If we shift our attention from the intellectual project of development economics that Hirschman had in mind, whose success or failure after all depended on many disparate factors, to the legacy of other aspects of Hirschman's view of development—namely, his reformist attitude and methodology—the connections between the two are clearly visible. Although Hirschman and Rodrik expressed different ideas about whether development economics should exist as a separate disciplinary field (and indeed whether there ever existed "one" economic theory), they show remarkable affinities on important methodological questions.

Hirschman's effort to understand how policy making actually works in practice, for example, is a central characteristic of Rodrik's work on development issues and international political economy. In his theoretical credo, mentioned previously, Rodrik refers to the many differences between his analysis and the majority consensus: "If I often depart from the consensus that 'mainstream' economists have reached in matters of development policy, this has less to do with different modes of analysis than with different readings of the evidence and with different evaluations of the 'political economy' of developing nations."[53] If we add to this the importance that Rodrik has consistently given to in-depth historical analysis to understand the particulars of how social and economic change takes place in a specific situation, we start to see the deep consonances between Hirschman's approach and Rodrik's.[54]

In a number of interventions, Rodrik underscored how development studies are increasingly diagnostic rather than presumptive, focusing on detailed studies of what works and what does not and disregarding comprehensive explanations. He also highlighted the importance of context-specific analysis and the focus on bottlenecks and constraints that inhibit growth in specific situations; the importance of monitoring and evaluation; the suspicion against "best practices" or universal remedies; and the emphasis on selective, relatively narrowly targeted reforms—in his words, "hitting the right targets and not doing everything at once."[55]

Hirschman's legacy in development economics continues to grow with the relevance of more sophisticated approaches such as Rodrik's, more so than in the 1980s and 1990s (the years of the mainstream, neoliberal Washington Consensus), when the impression was that Hirschman's development work was not very relevant to practice.[56]

Perhaps an exception to this oscillating interest in Hirschman is the steady attention accorded to his work on Latin American development issues. The literature here is vast and considers Hirschman as an essential reference, both for examining development policies in Latin America historically and for generating new thinking about current development strategies for the region. A particularly well-documented example of historical analysis is the account of how, in the second half of the 1970s, Hirschman and Guillermo O'Donnell debated the theory of the bureaucratic-authoritarian state in Latin America in the broader context of the so-called era of the developmental state.[57] From that analysis, Augustin Ferraro and Miguel Centeno have recently concluded that, contrary to common wisdom, Latin American developmentalist states were quite successful, and that their crisis stemmed from increasingly "arbitrary, erratic, and authoritarian policy styles."[58] As Ferraro and Centeno argue, this historical analysis may have important repercussions on the institutional development of Latin American countries in the next decades. An example of new development thinking is the symposium that the Inter-American Development Bank sponsored as an opportunity to generate new ideas about development strategies for Latin America, starting from the work of Albert Hirschman. A more recent symposium on the relevance of Hirschman's work for Latin America (and Colombia in particular) is the conference co-organized by the Universidad de Los Andes and the Colombian Banco de la *República* in Bogotá, with interventions by Miguel Urrutia, José Antonio Ocampo, and others.[59]

David Ellerman's analysis of development aid policies by the World Bank extends Hirschman's observations beyond Latin America. Ellerman's book discusses the cognitive assumptions behind the theory of unbalanced growth, interpreted as a learning process in a situation characterized by uncertainty and widespread lack of information. If this is the typical situation in which development organizations work, Ellerman suggests that epistemological perspectives such as Herbert Simon's bounded rationality, Lindblom's analysis of policy making as muddling through, Donald Schön's theory of decentralized social learning, among others, should be used together with Hirschman's perspective in a more realistic approach to development lending and policy making.[60] Interestingly, however, Ellerman also notes that the development practices of large organizations are difficult to change, and thus Hirschman's vision still remains at the margins. As he put it, "the language has changed more than the substance."[61]

But the reverse has actually happened with some of Hirschman's development concepts. The concept of linkages, for example, has encountered wide success and has been adopted by a vast literature. At the same time, it has been adapted and enlarged to contain a much broader spectrum of phenomena than originally envisaged by Hirschman in *Strategy*. In such cases, the language has remained the same; perhaps its substance has not changed outright, but it has certainly grown.[62]

A NOVEL SOCIAL SCIENCE

Hirschman's interest in disciplinary trespassing was visible from his very first book. In the early 1970s, two founders of the then new and thriving field of international political economy lamented the persistent separation, against any logic, of political and economic analyses in international studies:

It is commonplace to observe that international politics and economics are closely linked to one another, and that sophisticated analysis of either requires some understanding of both. Nevertheless, few writers actually relate the two. Economists tend to assume the political structure, ignore politics entirely, or at best, attempt to analyze its effects on economic processes through the use of highly simplified political notions. Political scientists are even more guilty of disciplinary tunnel-vision. Most professional students of international politics know relatively little about international economics. Generally, like neophytes at three-dimensional tic-tac-toe, political analysts take formal cognizance of economic planes of power, but in fact succumb to the habit of playing the game on the familiar military-diplomatic plane.[63]

With *National Power and the Structure of Foreign Trade*, Hirschman bridged this gap, thirty years in advance. A few months before its publication, Condliffe remarked upon the spirit that had animated Hirschman and his colleagues: perhaps in the world prior to World War II, "the balance of power and the balance of payments" were the governing concepts of two separate spheres of thought and action; it was essential to recognize, however, that after World War II it would be "impossible . . . to revert to this separation of international economics from international politics."[64]

Interestingly, Condliffe suggested that a distinct continental European sensitivity might have been the basis of this easier interdisciplinary attitude of Hirschman and his colleagues. Throughout the long nineteenth century, the diplomatic practice of English-speaking countries had been based largely upon the philosophy of laissez-faire, seeking to keep government intervention in economic matters to a minimum. Although trade, of course, was never entirely divorced from national policy, it is worth noting that neither the Foreign Office nor the Department of State had any economic staff.

The situation on the European continent, however, was different, and the separation of economics and politics, in both domestic and foreign policy, was never so clear in continental Europe. The strategic element was always important in economic planning and international economic relations, while the multilateral trading system, the foundation of British economic power, continued to expand. Condliffe observed, "While the balance of power in Europe was visibly shifting, the balancing of international payments continued to be regulated through the monetary mechanism of the international gold standard," but only a few noticed that at the time.[65]

Those early reflections and scholarly experiences were clearly important for Hirschman, who always moved across disciplinary fields like the moral philosophers of the modern era, blessed by having lived well before disciplinary silos would sclerotize the university system. In *National Power*, crossing disciplinary boundaries made it possible to discuss the political dimension of international trade in a novel fashion; in the development trilogy, it opened new vistas on different approaches to individual and social promotion with the help of anthropological literature (in *Strategy*, thanks to Sarah's essential input), the policy dimension of development strategies (in *Journeys*), and the introduction of epistemological uncertainty in project management (*Development Projects Observed*). In a 1984 article programmatically titled "Against Parsimony: Three Easy Ways of Complicating Some Categories of Economic Discourse," Hirschman reexamined some ideas that he had introduced two years before in *Shifting Involvements*, such as the concept of metapreferences. Originally discussed in the realm of philosophy, metapreferences demonstrate some important limits of standard economic theory. First, Hirschman argued, standard economic concepts such as revealed preferences and the rational actor make it impossible to discuss in any serious way how values shape and modify human action—values have a different impact than changes in simple, uncomplicated preferences such as the choice between pears and apples. Second, at the policy level, treating values like simple preferences might suggest relatively inefficient ways to overcome certain collective problems, such as pollution. Laws, Hirschman argued, shape values and affect collective behaviors at a much deeper level than, say, actions that make industrialists' likelihood to pollute more costly, precisely because actions that address only a demand schedule have a much lesser impact as value molders.

A similar case can be made for different types of activity, such as instrumental and noninstrumental activity. The former refers to activities in which means and ends, and costs and rewards, are clearly defined and separated. They are the natural territory of standard economic analysis. But many activities are characterized by a much less neat separation between means and ends, or between the costs we incur to reach our ends and the rewards we obtain from the activity. The neglect of noninstrumental activities and the "fusion of striving and attaining" that often characterizes them, for example, is responsible for the "trained incapacity" (to use Veblen's expression) of mainstream economists to explain convincingly collective action.[66] Even typical instrumental economic action such as routine work has a component of noninstrumentality that is very important in seeking to explain fluctuations in labor productivity and the effectiveness of industrial management.

Clearly, for Hirschman, the question of collective social change was particularly important. His focus on the collective dimension of social action often took the form of a lack of patience with the concept of the free rider. Perhaps this concept had some usefulness in "normal times," Hirschman argued, when private life claims the time and energy of citizens who may be nonetheless interested in policy decisions about public goods. But as Hirschman put it in 1971 (with appropriate reference to a 1964 hit), "the times . . . are seldom wholly normal; on quite a few occasions . . . they have been abnormal and 'a-changin'." "[67] The practice of economics-cum-politics-cum-social-psychology was for Hirschman the only way to address the problem of social change and collective action in a meaningful way.

Public morality and civic behavior are thus, not unexpectedly, Hirschman's third example from "Against Parsimony." They help explain, for example, the economics of blood donations, and many other mechanisms based on trust and the respect of certain moral norms that are actually vital for the well-functioning of a market. Disregarding public morality comes at the risk of seeing it atrophy, but insisting too much on it also backfires, for it cannot grow indefinitely and it may thus become scarce if requested in excessively high doses. Hirschman summarized the conundrum:

Love, benevolence, and civic spirit are neither scarce factors in fixed supply, nor do they act like skills and abilities that improve and expand more or less indefinitely with practice. Rather, they exhibit a complex, composite behavior: they atrophy when not adequately practiced and appealed to by the ruling socioeconomic regime, yet will once again make themselves scarce when preached and relied on to excess. To make matters worse, the precise location of these two danger zones . . . is by no means known, nor are these zones ever stable.[68]

Typically, as we have come to know Hirschman's way of reasoning, one must acquire a sensitivity for understanding these hidden thresholds and how they vary by time and place.

Hirschman's method, we can conclude, was meant not so much to increase our predictive abilities as to make the analysis of society and social change more realistic and convincing. As Hirschman wrote in the conclusion to his 1984 article, "all the complications flow from a single source—the incredible complexity of human nature which was disregarded by traditional theory for very good reasons, but which must be spoon-fed back into the traditional findings for the sake of greater realism."[69] The human being is not just an efficient economic agent, a "superior statistician" as Kenneth Arrow put it, but is capable of arguing and elaborating opinions and values, is self-reflective, and is inhabited by inner tensions between egotism and altruism, self-interest and civic-mindedness, and the drive toward both instrumental and noninstrumental actions. All these behaviors affect economic processes and, Hirschman argued, must therefore be reincorporated into economics and the broader field of social science.

Hirschman's critique of excessively parsimonious models, however, did not mean that he had an intolerance for modeling or theoretical thinking. Hirschman noted as much in a 1992 workshop on his work, in which he listed with evident pride the many theoretical notions he had elaborated throughout his scholarly life. Indeed, Hirschman considered it improper to be described as an atheoretical or antitheoretical social scientist. Even *institutional* was a term he considered limiting and not to the point, and we need not dig far to find paradigms, theories, principles, and broad analytical categories in his work. Indeed, many of his books put these categories center stage, starting with the title (*Exit Voice, and Loyalty*; *The Passions and the Interests*; *The Rhetoric of Reaction: Perversity, Futility, Jeopardy*), and when the theoretical approach is not immediately declared on the front cover (*The Strategy of Economic Development*; *Development Projects Observed*), it becomes evident at first reading.[70]

Hirschman's theorizing was not aimed at producing tight and imposing laws of social change, but at building middle-range models, abstract enough to isolate specific elements and show their explanatory potential, but not so particularistic as to abdicate their analytical role.[71] All Hirschman's models and principles are interpretive lenses that can help us make sense of historical processes, but they need to be fed with historical material to be of any use. Contextualization is fundamental to using Hirschman's analyses properly, and to assessing their capacity to generate new knowledge and propose useful novel perspectives. Projects, for Hirschman, are "unique constellations" of events, and so are processes of policy making, specific debates on welfare policies or negotiations about the quality of public services, and the political support that a government is able to muster in the face of increasing domestic inequality. They are "amenable to paradigmatic thinking," he wrote, but "only in a very special sense."[72]

Hirschman's models do not offer any ready-made prediction about where a certain situation will lead. What they do is help frame the analysis in order to make the debate and policy making more informed. But this is possible only through the study of the historical, specific material and ideological conditions of a certain situation. It is an exercise that helps the observer refine her sensitivity for the complexity of social processes, a sensitivity that, as we have seen in many passages, Hirschman considers a tacit knowledge that can grow only from experience. But when it grows, it is essential to that openness of mind and curiosity for the surprises of history that enlarge the spaces for political action—it is, in other words, one of the principal sources of Hirschman's possibilism.

SELF-SUBVERSION

In the final chapter of *The Rhetoric of Reaction*, Hirschman explored how the perversity, futility, and jeopardy theses, which he had analyzed at length with respect to conservative and neoconservative positions in public debate, had their mirror images in certain specific rhetorical constructs of progressive discourse. As a result, Hirschman wrote a chapter, not initially planned, that in some ways subverted the original intent of his book.

That was an exercise in what, Hirschman would call "self-subversion." Rehabilitating an otherwise derogatory Cold War term (subversion) and playing with it in the reflexive mode, Hirschman described his aptitude for arguing against his own propositions (remember his "it ain't necessarily so" reaction to other people's theories). Indeed, Hirschman noticed, this is a common trait among many scholars.[73]

What Hirschman found to be a characteristic peculiar to his own work was that he maintained a habit of reconsidering and qualifying his past assertions, and even pursuing the opposite line of reasoning, as opposed to looking exclusively for evidence confirming his core theories. We have encountered many examples of this attitude throughout this volume. In chapter 5, for example, we noticed how Hirschman qualified the concepts of exit and voice in his analysis of the revolutions of 1989. Presented as alternative behaviors in his original 1970 book, exit and voice were mutually reinforcing in the 1989 sequence of massive flight to the West (exit) and growing mass demonstrations against the Communist regime (voice). As this example shows, however, this and other acts of self-subversion did not result in the complete disqualification of Hirschman's original theories. Hirschman considered such self-subversion "rewarding and enriching," for instead of refuting the original thesis, it helped "define new domains of the social world where the originally postulated relationships do not hold."[74] This self-subversive attitude, in other words, enhances the ability to interpret the world rather than disrupting it.

This was for Hirschman another important attitude on which to build a more democratic society, based on civil confrontation and a deeply rooted trust in the deliberative power of society. "I believe," he wrote, "that what I have here called self-subversion can make a contribution to a more democratic culture in which citizens not only have the right to their individual opinions and convictions but, more important, are ready to question them in the light of new arguments and evidence."[75]

NOTES

PREFACE

1. Hirschman 1994c, 278.
2. Adelman 2013.
3. Adelman 2013, 9–10.
4. See, for example, *Desarrollo y Sociedad*, vol. 62 (2008); and the symposiums on Hirschman in *Humanity* 6, no. 2 (Summer 2015), ed. Michele Alacevich, and in *Research in the History of Economic Thought and Methodology*, vol. 34B (2016), ed. Marina Bianchi and Maurizio Franzini.
5. Hirschman 1998, 8.
6. Adelman 2013, xiv.
7. Adelman 2013, 580, 590.

1. THE FORMATION OF AN INTERNATIONAL POLITICAL ECONOMIST

1. U. Hirschmann 1993, 37; here and in other quotes from non-English literature, the translation is mine unless otherwise specified.
2. The characterization is by Albert Hirschman, as quoted in Adelman 2013, 31; see also Ursula's memoir, U. Hirschmann 1993, 77–93.
3. Adelman 2013, 21–25.
4. U. Hirschmann 1993, 66.
5. On the very recent rediscovery of Gerty Simon, see Mark Brown, "UK Show Revives Lost Work of Photographer Who Fled Nazis," *Guardian*, May 26, 2019, https://www.theguardian.com/artanddesign/2019/may/26/gerty-simon-uk-show -revives-lost-work-of-photographer-who-fled-nazis.

6. Adelman 2013, 46.
7. Adelman 2013, 18.
8. U. Hirschmann 1993, 81.
9. Adelman 2013, 67.
10. Adelman 2013, 60.
11. Erna von Pustau in conversation with Pearl Buck, in Pearl S. Buck, *How It Happens: Talk About the German People, 1914–1933* (New York: John Day, 1947), as quoted in Overy 2017, 130.
12. On the crisis of the Weimar Republic, see Evans 2004, on which I rely for facts and data; see also Calvocoressi, Wint, and Pritchard 1989.
13. For a concise but very clear discussion of the German interwar fragility and the Great Crash, see Clavin 2000, 88–109.
14. Feinstein, Temin, and Toniolo 1997, 106.
15. Quoted in Mazower 2000, 114.
16. Evans 2004, 237.
17. Adelman 2013, 49.
18. Evans 2004, 264.
19. Hirschman 1994a; Adelman 2013, 65.
20. Hirschman 1994a, 67.
21. Hirschman 1994a, 53.
22. Hirschman 1994a, 51–52, quote at 55.
23. Adelman 2013, 76.
24. Evans 2004, 354.
25. Hirschman as quoted in Adelman 2013, 80.
26. Adelman 2013, 87.
27. Hirschman 1989a, 113.
28. Adelman 2013, 88.
29. Adelman 2013, 90.
30. Hirschman 1989a, 116.
31. Hirschman 1989a, 116.
32. Adelman 2013, 98.
33. Quoted in Mouré 1991, 27.
34. Mouré 1991, 31–38.
35. Hirschman 1994a, 60.
36. "Hans Landsberg, 88: Economist, Expert in Energy Data Analysis," *Los Angeles Times*, October 23, 2001, https://www.latimes.com/archives/la-xpm-2001-oct-23 -me-60629-story.html; Carson 1993.
37. Hirschman 1988b, 102.
38. See, for example, Hayek 1935.
39. Hirschman 1994a, 61.
40. Albert O. Hirschmann, ca. 1943, as quoted in Adelman 2013, 133.
41. Adelman 2013, 134.
42. O. Albert Hirschmann, "Curriculum Vitae," undated but ca. 1942, Harvard University Archives, Department of Economics, Correspondence & Papers 1902–1950, Box 5, Folder "H," published online by Irwin Collier, accessed on September 29, 2019, http://www.irwincollier.com/harvard-curriculum-vitae-submitted -by-albert-o-hirschman-ca-1942/.

43. Albert Hirschman to Pierpaolo Luzzatto Fegiz, April 22, 1983, AOHP (emphasis original); see also Department of Defense, Personnel Security Questionnaire submitted by Albert O. Hirschman, 1 July 1957, AOHP, in which the University of Trieste degree is described as a "Doctorate." See also Hirschman 1994a, 60; Adelman 2013, 142–143.

44. On Renzo Fubini, see Da Empoli 1998; Fubini 2014.

45. Hirschmann 1938a [2004], 89.

46. Hirschmann 1938a [2004], 85.

47. Hirschmann 1938a [2004], 10.

48. Hirschmann 1938a [2004], 63.

49. De Cecco 2004; Hirschmann 1939a [1987b].

50. Hirschmann 1938b.

51. Luzzatto-Fegiz 1937, 111.

52. "La trama giudaico-antifascista stroncata dalla vigile azione della polizia," *Corriere della Sera*, October 18, 1938, 5. *La difesa della razza* reported an extract from the article published in *Corriere della Sera*, adding comments on the dangers that Jewish culture posed to the Italian academic system, "Eredità ebraica," *La difesa della razza*, Anno 2, no. 1, 5 November XVII (1938), 46.

53. "Dal diario di Pierpaolo Luzzatto Fegiz," 31 ottobre 1937, attached to Pierpaolo Luzzatto Fegiz to Albert O. Hirshman [*sic*], 11 marzo 1983, AOHP.

54. Fubini 2014, 38–39, 174–175. Mortara was also expelled and emigrated to Brazil; see Baffigi and Magnani 2009.

55. In Fubini's application for a Rockefeller Foundation fellowship in 1939, ultimately rejected on the very basis that he could not show that he would return to a proper job, he proposed as a research topic the subject of Hirschmann's thesis, the franc Poincaré; see Fubini 2014, 50, 178–181.

56. Hirschmann 1938c, 1938d.

57. Hirschman 1987a, 118.

58. Hirschman 1987a, 117–119.

59. Adelman 2013, 144–145.

60. Marino 1999, 78.

61. Giuseppe Berti, "Elementi di un'inchiesta sul lavoro dei quadri negli anni 1935–38," mimeo, Arch. PCI, posiz. 1496, quoted in Finzi 2004, 115–116. Finzi accessed the "Hirschmann" folder in the historical archive of the University of Trieste and offers much interesting information on his years there.

62. Hirschman 1994a, 68; 1997, 36.

63. O. Albert Hirschmann, "Curriculum Vitae"; Hirschman 1987a, 118; 1997, 36–37. On the Institut scientifique de recherches économiques et sociales, see Rist 1934. Like the Oxford Institute of Statistics, the Institut scientifique de recherches économiques et sociales was funded by the Rockefeller Foundation; see Craver 1986.

64. Jean Albert [Otto Albert Hirschmann] 1938e, 1236.

65. Hirschmann 1938f, 255.

66. See also J. B. Condliffe, "Memorandum on a Programme of International Economic Research," confidential memo prepared for the Geneva Research Centre, mimeo [date not available but either 1937 or 1938]; J. B. Condliffe, "A Survey of International Research in Europe," confidential, mimeo [date not available but either 1937 or 1938].

67. Fleming 1998.
68. "Memoranda Submitted to the Twelfth Session of the International Studies Conference," attached at the beginning of International Studies Conference 1939.
69. Condliffe 1940, 395–396.
70. Piatier 1939, 1.
71. International Studies Conference 1938, 46.
72. International Studies Conference 1938, 10–11.
73. Questore di Trieste, Antonio Gorgoni, all'On.le Ministero dell'Interno, Direzione Generale della P.S.—Divisione Polizia Politica, Roma, "Oggetto: Movimento socialista," Assicurata Riservatissima, doppia busta, 8 settembre 1938, AOHP.
74. Urgentissimo Espresso, Questori, Padova-Vicenza-Verona-Belluno-Alessandria-Aosta-Cuneo-Novara-Torino-Vercelli, 23 settembre 1938, 500.31475, AOHP.
75. Not only is Hirschmann's Italian memorandum unsigned. The list of memorandums available in Piatier 1939, i, reports authors of all memorandums except the Italian one. Moreover, the summary report, authored by André Piatier, reports the names of authors of the national reports but never cites Hirschmann; see Piatier 1939. The Italian report is listed as authored by O. A. Hirschmann in Condliffe 1940, 398. The report was first published only fifty years later, in a collection of early essays by Hirschman in collaboration with Pier Francesco Asso and Marcello De Cecco, who also wrote an introduction; see Hirschman 1987b.
76. Hirschmann 1939a, 2–3.
77. Hirschmann 1939a, 4.
78. Hirschmann 1939a, 9.
79. Hirschman 1938b.
80. Hirschmann 1939a, 71.
81. Hirschmann 1939a, 73.
82. Hirschmann 1939a, 62.
83. Ellis 1934.
84. Hirschmann 1939b.
85. Hirschmann 1939b, 1; translation by Pier Francesco Asso, 111.
86. Asso 1988.
87. Asso 1988, 85.
88. Asso 1988; see also Condliffe 1940, 282–283.
89. Hirschmann 1939b, 14 and table II.
90. Hirschmann 1939b, 15; translation by Pier Francesco Asso, 122.
91. Condliffe 1940.
92. O. A. Hirschmann to Professor Condliffe, February 28, 1940, JBCP.
93. Otto A. Hirschmann to Professor Condliffe, October 7, 1939, JBCP.
94. On this episode, see Fry 1945; Marino 1999; Isenberg 2001; McClafferty 2008. There is also a 2001 movie, *Varian's War*, directed by Lionel Chetwynd, with William Hurt and Julia Ormond. Fry's volume was reprinted in 1993 with an introduction by Hirschman; see Hirschman 1993a.
95. Isenberg 2001, 26.
96. Marino 1999, 115.
97. "The Emergency Rescue Committee in France," extracts from letters written to the New York office by the ERC representative in Marseille, between the end of September and the beginning of December 1940, VFC.

98. Varian M. Fry to Otto Albert Hirschman, November 30, 1941, VFC.

99. Fry 1945, 26.

100. Fry 1945, 24.

101. Isenberg 2001, 71; Marino 1999, 122.

102. Gold 1980, 160, 158.

103. Hirschman's self-description, as reported in Isenberg 2001, 29.

104. Otto Albert Hirschmann to Mr. Wheeler-Bennett, British Press Service, 30 Rockefeller Plaza, New York City, January 17, 1941, VFC; see also Fittko 1991.

105. "Auxiliary Services," undated but second half of 1941, VFC; see also Isenberg 2001; Marino 1999.

106. Marino 1999, 211.

107. "Auxiliary Services."

108. Varian Fry to Mildred Adams, September 1940, VFC.

109. From an unsigned report on their vicissitudes dated February 14, 1941, VFC.

110. Unsigned report, February 14, 1941, VFC.

111. Hirschman 1993b; see also O. Albert Hirschmann to Professor Condliffe, January 14, 1941, JBCP.

112. Hirschman 1994a, 77.

113. Varian Fry to Eileen Fry, February 9, 1941, VFC.

114. Fry 1945, 151.

115. These events are documented in Alfred Hamilton Barr Jr. to Archibald MacLeish, May 9, 1941; Hugh S. Fullerton, American General Consul in France, to Varian Fry, June 23, 1941; "Paraphrase of Telegram Sent to Department of State through Embassy in Vichy by American Consulate at Marseille on or about June 13, 1941," attached to Hugh S. Fullerton, American General Consul in France, to Varian Fry, June 23, 1941; Varian M. Fry to Frank Kingdon, President of the Emergency Rescue Committee, June 24, 1941, all in VFC.

116. "Memorandum," September 25, 1942, VFC.

117. Gold 1980, 398–400.

2. THE POLITICS OF POWER

1. O. Albert Hirschmann to Professor Condliffe, January 14, 1941, JBCP.

2. Hirschmann to Condliffe, January 26, 1941.

3. Gerschenkron 1943. On Gerschenkron, see Dawidoff 2002 and McCloskey 1992.

4. Lind Olsen 2003.

5. "Antonin Basch, World Bank Aide," *New York Times*, March 19, 1971, 43.

6. Adelman 2013, 193.

7. Albert Hirschman to Ursula, July 21, 1941, quoted in Adelman 2013, 195.

8. Information about the reports that were being prepared for the Trade Regulation Project comes from Inter-Allied Information Center, Section for Information on Studies in Postwar Reconstruction, *Research and Postwar Planning in the U.S.A. List of Agencies. Bibliography*, New York [publisher and publication date not provided, probably 1942].

9. Hirschman 1943a, 1943b.

10. On this debate, see Rosenboim 2017.

11. Gerschenkron 1943, 173.
12. Albert H. to Professor Condliffe, July 6, 1942, JBCP.
13. Condliffe 1940, 16.
14. Condliffe 1940, 16–17.
15. Toynbee 1939; Staley 1939; Condliffe 1940, 56.
16. Condliffe 1943a, xi.
17. Hirschman 1945, ix.
18. Hirschman 1945, 12.
19. Hirschman 1945, 16. Lionel Robbins also used the word "politicalization," adding that it was the borrowing of "a very ugly word from a people who have carried this thing further than most." Robbins 1937, 91.
20. Hirschman 1945, 18–29.
21. See also Condliffe's reflections in International Studies Conference 1938, 23.
22. Hirschman 1945, 30–31.
23. Viner 1940, 52.
24. Viner 1940, 52–53.
25. Viner 1940, 53.
26. Hirschman 1945, 34–40. Another work that discusses the "Nazi methods of economic penetration" in the Danube Basin and the Balkans is Einzig 1938 (quote at 17). See also Royal Institute of International Affairs 1939, 1940.
27. Hirschman 1945, 39.
28. Asso 1988, 109.
29. Hirschman 1945, 75.
30. Albert H. to Professor Condliffe, August 18, 1942, JBCP.
31. Hirschman 1945, 79.
32. Hirschman and Bird 1968, 14.
33. Condliffe 1940, 39.
34. Condliffe 1940, 44; Hirschman 1945, 75.
35. Condliffe 1940, 392.
36. Laves 1940, 174; Carr 1942, 259.
37. Meade 1940, 179.
38. Meade 1940, 9–10.
39. Basch 1941, 182.
40. See, for example, the evolution of Condliffe's proposals in Condliffe 1940, 1942, 1943b, 1946.
41. For a short note on the genealogy of this index, see Hirschman 1964.
42. As mentioned, this chapter had already appeared as Hirschman 1943b.
43. Hirschman 1945, 146.
44. See Prebisch 1950 and Singer 1950.
45. Hirschman 1978.
46. Hirschman 1945, 27 (emphasis added).
47. Oliver 1946, 304.
48. Mann 1946, 91; Brown 1947, 91; Buck 1946, 223; Weiller 1954, 119.
49. Hoselitz 1948, 269; Gottlieb 1949, 159.
50. Brown 1947, 91; Buck 1946; Mann 1946.
51. Florinsky 1946, 274.
52. Oliver 1946, 304.

53. Hirschman 1978, 46.
54. Stinebower 1946, 420.
55. Bidwell 1945, 19.
56. Hirschman 1945, 78.
57. Hirschman 1945, 75.
58. Paul Valéry, *Regards sur le monde actuel* (Paris: Librairie Stock, 1931), 55, in Hirschman 1945, 80.
59. See, for example, Michaely 1960, 1962; Kindleberger 1962; Murphy 1961; Spiegelglas 1961; Kuznets 1964.
60. Stolper 1946, 562.
61. Hirschman 1979a, v–vi.
62. Quoted in Cohen 1990, 263.
63. Baldwin 1985, 53.
64. Quoted in Cohen 2007, 197.
65. Cohen 2008, 21.
66. Keohane and Nye 1972.
67. Krasner 1976; see the reference in Cohen 2008, 74.
68. Kindleberger 1973.
69. Hirschman 1981b.
70. Hirschman 1978.
71. Hirschman 1978, 49.
72. Hirschman 1978, 47.
73. Hirschman 1978, 49–50.
74. Baldwin 1985, 212.
75. Albert O. Hirschman to Professor Condliffe, December 22, 1941, JBCP.
76. Albert H. to Professor Condliffe, April 29, 1943; Albert Hirschman to Professor Condliffe, May 29, 1943, JBCP.
77. Albert H. to Professor Condliffe, April 7, 1943, JBCP.
78. Albert Hirschman to Sarah, June 25, 1944, and Hirschman's entry in his personal diary, both as reported in Adelman 2013, 231.
79. Hirschman 1970a, v.
80. To make ends meet, during the spring of 1946 Hirschman worked as an adjunct professor at American University in Washington, D.C., teaching a course on Contemporary World Politics. Albert H. to Professor Condliffe, April 15, 1946, JBCP.
81. Quoted in Adelman 2013, 288.
82. For example, Hirschman 1947a, 1949a, 1950a, 1950b.
83. Hirschman 1947b, 1947c; first published in Hirschman 1987b.
84. See, for example, the detailed analyses about data unreliability on trade patterns in Europe in Hirschman 1947d and Hirschman and Roberts 1947.
85. Hirschman 1947b, 15.
86. Hirschman 1947b, 15.
87. Hirschman 1947a, 6.
88. Hirschman 1948a, 8. An expanded version of this report was published as Hirschman 1948b.
89. Hirschman 1948a, 8.
90. Hirschman 1948a, 8 (emphasis original).

91. Hirschman 1948c. Together with Hirschman 1948f, this report was published as Hirschman 1948d. A formal elaboration of some of these aspects is in Hirschman 1949b.

92. Hirschman 1948e, 16 (emphasis original).

93. Hirschman 1948e, 3.

94. Hirschman 1948e, 13.

95. See also Asso and De Cecco 1987; Meldolesi 1990.

96. Some margin, however, was contemplated. As Diebold reports, "To avoid the rigidities . . . of exact bilateral balancing, each country usually agreed to hold the other's currency up to a certain amount. But to prevent the trade from becoming too one-sided, the agreement often provided that if one country's trade debts to the other exceeded a specified amount the balance was to be paid in dollars or in gold" Diebold 1952, 20.

97. Diebold 1952, 15.

98. Carli 1996, 72.

99. Eichengreen 2007, 73; Diebold 1952, 19. This and subsequent paragraphs are a synthesis of sections 3–5 of Alacevich 2014.

100. Hirschman 1947e, 358.

101. Hirschman 1947e.

102. Bissell 1996, 31 (emphasis added).

103. Milward 1984, 285.

104. Marjolin quoted in Bissell 1996, 57. For an analysis of the EPU, see Diebold 1952, 87–136; Eichengreen 1993, 1995; Kaplan and Schleiminger 1989.

105. Hirschman 1997; Theodore Geiger, "Marshall Plan Experiences of Theodore Geiger," mimeo prepared for the Reunion and Conference to celebrate the fiftieth anniversary of the Marshall Plan, sponsored by the Elliott School of International Affairs, George Washington University, Monday, June 2, 1997, AOHP. For a discussion of the ECA group in the establishment of the EPU, see Milward 1984, 282–298; Hogan 1987, esp. 271–273; Bissell 1996.

106. Albert O. Hirschman, "Proposal for the Establishment of a European Monetary Authority," AOHP.

107. Hirschman 1950b, 1.

108. Hirschman 1950b; Flexner 1955.

109. Albert O. Hirschman, "Harmonization of Economic Policies," October 16, 1950, AOHP.

110. Hirschman, "Harmonization of Economic Policies."

111. Flexner 1955, 61.

112. Diebold 1952, 410.

113. Bissell 1996, 65.

114. Albert O. Hirschman to Governor Szymczak, "Interim Appraisal of EPU," March 21, 1951, AOHP. See also AOH, "O.E.E.C. Memorandum on 'Urgent Economic Problems,' " October 9, 1950, AOHP.

115. On Manlio Rossi-Doria, see Bernardi 2010; Misiani 2010.

116. Albert O. Hirschman to Manlio Rossi-Doria, July 13, 1951, in Rossi-Doria 2011, 64.

117. Hirschman to Rossi-Doria, July 13, 1951, 64.

118. Hirschman to Rossi-Doria, July 13, 1951, 66.

119. Hirschman to Rossi-Doria, July 13, 1951, 64.

120. Hirschman 1997, 42–43.

3. PIONEER OF DEVELOPMENT

1. Albert O. Hirschman to H. W. Singer, March 29, 1982, AOHP; Hirschman 1950c and 1952.
2. Hirschman and Solomon 1950, 1.
3. Hirschman 1994a, 81.
4. International Bank for Reconstruction and Development (IBRD; the World Bank) 1950a, xv. For an analysis of the World Bank 1949 mission to Colombia and Hirschman's experience in Colombia, see Alacevich 2009, 2011.
5. IBRD 1950a, 1950b. On Lauchlin Currie, see Sandilands 1990.
6. Currie 1950, 5.
7. Albert O. Hirschman to Mr. Richard H. Demuth, August 23, 1952, WBGA.
8. Albert O. Hirschman to Mr. J. Burke Knapp, September 20, 1952, WBGA.
9. Albert O. Hirschman to Mr. J. Burke Knapp, September 20, 1952, WBGA.
10. J. Burke Knapp to Mr. Albert O. Hirschman, November 7, 1952, WBGA.
11. J. Burke Knapp to Mr. Albert O. Hirschman, November 7, 1952, WBGA.
12. See the letters of Albert O. Hirschman to Professor Condliffe, December 29, 1952; June 30, 1953; May 3, 1956; and Albert to Jack [Condliffe], April 7, 1957, JBCP. Quotes from Adelman 2013 are at 336, 363, and 419.
13. Hirschman 1954a, 540.
14. Hirschman 1994a, 81–82.
15. Hirschman and Kalmanoff 1956; Albert O. Hirschman to J. Burke Knapp, May 19, 1954, AOHP. See also the reports by Albert Hirschman and George Kalmanoff, "Present and Prospect Financial Position of the Empresas Municipales de Cali," February 25, 1955; "La demanda para gas en Cali y en el Valle del Cauca," February 1956; "Situacion financiera actual y prospective de las Empresas Municipales de Cali," March 1956; "The Market for Paper and Pulp in Colombia," June 1956; "El nivel de remuneraciones para posiciones directivas en la empresa privada en Colombia," August 1956, all in AOHP.
16. Albert H. to Professor Condliffe, December 18, 1945, JBCP.
17. Albert O. Hirschman to J. Burke Knapp, "Personal," May 1, 1954, AOHP (emphasis original).
18. Emilio Toro to Mr. Robert L. Garner, November 28, 1952, WBGA.
19. Hirschman 1954b, 47.
20. Lloyd G. Reynolds to Albert O. Hirschman, August 21, 1956; Flora M. Rhind to Provost E. S. Furniss, April 12, 1957; Secretary of Yale Corporation, June 10, 1957, all in AOHP.
21. Hirschman 1958, v, vi.
22. Hirschman 1984a, 94.
23. Albert O. Hirschman, "Case Studies of Instances of Successful Economic Development in Colombia," March 8, 1954, AOHP; see also Albert O. Hirschman to Professor Condliffe, April 18, 1953, JBCP.
24. Albert O. Hirschman to Professor Condliffe, April 18, 1953, JBCP.
25. Hirschman 1958, 50.
26. Rosenstein-Rodan 1943, 202.
27. Rosenstein-Rodan 1943, 204.
28. Rosenstein-Rodan 1943, 206.

29. Lewis 1954, 140–142, 146–147.

30. Lewis 1954, 155.

31. The scholar who most contributed to the divulgation of the "takeoff" metaphor is arguably Walt W. Rostow 1960.

32. Nurkse [1953] 1962, 11.

33. Nurkse [1953] 1962, 13.

34. Hirschman 1984a, 87.

35. See Hirschman 1971a, 1971b. For a discussion of Hirschman's view of visiting economists in less developed countries, see Bianchi 2011.

36. For a discussion of the significance of the work of Chatham House for the global development discourse, see Alacevich 2018. For an analysis of development debates in interwar central Europe, especially the role of Manoilescu, see Love 1996.

37. Rosenstein-Rodan 1957, 1961; Nurkse 1961, 74.

38. Adelman 2013, 333.

39. Hirschman 1958, 51–52 (emphasis original).

40. Hirschman 1958, 5. This concept was not completely new. It was also present in the writings of the scholars whom Hirschman criticized. The attention given by Rosenstein-Rodan and Nurkse to "disguised unemployment" in agriculture was clearly an attempt to bring to light hidden or badly utilized resources.

41. Streeten 1959, 182–183.

42. Hirschman 1958, 25.

43. Hirschman 1958, 25. Hirschman noted that his book and Streeten's article were written independently, but Streeten acknowledged that he read Hirschman's book after writing a first draft of the paper and that the final version thus benefited from Hirschman's ideas; see Hirschman 1984a, 87 n. 1, and Paul P. Streeten to Albert Hirschman, November 4, 1982, AOHP.

44. Hirschman 1958, 25.

45. Hirschman 1958, 25.

46. Hirschman 1965, 386.

47. Gershenkron 1962, which contains important essays written in 1952 and 1957.

48. Hirschman 1965.

49. Hirschman 1958, 28.

50. Hirschman 1965, 391. See also Hirschman 1984a, 91–94.

51. I am grateful to Ilene Grabel for suggesting that I stress this point.

52. Hirschman 1977a, 80.

53. Hirschman 1958, 105–108; Chenery and Watanabe 1958.

54. Hirschman 1985a offers a summary of the linkages approach.

55. Hirschman 1958, 122 (emphasis original).

56. Hirschman 1958, 124.

57. Hirschman 1958, 109.

58. Hirschman 1977a; 1985a, 64–66; Watkins 1963.

59. Hirschman 1977a.

60. Hirschman 1958, 209.

61. Hirschman 1958, 210.

62. Hirschman 1977a, 90–91.

63. See, for example, Higgins, Kafka, and Britnell 1959.

64. Mukherji 1959, 85; Goodman 1959, 468; Hill 1959, 72.

65. Reubens 1959, 462; Frank 1960.
66. Jacques J. Polak to Albert O. Hirschman, August 10, 1959, AOHP, and letters from the mentioned individuals.
67. Roy Harrod to Albert Hirschman, September 8, 1963, AOHP. *Legenda* is a Latin gerundive meaning "to be read."
68. Knox 1960, 99.
69. Watkins 1961, 111.
70. Chenery 1959, 1064.
71. Chenery 1959, 1064–1065.
72. Goodman 1959, 468. For an assessment of Chenery's reading of *Strategy*, see De Marchi 2016.
73. Shannon 1959, 125.
74. Higgins 1960, 114.
75. Lewis 1955, 384.
76. Lewis 1955, 264–265.
77. Mannheim 1936, 265.
78. Staley 1939, 149.
79. Dasgupta 1965.
80. Galbraith 1958, 591.
81. Rosenstein-Rodan 1963, 1.
82. Hirschman and Bird 1968.
83. Hirschman and Bird 1968, 8.
84. Singer 1965.
85. Hirschman and Bird 1968, 9.
86. Harberger 1972, 637.
87. Harberger 1972, 637.
88. Hirschman 1994a, 81.
89. Transcript of oral history interview with Paul Rosenstein-Rodan held on August 14, 1961, Oral History Program, WBGA.
90. Harberger 1972; Singer 1965; Hirschman 1968b.
91. Little 1982, 44.
92. Recent examples are Meier 2005 and Clark 2006 (see, for example, the entry on Albert O. Hirschman by Osvaldo Feinstein).
93. Krugman 1994, 40; see also Krugman 1993.
94. Hirschman 1958, v. For a reassessment of the conflict between Currie and Hirschman in Colombia, see Álvarez, Guiot-Isaac, and Hurtado 2020.
95. IBRD 1950a, 423–425.
96. IBRD 1950a, 427.
97. Comité de Desarrollo Economico, *Informe de la mision para el Comité. Fomento de una industria colombiana de acero*, draft, December 15, 1950, LBCP.
98. Comité de Desarrollo Economico, *Informe preliminar sobre el establecimiento de una planta siderurgica*, Bogotá, Diciembre 14 de 1950, LBCP.
99. Hirschman 1954b.
100. Hirschman 1954b, 49.
101. Hirschman 1958, chap. 10.
102. George Rosen, "The Plan for Industry," Center for International Studies, MIT, Economic Development, India Project, A/56-36, September 1956.

103. Merton [1961] 1973, 56.
104. Merton [1961] 1973, 56.
105. Killick 1978, 19
106. Merton [1961] 1973, 51.
107. Hirschman 1958, 51.
108. Sen 1960, 591.
109. Sen 1960, 592 (emphasis original).
110. Hirschman 1958, ix (emphasis original).
111. William Diebold, Jr. to Albert O. Hirschman, August 17, 1983, AOHP.
112. Diebold, Jr. to Hirschman, August 17, 1983. See Currie 1981.
113. Streeten 1986, 240.
114. Streeten 1986, 243.
115. Paul P. Streeten, personal email communication, October 15, 2004.

4. REMAKING DEVELOPMENT ECONOMICS

1. For introductory texts on development economics, see Arndt 1987; Meier 2001, 2005; Meier and Seers 1984; Oman and Wignaraja 1991; Hirschman 1981b. For a reassessment of early development debates, see Alacevich 2011. A recent assessment is Alacevich and Boianovsky 2018.
2. Hirschman 1981b.
3. Hirschman 1968a, vii–viii.
4. Tendler 1968.
5. Hirschman 1963, 1.
6. Hirschman 1963, 2.
7. Hirschman 1980a, 171–172.
8. Hirschman 1967a, 3.
9. Hirschman 1963, 227.
10. Hirschman 1963, 228.
11. Hirschman 1961a, 1961b.
12. Adelman 2013, 369.
13. Albert O. Hirschman, "Making the Best of Inflation," paper delivered at the Conference on Inflation and Growth in Latin America, Rio de Janeiro, Brazil, January 3–11, 1963, AOHP.
14. Hirschman 1963, 232.
15. Albert O. Hirschman, "Making the Best of Inflation," paper delivered at the Conference on Inflation and Growth in Latin America, Rio de Janeiro, Brazil, January 3–11, 1963, AOHP.
16. Hirschman 1963, 242.
17. Hirschman 1963, 256.
18. Hirschman 1963, 256.
19. Hirschman 1963, 260.
20. Hirschman 1963, 4.
21. Hirschman 1963, 4.
22. Olson 1965.
23. Seers 1964, 158.

24. Seers 1964, 159.
25. Seers 1964, 159–160.
26. Adelman 2013, 383.
27. Don K. Price to Albert O. Hirschman, November 12, 1963; Albert O. Hirschman to Dean Price, December 9, 1963; Harold Barger to Albert O. Hirschman, December 30, 1963; Don K. Price to Albert O. Hirschman, March 9, 1964; Harvard University News office, Morning Papers of Thursday, March 19, 1964, all in AOHP.
28. See Feijoó and Hirschman 1984 and the website of the project, now a nonprofit corporation, https://peopleandstories.org.
29. Albert O. Hirschman to J. Burke Knapp, March 14, 1963, AOHP.
30. Albert O. Hirschman, "A Study of Completed Investment Projects Which Have Received Financial Support from the World Bank," June 1963, WBGA.
31. Hirschman 1967a, 1.
32. Hirschman 1967a, 4.
33. Albert O. Hirschman, "A Study of Completed Investment Projects Which Have Received Financial Support from the World Bank," June 5, 1963, WBGA.
34. Hirschman 1967a, 3.
35. Dragoslav Avramovic to Department Heads, IBRD and IFC, "Investment in Developing Countries—Effects, Expectations and Reality," February 18, 1964, WBGA.
36. Robert E. Asher to Robert D. Calkins, "Hirschman Project," April 8, 1964, AOHP.
37. P. M. Mathew to William Diamond, "Investment in Developing Countries—Effects, Expectations and Reality," February 24, 1964, WBGA.
38. Robert F. Skillings to Syed S. Husain, "Professor Hirschman's Forthcoming Study," February 26, 1964, WBGA.
39. IBRD 1972.
40. Transcript of Interview with Robert Picciotto, by William H. Becker and Marie T. Zenni, held on November 1, 2000, Oral History Program, WBGA, 16.
41. Hirschman 1958, vi; 1963, ix.
42. Albert O. Hirschman to Don K. Price, October 19, 1964, AOHP.
43. Albert O. Hirschman, "A Study of Selected World Bank Projects—Some Interim Observations," August 1965, WBGA.
44. Hirschman, "A Study of Selected World Bank Projects."
45. Hirschman, "A Study of Selected World Bank Projects."
46. "Ideas—Miscellaneous," no date, AOHP.
47. Hirschman, "A Study of Selected World Bank Projects."
48. "Ideas—Miscellaneous," no date, AOHP.
49. "Uganda," no date, AOHP.
50. Sarah Hirschman, "Latin America," April 19, 1965, AOHP.
51. Sarah Hirschman, "Nigeria," August 18, 1965, AOHP.
52. "Ideas—Miscellaneous," no date, AOHP.
53. Sarah Hirschman, "Latin America," April 19, 1965, AOHP.
54. Hirschman, "A Study of Selected World Bank Projects.".
55. Sarah Hirschman, "Ethiopia," August 19, 1965, AOHP.
56. Hirschman, "A Study of Selected World Bank Projects."
57. Sarah Hirschman, "Ethiopia," August 19, 1965, AOHP.
58. "Ideas—Miscellaneous," no date, AOHP.

59. A. D. Spottswood to Bernard Chadenet, "Comments on Dr. Hirschman's 'Interim Observations,'" September 8, 1965, WBGA.
60. D. S. Ballantine to B. Chadenet, "Comment on Interim Observations by A. O. Hirschman," September 15, 1965, WBGA.
61. P. A. Reid to L. J. C. Evans, November 16, 1965, WBGA.
62. Hirschman, "A Study of Selected World Bank Projects."
63. A. D. Spottswood to Bernard Chadenet, "Comments on Dr. Hirschman's 'Interim Observations,'" September 8, 1965, WBGA.
64. C. P. McMeekan to H. B. Ripman, "Project Study—A. O. Hirschman," September 22, 1965, WBGA.
65. Hans A. Adler to Warren C. Baum, "Comments on Professor Hirschman's 'Study of Selected World Bank Projects—Some Interim Observations,'" September 22, 1965, WBGA.
66. Hirschman, "A Study of Selected World Bank Projects."
67. A. D. Spottswood to Bernard Chadenet, "Comments on Dr. Hirschman's 'Interim Observations,'" September 8, 1965, WBGA (emphasis original).
68. C. P. McMeekan to H. B. Ripman, "Project Study—A. O. Hirschman," September 22, 1965, WBGA.
69. D. S. Ballantine to B. Chadenet, "Comment on Interim Observations by A. O. Hirschman," September 15, 1965, WBGA.
70. Hirschman, "A Study of Selected World Bank Projects."
71. Dragoslav Avramovic to Department Heads, IBRD and IFC, "Investment in Developing Countries—Effects, Expectations and Reality," February 18, 1964, WBGA.
72. Hirschman, "A Study of Selected World Bank Projects."
73. A. D. Spottswood to Bernard Chadenet, "Comments on Dr. Hirschman's 'Interim Observations,'" September 8, 1965, WBGA.
74. Hans A. Adler to Warren C. Baum, "Comments on Professor Hirschman's 'Study of Selected World Bank Projects—Some Interim Observations,'" September 22, 1965, WBGA.
75. Reported in Robert E. Asher to Albert O. Hirschman, May 27, 1966, WBGA.
76. Asher 1962, 217.
77. Albert O. Hirschman to his daughters Katia and Lisa, April 4, 1965, AOHP (emphasis original).
78. Original Italian, Albert Hirschman to Katia and Lisa, April 4, 1965, AOHP.
79. "Advisory Committee for *Development Projects Observed* by Albert O. Hirschman," September 21, 1966, AOHP. "The Principle of the Hiding Hand" was also published as a stand-alone piece in *The Public Interest*, Hirschman 1967b.
80. Walter S. Salant to Albert O. Hirschman, "More on 'The Hiding Hand' and other comments on *Development Projects Observed*," January 26, 1967, AOHP.
81. Hirschman 1994b, ix.
82. Albert O. Hirschman to Katia and Lisa, January 1, 1965, AOHP (emphasis original).
83. Hirschman 1967a, 161.
84. Hirschman 1967a, 162.
85. Hirschman 1967a, 169.
86. Hirschman 1967a, 179.
87. Hirschman 1967a, 186 (emphasis original).
88. Richard H. Demuth to Robert E. Asher, September 13, 1966, WBGA.

89. Killick 1978, 27 (emphasis original).
90. Herman G. van der Tak to Albert O. Hirschman, December 20, 1966, WBGA.
91. Porter 1995, 148–189.
92. Marglin 1967, 18; see also Porter 1995.
93. Hammond 1966, 222.
94. Little and Mirrlees 1968, 1974.
95. Kornai 1979, 76.
96. Dasgupta, Marglin, and Sen 1972.
97. Dasgupta 1972, 41; Kornai 1979, 76. On the differences between the two approaches, see, for example, the comparison of OECD and UNIDO approaches by Dasgupta 1972, and a critique of the OECD volume by Frances Stewart and Paul Streeten 1972.
98. Hirschman and Lindblom 1962, 83–84.
99. UNESCO 1978, 124.
100. Schaffer and Lamb 1978, esp. 70–79.
101. Hall 1980, 8.
102. Little and Mirrlees 1974, 379.
103. Squire and Van der Tak 1975.
104. Cracknell 1984, 17–18.
105. Mario Piccagli to H. B. Ripman, "Comments on Mr. Hirschman's Observations," September 22, 1965, AOHP.
106. Warren C. Baum to B. Chadenet, "Comments on Mr. Hirschman's Paper," September 17, 1965, WBGA.
107. D. S. Ballantine to B. Chadenet, "Comment on Interim Observations by A. O. Hirschman," September 15, 1965, WBGA.
108. Cited in Grasso, Wasty, and Weaving 2003, 43.
109. Köpp 2003, 55.
110. Sunstein 2015, xi.
111. Sunstein 2013.
112. See, for example, Sunstein 1999, 23, 46.
113. Sunstein 2018, xi (emphasis original).
114. Streeten 1984, 116; Picciotto 1994, 221–222.
115. Picciotto 1994, 222 (emphasis original).
116. Sunstein 2015, xii; Sandilands 2015, 32.
117. Picciotto 1994, 224.
118. For the entire discussion, see Sunstein 2015; Flyvbjerg and Sunstein 2016, 991; Flyvbjerg 2016, 2018; Ika 2018; Lepenies 2018; Room 2018.
119. Gasper 1986, 473, 470.
120. Kenyon and Criscuolo 2017. Honig 2018 offers new and stimulating perspectives on how foreign aid organizations can effectively implement aid projects in an uncertain environment.

5. AN INTERDISCIPLINARY SOCIAL SCIENCE

1. Hirschman 1971a, ix.
2. Hirschman 1971a.
3. Hirschman 1970a.

4. Hirschman 1971b, 2.
5. Hirschman 1970a, 15.
6. Hirschman 1971b, 8.
7. Hirschman 1971b, 24, 10.
8. As reported by one of Hoffman's assistants, Marge Fonyi, in Murphy 2006, 112.
9. Hirschman 1963, 238.
10. Hirschman 1970b, 336–337 (emphasis original).
11. Hirschman 1963, 238.
12. Hirschman 1968b, 88–89. For earlier discussions of this failure complex or self-incriminating attitude, see Hirschman 1961b, 1963.
13. ECLA 1950; Prebisch 1950; Singer 1950; Hadass and Williamson 2003.
14. Furtado 1966.
15. Hirschman 1968b.
16. Hirschman 1968b, 32.
17. Hirschman 1968b, 9.
18. Hirschman 1968c, 926 (emphasis added).
19. Hirschman 1968c, 930 (emphasis original).
20. Hirschman 1990a.
21. Hirschman 1968c, 932.
22. da Conceição Tavares 1964; Macario 1964; Furtado 1966. See also the discussion of the critic of ISI from the left in Love 1996.
23. Little, Scitovsky, and Scott 1970.
24. John Knapp, for example, wrote of "excess borrowing" on the part of developing nations. Knapp 1957.
25. Hirschman and Lindblom 1962, 222.
26. Hirschman 1969, 6.
27. Hirschman 1969, 6.
28. Hirschman 1969, 11.
29. Hirschman 1969, 13.
30. Hirschman 1969, 15.
31. Zahniser and Weis 1989, 181.
32. Milton S. Eisenhower, Report to the President, "United States-Latin American Relations," December 27, 1958, Department of State Publication 6764, 1959, 15.
33. Hirschman 1960, 61.
34. John F. Kennedy, "Address at a White House Reception for Members of Congress and for the Diplomatic Corps of the Latin American Republics," March 13, 1961, accessed November 11, 2019, https://www.jfklibrary.org/archives/other-resources/john-f-kennedy-speeches/latin-american-diplomats-washington-dc-19610313.
35. Hirschman 1961c, 179.
36. Adelman 2013, 413.
37. Hirschman and Bird 1968, 3.
38. "A Modest Proposal," undated, AOHP.
39. Hirschman and Bird 1968, 21.
40. As this list makes clear, development debates in those years were strikingly and nearly wholly dominated by men.
41. Sherman Robinson, Rapporteur, "Institute of Politics: Study Group on Foreign Aid," Report of the Meeting of December 4, 1967, AOHP.

42. Stanley Please to Alexander Stevenson, "Foreign Aid—A Critique and a Proposal," paper Prepared by Albert O. Hirschman and Richard M. Bird, December 26, 1967, AOHP; John A. Holsen to Alexander Stevenson, A Reaction to Hirschman and Bird ("Foreign Aid—A Critique and a Proposal"), December 26, 1967, AOHP.
43. Alexander Stevenson to Albert O. Hirschman, December 29, 1967, AOHP.
44. Fritz Machlup to Albert O. Hirschman, February 20, 1968, AOHP.
45. Albert Hirschman to Fritz Machlup, January 28, 1968, AOHP.
46. Albert O. Hirschman to Robert Heilbroner, August 15, 1969, AOHP.
47. Albert O. Hirschman to Martin M. Rosen, June 8, 1961; Martin M. Rosen to Albert O. Hirschman, July 6, 1961, AOHP.
48. Samuel Bowles to Albert O. Hirschman, January 14, 1970, AOHP.
49. Albert O. Hirschman to Samuel Bowles, January 22, 1970, AOHP.
50. Adelman 2013, 422–433.
51. Adelman 2013, 423.
52. Albert O. Hirschman to Ursula Hirschmann, September 8, 1968, quoted in Adelman 2013, 428.
53. Hirschman 1967a, p. 148.
54. Adelman 2013, 393.
55. Adelman 2013, 393.
56. Hirschman 1958, 142.
57. Hirschman 1967a, 147.
58. Hirschman 1970a, vii.
59. Lazear 1999, 12.
60. Becker 1957, 1960, 1964, 1976, 1981; Gilber and Becker 1975; Stigler and Becker 1977.
61. Hirschman 1990b, 158–159.
62. Hirschman 1970a, 16.
63. Milton Friedman, quoted in Hirschman 1970a, 16.
64. Hirschman 1970a, 17.
65. Hirschman 1970a, 18 (emphasis original).
66. Hirschman 1970a, 19 (emphasis original).
67. Hirschman 1970a, 19.
68. Hirschman 1974, 8.
69. Barry 1974, 85–86.
70. Rokkan 1974a, 27.
71. Hirschman 1970a, 1 (emphasis original).
72. Hirschman 1970a, 3.
73. Hirschman 1970a, 25.
74. Hirschman 1970a, 107–108.
75. Adelman 2013, 435–437.
76. We could also speculate that once the decision to exit is acted upon, some inertia and path dependence sets in, such that moving back later to the public school becomes nonviable. In other words, the costs of reversing exit become or are perceived as too high.
77. Hirschman 1970a, 79.
78. Hirschman 1970a, 80.
79. Hirschman 1970a, 59 (emphasis original).

80. Hirschman 1970a, 59–61. By encouraging political emigration, however, dictatorial regimes risk exacerbating the so-called autocrat's dilemma.
81. Hirschman 1970a, 53.
82. Hirschman 1970a, 54.
83. Hotelling 1929, 45.
84. Hotelling 1929.
85. Hirschman 1970a, 72.
86. Psychologist Philip Zimbardo and one of his graduate students, Mark Snyder, designed an experiment in collaboration with Hirschman on "The Effects of Severity of Initiation on Activism." The experiment was never enacted, but two years later, Zimbardo conducted what has become famous as the Stanford Prison Experiment, in which college students were divided into two groups of guards and prisoners to reproduce the dynamics of a prison. The Hirschman-Snyder-Zimbardo experiment is reproduced as Appendix E of Hirschman 1970a, 146–155.
87. Adelman 2013, 446.
88. Hirschman 1994d, 206.
89. Hirschman 1994d, 211.
90. Hirschman 1994d, 216.
91. Baer 1970, 814.
92. Hanson 1970, 1275.
93. Deutsch 1971, 25.
94. Barry 1974, 79.
95. Barry 1974, 79, 82.
96. Rokkan 1974a, 27.
97. See in particular Williamson 1975, 1976, and the comments by Nelson 1976.
98. Matthews and Prothro 1966, 450.
99. Orbell and Uno 1972. The concepts of exit and voice were also used to study citizen satisfaction and dissatisfaction with urban services by Lyons, Lowery, and Hoogland DeHoog 1992. A more recent analysis of citizens' reaction to urban services that relies extensively on Hirschman's framework is Dowding and John 2012.
100. See, for example, Migdal 1980; Peleg and Waxman 2011; Ophir 2019; and Zolberg, Suhrke, and Aguayo 1989.
101. Rokkan 1975. For a further reflection on this point, see Rokkan 1974b. For a description of this top-down approach within nations, see Coleman 1974. For Hirschman's later reflections on areas of application of the exit-voice dichotomy, see Hirschman 1986a, esp. 85–99.
102. Barry 1974, 92–95.
103. Olson [1965] 1971, 159–162.
104. Hirschman 1994a, 108.
105. Tullock 1970.
106. Mancur Olson to Albert O. Hirschman, February 20, 1973, quoted in Adelman 2013, 448.
107. Hirschman 1974, 9 (emphasis original).
108. Hirschman 1974, 10.
109. Hirschman 1993c.
110. Adelman 2013, 621.
111. Hirschman 1993c, 198.

112. Hirschman 1993c, 198.
113. Hirschman 1993c, 202.
114. O'Donnell 1986, 252.
115. O'Donnell 1986, 254.
116. O'Donnell 1986, 260.
117. O'Donnell 1986, 261.

6. THE HISTORY AND THEORY OF MARKET SOCIETIES

1. Marx 1859 [1904], 12–13.
2. Hirschman 1979b, xv.
3. Rostow 1960 [1990], 134.
4. Adelman and Morris 1973, vii.
5. Adelman and Morris 1973, 139.
6. Adelman and Morris 1973, 188.
7. Adelman and Morris 1973, 192.
8. O'Donnell 1973, 8.
9. O'Donnell 1973; Collier 1979.
10. O'Donnell 1973, 84.
11. O'Donnell 1973, 91.
12. O'Donnell 1973, 91.
13. Collier 1979.
14. Hirschman 1979c, 61–62.
15. "A Conversation with Clifford Geertz, Albert Hirschman and Colleagues on 'The Hungry, Crowded, Competitive World,'" Institute for Advanced Study, Princeton, NJ, January 26, 1976, AOHP.
16. Hirschman 1975, 386, 402.
17. Albert O. Hirschman, "Lisa's Questions," 1998, AOHP. Adelman describes how Hirschman used the Joint Committee on Latin American Studies "as a rescue instrument," and the fellowship program at the Institute in Princeton "as a haven for persecuted social scientists." Adelman 2013, 470.
18. "Where We Went Wrong," The Four W Club, founded by A.O.H., 1972, AOHP.
19. Hirschman 1973, 533.
20. Hirschman 1973, 544.
21. Hirschman 1973, 561.
22. Hirschman 1973, 561.
23. Adelman 2013, 465–467.
24. Hirschman 1977b [1997], 3.
25. Schumpeter 1942 [2008], 127–128.
26. Hazard 1952 [1990], xv. I am indebted to Castrillón 2013 for the references to Schumpeter and Hazard.
27. Hirschman 1977b [1997], 3–4.
28. Machiavelli, quoted in Hirschman 1977b [1997], 13.
29. Vico, quoted in Hirschman 1977b [1997], 14.
30. Vico, quoted in Hirschman 1977b [1997], 17.
31. Schelling 1978.

32. Hirschman 1977b [1997], 31.

33. Hirschman 1985a, 36–37.

34. Hirschman 1985b, 39.

35. Hirschman 1977b [1997], 59.

36. Hirschman 1977b [1997], 59.

37. Montesquieu, quoted in Hirschman 1977b [1997], 60.

38. Machiavelli, quoted in Hirschman 1977b [1997], 13.

39. Steuart, quoted in Hirschman 1977b [1997], 84–85.

40. Hirschman 1977b [1997], 102 (emphasis original).

41. Smith 1776 [1976], III.iv.4–5.

42. Smith, quoted in Hirschman 1977b [1997], 108.

43. Hirschman 1977b [1997], 112.

44. Hirschman 1977b [1997], 62; Marx's quote is from the same page.

45. Hirschman 1979c, 62.

46. Hirschman 1977b [1997], 117.

47. Hirschman 1977b [1997], 122.

48. Tocqueville, quoted in Hirschman 1977b [1997], 124.

49. Tocqueville, quoted in Hirschman 1979c, 62–63.

50. Hirschman 1979c, 63.

51. Ryan 1977, 535.

52. Seddig 1978, 339; Coser 1978, 397.

53. See, for example, Elster 1978; Bertilsson and Eyerman 1979; Suttle 1987; Martin 1990; Hoffman 1991; Elster 1994; Daston 1994; Inayatullah 1997; Bowles 1998; Force 2003; Mathiowetz 2007; Bridel 2009; Friedman 2011.

54. Keohane 1978, 776.

55. De Vries 1979, 140.

56. Stillman 1978.

57. Hirschman 1977b [1997], 131.

58. Hirschman 1977b [1997], 131.

59. Hirschman 1977b [1997], 130 (emphasis original).

60. Keohane 1978; Supple 1978; Schneider 1978, 402; Stillman 1978, 1028.

61. Kaiser 1979, 421.

62. Wuthnow 1979.

63. Poggi 1978, 398.

64. Poggi 1978, 399.

65. Supple 1978.

66. Schneider 1978, 401–402.

67. Michael Walzer to Albert O. Hirschman, July 19, 1973; Albert O. Hirschman to Michael Walzer, August 1, 1973; Quentin Skinner to Albert Hirschman, undated, all in AOHP.

68. Wuthnow 1979, 427.

69. Wuthnow 1979, 428.

70. Wuthnow 1979, 429.

71. Pocock 1981, 50.

72. Hirschman 1977b [1997], 42; see also Hampsher-Monk 1984, 104.

73. Pocock 1981, 53.

74. Pocock 1981, 52; 1975, vii–viii.

75. Hampsher-Monk 1984, 89.
76. Wuthnow 1979, 430.
77. Gellner 1979, 469.
78. Gellner 1979, 469.
79. De Vries 1979, 141.
80. Luis Eduardo Nieto Arteta, quoted in Hirschman 1979c, 64.
81. Hirschman 1979c, 83.
82. Hirschman 1979c, 85–86.
83. Hirschman 1979c, 91–92.
84. Hirschman 1979c, 98.
85. Hirschman 1979c, 94–95.
86. Lindberg 1985; Maier 1985.
87. Hirschman 1985c.
88. Albert O. Hirschman to Michael Walzer, August 1, 1973, AOHP.
89. Hirschman 1982a.
90. Hirschman 1982a, 1480.
91. Hirschman 1982a, 1464.
92. Hirschman 1982a, 1463.
93. Hirschman 1982a, 1470.
94. Karl Marx and Frederick Engels, "Address of the Central Committee to the Communist League," March 1850, accessed on December 26, 2019, https://www.marxists .org/archive/marx/works/1847/communist-league/1850-ad1.htm.
95. Karl Marx and Frederick Engels, "Manifesto of the Communist Party," February 1848, accessed on December 26, 2019, https://www.marxists.org/archive/marx/works /download/pdf/Manifesto.pdf.
96. Schumpeter, quoted in Hirschman 1982a, 1469.
97. Hirschman 1982a, 1473.
98. Hirschman 1982a, 1473–1474 (emphasis original).
99. See, for example, Frank 1967.
100. Hartz, quoted in Hirschman 1982a, 1479.
101. Hirschman 1982a, 1481 (emphasis added).
102. Hirschman 1982a, 1481 (emphasis original).
103. Hirschman 1982a, 1483.
104. Hirschman 1982a, 1483.

7. THE WORKING OF DEMOCRACY

1. Rodgers 2011, 3.
2. Hirschman 1982b [2002], 3.
3. Hirschman 1982b [2002], xv.
4. Hirschman 1982b [2002], 3.
5. Hirschman 1982b [2002], 12.
6. See, for example, Simon 1957; Cyert and De Groot 1975.
7. Hirschman 1982b [2002], 10.
8. Scitovsky 1976.
9. Lane 1978, 814–815.

10. Hirschman 1982b [2002], 33.
11. Hirschman 1982b [2002], 33.
12. Hirschman 1982b [2002], 41.
13. O'Connor 1973; Hirsch 1976; Murray 1984 [1994]. See also Habermas 1975.
14. Hirschman 1980b, 113.
15. See Katznelson 1980.
16. Hirschman 1980b.
17. Hirschman 1980b, 115.
18. Hirschman 1980b, 115.
19. Frankfurt 1971, 6.
20. Frankfurt 1971, 7.
21. Sen 1977, 322.
22. Sen 1972, 1977.
23. Hirschman 1984b, 145 (emphasis original).
24. Hirschman 1982b [2002], 65.
25. See Olson 1965 [1971]; Scitovsky 1976; and Hirschman's discussion, Hirschman 1982b [2002], esp. 77–87.
26. Hirschman 1982b [2002], 92.
27. On the usefulness of this kind of middle-range model, like Olson's *Logic of Collective Action* but also many of Hirschman's own analyses, see Boudon 1982.
28. Hirschman 1982b [2002].
29. Hirschman 1982b [2002], 95.
30. Hirschman 1982b [2002], 95.
31. Hirschman 1982b [2002], 132.
32. Hirschman 1982b [2002], 134 (emphasis original).
33. O'Donnell 1986, 257.
34. O'Donnell 1986, 257.
35. See, for example, Buttrick 1982; Ginzberg 1982; Schott 1983; Bolton 1984.
36. Boudon 1986, 238.
37. Hirschman 1982b [2002], 4.
38. Hirschman 1982b [2002], 4, 8.
39. Axinn 1983, 242.
40. Stinchcombe 1983, 691.
41. Hickerson 1983, 259. See also Schott 1983; Smith 1983.
42. Maier 2017, 5.
43. Greek 1983.
44. Maier 2017, 5.
45. Stinchcombe 1983, 690.
46. Paci 1982, referring especially to Weisbrod 1978.
47. Hirschman 1982b [2002], 6, 15.
48. Paci 1982.
49. For instance, Maser 1984.
50. Stinchcombe 1983, 689.
51. Stinchcombe 1983, 691; see also Scitovsky 1983.
52. Ginzberg 1982.
53. Hirschman 1982b [2002], 21.
54. Tarrow 1988, 422.

55. Stinchcombe 1983, 691.
56. Hirschman 1984c, 47.
57. Tilly 1978, 73.
58. Moore 1966; Wolf 1969.
59. Hirschman 1984c, 8.
60. The Inter-American Foundation is still active; see www.iaf.gov.
61. Smith 1776 [1976], II.iii.28.
62. Hirschman 1984c, ix.
63. Hirschman 1984c, 36.
64. Hirschman 1984c, 41.
65. Hirschman 1984c, 57.
66. Hirschman 1984c, 95.
67. O'Donnell 1983, 17–18 (emphasis original).
68. Hirschman 1984c, 58–77, quote at 59.
69. Hirschman 1984c, 33.
70. Hirschman 1963, 271.
71. Hirschman 1984c, 33 (emphasis original).
72. Hirschman 1984c, 66–68.
73. Hirschman 1984c, 43.
74. Hirschman 1984c, 43 (emphasis original).
75. Hirschman 1994b, xvii.
76. Hirschman 1984c, 48.
77. Hirschman 1984c, 49 (emphasis original).
78. See also Tendler 1983b.
79. Tendler 1982, 95.
80. Tendler 1982, 97.
81. On the 1970s birth of human rights, see Moyn 2010; this view has been challenged, for example by Sikkink 2017. On the far from linear relationship among human rights, basic need, and economic inequality, see Moyn 2018.
82. Hirschman 1984c, 101 (emphasis original).
83. Hirschman 1984c, 97 (emphasis original).
84. Tendler 1982, 95.
85. Hirschman 1984c, 97–98 (emphasis original).
86. Hirschman 1984c, 99.
87. See the considerations in Bray 1991. Exceptions are Siebel and Massing 1976; Cernea 1981.
88. Tendler 1983a, 260.
89. Hirschman 1985d, 177.
90. Hirschman 1985d, 176.
91. Huntington 1991, 42 (emphasis original).
92. Hirschman 1985d, 177.
93. Hirschman 1985d, 181.
94. On Hirschman's continuing attention to Latin America, see, for example, Hirschman 1987c.
95. Harpham and Scotch 1988, 194.
96. Harpham and Scotch 1988, 194.
97. Schwartz 1983.

98. Murray 1984 [1994], 8.
99. Murray 1984 [1994], 9.
100. Ford Foundation 1989, v.
101. Meyer 1989, 40–41, 45.
102. Katznelson, Geiger, and Kryder 1993; Katznelson and Pietrykowski 1991; Skocpol 1991, 1992a, 1992b, 1993, 1995; Skocpol, Howard, Goodrich Lehmann, and Abend-Wein 1993.
103. Hirschman 1991, x.
104. Merton 1936, 894.
105. Hirschman 1991, 7.
106. Hirschman 1991, 7.
107. Hirschman 1993d, 294.
108. Smith 1776 [1976], I.ii.2.
109. Hirschman 1991, 36–37.
110. Sen 1993, 132.
111. Hirschman 1993d.
112. Hirschman 1991, 117.
113. Hirschman 1993d, 297–302.
114. Hirschman 1993d, 311.
115. Hirschman 1993d, 312 (emphasis original).
116. Hirschman 1993d, 312–313 (emphasis original).
117. Hirschman 1991, 168.
118. Harvard Law Review 1994; Sender 1994; Eldridge 1996.
119. Wolfe 1992, 31–32; DiIulio 1992, 720.
120. Garver 1991, p. 49.
121. DiIulio 1992, 722.
122. Harvard Law Review 1991, 588.
123. Hirschman 1991, x–xi.
124. Lynn 1992, 651.
125. Bronner 1993, 135.
126. Dunn 1991, 523.
127. Boudon 1992, 92.
128. Boudon 1992, 93.
129. Boudon 1992, 90.
130. Boudon 1992, 93.
131. Boudon 1992, 95.
132. Adelman 2013, 636.
133. Hirschman 1992, 96.
134. Hirschman 1992, 97.
135. Muller 1991, 85.
136. Muller 1991, 91.
137. Muller 1991, 92.
138. Muller 1991, 83.
139. Clifford Geertz, quoted in Adelman 2013, 601. More generally, this section draws on Adelman 2013, chap. 20.
140. Hirschman 1986b, 1995, 1998.
141. Adelman 2013, 600.

142. Adelman 2013, 599.

143. Adelman 2013, 613.

144. Adelman 2013, 613.

145. Personal communication from an economist consulted for the Nobel nominations in the 1980s.

146. Adelman 2013, 644.

8. THE LEGACY OF ALBERT HIRSCHMAN

1. "Exit Albert Hirschman," *Economist* 405, no. 8816 (December 22, 2012): 97; Cass R. Sunstein, "An Original Thinker of Our Time," *New York Review of Books*, May 23, 2013; Malcolm Gladwell, "The Gift of Doubt," *New Yorker*, June 24, 2013.

2. "Exit Albert Hirschman," 97.

3. McPherson 1986, 307.

4. Anonymous reviewers remarked that I should specify that here I am referring to Groucho Marx, not Karl.

5. Hirschman 1994a, 110.

6. Hirschman 1988a.

7. Hirschman 1987a.

8. Hirschman 1987a, 118.

9. Hirschman 1987a, 118. Some of Colorni's writings have recently been translated into English; see Colorni 2019a, 2019b.

10. Manlio Rossi-Doria to his wife, Irene Nunberg, March 11, 1942, quoted in Omiccioli 2018, 180.

11. U. Hirschmann 1993, 146.

12. Hirschman 1987a, 118–119 (emphasis original).

13. McPherson 1986, 307.

14. McPherson 1986, 307.

15. Hirschman 1994c, 278.

16. Hirschman 1987a, 119.

17. Hirschman 1989b, 77 (emphasis original).

18. Hirschman 1989b, 77.

19. Hirschman 1971a, 27.

20. Hirschman 1971a, 28.

21. Hirschman 1971a, 29.

22. Hirschman 1971a, 28.

23. Paul Valéry, *Regards sur le monde actuel* (Paris: Librairie Stock, Delamain et Boutellau, 1931), 55, quoted in Hirschman 1945, 80.

24. Hirschman 1970b, 335, 340.

25. Hirschman 1980a, 171–172.

26. Hirschman 1990a, 20.

27. Hirschman 1971a, 37.

28. With the exceptions of Meldolesi 1990, 1995; Roncaglia 2014.

29. Grabel 2017, 52–53.

30. Grabel 2017, 53.

31. Grabel 2017, 4–5.

32. Grabel 2017, 9.
33. Sikkink 2017, 9.
34. Sikkink 2017, 153.
35. Sikkink 2017, 43.
36. Hirschman 1980c, 294 (emphasis original).
37. Hirschman 1980c, 296.
38. As quoted in Hirschman 1980c, 303.
39. Hirschman 1980c, 303–304. On Hirschman's views on morality and the social sciences, see also Hess 1999; Trigilia 2014.
40. Hirschman 1980c, 305.
41. Hirschman 1980c, 305–306.
42. Hirschman 1980c, 306.
43. Hirschman 1981b, 3.
44. Hirschman 1981b, 3.
45. Hirschman 1981b, 3.
46. Hirschman 1981b, 4.
47. Hirschman 1963, 256.
48. Collected in Frank 1967, 1969.
49. Backhouse and Cherrier 2017.
50. Gillis et al. 1983, xv–xvi.
51. Agénor and Montiel 1996, 3–4; Dornbusch 1996, xxi.
52. Rodrik 2007a, 3.
53. Rodrik 2007a, 3.
54. Rodrik 2003.
55. Rodrik, 2007b, 5; Rodrik 2008.
56. Rodwin and Schön 1994, 288.
57. See O'Donnell 1973; Hirschman 1979b.
58. Ferraro and Centeno 2019, 423.
59. See the articles in *Development y Sociedad*, vol. 62 (2008).
60. Ellerman 2005. See also Ellerman 2001, 2004.
61. Ellerman 2005, 209.
62. The same can be argued for Hirschman's tunnel effect.
63. Keohane and Nye 1973, 115.
64. Condliffe 1944, 3.
65. Condliffe 1944, 2.
66. Hirschman 1984b, 19.
67. Hirschman 1971b, 5.
68. Hirschman 1984b, 26.
69. Hirschman 1984b, 28.
70. Hirschman 1994c.
71. See also the opening considerations in Pasquino 2014.
72. Hirschman 1970b, 339.
73. Hirschman 1994c, 278.
74. Hirschman 1994c, 282.
75. Hirschman 1994c, 282.

ABBREVIATIONS

AOHP: Albert O. Hirschman Papers, Seeley G. Mudd Manuscript Library, Princeton University, Princeton, NJ

JBCP: John B. Condliffe Papers, The Bancroft Library, University of California, Berkeley

LBCP: Lauchlin B. Currie Papers, David M. Rubenstein Rare Book & Manuscript Library, Duke University, Durham, NC

VFC: Varian Fry Collection, Rare Book and Manuscript Library, Columbia University, New York

WBGA: World Bank Group Archives, Washington, DC

BIBLIOGRAPHY

NOTE ON SOURCES:

In writing this book, I have used modified excerpts of articles I wrote in the past ten years. This material, embedded in the manuscript, originally appeared in the following publications:

"Theory and Practice in Development Economics." *History of Political Economy* 49, Supplement (2017): 264–291.

"Albert O. Hirschman and the Rise and Decline of Development Economics." *Research in the History of Economic Thought and Methodology*, Vol. 34B (2016), 13–39. Republished in slightly different form as "Albert Hirschman." In *Elgar Handbook of Alternative Theories of Economic Development*, ed. Jayati Ghosh, Rainer Kattel, and Erik Reinert, 456–474. Cheltenham, UK: Edward Elgar, 2016.

"Visualizing Uncertainties, or How Albert Hirschman and the World Bank Disagreed on Project Appraisal and What This Says About the End of 'High Development Theory.'" *Journal of the History of Economic Thought* 36, no. 2 (June 2014): 137–168.

"Il Piano Marshall, l'Italia e il Mezzogiorno." In *La Cassa per il Mezzogiorno: Dal recupero dell'archivio alla promozione della ricerca*. Rome: Svimez, 2014.

"Early Development Debates Revisited." *Journal of the History of Economic Thought* 33, no. 2 (June 2011): 145–171.

All these materials are reprinted with permission.

SOURCES

Adelman, Irma, and Cynthia Taft Morris. 1973. *Economic Growth and Social Equity in Developing Countries*. Stanford, CA: Stanford University Press.

Adelman, Jeremy. 2013. *Worldly Philosopher: The Odyssey of Albert O. Hirschman.* Princeton, NJ: Princeton University Press.

Agénor, Pierre-Richard, and Peter J. Montiel. 1996. *Development Macroeconomics.* Princeton, NJ: Princeton University Press.

Alacevich, Michele. 2018. "Planning Peace: The European Roots of the Post-War Global Development Challenge." *Past & Present* 239 (1): 220–264.

———. 2014. "Il Piano Marshall, l'Italia e il Mezzogiorno." In *La Cassa per il Mezzogiorno: Dal recupero dell'archivio alla promozione della ricerca.* Rome: Svimez, 2014.

———. 2011. "The World Bank and the Politics of Productivity: The Debate on Economic Growth, Poverty, and Living Standards in the 1950s." *Journal of Global History* 6 (1): 53–74.

———. 2009. *The Political Economy of the World Bank: The Early Years.* Stanford, CA: Stanford University Press.

Alacevich, Michele, and Mauro Boianvosky, eds. 2018. *The Political Economy of Development Economics: A Historical Perspective,* Supplement to *History of Political Economy* 50, Durham, NC: Duke University Press.

Álvarez, Andrés, Andrés M. Guiot-Isaac, and Jimena Hurtado. 2020. "The Quarrel of Policy Advisers That Became Development Experts: Currie and Hirschman in Colombia." *History of Political Economy* 52 (2): 275–306.

Arndt, Heinz W. 1987. *Economic Development: The History of an Idea.* Chicago: University of Chicago Press.

Asher, Robert E. 1962. "In Conclusion." In *Development of the Emerging Countries. An Agenda for Research,* ed. Robert E. Asher et al., 215–226. Washington, DC: Brookings Institution.

Asso, Pier Francesco. 1988. "Bilateralism, Trade Agreements and Political Economists in the 1930s: Theories and Events Underlying Hirschman's Index." *Political Economy: Studies in the Surplus Approach* 4 (1): 83–110. http://www.centrosraffa.org/pe/4,1/4,1.4.%20Asso.pdf.

Asso, Pier Francesco, and Marcello De Cecco. 1987. "Introduzione." In *Potenza nazionale e commercio estero: Gli anni trenta, l'Italia e la ricostruzione,* by Albert O. Hirschman. Bologna: Il Mulino.

Axinn, Sidney. 1983. "Review of: *Shifting Involvements: Private Interest and Public Action* by Albert O. Hirschman." *Annals of the American Academy of Political and Social Science* 467 (May): 241–242.

Backhouse, Roger E., and Béatrice Cherrier. 2017. "The Age of the Applied Economist: The Transformation of Economics Since the 1970s." *History of Political Economy* 49 (Supplement): 1–33.

Baer, Werner. 1970. "Review of *Exit, Voice, and Loyalty: Responses to Decline in Firms, Organizations, and States* by Albert O. Hirschman." *Journal of Economic Literature* 8, no. 3 (September): 811–814.

Baffigi, Alberto, and Marco Magnani. 2009. *Giorgio Mortara,* in *Le leggi antiebraiche del 1938, le società scientifiche e la scuola in Italia,* Atti del Convegno, Roma, 26–27 novembre 2008, 237–254. Rome: Biblioteca dell'Accademia Nazionale delle Scienze.

Baldwin, David A. 1985. *Economic Statecraft.* Princeton, NJ: Princeton University Press.

Barry, Brian. 1974. "Review of *Exit, Voice, and Loyalty: Responses to Decline in Firms, Organization, and States* by Albert O. Hirschman." *British Journal of Political Science* 4, no. 1 (January): 79–107.

Basch, Antonín. 1941. *The New Economic Warfare*. New York: Columbia University Press.

Becker, Gary S. 1981. *A Treatise on the Family*. Cambridge, MA: Harvard University Press.

———. 1976. *The Economic Approach to Human Behavior*. Chicago: University of Chicago Press.

———. 1964. *Human Capital*. New York: Columbia University Press.

———. 1960. "An Economic Analysis of Fertility." In *Demographic and Economic Change in Developed Countries*, A Conference of Universities–National Bureau Committee for Economic Research, 209–240. New York: Columbia University Press.

———. 1957. *The Economics of Discrimination*. Chicago: University of Chicago Press.

Bernardi, Emanuele. 2010. *Riforme e democrazia. Manlio Rossi-Doria dal fascismo al centro-sinistra*. Soveria Mannelli, Italy: Rubbettino.

Bertilsson, Margareta and Ron Eyerman. 1979. "Interest as a Problematic Concept in Marxist Social Science." *Acta Sociologica* 22, no. 4: 361–375.

Bianchi, Ana Maria. 2011. "Visiting-Economists Through Hirschman's Eyes." *European Journal of the History of Economic Thought* 18, no. 2 (May): 217–242.

Bidwell, Percy W. 1945. "A Commercial Policy for the United Nations." Papers Submitted to the Committee on International Economic Policy, in cooperation with the Carnegie Endowment for International Peace, No. 6 (February 7, 1945). New York: Committee on International Economic Policy.

Bissell, Richard M., Jr., with Jonathan E. Lewis and Frances T. Pudlo. 1996. *Reflections of a Cold Warrior: From Yalta to the Bay of Pigs*. New Haven, CT: Yale University Press.

Bolton, Craig J. 1984. "Review of: *Shifting Involvements, Private Interest and Public Action* by Albert O. Hirschman." *Social Science Quarterly* 65, no. 1 (March): 216–217.

Boudon, Raymond. 1992. "La rhétorique est-elle réactionnaire?" *Le Débat* 1992/2 (69): 87–95.

———. 1986. *Theories of Social Change: A Critical Appraisal*. Cambridge, UK: Polity Press.

———. 1982. "Intérêts privés et action publique." *Analyses de la Sedeis* 29 (September): 1–4.

Bowles, Samuel. 1998. "Endogenous Preferences: The Cultural Consequences of Markets and Other Economic Institutions." *Journal of Economic Literature* 36, no. 1 (March): 75–111.

Bray, David Barton. 1991. " 'Defiance' and the Search for Sustainable Small Farmer Organizations: A Paraguayan Case Study and a Research Agenda." *Human Organization* 50, no. 2 (Summer): 125–135.

Bridel, Pascal. 2009. " 'Passions et intérêts revisités: La suppression des 'sentiments' est-elle à l'origine de l'économie politique?" *Revue européenne des sciences sociales* 47 (144): 135–150.

Bronner, Stephen Eric. 1993. "Review of *The Rhetoric of Reaction: Perversity, Futility, Jeopardy* by Albert O. Hirschman." *Political Theory* 21, no. 1 (February): 132–135.

Brown, A. J. 1947. "Review of *National Power and the Structure of Foreign Trade* by Albert O. Hirschmann [sic]." *International Affairs* 23, no. 1 (January): 91–92.

Buck, Philip W. 1946. "Review of *National Power and the Structure of Foreign Trade* by Albert O. Hirschman." *Annals of the American Academy of Political and Social Science* 244 (March): 222–223.

Buttrick, John A. 1982. "Review of: *Shifting Involvements: Private Interest and Public Action* by Albert O. Hirschman." *Canadian Journal of Political Science / Revue canadienne de science politique* 15, no. 4 (December): 837–838.

Calvocoressi, Peter, Guy Wint, and John Pritchard. 1989. *Total War. The Causes and Courses of the Second World War*. Rev. 2nd ed. New York: Viking.

Carli, Guido. 1996. *Cinquant'anni di vita italiana*. Rome: Laterza.

Carr, Edward Hallett. 1942. *Conditions of Peace*. New York: Macmillan.

Carson, Carol S. 1993. "IN MEMORIAM George Jaszi (1915–1992)." *Review of Income and Wealth* 39 (2): 225–227.

Castrillón, Alberto. 2013. "Mercado y virtud o cómo complicar la economia: A propósito de *Las Pasiones y Los Intereses*, de Albert Hirschman." *Revista de Economía Institucional* 15 (28): 79–93.

Cernea, Michael. 1981. "Modernization and Development Potential of Traditional Grass Roots Peasant Organizations." In *Direction of Change: Modernization Theory, Research, and Realities*, ed. Mustafa O. Attir, Burkart Holzner, and Zdenek Suda, 121–139. Boulder, CO: Westview Press.

Chenery, Hollis B. 1959. "Review of *The Design of Development* by Jan Tinbergen; *The Strategy of Economic Development* by Albert O. Hirschman." *American Economic Review* 49, no. 5 (December): 1063–1065.

Chenery, Hollis B., and Tsunehiko Watanabe. 1958. "International Comparisons of the Structure of Production." *Econometrica* 26, no. 4 (October): 487–521.

Clark, David A., ed. 2006. *The Elgar Companion to Development Studies*. Cheltenham, UK: Edward Elgar.

Clavin, Patricia. 2000. *The Great Depression in Europe, 1929–1939*. Basingstoke, UK: Macmillan.

Cohen, Benjamin J. 2008. *International Political Economy: An Intellectual History*. Princeton, NJ: Princeton University Press.

——. 2007. "The Transatlantic Divide: Why Are American and British IPE So Different?" *Review of International Political Economy* 14, no. 2 (May): 197–219.

——. 1990. "The Political Economy of International Trade." *International Organization* 44, no. 2 (Spring): 261–281.

Coleman, James S. 1974. "Processes of Concentration and Dispersal of Power in Social Systems." *Social Science Information* 13, no. 2 (February): 7–18.

Collier, David. 1979. "Introduction." In *The New Authoritarianism in Latin America*, ed. David Collier, 3–16. Princeton, NJ: Princeton University Press.

Colorni, Eugenio. 2019a. *Critical Thinking in Action: Excerpts from Political Writings and Correspondence*, ed. Luca Meldolesi and Nicoletta Stame. New York: Bordighera Press.

——. 2019b. *The Discovery of the Possible: Excerpts from Political Writings and Correspondence II*, ed. Luca Meldolesi and Nicoletta Stame. New York: Bordighera Press.

Condliffe, John B. 1946. "Proposals for Consideration by an International Conference on Trade and Employment." *National Economic Problems*, No. 423. New York: American Enterprise Association.

——. 1944. "The Foreign Economic Policy of the United States." Memorandum No. 11, September 25, 1944, Yale Institute of International Studies.

——. 1943a. "Introduction: East of the Rhine." In *The Danube Basin and the German Economic Sphere*, by Antonín Basch. New York: Columbia University Press.

——. 1943b. *Problems of Economic Reorganization*. New York: Commission to Study the Organization of Peace.

——. 1942. *Agenda for a Postwar World*. New York: Norton.

——. 1940. *The Reconstruction of World Trade*. New York: Norton.

Coser, Lewis A. 1978. "A Superb Contribution to the History of Ideas, Review of *The Passions and the Interests: Political Arguments for Capitalism Before Its Triumph* by Albert O. Hirschman. *Contemporary Sociology* 7, no. 4 (July): 395–397.

Cracknell, Basil E. 1984. "Learning Lessons from Experience: The Role of Evaluation in the Administration of the U.K. Aid Programme." *Public Administration and Development* 4, no. 1 (January/March): 15–20.

Craver, Earlene. 1986. "Patronage and the Directions of Research in Economics: The Rockefeller Foundation in Europe, 1924–1938." *Minerva* 24, no. 2/3 (June): 205–222.

Currie, Lauchlin B. 1981. *The Role of Economic Advisers in Developing Countries*. Westport, CT: Greenwood Press.

——. 1950. "Some Prerequisites for Success of the Point Four Program." Address before the American Academy of Political and Social Sciences, Bellevue Stratford Hotel, Philadelphia, April 15. Published in *Annals of the American Academy of Political and Social Sciences*, no. 270 (July): 102–109.

Cyert, Richard M., and Morris H. De Groot. 1975. "Adaptive Utility." In *Adaptive Economic Models*, ed. R. H. Day and T. Groves, 223–246. New York: Free Press.

da Conceição Tavares, Maria. 1964. "The Growth and Decline of Import Substitution in Brazil." *Economic Bulletin for Latin America* 9, no. 1 (March): 1–61.

Da Empoli, Domenico. 1998. "Fubini, Renzo." *Dizionario Biografico degli Italiani*, Vol. 50. http://www.treccani.it/enciclopedia/renzo-fubini_(Dizionario-Biografico).

Dasgupta, Amiya Kumar. 1965. *Planning and Economic Growth*. London: George Allen & Unwin.

Dasgupta, Partha. 1972. "A Comparative Analysis of the UNIDO Guidelines and the OECD Manual." *Bulletin of the Oxford University Institute of Economics and Statistics* 34, no. 1 (February): 33–51.

Dasgupta, Partha, Stephen A. Marglin, and Amartya K. Sen. 1972. *Guidelines for Project Evaluation*. New York: United Nations.

Daston, Lorraine. 1994. "Enlightenment Calculations." *Critical Inquiry* 21, no. 1 (Autumn): 182–202.

Dawidoff, Nicholas. 2002. *The Fly Swatter. How My Grandfather Made His Way in the World*. New York: Pantheon.

De Cecco, Marcello. 2004. "Prefazione." In Otto A. Hirschmann, *Il Franco Poincaré e la sua svalutazione*, a cura di Giorgio Gilibert, vii–xv. Rome: Edizioni di Storia e Letteratura, 2004.

De Marchi, Neil. 2016. "Models and Misperceptions: Chenery, Hirschman and Tinbergen on Development Planning." *Research in the History of Economic Thought and Methodology*, Vol. 34B, 91–99.

Deutsch, Karl W. 1971. "On Political Theory and Political Action." *American Political Science Review* 65, no. 1 (March): 11–27.

De Vries, Jan. 1979. "Spotlight on Capitalism: A Review Article of *The Passions and the Interests: Political Arguments for Capitalism Before Its Triumph* by Albert O. Hirschman; and *Afterthoughts on Material Civilization and Capitalism* by Fernand Braudel." *Comparative Studies in Society and History* 21, no. 1 (January): 139–143.

Diebold, William, Jr. 1952. *Trade and Payments in Western Europe: A Study in Economic Cooperation, 1947–51*. New York: Council on Foreign Relations.

DiIulio, John J., Jr. 1992. "Review of *The Rhetoric of Reaction: Perversity, Futility, Jeopardy* by Albert O. Hirschman." *Journal of Policy Analysis and Management* 11, no. 4 (Autumn): 720–723.

Dornbusch, Rudiger. 1996. "Foreword." In *Development Macroeconomics*, by Pierre-Richard Agénor and Peter J. Montiel. Princeton, NJ: Princeton University Press.

Dowding, Keith, and Peter John. 2012. *Exits, Voices and Social Investment: Citizens' Reaction to Public Services*. Cambridge: Cambridge University Press.

Dunn, John. 1991. "Review: *The Rhetoric of Reaction: Perversity, Futility, Jeopardy* by Albert O. Hirschman." *Government and Opposition* 26, no. 4 (Autumn): 520–525.

Economic Commission for Latin America (ECLA). 1950. *Economic Survey of Latin America, 1949*. New York: United Nations.

Eichengreen, Barry. 2007. *The European Economy Since 1945: Coordinated Capitalism and Beyond*. Princeton, NJ: Princeton University Press.

——. 1995. "The European Payments Union: An Efficient Mechanism for Rebuilding Europe's Trade?" In *Europe's Postwar Recovery*, ed. Barry Eichengreen, 169–196. Cambridge: Cambridge University Press, 1995.

——. 1993. *Reconstructing Europe's Trade and Payments: The European Payments Union*. Manchester: Manchester University Press.

Einzig, Paul. 1938. *Bloodless Invasion. German Economic Penetration Into the Danubian States and the Balkans*. London: Duckworth.

Eldridge, John. 1996. "Review of *Rhetoric and Marxism* by James Arnt Aune." *American Journal of Sociology* 101, no. 5 (March): 1461–1462.

Ellerman, David. 2005. *Helping People Help Themselves: From the World Bank to an Alternative Philosophy of Development Assistance*. Ann Arbor: University of Michigan Press.

——. 2004. "Revisiting Hirschman on Development Assistance and Unbalanced Growth." *Eastern Economics Journal* 30, no. 2 (Spring): 311–331.

——. 2001. "Helping People Help Themselves: Toward a Theory of Autonomy-Compatible Help." World Bank Policy Research Working Paper No. 2693. Washington, DC: World Bank.

Ellis, Howard S. 1934. *German Monetary Theory, 1905–1933*. Cambridge, MA: Harvard University Press.

Elster, Jon. 1994. "Rationality, Emotions, and Social Norms." *Synthese* 98, no. 1 (January): 21–49.

——. 1978. "Exploring Exploitation." *Journal of Peace Research* 15 (1): 3–17.

Evans, Richard J. 2004. *The Coming of the Third Reich*. New York: Penguin.

Feijóo, María del Carmen, and Sarah Hirschman. 1984. *Gente y Cuentos: educación popular y literature*. Buenos Aires: Centro de Estudios de Estado y Sociedad.

Feinstein, Charles H., Peter Temin, and Gianni Toniolo. 1997. *The European Economy Between the Wars*. New York: Oxford University Press.

Ferraro, Agustin E., and Miguel A. Centeno. 2019. "Authoritarianism, Democracy, and Development in Latin America and Spain, 1930–1990." In *State and Nation Making in Latin America and Spain: The Rise and Fall of the Developmental State*, ed. Agustin E. Ferraro and Miguel A. Centeno, 405–427. Cambridge: Cambridge University Press.

Finzi, Roberto. 2004. "Uno studioso studente a Trieste: Otto Albert Hirschman." In *Otto A. Hirschmann. Il Franco Poincaré e la sua svalutazione*, a cura di Giorgio Gilibert, 109–134. Rome: Edizioni di Storia e Letteratura.

Fittko, Lisa. 1991. *Escape Through the Pyrenees*. Evanston, IL: Northwestern University Press.

Fleming, Grant. 1998. "Condliffe, John Bell." *Dictionary of New Zealand Biography*. https://teara.govt.nz/en/biographies/4c28/condliffe-john-bell.

Flexner, Kurt Fisher. 1955. "The European Payments Union from 1950 to 1954: An Analysis and Evaluation." PhD diss., Faculty of Political Science, Columbia University.

Florinsky, Michael T. 1946. "Review of *National Power and the Structure of Foreign Trade* by Albert O. Hirschman." *Political Science Quarterly* 61, no. 2 (June): 272–274.

Flyvbjerg, Bent. 2018. "Planning Fallacy or Hiding Hand: Which Is the Better Explanation?" *World Development* 103 (March): 383–386.

——. 2016. "Did Megaproject Research Pioneer Behavioral Economics? The Case of Albert O. Hirschman." In *The Oxford Handbook of Megaproject Management*, ed. Bent Flyvbjerg, 155–193. Oxford: Oxford University Press.

Flyvbjerg, Bent, and Cass R. Sunstein. 2016. "The Principle of the Malevolent Hiding Hand; or, the Planning Fallacy Writ Large." *Social Research* 83, no. 4 (Winter): 979–1004.

Force, Pierre. 2003. *Self-Interest Before Adam Smith: A Genealogy of Economic Science*. Cambridge: Cambridge University Press.

Ford Foundation. 1989. *The Common Good: Social Welfare and the American Future: Policy Recommendations of the Executive Panel*. New York: Ford Foundation.

Foxley, Alejandro, Michael S. McPherson, and Guillermo O'Donnell, eds. 1986. *Development, Democracy, and the Art of Trespassing: Essays in Honor of Albert O. Hirschman*. Notre Dame, IN: University of Notre Dame Press.

Frank, Andre Gunder. 1969. *Latin America: Underdevelopment or Revolution: Essays on the Development of Underdevelopment and the Immediate Enemy*. New York: Monthly Review Press.

——. 1967. *Capitalism and Underdevelopment in Latin America: Historical Studies of Chile and Brazil*. New York: Monthly Review Press.

——. 1960. "Built in Destabilization: A. O. Hirschman's *Strategy of Economic Development*." *Economic Development and Cultural Change* 8, no. 4, part 1 (July): 433–440.

Frankfurt, Harry G. 1971. "Freedom of the Will and the Concept of a Person." *Journal of Philosophy* 68, no. 1 (January): 5–20.

Friedman, Benjamin M. 2011. "Economics: A Moral Inquiry with Religious Origins." *American Economic Review* 101, no. 3 (May): 166–170.

Fry, Varian. 1945. *Surrender on Demand*. New York: Random House.

Fubini, Federico. 2014. *La via di fuga: Storia di Renzo Fubini*. Milan: Mondadori.

Furtado, Celso. 1966. "U.S. Hegemony and the Future of Latin America." *World Today* 22, no. 9 (September): 375–385.

Galbraith, John K. 1958. "Rival Economic Theories in India." *Foreign Affairs* 36 (4): 587–596.

Gasper, Des. 1986. "Programme Appraisal and Evaluation: The Hiding Hand and Other Stories." *Public Administration and Development* 6, no. 4 (October/December): 467–474.

Garver, Eugene. 1991. "Review of *The Rhetoric of Reaction: Perversity, Futility, Jeopardy* by Albert O. Hirschman." *Rhetoric Society Quarterly* 21, no. 4 (Autumn): 46–51.

Gellner, Ernest. 1979. "The Withering Away of the Dentistry State: Review of *The Passions and the Interests: Political Arguments for Capitalism Before Its Triumph* by Albert O. Hirschman." *Review (Fernand Braudel Center)* 2, no. 3 (Winter): 461–472.

Gerschenkron, Alexander. 1962. *Economic Backwardness in Historical Perspective*. Cambridge, MA: Belknap Press.

——. 1943. *Bread and Democracy in Germany*. Berkeley: University of California Press.

Ghez, Gilber R., and Gary S. Becker. 1975. *The Allocation of Time and Goods Over the Life Cycle*. New York: Columbia University Press.

Gillis, Malcolm, Dwight H. Perkins, Michael Roemer, and Donald R. Snodgrass. 1983. *Economics of Development*. New York: Norton.

Ginzberg, Eli. 1982. "Review of: *Shifting Involvements: Private Interest and Public Action* by Albert O. Hirschman." *Journal of Economic Literature* 20, no. 4 (December): 1563–1564.

Gold, Mary Jayne. 1980. *Crossroads Marseilles 1940*. New York: Doubleday.

Goodman, Bernard. 1959. "Review of *The Strategy of Economic Development* by Albert O. Hirschman." *Journal of Farm Economics* 41, no. 2 (May): 468–469.

Gottlieb, M. 1949. "Optimum Population, Foreign Trade and World Economy." *Population Studies* 3, no. 2 (September): 151–169.

Grabel, Ilene. 2017. *When Things Don't Fall Apart: Global Financial Governance and Developmental Finance in an Age of Productive Incoherence*. Cambridge, MA: MIT Press.

Grasso, Patrick G., Sulaiman S. Wasty, and Rachel V. Weaving, eds. 2003. *World Bank Operations Evaluation Department: The First 30 Years*. Washington, DC: World Bank.

Greek, Cecil E. 1983. "Review of: *Shifting Involvements: Private Interest and Public Action* by Albert O. Hirschman." *Contemporary Sociology* 12, no. 6 (November): 671.

Habermas, Jürgen. 1975. *Legitimation Crisis*. Boston: Beacon Press.

Hadass, Yael S., and Jeffrey G. Williamson. 2003. "Terms-of-Trade Shocks and Economic Performance, 1870–1940: Prebisch and Singer Revisited." *Economic Development and Cultural Change* 51, no. 3 (April): 629–656.

Hall, Peter. 1980. *Great Planning Disasters*. London: Weidenfeld and Nicolson.

Hammond, Richard J. 1966. "Convention and Limitation in Benefit-Cost Analysis." *National Resources Journal* 6, no. 2 (April): 195–222.

Hampsher-Monk, Iain. 1984. "Political Languages in Time—The Work of J. G. A. Pocock." *British Journal of Political Science* 14, no. 1 (January): 89–116.

Hanson, Roger A. 1970. "Review of Albert O. Hirschman, *Exit, Voice, and Loyalty: Responses to Decline in Firms, Organizations, and States*." *American Political Science Review* 64, no. 4 (December): 1274–1276.

Harberger, Arnold C. 1972. "Issues Concerning Capital Assistance to Less-Developed Countries." *Economic Development and Cultural Change* 20, no. 4 (July): 631–640.

Harpham, Edward J., and Richard K. Scotch. 1988. "Rethinking the War on Poverty: The Ideology of Social Welfare Reform." *Western Political Quarterly* 41, no. 1 (March): 193–207.

Harvard Law Review. 1994. "Dethroning the Welfare Queen: The Rhetoric of Reform." *Harvard Law Review* 107, no. 8 (June): 2013–2030.

——. 1991. "Review: *The Rhetoric of Reaction: Perversity, Futility, Jeopardy* by Albert O. Hirschman." *Harvard Law Review* 105, no. 2 (December): 585–590.

Hayek, Friedrich A., ed. 1935. *Collectivist Economic Planning: Critical Studies on the Possibilities of Socialism*. London: Routledge.

Hazard, Paul. 1952 [1990]. *The European Mind: The Critical Years, 1680–1715*. New York: Fordham University Press.

Hess, Andreas. 1999. " 'The Economy of Morals and Its Applications': An Attempt to Understand Some Central Concepts in the Work of Albert O. Hirschman." *Review of International Political Economy* 6, no. 3 (Autumn): 338–359.

Hickerson, Steven R. 1983. "Review of: *Shifting Involvements: Private Interest and Public Action* by Albert O. Hirschman." *Journal of Economic Issues* 17, no. 1 (March): 256–259.

Higgins, Benjamin. 1960. "Review of *The Strategy of Economic Development* by Albert O. Hirschman." *Social Research* 27, no. 1 (Spring): 112–115.

Higgins, Benjamin, Alexandre Kafka, and George E. Britnell. 1959. "Discussion." *American Economic Review* 49, no. 2 (May): 169–178.

Hill, Lewis E. 1959. "Review of *The Strategy of Economic Development* by Albert O. Hirschman." *Southern Economic Journal* 26, no. 1 (July): 72.

Hirsch, Fred. 1976. *Social Limits to Growth*. Cambridge, MA: Harvard University Press.

Hirschman, Albert O. 1998. *Crossing Boundaries: Selected Writings*. New York: Zone Books.

——. 1997. "Fifty Years After the Marshall Plan: Two Posthumous Memoirs and Some Personal Recollections." In Hirschman 1998, 33–43.

——. 1995. *A Propensity to Self-Subversion*. Cambridge, MA: Harvard University Press.

——. 1994a. "Trespassing: Places and Ideas in the Course of a Life." Interview with Carmine Donzelli, Marta Petrusewicz and Claudia Rusconi. In Hirschman 1998, 45–110. [Original edition: Albert O. Hirschman. *Passaggi di Frontiera. I luoghi e le idee di un percorso di vita*, a cura di Carmine Donzelli, Marta Petrusewicz e Claudia Rusconi. Rome: Donzelli Editore, 1994.]

——. 1994b. "A Hidden Ambition." In *Development Projects Observed*, 2015 ed., xv–xx. Washington, DC: Brookings Institution.

——. 1994c. "A Propensity to Self-Subversion." In Rodwin and Schön 1994, 277–283.

——. 1994d. "Social Conflicts as Pillars of Democratic Market Society." *Political Theory* 22, no. 2 (May): 203–218.

——. 1993a. "Introduction." In Varian Fry, *Assignment: Rescue*. New York: Scholastic.

——. 1993b. "Escaping Over the Pyrenees, 1940–41." In Hirschman 1995, 123–126.

——. 1993c. "Exit, Voice, and the Fate of the German Democratic Republic: An Essay in Conceptual History." *World Politics* 45, no. 2 (January): 173–202.

——. 1993d. " 'The Rhetoric of Reaction'—Two Years Later." *Government and Opposition* 28, no. 3 (Summer): 292–314.

——. 1992. "L'argument intransigeant comme idée reçue: En guise de réponse à Raymond Boudon." *Le Débat* 1992/2 (69): 96–102.

——. 1991. *The Rhetoric of Reaction: Perversity, Futility, Jeopardy*. Cambridge, MA: Belknap Press.

——. 1990a. "Good News Is Not Bad News." *New York Review of Books*, October 11, 1990, 20–22.

——. 1990b. "Albert O. Hirschman." Interview by Richard Swedberg. In *Economics and Sociology: Redefining Their Boundaries: Conversations with Economists and Sociologists*, by Richard Swedberg, 152–166. Princeton, NJ: Princeton University Press.

——. 1989a. "Studies in Paris, 1933–1935." In Hirschman 1995, 113–116.

——. 1989b. "Having Opinions—One of the Elements of Well-Being?" *American Economic Review* 79, no. 2 (May): 75–79.

——. 1988a, "My Father and Weltanschauung, circa 1928." In Hirschman 1995, 111–112.

——. 1988b. "Four Reencounters." In Hirschman 1995, 95–110.

——. 1987a. "Doubt and Antifascist Action in Italy, 1936–1938." In Hirschman 1995, 117–119.

——. 1987b. *Potenza nazionale e commercio estero: Gli anni trenta, l'Italia e la ricostruzione*. Ed. Pier Francesco Asso and Marcello De Cecco. Bologna: Il Mulino.

——. 1987c. "The Political Economy of Latin American Development: Seven Exercises in Retrospection." *Latin American Research Review* 22 (3): 7–36.

——. 1986a. "*Exit and Voice*: An Expanding Sphere of Influence." In Hirschman 1986b, 77–101.

——. 1986b. *Rival Views of Market Society and Other Recent Essays*. Cambridge, MA: Harvard University Press [paperback ed. 1992].

—— O. 1985a. "Linkages in Economic Development." In Hirschman 1986b, 56–76.

——. 1985b. "The Concept of Interest: From Euphemism to Tautology." In Hirschman 1986b, 35–55.

——. 1985c. "Reflections on Latin American Experience." In Lindberg and Maier 1985, 53–77.

——. 1985d. "Notes on Consolidating Democracy in Latin America." In Hirschman 1986b, 176–182.

——. 1984a. "A Dissenter's Confession: *The Strategy of Economic Development* Revisited." In Meier and Seers 1984, 87–111.

——. 1984b. "Against Parsimony: Three Easy Ways of Complicating Some Categories of Economic Discourse." *Bulletin of the American Academy of Arts and Sciences* 37, no. 8 (May): 11–28.

——. 1984c. *Getting Ahead Collectively: Grassroots Experiences in Latin America*. New York: Pergamon Press.

——. 1982a. "Rival Interpretations of Market Society: Civilizing, Destructive, or Feeble?" *Journal of Economic Literature* 20, no. 4 (December): 1463–1484.

——. 1982b. *Shifting Involvements: Private Interest and Public Action*. Princeton, NJ: Princeton University Press [2002, twentieth-anniversary edition].

——. 1981a. *Essays in Trespassing: Economics to Politics and Beyond*. Cambridge, MA: Harvard University Press.

——. 1981b. "The Rise and Decline of Development Economics." In Hirschman 1981a, 1–24.

——. 1980a. "In Defense of Possibilism." In Hirschman 1986b, 171–175.

——. 1980b. "The Welfare State in Trouble: Systemic Crisis or Growing Pains?" *American Economic Review* 70, no. 2 (May): 113–116.

——. 1980c. "Morality and the Social Sciences: A Durable Tension." In Hirschman 1981a, 294–306.

——. 1979a. "Preface to the Expanded Edition." In *National Power and the Structure of Foreign Trade*, v–xii. Berkeley: University of California Press, [1945] 1980.

——. 1979b. "Foreword." In *Toward a New Strategy for Development: A Rothko Chapel Colloquium*, ed. Albert O. Hirschman et al., xv–xviii. New York: Pergamon Press.

——. 1979c. "The Turn to Authoritarianism in Latin America and the Search for Its Economic Determinants." In *The New Authoritarianism in Latin America*, ed. David Collier, 61–98. Princeton, NJ: Princeton University Press.

——. 1978. "Beyond Asymmetry: Critical Notes on Myself as a Young Man and on Some Other Old Friends." *International Organization* 32, no. 1 (Winter): 45–50.

———. 1977a. "A Generalized Linkage Approach to Development, with Special Reference to Staples." *Economic Development and Cultural Change* 25, supplement (August): 67–98.

———. 1977b. *The Passions and the Interests: Political Arguments for Capitalism Before Its Triumph*. Princeton, NJ: Princeton University Press [1997, twentieth anniversary edition].

———. 1975. "Policymaking and Policy Analysis in Latin America—A Return Journey." *Policy Sciences* 6, no. 4 (December): 385–402.

———. 1974. "'Exit, Voice, and Loyalty': Further Reflections and a Survey of Recent Contributions." *Social Science Information* 13, no. 1 (February): 7–26.

———. 1973. "The Changing Tolerance for Income Inequality in the Course of Economic Development." *Quarterly Journal of Economics* 87, no. 4 (November): 544–566.

———. 1971a. *A Bias for Hope: Essays on Development and Latin America*. New Haven, CT: Yale University Press.

———. 1971b. "Introduction: Political Economics and Possibilism." In Hirschman 1971a, 1–37.

———. 1970a. *Exit, Voice, and Loyalty: Responses to Decline in Firms, Organizations, and States*. Cambridge, MA: Harvard University Press.

———. 1970b. "The Search for Paradigms as a Hindrance to Understanding." *World Politics* 22, no. 3 (April): 329–343.

———. 1969. "How to Divest in Latin America, and Why." *Essays in International Finance*, no. 76 (November), International Finance Section, Department of Economics, Princeton University.

———. 1968a. "Foreword." In *Electric Power in Brazil: Entrepreneurship in the Public Sector*, by Judith Tendler. Cambridge, MA: Harvard University Press, vii–x.

———. 1968b. "The Political Economy of Import-Substituting Industrialization in Latin America." *Quarterly Journal of Economics* 82, no. 1 (February): 1–32.

———. 1968c. "Underdevelopment, Obstacles to the Perception of Change, and Leadership." *Daedalus* 97, no. 3 (Summer): 925–937.

———. 1967a. *Development Projects Observed*. Washington, DC: Brookings Institution Press.

———. 1967b. "The Principle of the Hiding Hand." *Public Interest* 6 (Winter): 10–23.

———. 1965. "Obstacles to Development: A Classification and a Quasi-Vanishing Act." *Economic Development and Cultural Change* 13, no. 4, part 1 (July): 385–393.

———. 1964. "The Paternity of an Index." *American Economic Review* 54, no. 5 (September): 761–762.

———. 1963. *Journeys Toward Progress*. New York: Twentieth Century Fund.

———, ed. 1961a. *Latin American Issues: Essays and Comments*. New York: Twentieth Century Fund.

———. 1961b. "Ideologies of Economic Development in Latin America." In Hirschman 1961a, 3–42.

———. 1961c. "Second Thoughts on the Alliance for Progress." In Hirschman 1971a, 175–182.

———. 1960. "Abrazo Versus Coexistence." In Hirschman 1961a, 59–63.

———. 1958. *The Strategy of Economic Development*. New Haven, CT: Yale University Press [1961 ed. with new preface].

———. 1954a. "Guia para el análisis y la confección de recomendaciones sobre la situación monetaria." *Economia Colombiana*, Año I, vol. 2 (October): 531–540.

——. 1954b. "Economics and Investment Planning: Reflections Based on Experience in Colombia." In Hirschman 1971a, pp. 41–62.

——. 1952. "Effects of Industrialization on the Markets of Industrial Countries." In *The Progress of Underdeveloped Areas*, ed. Bert F. Hoselitz, 270–283. Chicago: University of Chicago Press.

——. 1950a. "Multilateralism and European Integration." *Review of Foreign Developments*, April 25, 1950, Board of Governors of the Federal Reserve System, Division of Research and Statistics, International Section, 1–19.

——. 1950b. "The European Payments Union." *Review of Foreign Developments*, August 15, 1950, Board of Governors of the Federal Reserve System, Division of International Finance, 1–9.

——. 1950c. "The Long-Run Effect of Development and Industrialization Abroad on the United State." *Review of Foreign Developments*, July 25, 1950, 1–17.

——. 1949a. "The New Intra-European Payments Scheme." *Review of Foreign Developments*, July 19, 1949, Board of Governors of the Federal Reserve System, Division of Research and Statistics, International Section, 1–5.

——. 1949b. "Devaluation and the Trade Balance: A Note." *Review of Economics and Statistics* 31, no. 1 (February): 50–53.

——. 1948a. "Credit Restrictions and Deflation in Italy." *Review of Foreign Developments*, April 20, 1948, Board of Governors of the Federal Reserve System, Division of Research and Statistics, International Section, 5–9.

——. 1948b. "Inflation and Deflation in Italy." *American Economic Review* 38, no. 4 (September): 598–606.

——. 1948c. "Inflation and Balance of Payments Deficit." *Review of Foreign Developments*, August 24, 1948, Board of Governors of the Federal Reserve System, Division of Research and Statistics, International Section, 6–8.

——. 1948d. "Disinflation, Discrimination, and the Dollar Shortage." *American Economic Review* 38, no. 5 (December): 886–892.

——. 1948e. "Economic and Financial Conditions in Italy." *Review of Foreign Developments*, December 14, 1948, Board of Governors of the Federal Reserve System, Division of Research and Statistics, International Section, 1–17.

——. 1948f. "Dollar Shortage and Discrimination." *Review of Foreign Developments*, September 7, 1948, Board of Governors of the Federal Reserve System, Division of Research and Statistics, International Section, 1–4.

——. 1947a. "Swiss Foreign Economic Policy." *Review of Foreign Developments*, June 3, 1947, Board of Governors of the Federal Reserve System, Division of Research and Statistics, International Section, 13–20.

——. 1947b. "Exchange Control in Italy." *Review of Foreign Developments*, March 11, 1947, Board of Governors of the Federal Reserve System, Division of Research and Statistics, International Section, 11–17.

——. 1947c. "Exchange Control in Italy—II." *Review of Foreign Developments*, May 6, 1947, Board of Governors of the Federal Reserve System, Division of Research and Statistics, International Section, 11–14.

——. 1947d. "Trade Structure of the 'Marshall Plan Countries.'" *Review of Foreign Developments*, August 12, 1947, Board of Governors of the Federal Reserve System, Division of Research and Statistics, International Section, 7–11.

——. 1947e. "France and Italy: Patterns of Reconstruction." *Federal Reserve Bulletin* 33, no. 4 (April): 353–366.

——. 1945. *National Power and the Structure of Foreign Trade.* Berkeley: University of California Press.

——. 1943a. "On Measures of Dispersion for a Finite Distribution." *Journal of the American Statistical Association* 38, no. 223 (September): 346–352.

——. 1943b. "The Commodity Structure of World Trade." *Quarterly Journal of Economics* 57, no. 4 (August): 565–595.

Hirschmann, Otto Albert [not mentioned as author]. 1939a. "Mèmoire sur le Contrôle des Changes en Italie," juin 1939, Conférence permanente des hautes études internationales, XIIème session, Bergen 1939, Conférence générale d'études sur les politiques économiques et la paix. Paris: Institut International de Coopération Intellectuelle. Société des Nations, in International Studies Conference, Twelfth Session, 1939, *General Study Conference on Economic Policies in Relation to World Peace*, Memoranda, Exchange Control No. 1–5. Paris: International Institute of Intellectual Co-operation, League of Nations. An Italian translation is available in Hirschman 1987b, 161–255.

——. 1939b. "Étude statistique sur la tendance du Commerce extérieur vers l'équilibre et le bilatéralism," aoÛt 1939, Conférence permanente des hautes études internationales, XIIème session, Bergen 1939, Conférence générale d'études sur les politiques économiques et la paix. Paris: Institut International de Coopération Intellectuelle, Société des Nations. In International Studies Conference, Twelfth Session, 1939, *General Study Conference on Economic Policies in Relation to World Peace*, Memoranda, Exchange Control No. 7–8. Paris: International Institute of Intellectual Co-operation, League of Nations. Also available at https://colornihirschman.org/dossier/article/75/etude-statistique-sur-la-tendence-du-commerce-exterieur-vers-lequilibre-et-le-bilateralisme. English translation from the French original by Pier Francesco Asso: Albert O. Hirschman. 1988. "Statistical Study of the Trend of Foreign Trade Toward Equilibrium and Bilateralism." *Political Economy. Studies in the Surplus Approach* 4 (1): 111–124. http://www.centrosraffa.org/pe/4,1/4,1.5.%20Hirschman.pdf.

——. 1938a. *Il franco Poincaré e la sua svalutazione*, a cura di Giorgio Gilibert. Rome: Edizioni di Storia e Letteratura, 2004.

——. 1938b. "Nota su due recenti tavole di nuzialità della popolazione italiana." *Giornale degli Economisti e Rivista di Statistica*, Serie quarta, 78, no. 1 (January): 40–47.

—— [unsigned]. 1938c. "Les Finances et l'économie italiennes—Situation actuelle et perspectives." *Bulletin Quotidien*, Supplément, no. 123 (1 juin 1938), Société d'Études et d'Informations Économiques.

—— [unsigned]. 1938d. "L'Industrie textile italienne et l'autarcie." *Bulletin Quotidien*, Supplément, no. 248 (2 novembre 1938), Société d'Études et d'Informations Économiques.

—— [under the pseudonym Jean Albert]. 1938e. "Crise de la colonisation italienne en Éthiopie." *L'Europe Nouvelle* 21, no. 1083 (12 novembre 1938): 1235–1236.

—— [unsigned]. 1938f. "Italie." *L'Activité Économique* 4, no. 15 (31 octobre 1938): 250–255.

Hirschmann, Ursula. 1993. *Noi Senzapatria.* Bologna: Il Mulino.

Hirschman, Albert O., and Richard M. Bird. 1968. "Foreign Aid—A Critique and a Proposal." Essays in International Finance No. 69 (July). Princeton, NJ: Princeton University, Department of Economics, International Finance Section.

Hirschman, Alberto [*sic*] O., and George Kalmanoff. 1956. "Demanda de energia electrica para la C.V.C." *Economia Colombiana*, Año III, vol. 9 (June): 507–519.

Hirschman, Albert O., and Charles E. Lindblom. 1962. "Economic Development, Research and Development, Policy Making: Some Converging Views." *Behavioral Science* 7, no. 2 (April): 211–222.

Hirschman, Albert O., and M. J. Roberts. 1947. "Trade and Credit Arrangements Between the 'Marshall Plan Countries.' " *Review of Foreign Developments*, August 26, 1947, Board of Governors of the Federal Reserve System, Division of Research and Statistics, International Section, 8–11.

Hirschman, Albert O., and Robert Solomon. 1950. "The Influence of U.S. Economic Conditions on Foreign Countries." *Review of Foreign Developments*, September 12, 1950, Board of Governors of the Federal Reserve System, Division of International Finance, 1–20.

Hoffman, Paul. 1991. "Three Dualist Theories of the Passions." *Philosophical Topics* 19, no. 1 (Spring): 153–200.

Hogan, Michael J. 1987. *The Marshall Plan: America, Britain, and the Reconstruction of Western Europe, 1947–1952*. Cambridge: Cambridge University Press.

Honig, Dan. 2018. *Navigation by Judgment: Why and When Top Down Management of Foreign Aid Doesn't Work*. New York: Oxford University Press.

Hoselitz, Bert F. 1948. "Review of *Problèmes d'économie internationale: Les Échanges du capitalisme libéral* by Jean Weiller." *Journal of Political Economy* 56, no. 3 (June): 269–271.

Hotelling, Harold. 1929. "Stability in Competition." *Economic Journal* 39, no. 153 (March): 41–57.

Huntington, Samuel P. 1991. *The Third Wave: Democratization in the Late Twentieth Century*. Norman: University of Oklahoma Press.

IBRD: see International Bank for Reconstruction and Development.

Ika, Lavagnon A. 2018. "Beneficial or Detrimental Ignorance: The Straw Man Fallacy of Flyvbjerg's Test of Hirschman's Hiding Hand." *World Development* 103 (March): 369–382.

Inayatullah, Naeem. 1997. "Theories of Spontaneous Disorder." *Review of International Political Economy* 4, no. 2 (Summer): 319–348.

International Bank for Reconstruction and Development (IBRD). 1972. "Operations Evaluation Report: Electric Power." March 10, 1972, Report No. 2–17, Programming & Budgeting Department, Operations Evaluation Division.

——. 1950a. *The Basis of a Development Program for Colombia: Report of a Mission Headed by Lauchlin Currie, and Sponsored by the International Bank for Reconstruction and Development in Collaboration with the Government of Colombia*. Washington, DC: IBRD.

——. 1950b. *The Basis of a Development Program for Colombia: Report of a Mission: The Summary*. Washington, DC: IBRD.

International Studies Conference. 1939. *Twelfth Session, 1939, General Study Conference on Economic Policies in Relation to World Peace*, Memoranda, Argentine No. 1, Australia No. 1–5. Paris: International Institute of Intellectual Co-operation, League of Nations.

——. 1938. *Economic Policies in Relation to World Peace. A record of the meetings held in Prague on May 25th and 26th 1938*. Paris: International Institute of Intellectual Co-operation, League of Nations.

Isenberg, Sheila. 2001. *A Hero of Our Own: The Story of Varian Fry*. New York: Random House.

Kaiser, Thomas E. 1979. "Review of *The Passions and the Interests: Political Arguments for Capitalism Before Its Triumph* by Albert O. Hirschman." *Eighteenth-Century Studies* 12, no. 3 (Spring): 419–422.

Kaplan, Jacob J., and Günther Schleiminger. 1989. *The European Payments Union: Financial Diplomacy in the 1950s*. Oxford: Clarendon Press.

Katznelson, Ira. 1980. "Accounts of the Welfare State and the New Mood." *American Economic Review* 70, no. 2 (May): 117–122.

Katznelson, Ira, Kim Geiger, and Daniel Kryder. 1993. "Limiting Liberalism: The Southern Veto in Congress, 1933–1950." *Political Science Quarterly* 108, no. 2 (Summer): 283–306.

Katznelson, Ira, and Bruce Pietrykowski. 1991. "Rebuilding the American State: Evidence from the 1940s." *Studies in American Political Development* 5, no. 2 (Fall): 301–339.

Kenyon, Tom, and Alberto Criscuolo. 2017. "Social Learning and the World Bank." Paper prepared for the First Hirschman-Colorni Conference, Boston University, October 6–7, 2017.

Keohane, Nannerl O. 1978. "Review of *The Passions and the Interests: Political Arguments for Capitalism Before Its Triumph* by Albert O. Hirschman." *Journal of Interdisciplinary History* 8, no. 4 (Spring): 776–778.

Keohane, Robert O., and Joseph S. Nye. 1973. "World Politics and the International Economic System." In *The Future of the International Economic Order: An Agenda for Research*, by C. Fred Bergsten, 115–179. Lexington, MA: Lexington Books.

——, eds. 1972. *Transnational Relations and World Politics*. Cambridge, MA: Harvard University Press.

Killick, Tony. 1978. *Economic Development in Action: A Study of Economic Policies in Ghana*. London: Heinemann.

Kindleberger, Charles P. 1973. *The World in Depression 1929–1939*. Berkeley: University of California Press.

—— 1962. *Foreign Trade and the National Economy*. New Haven, CT: Yale University Press.

Knapp, John. 1957. "Capital Exports and Growth." *Economic Journal* 67, no. 267 (September): 432–444.

Knox, A. D. 1960. "Review of *The Strategy of Economic Development* by Albert O. Hirschman." *International Affairs* 36, no. 1 (January): 99–100.

Köpp, H. Eberhard. 2003. "Promoting Professional and Personal Trust in OED." in Grasso, Wasty, and Weaving 2003, 55–60.

Kornai, János. 1979. "Appraisal of Project Appraisal." In *Economics and Human Welfare: Essays in Honor of Tibor Scitovsky*, ed. Michael J. Boskin, 75–99. New York: Academic Press.

Krasner, Stephen D. 1976. "State Power and the Structure of International Trade." *World Politics* 28, no. 3 (April): 317–347.

Krugman, Paul. 1994. "The Fall and Rise of Development Economics." In Rodwin and Schön 1994, 39–58.

——. 1993. "Toward a Counter-Counterrevolution in Development Theory." In *Proceedings of the World Bank Annual Conference on Development Economics 1992*, ed. Lawrence H. Summers and Shekhar Shah, 15–61. Washington, DC: World Bank.

Kuznets, Simon. 1964. "Quantitative Aspects of the Economic Growth of Nations: IX. Level and Structure of Foreign Trade: Comparisons for Recent Years." *Economic Development and Cultural Change* 13, no. 1, part 2 (October): 1–106.

Lane, Robert E. 1978. "Markets and the Satisfaction of Human Wants." *Journal of Economic Issues* 12, no. 4 (December): 799–827.

Laves, Walter H. C. 1940. "The Institutional Requirements for a More Stable World Order." In *The Foundations of a More Stable Order*, ed. Walter H. C. Laves, 157–185. Chicago: University of Chicago Press, 1941.

Lazear, Edward P. 1999. "Economic Imperialism." *NBER Working Paper Series*, 7300 (August).

Lepenies, Philipp H. 2018. "Statistical Tests as a Hindrance to Understanding What the Controversy Around the 'Hiding Hand' Reveals About Research in the Social Sciences and Conceals About Project Management." *World Development* 103 (March): 360–365.

Lewis, W. Arthur. 1955. *The Theory of Economic Growth*. London: Allen & Unwin.

——. 1954. "Economic Development with Unlimited Supply of Labour." *Manchester School of Economic and Social Studies* 22, no. 2 (May): 139–191.

Lindberg, Leon N. 1985. "Models of Inflation-Disinflation Process." In Lindberg and Maier 1985, 25–50.

Lindberg, Leon N., and Charles S. Maier, eds. 1985. *The Politics of Inflation and Economic Stagnation: Theoretical Approaches and International Case Studies*. Washington, DC: Brookings Institution.

Lind Olsen, Pernille. 2003. "Nonny Wright (1909–2003)." *Dansk kvindehistorie: Dansk kvindebiografisk leksikon*. Accessed September 30, 2019. http://www.kvinfo.dk /side/597/bio/1693/origin/170/.

Little, Ian M. D. 1982. *Economic Development: Theory, Policy, and International Relations*. New York: Basic Books.

Little, Ian M. D., and James A. Mirrlees. 1974. *Project Appraisal and Planning for Developing Countries*. New York: Basic Books.

——. 1968. *Manual of Industrial Project Analysis in Developing Countries, Vol. II, Social Cost Benefit Analysis*. Paris: Development Centre of the Organisation for Economic Co-operation and Development.

Little, Ian M. D., Tibor Scitovsky, and Maurice Scott. 1970. *Industry and Trade in Some Developing Countries: A Comparative Study*. London: Oxford University Press.

Love, Joseph L. 1996. *Crafting the Third World: Theorizing Underdevelopment in Rumania and Brazil*. Stanford, CA: Stanford University Press.

Luzzatto-Fegiz, Pierpaolo. 1937. "La Politica Demografica del Fascismo." *Annali di Economia*, Vol. 12, Dieci anni di Economia fascista: 1926–1935: La formazione dell'Economia corporativa, 109–124.

Lynn, Laurence E., Jr. 1992. "Welfare Reform and the Revival of Ideology: An Essay Review." *Social Service Review* 66, no. 4 (December): 642–654.

Lyons, William E., David Lowery, and Ruth Hoogland DeHoog. 1992. *The Politics of Dissatisfaction: Citizens, Services, and Urban Institutions*. Armonk, NY: M. E. Sharpe.

Macario, Santiago. 1964. "Protectionism and Industrialization in Latin America." *Economic Bulletin for Latin America* 9, no. 1 (March): 62–102.

Maier, Charles S. 2017. "On the Applicability of Albert Hirschman's Shifting Involvements for the Historian: Notes for a Research Proposal." Paper presented at the Conference on Albert Hirschman's Legacy: Theory and Practice, Boston University, October 6–7, 2017.

——. 1985. "Inflation and Stagnation as Politics and History." In Lindberg and Maier 1985, 3–24.

Mann, Fritz Karl. 1946. "Review of *National Power and the Structure of Foreign Trade* by Albert O. Hirschman." *Journal of Economic History* 6, no. 1 (May): 91–93.

Mannheim, Karl. 1936. *Ideology and Utopia: An Introduction to the Sociology of Knowledge*. New York: Harcourt, Brace.

Marglin, Stephen A. 1967. *Public Investment Criteria: Benefit-Cost Analysis for Planned Economic Growth*. London: George Allen & Unwin.

Marino, Andy. 1999. *American Pimpernel: The Man Who Saved the Artists on Hitler's Death List*. London: Hutchinson.

Martin, David A. 1990. "Economics as Ideology: On Making 'The Invisible Hand' Invisible." *Review of Social Economy* 48, no. 3 (Fall): 272–287.

Maser, Steven M. 1984. "Review of: *Shifting Involvements: Private Interests and Public Action* by Albert O. Hirschman." *American Political Science Review* 78, no. 2 (June): 590–591.

Mathiowetz, Dean. 2007. "The Juridical Subject of 'Interest.'" *Political Theory* 35, no. 4 (August): 468–493.

Matthews, Donald R., and James W. Prothro. 1966. *Negroes and the New Southern Politics*. New York: Harcourt, Brace and World.

Marx, Karl. 1859 [1904]. *A Contribution to the Critique of Political Economy*. Translated by N. I. Stone. Chicago: Charles H. Kerr.

Mazower, Mark. 2000. *Dark Continent: Europe's Twentieth Century*. New York: Vintage.

McClafferty, Carla Killough. 2008. *In Defiance of Hitler: The Secret Mission of Varian Fry*. New York: Farrar, Straus and Giroux.

McCloskey, Deirdre N. 1992. "Alexander Gerschenkron." *American Scholar* 61, no. 2 (Spring): 241–246.

McPherson, Michael S. 1986. "The Social Scientist as Constructive Skeptic: On Hirschman's Role." In Foxley, McPherson, and O'Donnell 1986, 305–315.

Meade, James E. 1940. *The Economic Basis of a Durable Peace*. New York: Oxford University Press.

Meier, Gerald M. 2005. *Biography of a Subject: An Evolution of Development Economics*. New York: Oxford University Press.

——. 2001. "The Old Generation of Development Economists and the New." In *Frontiers of Development Economics: The Future in Perspective*, ed. Gerald M. Meier and Joseph E. Stiglitz, 13–50. New York: Oxford University Press.

Meier, Gerald M., and Dudley Seers. 1984. *Pioneers in Development*. New York: Oxford University Press.

Meldolesi, Luca. 1995. *Discovering the Possible: The Surprising World of Albert O. Hirschman*. Notre Dame, IN: University of Notre Dame Press.

——. 1990. "Una passione per il possibile." In *Tre continenti: Economia politica e sviluppo della democrazia in Europa, Stati Uniti e America Latina*, by Albert O. Hirschman. Turin: Einaudi.

Merton, Robert K. 1973. "Social Conflict Over Styles of Sociological Work." In *The Sociology of Science: Theoretical and Empirical Investigations*, 47–69. Chicago: University of Chicago Press. [Originally published in Fourth World Congress of Sociology, *Transactions* 3 (1961): 21–46. Louvain, Belgium: International Sociological Association.]

——. 1936. "The Unanticipated Consequences of Purposive Social Action." *American Sociological Review* 1, no. 6 (December): 894–904.

Meyer, Jack A. 1989. "Statement." In *Public Investment in Human and Physical Infra-structure*. Hearing Before the Joint Economic Committee, Congress of the United States, One Hundred First Congress, First Session, July 19, 1989. Washington, DC: Government Printing Office, 1990.

Michaely, Michael. 1962. *Concentration in International Trade*. Amsterdam: North-Holland.

——. 1960. "The Shares of Countries in World Trade." *Review of Economics and Statistics* 42, no. 3 (August): 307–317.

Migdal, Joel S. 1980. *Palestinian Society and Politics*. Princeton, NJ: Princeton University Press.

Milward, Alan S. 1984. *The Reconstruction of Western Europe, 1945–51*. Berkeley: University of California Press.

Misiani, Simone. 2010. *Manlio Rossi-Doria: un riformatore del Novecento*. Soveria Mannelli, Italy: Rubbettino.

Moore, Barrington, Jr. 1966. *Social Origins of Dictatorship and Democracy: Lord and Peasant in the Making of the Modern World*. Boston: Beacon Press.

Mouré, Kenneth. 1991. *Managing the Franc Poincaré: Economic Understanding and Political Constraint in French Monetary Policy, 1928–1936*. Cambridge: Cambridge University Press.

Moyn, Samuel. 2018. *Not Enough: Human Rights in an Unequal World*. Cambridge, MA: Harvard University Press.

——. 2010. *The Last Utopia: Human Rights in History*. Cambridge, MA: Harvard University Press.

Mukherji, V. 1959. "Review of *The Strategy of Economic Development* by Albert O. Hirschman." *Indian Economic Review* 4, no. 3 (February): 84–89.

Muller, Jerry Z. 1991. "Albert Hirschman's Rhetoric of Recrimination." *Public Interest* 104 (Summer): 81–92.

Murphy, Craig N. 2006. *The United Nations Development Programme: A Better Way?* New York: Cambridge University Press.

Murphy, George G. S. 1961. "On Satelliteship." *Journal of Economic History* 21, no. 4 (December): 641–651.

Murray, Charles. 1984 [1994]. *Losing Ground: American Special Policy 1950–1980*. New York: Basic Books.

Nelson, Richard R. 1976. "Discussion." *American Economic Review* 66, no. 2 (May): 389–391.

Nurkse, Ragnar. 1961. "Further Comments on Professor Rosenstein-Rodan's Paper." In *Economic Development for Latin America*, ed. Howard S. Ellis and Henry C. Wallich, 74–78. New York: St. Martin's.

——. [1953] 1962. *Problems of Capital Formation in Underdeveloped Countries*. 3rd ed. Oxford: Basil Blackwell and Mott.

O'Connor, James. 1973. *The Fiscal Crisis of the State*. New York: St. Martin's Press.

O'Donnell, Guillermo. 1986. "On the Fruitful Convergences of Hirschman's *Exit, Voice, and Loyalty* and *Shifting Involvements*: Reflections from the Recent Argentinian Experience." in Foxley, McPherson, and O'Donnell 1986, 249–268.

——. 1983. "Democracia en la Argentina: Micro y Macro." Working Paper No. 2 (December), Kellogg Institute for International Studies. Accessed on January 3, 2020. https://kellogg.nd.edu/sites/default/files/old_files/documents/002_0.pdf.

——. 1973. *Modernization and Bureaucratic-Authoritarianism: Studies in South American Politics*. Berkeley, CA: Institute of International Studies.

Oliver, Henry. 1946. "Review of *National Power and the Structure of Foreign Trade* by Albert Hirschman." *Southern Economic Journal* 12, no. 3 (January): 304–305.

Olson, Mancur. 1965 [1971]. *The Logic of Collective Action*. Cambridge, MA: Harvard University Press.

——. 1965. "Some Social and Political Implications of Economic Development." *World Politics* 17 (3): 525–554.

Oman, Charles P., and Ganeshan Wignaraja. 1991. *The Postwar Evolution of Development Thinking*. Basingstoke, UK: Macmillan.

Omiccioli, Massimo. 2018. *La "strana" biblioteca di uno "strano" economista: Viaggio tra i libri di Ernesto Rossi*. Rome: Banca d'Italia.

Ophir, Adi. 2019. "Exit, Voice, Loyalty: The Case of the BDS." *Philosophy and Social Criticism*, first published online November 14, 2019.

Orbell, John M., and Toro Uno. 1972. "A Theory of Neighborhood Problem Solving: Political Actions vs. Residential Mobility." *American Political Science Review* 66, no. 2 (June): 471–489.

Overy, Richard. 2017. *The Inter-War Crisis*. 3rd ed. London: Routledge.

Paci, Massimo. 1982. "Onde lunghe nello sviluppo dei sistemi di welfare." *Stato e mercato*, no. 6 (December): 345–400.

Pasquino, Gianfranco. 2014. "Hirschman politologo (per necessità e virtù)." *Moneta e Credito* 67 (266): 167–189.

Peleg, Ilan, and Dov Waxman. 2011. *Israel's Palestinians: The Conflict Within*. Cambridge: Cambridge University Press.

Piatier, André. 1939. "Report on the Study of Exchange Control." In International Studies Conference, Twelfth Session, Bergen, August 27–September 2, 1939, *Economic Policies in Relation to World Peace*, Memoranda, Exchange Control No. 7–8. Paris: International Institute of Intellectual Co-operation, League of Nations.

Picciotto, Robert. 1994. "Visibility and Disappointment: The New Role of Development Evaluation." In Rodwin and Schön 1994, 210–230.

Pocock, J. G. A. 1981. "The Machiavellian Moment Revisited: A Study in History and Ideology." *Journal of Modern History* 53, no. 1 (March): 49–72.

——. 1975. *The Machiavellian Moment: Florentine Political Thought and the Atlantic Republican Tradition*. Princeton, NJ: Princeton University Press.

Poggi, Gianfranco. 1978. "Economy and Polity: A Chastened Reflection of Past Hopes: A Review of *The Passions and the Interests: Political Arguments for Capitalism Before Its Triumph*, by Albert O. Hirschman." *Contemporary Sociology* 7, no. 4 (July): 397–399.

Porter, Theodore M. 1995. *Trust in Numbers: The Pursuit of Objectivity in Science and Public Life*. Princeton, NJ: Princeton University Press.

Prebisch, Raúl. 1950. *The Economic Development of Latin America and Its Principal Problems*. UN document no. E/CN.12/89/Rev.1. Lake Success, NY: United Nations.

Reubens, Edwin P. 1959. "Review of *Economic Planning in Underdeveloped Areas: Government and Business* by Edward S. Mason; *The Strategy of Economic Development* by Albert O. Hirschman." *Political Science Quarterly* 74, no. 3 (September): 461–463.

Rist, Charles. 1934. "L'Institut scientifique de recherches économiques et sociales." *Revue d'économie politique* 48 (6): 1769–1774.

Robbins, Lionel. 1937. *Economic Planning and International Order*. London: Macmillan.

Rodgers, Daniel T. 2011. *Age of Fracture*. Cambridge, MA: Belknap Press.

Rodrik, Dani. 2008. "The New Development Economics: We Shall Experiment, but How Shall We Learn?" Paper presented at the Brookings Development Conference, May 29–30, 2008.

——. 2007a. *One Economics, Many Recipes: Globalization, Institutions, and Economic Growth*. Princeton, NJ: Princeton University Press.

——. 2007b. "One Economics, Many Recipes: What We Have Learned Since Albert Hirschman." *Items and Issues* 6 (1–2): 1–7.

——, ed. 2003. *In Search of Prosperity: Analytical Narratives on Economic Growth*. Princeton, NJ: Princeton University Press.

Rodwin, Lloyd, and Donald A. Schön, eds. 1994. *Rethinking the Development Experience: Essays Provoked by the Work of Albert O. Hirschman*. Washington, DC: Brookings Institution.

Rokkan, Stein. 1975. "Dimensions of State Formation and Nation-Building: A Possible Paradigm for Research on Variations within Europe." In Charles Tilly, ed., *The Formation of National States in Western Europe*, Princeton, NJ: Princeton University Press, 1975, pp. 562–600.

——. 1974a. "Politics Between Economy and Culture: An International Seminar on Albert O. Hirschman's *Exit, Voice and Loyalty*." *Social Science Information* 13, no. 1 (February): 27–38.

——. 1974b. "Entries, Voices, Exits: Towards a Possible Generalization of the Hirschman Model." *Social Science Information* 13, no. 1 (February): 39–53.

Roncaglia, Alessandro. 2014. "Hirschman e l'Italia." *Moneta e Credito* 67 (266): 153–157.

Room, Graham. 2018. "The Hiding Hand: A Rejoinder to Flyvbjerg on Hirschman." *World Development* 103 (March): 366–368.

Rosenboim, Or. 2017. *The Emergence of Globalism. Visions of World Order in Britain and the United States, 1939–1950*. Princeton, NJ: Princeton University Press.

Rosenstein-Rodan, Paul N. 1963. "National Planning." Unpublished manuscript, Massachusetts Institute of Technology, November 1963.

——. 1961. "Notes on the Theory of the 'Big Push.' " In *Economic Development for Latin America*, ed. Howard S. Ellis and Henry C. Wallich, 57–67. New York: St. Martin's.

——. 1957. "Notes on the Theory of the 'Big Push.' " Italy Project, MIT Center for International Studies.

——. 1943. "Problems of Industrialisation of Eastern and South-Eastern Europe." *Economic Journal* 53, no. 210/211 (June–September): 202–211.

Rossi-Doria, Manlio. 2011. *Una vita per il sud: Dialoghi epistolari 1944–1987*, ed. Emanuele Bernardi. Rome: Donzelli.

Rostow, Walt W. 1960 [1990]. *The Stages of Economic Growth: A Non-Communist Manifesto*. Cambridge: Cambridge University Press.

Royal Institute of International Affairs. 1940. *South-Eastern Europe. A Brief Survey*. Information Department Papers No. 26. London: Royal Institute of International Affairs.

——. 1939. *South-Eastern Europe. A Political and Economic Survey*. Prepared by the Information Department of the Royal Institute of International Affairs in collaboration with the London and Cambridge Economic Service. London: Royal Institute of International Affairs.

Ryan, Alan. 1977. "Review of *The Passions and the Interests* by Albert O. Hirschman." *Political Theory* 5, no. 4 (November): 535–538.

Sandilands, Roger J. 2015. "The 1949 World Bank Mission to Colombia and the Competing Visions of Lauchlin Currie (1902–1993) and Albert Hirschman (1915–2012)." *History of Economic Thought and Policy* 2015 (1): 21–37.

——. 1990. *The Life and Political Economy of Lauchlin Currie: New Dealer, Presidential Adviser, and Development Economist.* Durham, NC: Duke University Press.

Schaffer, Bernard, and Geoff Lamb. 1978. *Can Equity Be Organized? Equity, Development Analysis and Planning.* Paris: UNESCO.

Schelling, Thomas C. 1978. *Micromotives and Macrobehaviors.* New York: Norton.

Schneider, Louis. 1978. "On Human Nature, Economy, and Society: Review of *The Passions and the Interests: Political Arguments for Capitalism Before Its Triumph*, by Albert O. Hirschman." *Contemporary Sociology* 7, no. 4 (July): 400–402.

Schott, Kerry. 1983. "Review of: *Shifting Involvements: Private Interest and Public Action* by Albert Hirschman." *Economic Journal* 93, no. 372 (December): 941–942.

Schumpeter, Joseph A. 1942 [2008]. *Capitalism, Socialism and Democracy.* New York: Harper.

Schwarz, John E. 1983. *America's Hidden Success: A Reassessment of Twenty Years of Public Policy.* New York: Norton.

Scitovsky, Tibor. 1983. "Review of: *Shifting Involvements: Private Interest and Public Action* by Albert O. Hirschman." *Economica* (New Series) 50, no. 199 (August): 372–373.

——. 1976. *The Joyless Economy: An Inquiry Into Human Satisfaction and Consumer Dissatisfaction.* New York: Oxford University Press.

Seddig, Robert G. 1978. "Review of *The Passions and the Interests: Political Arguments for Capitalism Before Its Triumph* by Albert O. Hirschman." *Annals of the American Academy of Political and Social Science* 435 (January): 339–340.

Seers, Dudley. 1964. "Review of *Journeys Toward Progress: Studies of Economic Policy-Making in Latin America* by Albert O. Hirschman." *American Economic Review* 54 (2): 157–160.

Sen, Amartya K. 1993. "On the Darwinian View of Progress." *Population and Development Review* 19, no. 1 (March): 123–137.

——. 1977. "Rational Fools: A Critique of the Behavioral Foundations of Economic Theory." *Philosophy & Public Affairs* 6, no. 4 (Summer): 317–344.

——. 1972. "Choice, Orderings and Morality." In *Choice, Welfare and Measurement*, 74–83. Cambridge, MA: Harvard University Press.

——. 1960. "Review of *The Strategy of Economic Development*, by A. O. Hirschman; *The Struggle for a Higher Standard of Living: The Problems of the Underdeveloped Countries*, by W. Brand; and *Public Enterprise and Economic Development*, by A. H. Hanson." *Economic Journal* 70, no. 279 (September): 590–594.

Sender, John. 1994. "Economic Restructuring in South Africa: Reactionary Rhetoric Prevails." *Journal of Southern African Studies* 20, no. 4 (December): 539–543.

Shannon, Lyle W. 1959. "Review of *The Strategy of Economic Development* by Albert O. Hirschman." *Annals of the American Academy of Political and Social Science* 325 (September): 125–126.

Siebel, H. D., and Andreas Massing. 1976. *Traditional Organizations and Economic Development.* New York: Praeger.

Sikkink, Kathryn. 2017. *Evidence for Hope: Making Human Rights Work in the Twenty-First Century.* Princeton, NJ: Princeton University Press.

Simon, Herbert A. 1957. *Models of Man*. New York: Wiley.

Singer, Hans W. 1965. "External Aid: For Plans or Projects?" *Economic Journal* 75, no. 299 (September): 539–545.

——. 1950. "The Distribution of Gains Between Investing and Borrowing Countries." *American Economic Review* 40, no. 2 (May): 473–485.

Skocpol, Theda. 1995. *Social Policy in the United States: Future Possibilities in Historical Perspective*. Princeton, NJ: Princeton University Press.

——. 1993. "Is the Time Finally Ripe? Health Insurance Reforms in the 1990s." *Journal of Health Politics, Policy, and Law* 18 (Fall): 531–550.

——. 1992a. *Protecting Soldiers and Mothers: The Political Origins of Social Policy in the United States*. Cambridge, MA: Belknap Press.

——. 1992b. "State Formation and Social Policy in the United States." *American Behavioral Scientist* 35, no. 4/5 (March–June): 559–584.

——. 1991. "Targeting Within Universalism: Politically Viable Policies to Combat Poverty in the United States." In *The Urban Underclass*, ed. Christopher Jencks and Paul E. Peterson, 411–436. Washington, DC: Brookings Institution.

Skocpol, Theda, Christopher Howard, Susan Goodrich Lehmann, and Marjorie Abend-Wein. 1993. "Women's Associations and the Enactment of Mothers' Pensions in the United States." *American Political Science Review* 87 (3): 686–701.

Smith, Adam. 1776 [1976]. *An Inquiry Into the Nature and Causes of the Wealth of Nations*. Oxford: Oxford University Press.

Smith, Jan. 1983. "Review of: *Essays in Trespassing: Economics to Politics and Beyond* by Albert O. Hirschman; *Shifting Involvements: Private Interest and Public Action* by Albert O. Hirschman." *American Journal of Sociology* 89, no. 1 (July): 225–228.

Spiegelglas, Stephen. 1961. "The Commodity Structure of World Trade: Comment." *Quarterly Journal of Economics* 75, no. 1 (February): 157–165.

Squire, Lyn, and Herman G. Van der Tak. 1975. *Economic Analysis of Projects*. Baltimore: Johns Hopkins University Press.

Staley, Eugene A. 1939. *World Economy in Transition: Technology vs. Politics, Laissez Faire vs. Planning, Power vs. Welfare*. New York: Council on Foreign Relations.

Stewart, Frances, and Paul Streeten. 1972. "Little-Mirrlees Methods and Project Appraisal." *Bulletin of the Oxford University Institute of Economics and Statistics* 34, no. 1 (February): 75–91.

Stigler, George J., and Gary S. Becker. 1977. "De Gustibus Non Est Disputandum." *American Economic Review* 67, no. 2 (March): 76–90.

Stillman, Peter G. 1978. "Review of *The Passions and the Interests: Political Arguments for Capitalism Before Its Triumph* by Albert O. Hirschman." *American Political Science Review* 72, no. 3 (September): 1027–1028.

Stinchcombe, Arthur L. 1983. "Review of: *Shifting Involvements: Private Interests and Public Action* by Albert O. Hirschman." *Theory and Society* 12, no. 5 (September): 689–692.

Stinebower, Leroy D. 1946. "Review of *National Power and the Structure of Foreign Trade* by Albert O. Hirschman." *American Economic Review* 36, no. 3 (June): 418–420.

Stolper, Wolfgang F. 1946. "Review of *National Power and the Structure of Foreign Trade* by Albert O. Hirschman." *Journal of Political Economy* 54, no. 6 (December): 562–563.

Streeten, Paul P. 1986. "Suffering from Success." In Foxley, McPherson, and O'Donnell 1986, 239–246.

——. 1984. "Comment." In *Pioneers in Development*, ed. Gerald M. Meier and Dudley Seers, 115–118. New York: Oxford University Press.

——. 1959. "Unbalanced Growth." *Oxford Economic Papers* 11 (2): 167–190.

Sunstein, Cass R. 2018. *The Cost-Benefit Revolution*. Cambridge, MA: MIT Press.

——. 2015. "Albert Hirschman's Hiding Hand." Foreword to *Development Projects Observed*, by Albert O. Hirschman, vii–xiii. Washington, DC: Brookings Institution Press.

——. 2013. "An Original Thinker of Our Time." *New York Review of Books* 60, no. 9 (May 23, 2013): 14–17.

——. 1999. "Cognition and Cost-Benefit Analysis." John M. Olin Law & Economics Working Paper No. 85 (2nd Series), Law School, University of Chicago.

Supple, Barry. 1978. "Review of *The Passions and the Interests: Political Arguments for Capitalism Before Its Triumph* by Albert O. Hirschman." *Journal of Modern History* 50, no. 4 (December): 723–725.

Suttle, Bruce B. 1987. "The Passion of Self-Interest: The Development of the Idea and Its Changing Status." *American Journal of Economics and Sociology* 46, no. 4 (October): 459–472.

Tarrow, Sidney. 1988. "National Politics and Collective Action: Recent Theory and Research in Western Europe and the United States." *Annual Review of Sociology* 14: 421–440.

Tendler, Judith. 1983a. *What to Think About Cooperatives: A Guide from Bolivia* (in collaboration with Kevin Healy and Carol Michaels O'Laughlin). Arlington, VA: Inter-American Foundation.

——. 1983b. "Ventures in the Informal Sector, and How They Worked Out in Brazil." A.I.D. Evaluation Special Study No. 12 (March). Washington, DC: U.S. Agency for International Development.

——. 1982. "Turning Private Voluntary Organizations Into Development Agencies: Questions for Evaluation." A.I.D. Program Evaluation Discussion Paper No. 12 (April). Washington, DC: U.S. Agency for International Development.

——. 1968. *Electric Power in Brazil: Entrepreneurship in the Public Sector*. Cambridge, MA: Harvard University Press.

Tilly, Charles. 1978. *From Mobilization to Revolution*. New York: Random House.

Toynbee, Arnold J. 1939. "A Turning Point in History." *Foreign Affairs* 17, no. 2 (January): 305–320.

Trigilia, Carlo. 2014. "Albert Hirschman e la scienza socio-morale." *Moneta e Credito* 67 (266): 191–203.

Tullock, Gordon. 1970. "Review of *Exit, Voice and Loyalty: Responses to Decline in Firms, Organizations, and States* by Albert O. Hirschman." *Journal of Finance* 25, no. 5 (December): 1194–1195.

Viner, Jacob. 1940. "International Economic Relations and the World Order." June 26, 1940. In *The Foundations of a More Stable Order*, ed. Walter H. C. Laves, 33–73. Chicago: University of Chicago Press, 1941.

Watkins, Melville H. 1963. "A Staple Theory of Economic Growth." *Canadian Journal of Economics and Political Science / Revue canadienne d'économique et de science politique* 29, no. 2 (May): 141–158.

——. 1961. "Review of *The Strategy of Economic Development* by Albert O. Hirschman." *Canadian Journal of Economics and Political Science / Revue canadienne d'économique et de science politique* 27, no. 1 (February): 110–112.

Weiller, Jean. 1954. "Review of *British Overseas Trade, from 1700 to the 1930's* by Werner Schlote, W. O. Henderson and W. H. Chaloner." *Revue économique* 5, no. 1 (January): 118–119.

Weisbrod, Burton. 1978. *The Voluntary Nonprofit Sector: An Economic Analysis.* Washington, DC: Lexington Books.

Williamson, Oliver E. 1976. "The Economics of Internal Organization: Exit and Voice in Relation to Markets and Hierarchies." *American Economic Review* 66, no. 2 (May): 369–377.

——. 1975. *Markets and Hierarchies: Analysis and Antitrust Implications.* New York: Free Press.

Wolf, Eric. 1969. *Peasant Wars of the Twentieth Century.* New York: Harper & Row.

Wolfe, Alan. 1992. "Review of *The Rhetoric of Reaction: Perversity, Futility, Jeopardy* by Albert O. Hirschman." *Contemporary Sociology* 21, no. 1 (January): 30–32.

Wuthnow, Robert. 1979. "Legitimating the Capitalist World Order: Review of *The Livelihood of Man*, by Karl Polanyi and Harry W. Pearson, and *The Passions and the Interests: Political Arguments for Capitalism Before Its Triumph*, by Albert O. Hirschman." *American Journal of Sociology* 85, no. 2 (September): 424–430.

Zahniser, Marvin R., and W. Michael Weis. 1989. "A Diplomatic Pearl Harbor? Richard Nixon's Goodwill Mission to Latin America in 1958." *Diplomatic History* 13, no. 2 (Spring): 163–190.

Zolberg, Aristide R., Astrid Suhrke, and Sergio Aguayo. 1989. *Escape from Violence: Conflict and the Refugee Crisis in the Developing World.* New York: Oxford University Press.

INDEX

Page numbers in *italics* indicate illustrations or tables.